INGLORIOUS REVOLUTION

WILLIAM R. SUMMERHILL

Inglorious Revolution

POLITICAL INSTITUTIONS, SOVEREIGN DEBT, AND

FINANCIAL UNDERDEVELOPMENT IN IMPERIAL BRAZIL

Yale UNIVERSITY PRESS

NEW HAVEN AND LONDON

Yale University Press books may be purchased in quantity for educational, business, or
promotional use. For information, please e-mail sales.press@yale.edu (U.S. office) or
sales@yaleup.co.uk (U.K. office).

Set in Scala and Scala Sans types by Westchester Book Group.
Printed in the United States of America.

Library of Congress Cataloging-in-Publication Data
Summerhill, William Roderick.
  Inglorious revolution : political institutions, sovereign debt, and financial underdevelop-
ment in imperial Brazil / William R. Summerhill.
        pages   cm—(Yale series in economic and financial history)
  Includes bibliographical references and index.
  ISBN 978-0-300-13927-3 (alk. paper)
  1. Debts, Public—Brazil—History—19th century.   2. Brazil—Economic conditions—
19th century.   3.   Brazil—Economic policy—19th century.   4. Brazil—History—
Empire, 1822–1889.   I. Title.
  HJ8579.S86 2015
  330.981'04—dc23   2014045428
A catalogue record for this book is available from the British Library.

This paper meets the requirements of ANSI/NISO Z39.48-1992 (Permanence of Paper).

10 9 8 7 6 5 4 3 2 1

For Yolanda

CONTENTS

ACKNOWLEDGMENTS

THIS BOOK DRAWS on research funded by a U.S. National Endowment for the Humanities Summer Stipend, a U.S. Department of Education Fulbright-Hays Faculty Research Abroad Grant, and a National Fellowship from the Hoover Institution on War, Revolution, and Peace at Stanford University. Without the support of these organizations the book would simply not have been possible. I am grateful for the opportunity they provided.

My always rewarding sojourn in the research collections of Rio de Janeiro was invaluably aided by Flávio Luiz de Souza Santos. I appreciate his dedicated professionalism and skillful help. Natsumi Ishino and Giovanna Violi provided help in libraries and archives in London. Cala Dietrich, Renata Rodrigues, and Blanca Serna assisted with data entry. Caroline Shaw of the Rothschild Archive in London was especially accommodating. Sátiro Ferreira Nunes at the Arquivo Nacional in Rio de Janeiro greatly facilitated my research. I enjoyed unfettered access at two collections of the Ministry of Finance in Rio de Janeiro—the rare works section of the Biblioteca do Ministério da Fazenda and the archive of the Museu da Fazenda Federal—which made my research there a genuine pleasure.

The natural complexity of uprooting a family to reside in another country for an extended period of research is made easier only with the help of others. I am deeply obliged to Renato Perim Colistete, Maria Ana Quaglino, Glenn Rosen, Joseph Ryan, and Hado Steinbrecher.

At three locations the progress of the manuscript benefited from unusually rich intellectual environments in which to work. A year as a National Fellow at the Hoover Institution, combined with a stint at the Social Science History Institute at Stanford University, allowed me to develop the foundations of the study. Conversations with Stephen Haber, Douglass North, and Barry Weingast greatly aided the early stages and gave the project new energy at various points thereafter. In Rio de Janeiro, the Escola de Pós-Graduação em Economia of the Fundação Getúlio Vargas provided me with a place to complete the first draft of the manuscript. My time there allowed me to discuss a central theme of Brazilian history and political economy with a world-class group of social scientists. Their collegiality and curiosity spurred several lines of investigation I would not have otherwise pursued. I am indebted to Renato Fragelli Cardoso, the department chair, and to Samuel de Abreu Pessôa, who arranged my visit and pressed me on the present-day relevance of my otherwise antiquarian investigation. Since first arriving at UCLA, I have had the good fortune of participating in the activities that ultimately evolved into the Center for Economic History. Naomi Lamoreaux, Jean-Laurent Rosenthal, the late Kenneth Sokoloff, and Mary Yeager were central to its creation, guaranteeing the provision of scholarly public goods that represent the largest intellectual debt of this project. The Center's faculty, graduate students, and visitors provide a vibrant and ideal environment for investigators working in social science history.

Joseph Ryan and Alison Adams allowed me to draw on their respective findings on private borrowing and lending in nineteenth-century Rio de Janeiro. Daniel Waldenström, Ulisses Ruiz-de-Gamboa, and Mark Dincecco generously shared their econometric expertise. Parts of the manuscript and related papers were improved by suggestions received during presentations at the Von Gremp Workshop in Economic History at UCLA, the Lowe Institute of Political Economy at Claremont-McKenna College, the School of International and Areas Studies at the University of Oklahoma, the second Stanford conference on the Politics of Financial Development, the Instituto Brasileiro dos Mercados de Capitais (Belo Horizonte), the Departamento de Ciências Econômicas of the Universidade Federal do Rio Grande do Sul, the Departamento de Economia of the Universidade Federal de Pelotas, the Instituto de Pesquisa Econômica Aplicada, the Instituto de Economia of the Universidade Estadual de Campinas, the Departamento de Economia of the Faculdade de Economia e Administração of the Universidade de São Paulo, the Escola de Pós-Graduação em Economia of the Fundação Getúlio Vargas, the Instituto de Estudos em Política Econômica-Casa das Garças, the UCLA Center for Economic History conference on States and Capital Markets in Historical Perspective, the Economic History Workshop at Yale University, and the Hoover Institution Seminar on Collective Choice. A preliminary version of chapter 5 appeared as the working paper "Political Economics of the Domestic Debt in Nineteenth-Century Brazil," in Diretoria de Estudos Macroeconômicos, *Seminários* 180, Instituto de Pesquisa Econômica Aplicada (Rio de Janeiro, 2005).

Portions of the manuscript greatly benefited from conversations with and critical readings by Lee Alston, Edmar Bacha, Luís Catão, Mark Dincecco, Gustavo Franco, Carlos Gabriel Guimarães, Timothy Guinnane, Carlos Marichal, Leonardo Monasterio, Aldo Musacchio, Douglass North, Eustáquio Reis, Cláudio Shikida, the late Kenneth Sokoloff, David Stasavage, André Villela, John Wallis, and Barry Weingast. Renato Perim Colistete not only read and discussed the manuscript but also made possible a series of lectures at the Universidade de São Paulo, where I received invaluable feedback. Roderick Barman offered tremendously helpful suggestions on several portions of the book, along with information from his own research in progress, and in general shared his expertise on Brazilian history. Jeffrey Needell's insights on key segments came at a critical moment in the process of revision, and I am grateful for his intellectual generosity. Adalton Diniz helped make the Empire's fiscal system intelligible.

Howard Bodenhorn, Stephen Haber, Herbert Klein, Hendrik Kraay, Naomi Lamoreaux, Francisco Vidal Luna, Carlos Manuel Peláez, Samuel de Abreu Pessôa, James Robinson, and two readers at Yale University Press commented on one version or another of the entire study, saving me from many an error. I thank Eugene White, who read two versions of the manuscript and, as a series editor, provided essential support for the project. Richard Salvucci accompanied the development of this book over several years and allowed me to tap into his vast reservoir of knowledge on sovereign borrowing in Latin American history. Jean-Laurent

Rosenthal offered countless insights from the very start of this project and graciously tolerated a never-ending stream of queries. Stephen Haber's mentorship and encouragement were indispensable. As editor, William Frucht at Yale University Press made it possible to bring the book to fruition.

My family made the greatest contribution that one could hope for over the course of this project. Yolanda, Liam, and Samuel bore the brunt of my distraction with what probably looked to them like an odd scholarly fixation. They did so with patience, good humor, and an appreciation of collective adventures. I am indebted to them for their love, support, and companionship.

NOTE ON ORTHOGRAPHY AND CURRENCY

BECAUSE OF CHANGES in Portuguese spelling since the nineteenth century, contemporary and present spellings of many words and even of names differ. In titles of references and proper names I tried to adhere to original spellings. In some instances there is no unique original spelling. For example, the Banco do Brasil in its own publications sometimes spelled Brasil with an *s* and at other times with a *z*. Outside of proper names and titles, I use modern spellings.

The base unit of Brazilian currency by the early nineteenth century was the *milréis,* written as 1$000. One thousand milréis made up one *conto de réis,* or 1:000$000. The milréis was only rarely convertible to gold at a fixed rate of exchange; for most of the nineteenth century it floated freely against other currencies. With the emission of large quantities of paper money between 1809 and 1829, the value of the milréis in terms of the principal foreign currency, the pound sterling, declined steadily through 1831, then recovered some of the ground it had lost before starting a long downward slide in the late 1830s. In 1846 Brazilian legislation fixed "parity" at 27 English pence per milréis. This parity was notional, representing an exchange rate target that was not supported on a continuing basis. Where suitable, monetary values are expressed in original milréis. When compared to or summed with the external debt, they are reported in British pounds.

CHAPTER ONE

Introduction

IN 1824 THE constitutional monarchy of independent Brazil borrowed money in London for the first time. A syndicate of three merchant firms loaned it 1 million pounds sterling, raising the cash by issuing bonds. In return, the emissaries of Emperor Pedro I promised that the government would repay the loan over a period of thirty years and make interest payments of 5 percent a year to bondholders. The cabinet in Rio de Janeiro wanted to use the money to pay down the Treasury's debt to the Banco do Brasil. Instead the government spent the cash fighting the anticonstitutional revolt in the northeast. In January 1825 Brazil borrowed again, taking 2 million pounds sterling through Nathan Mayer Rothschild. Once again the money was supposed to settle debts within Brazil. And once again the funds were spent on war, underwriting the emperor's blockade of Buenos Aires. In 1829 the Treasury could not make its next interest payment on time. So with the authorization of the emperor's council of state, the minister in London turned again to the same bankers, who issued more bonds to cover the interest due. New money under such circumstances was not cheap. But the ability to borrow was a remarkable achievement, one that the Empire would repeat in London at least once per decade during hard times and as often as four times per decade in good times.

Had Brazil been like other Latin American borrowers it would have already been in default by 1830. Mexico, Peru, Colombia, Guatemala, Buenos Aires, and Chile all suspended payment on their debt in the 1820s and were cut off from new borrowing in London. Most of the Spanish American republics went on to become serial defaulters over the course of the century. For its part, Brazil repaid almost none of the principal it owed between 1829 and 1852. Its bondholders, however, always received interest. When in 1853 the first loans from the 1820s were about to come due, the Treasury did not have the 3 million pounds it needed to retire the remaining bonds. It had no trouble getting new credit, however. With the consent of the bondholders and the intermediation of N. M. Rothschild & Sons, the Empire extended its loans by another ten years. Its credit was so good that when the modified loan was about to come due in 1863 the government simply rolled the remaining balance into a new bond issue bearing a lower coupon rate than before. Rather strikingly, it executed the debt rollover in London during a complete breakdown in diplomatic relations with the British government. International politics aside, Brazil raised new cash and effectively extended the maturity of what remained from its original 1820s loans by yet another thirty years with no trouble. By that time Brazil was already on its eleventh London loan, involving four different financial intermediaries.

Brazil's good standing in credit markets was not restricted to London. At home the Treasury ran its first auction of domestic bonds (apólices) in 1828, shortly after parliament established the national debt. Slave traders and Rio de Janeiro's merchants were prominent buyers of the bonds. The new apólices provided lenders with annual interest payments of 6 percent in Brazilian currency (milréis) and were supposed to be paid off over thirty-three years. Relatively little of the initial tranche of apólices from 1828 had been retired when the parliament halted amortization in 1838. From that point forward the bonds were perpetuities. This change had little impact on the government's ability to borrow. Investors continued to absorb new issues in ever larger amounts through the politically turbulent 1830s and 1840s. By the early 1880s apólices had been bid so high that the current yield had fallen below the coupon rate. So with parliamentary sanction the finance minister converted the apólices from 6 percents to 5 percents in 1886, leveraging the government's high creditworthiness to reduce outlays on debt service. By then the government had borrowed in local currency from the domestic market for nearly sixty years, with no fixed date of redemption and without missing an interest payment.

From its first London loan in 1824 to the overthrow of the constitutional monarchy in 1889, Brazil accumulated a funded external debt in excess of 30 million pounds. Two-thirds of that had been refinanced in 1889, cutting the Empire's coupon rate to only 4 percent per year and extending the maturity of the bulk of the external debt out to fifty-six years. Domestic long-term credit was even more elastic: from the first Treasury auction in 1828 up to late 1889 the growth of the local funded debt outpaced the value of foreign borrowing, attaining some 435 million milréis, the equivalent of nearly 50 million pounds sterling.

If Brazil's ability to borrow and repay without default is one puzzle, the country's relative financial backwardness is another. The gap between Brazil's achievement in public finance and the condition of the nation's private financial markets was considerable. One basic indicator of the distinct fates of the two markets is the difference between the government's cost of borrowing and the interest rate that lenders charged in the private sector. Over the course of the century the state's borrowing costs fell appreciably in both London and Rio de Janeiro. From the late 1820s to the last London loan taken by the constitutional monarchy in 1889, Brazil's annual cost of capital in London fell from a peak of 13.9 percent in 1829 to only 5.12 percent in 1889.[1] The decline in borrowing costs was no less impressive in Rio de Janeiro, where they fell from 12 percent in 1831 to just 5.12 percent in 1889.[2] Average rates on secured loans in the private sector in Rio, however, remained well above 12 percent through 1850. Interest rate spreads between loans to businesses and those extended to governments are common. Thus, it is worth stressing that the private sector loans used in this comparison had much shorter maturities than government bonds (usually only around two years), suffered from less inflation risk as a result of their shorter maturities, and in nearly all instances were collateralized using real property, farmland, or slaves. By the standards of the era these were high-quality borrowers, for whom the interest rate tended to the low end of the range of borrowing costs. Borrowers who sought loans that were unsecured or for longer maturities faced higher costs or were rationed out of the market altogether.

When government borrowing costs declined sharply in the mid-1850s, rates on secured loans to individuals barely fell below 12 percent.

Only after the war against Paraguay (1864–70) did the average rate on private market loans fall, moving closer to 10 percent. Even then, loans at 18 percent and 24 percent a year were common. The overall average of the mortgage loan rates was biased downward by the Banco do Brasil's special mortgage operations (established in the mid-1860s), which consistently provided cheaper loans than other lenders. While public borrowing costs fell by more than half over a period of fifty years, the rate of interest on private loans hardly budged. Considering the main features of Brazil's capital market—the small number of commercial banks, high indices of bank concentration, and politicized and arbitrary access to the corporate form of the firm—high borrowing costs were one facet of a deeper and broader problem in the political economy of business finance. Private borrowing costs in Brazil were high from the very beginning. And they remained so.

One would expect Imperial Brazil to have had a better overall financial outcome given its success in establishing sovereign creditworthiness. For the case of Britain, some economic historians have located the origins of modern financial development in the credibility-enhancing political changes wrought by the Glorious Revolution in 1688.[3] The institutional transformation that made Britain's parliament fiscally preeminent and established a credible commitment to honor sovereign debt also protected rights in financial property. Parliamentary sovereignty boosted private finance because it allowed greater access to the corporate form of the firm, helping to mobilize capital for business. While the details of the Glorious Revolution were British, the shift of fiscal authority toward representative assemblies was not limited to Britain. City-states had done so early on.[4] At the level of nations, the adoption of legislative controls over public finance in the Dutch Republic predated the British case, and the United States followed it. In all of these the institutional changes that made sovereign borrowing credible also helped foster successful long-term financial development.

Such success stories show how most states that borrowed and faithfully serviced their debt also underwent the broader financial development required for modern economic growth. Imperial Brazil did not. In this regard it was a remarkable failure. That no revolution in private finance transpired, despite the government's faithful servicing of its debt obligations over decades and the creation of a vibrant domestic market in government securities, is not merely an intriguing twist in the story. It warrants careful study. Had Brazil achieved financial development commensurate with its success as a sovereign borrower the gap in income and productivity between it and more economically advanced nations would have been reduced, perhaps considerably so. It serves as a powerful counterexample to the general proposition of North and Weingast that institutional changes that credibly commit government to honor its obligations *necessarily* result in the financial development needed to attain modern economic growth.[5] When one considers Brazil in light of Britain's experience the difference is shocking. In Brazil the establishment of credible debt after 1824 proved considerably less glorious in its implications for financial development than scholarly work on the British case would lead one to expect.

DEBT AND DEVELOPMENT

This book about Imperial Brazil (1822–89) addresses how the government could successfully commit to borrow without default, yet at the same time fail to achieve financial development of the type that would support sustained economic growth. Brazil's ability to borrow was not a result of unconventional economic attributes. (Indeed, it established a good record of debt repayment well before it emerged as the world's main coffee producer.) Despite some economic vibrancy in plantation agriculture, Brazil was relatively poor, exhibited low productivity by the standards of the advanced North Atlantic economies, had a low savings rate, relied on a mix of slave labor and low-wage free workers, and remained overwhelmingly agricultural more than a century after the Industrial Revolution had begun in Britain. On most counts it was a normal Latin American country. The chief exception was its sovereign creditworthiness. Because of its success with borrowing, the Imperial state could finance deficits, fight and win wars, and contribute to investments in infrastructure. Historically, few states have been able to borrow and then avoid default for appreciable intervals of time. In this regard the Empire's record represents a remarkable success.

Borrowing without default is no accident. Financiers do not lend to a government that will not repay. The prospect that lenders to Brazil would be repaid was good for two reasons. First, the state was sufficiently strong that it could command a portion of the economy's output via taxation and use it to service the debt. The concentration of tax authority in the hands of central government helped in this regard. Richard Salvucci astutely noted that Mexico's need to repay its London debt pushed it toward political centralization in the nineteenth century.[6] In Brazil, it was political centralization—and the fiscal capacity it implied—that helped make it possible to issue debt in London in the first place. Second, lenders were confident not only that Brazil could muster sufficient resources to pay but also that it would actually be willing to honor its debts. This was no small feat. Until the mid–twentieth century the doctrine of sovereign immunity made it impossible for creditors to take sovereign debtors in default to court. Moreover, whether a government repays has little to do with the economic results of its borrowing. Governments repay loans when they find it in their interest to do so. A few countries repay for centuries on end, while others default with shocking consistency. When borrowing is followed by shoddy fiscal practices and exacerbated by an adverse economic or political shock, it often culminates in a sharply reduced willingness to repay and then default.

To see just how exceptional the Empire was as a sovereign debtor, one need only consider the very recent past. The most recent rounds of crisis and default have seen far-flung states hammered by debt problems, with herculean efforts to limit the damage in the debtor countries through debt write-downs, international financial assistance, and debilitating austerity. Having defaulted in 1982, Mexico, by way of example, was saved from another default in 1994 only because of an external bailout. Brazil defaulted in 1983 and Bolivia in 1989. A decade later Ecuador defaulted (and then defaulted again a little more than a decade after that). In 1998 Russia's nearly decade-long boom turned to default. Ukraine soon followed. Argentine public finances collapsed early in the new millennium. The result was the largest sovereign default in history.

Recent problems with debt are not restricted to developing nations. Greece has been at the forefront of the fiscal crisis in Europe, its bondholders taking a 50 percent cut in their claims in hopes of staving off total default. Iceland and Ireland have flirted with default, Spain and Portugal have received bailouts to keep the banking sector from dragging their governments into default, and the public finances of Italy faced considerable pressure. Even the United States and Great Britain, nations whose governments have not reneged on debt in centuries, saw their credit ratings downgraded as banks and ratings agencies looked askance at rising debt and fiscal weakness.

Imperial Brazil is a striking exception to the history of debt and default in Latin America. Fiscal prudence and a political commitment to repay debt kept public finances on an even keel. This finding diverges fairly sharply from long-standing views. Early republican critics of the constitutional monarchy harped on its ostensible failure to balance its budgets and the debt that resulted.[7] Later scholars tended to echo this view. Caio Prado Junior argued that, because of continuous fiscal deficits, "Imperial Brazil, despite all of its advances, did not enjoy at any moment financial stability or security."[8] For Celso Furtado, the "few loans" taken after Brazil's independence "had unproductive goals, and as a result enormously aggravated the already precarious fiscal situation," while the "service on the external debt created serious fiscal difficulties, contributing to a reduction in public credit."[9] Even the eminent historian José Honório Rodrigues went so far as to assert that "all of the Empire's difficulties originated in the country's financial situation."[10]

Claims of persistent fiscal problems under the Empire fail to square with the history delineated in the chapters that follow. In the aftermath of independence Brazil enjoyed nearly seven decades of government borrowing without debt repudiation or default. Its credit was so good that it could borrow long in London at least once per decade before 1850 and multiple times per decade thereafter. Through the First Reign, the Regency, and nearly fifty years of the Second Reign, those who held the debt issued by Brazil received interest without fail. If King Philip II of Spain was the "borrower from hell," the Brazilian Empire was truly divine for its bondholders.[11] Using other people's money, including that of Rio's great slave traders as well as the money market in London, the Empire's statesmen secured recognition of the nation's independence by external powers, sustained the armed forces in early struggles against hostile neighbors, covered deficits, extended the basic institutions of governance across much of the national territory, beat back separatist movements and regional revolts, shored up and subsidized military allies inside neighboring countries, and defeated a hostile aggressor in a drawn-out, costly war. These requirements were too expensive and too urgent to be met solely from current tax revenues. Brazil shrewdly paid for state building by leveraging its future public revenues to secure long-term lending. The political economy of this borrowing remains a surprisingly neglected theme in the historiography of Imperial Brazil.[12]

SUMMARY OF THE ARGUMENT

The account given in this book runs in the following terms. With independence in 1822 Brazil's leaders confronted a two-pronged challenge: how to solve the fundamental problem of state building, and how to deal with a burdensome public debt bestowed by the Portuguese crown. The solution to these problems echoed that adopted in late-seventeenth-century England. Given that the Portuguese crown had used discretionary authority under absolutism to write down its debt and force loans from its subjects, the solution in Brazil was an institutional arrangement that limited the crown's ability to unilaterally conduct fiscal policy. The Constitution of 1824 created a parliament with authority over the budget and borrowing. Because the parliament's lower chamber was elected, it was necessarily responsive to the interests of the enfranchised elite. This allowed domestic debt holders to exercise influence over financial policy via a constitutionally defined veto point in the policy-making process. These formal political institutions constrained and ultimately eliminated the monarch's ability to unilaterally tax, spend, and debase the currency. Because of the creditworthiness conferred by institutional arrangements that supported repayment, Brazil was able to progressively increase its funded debt. Between 1824 and the end of the Empire in 1889, the government issued nearly 67 million pounds sterling overall in bonds in London. It also took out three loans at home and issued perpetual bonds in the domestic market. The value of this domestic debt eventually exceeded that of the government's foreign borrowing.

By the standards of emerging markets at the time, this degree of access to capital on both sides of the Atlantic was remarkable. It is widely accepted that, for sustained economic growth to occur, asset holders must be relatively secure in their ownership. The creation and extension of basic investor protections—limits on the sovereign's capacity to expropriate assets—play a central role in development. What Brazil did *not* get from its commitment to honor the property rights of creditors was the development of private financial markets to nourish entrepreneurs, farmers, and manufacturers. Indeed, a revolution in private finance proved far more elusive than the revolution in public finance. For sure, private-party financing existed. But there was precious little of it and almost no long-term sources of entrepreneurial capital. Business finance suffered from politicized market interventions that undermined the development of domestic capital markets. The national government heavily restricted access to the limited liability, joint-stock form of the corporation until 1882. The result was high barriers to entry in commercial banking, especially for note-issuing banks. These policies limited the options of entrepreneurs seeking to create or expand businesses and left firms constrained in their ability to raise capital.

The central government's dominance over all financial matters meant that Brazil's provinces could not tailor their own banking and business policies to best suit local needs. The Empire's extreme concentration of policy authority was the opposite of the situation that prevailed in the United States, where state governments had the independence to charter banks and corporations. The very institutional arrangements that made Brazil the most credible borrower in nineteenth-century Latin America made economic policies unresponsive to all but the most select among business interests, repressing financial innovation. Had the Empire been less politically centralized it probably would have liberalized incorporation before the 1880s and would have developed more financial intermediation. This counterfactual is neither as quixotic nor distant as it might first appear.[13] The loosening of restrictions on incorporation that began in the early 1880s had, by the end of the decade, boosted the growth in joint-stock companies and accelerated the rate of capital formation. The reach of the reform extended to industrial investment: annual machinery imports more than tripled in real terms in the 1880s.[14] The military government that replaced the constitutional monarchy transformed a simple loosening of credit into high inflation and an asset bubble. Even after the crash in the early 1890s, those manufacturers that had entered the capital market during the boom exhibited higher rates of productivity growth over the following decades.[15]

The impact on private finance of the state's restrictions is impossible to calculate with any semblance of quantitative precision. Yet the direction of the effect is not in doubt. Irrespective of the Empire's success with sovereign borrowing, the barriers to mobilizing capital via joint-stock companies left Brazil decades behind financially. When one considers what could have been achieved by permitting the use of corporate forms and banking practices already available elsewhere, the costs of such restrictions appear very high.

The supply of property rights on which financial development depends is a policy choice determined in the political arena. The extent of investor protection and the prospects for financial development were partly determined by the degree of accountability that politicians had to their constituents.[16] The Empire's electoral system enfranchised a relatively narrow slice of the population, mainly free adult males with proof of sufficient income. The most influential were property holders, men who held financial interests in Rio de Janeiro, or owned planting and ranching concerns in the provinces, or both. Elected officials responded only to a restricted set of economic interests. Many of the relations at the highest levels were as much personal as political. In such a setting financiers can command outsized influence over policy since they also command relatively scarce capital.[17] This might seem to bode well for financial interests. Yet low levels of political accountability, along with rent seeking by a privileged group of capitalists, rigidified the obstacles to financial development. A state that is strong enough to supply property rights is strong enough to abrogate them, or provide them only selectively.[18] This dilemma would bedevil Brazilian finance for most of the nineteenth century. The delinking of the revolution in public finance and the development of private capital markets that Brazil exhibited runs contrary to what one might expect. The potentially far-reaching economic benefits of the type that North and Weingast argued would result from the commitment to honor sovereign debt may be difficult to secure.

Britain's success made it seem as if credible sovereign borrowing and financial development necessarily went hand in hand. Translating sovereign commitment into broader financial development required more. After 1688 the British parliament not only safeguarded the property rights of state creditors but also proved responsive to demands from entrepreneurs for corporate charters that would allow them to create businesses and recruit capital.[19] For Brazil, independence from Portugal was an opportunity to foster a broad financial revolution of the type engendered in Britain after 1688 and in the United States following the War of Independence. That the Empire's new political institutions committed the state to honor sovereign debt yet stifled private financial markets meant that Brazil's constitutionalist rupture with Portuguese absolutism comprised, at least in financial terms, an "inglorious" revolution. The Empire firmly eschewed the model of the relatively permissive financial environment of Britain and the United States.

THE ISSUES

Imperial Brazil offers investigators a valuable case by which to examine a more general set of issues about government borrowing and financial development. Outside of a limited set of well-studied cases, detailed historical assessments of the financial consequences of institutions that honored sovereign debt remain in short supply. Four topics intersect with Brazil's early experience. The first of these is how new states create and sustain sovereign borrowing—a question that continues to occupy considerable interest among investigators in economics, political science, and economic history. Brazil appeared as a relatively high-quality sovereign borrower at the precise historical moment in which Spanish America was coming unglued. Considering Brazil in a Spanish American mirror suggests some of the benefits of credibly committing to debt repayment. Initial loans in the 1820s to Spanish American states gave way to defaults.[20] Peru was the first to succumb, in 1826. Gran Colombia and Chile followed, halting payments just a few months later. Buenos Aires staved off default, despite the Brazilian naval blockade, until 1829. By then any remaining optimism regarding Latin American sovereign bonds had been buried by the default in 1827 on the massive debt of the region's largest borrower, Mexico.[21] By 1829 every debtor state in Latin America except Brazil had defaulted on its London bondholders.[22]

Several countries that succeeded in borrowing again simply repeated the defaults of the 1820s at various intervals through the rest of the century.[23] Venezuela ultimately defaulted on external creditors at least four times before 1870, even after write-downs and refinancing. Mexico paid interest intermittently and rescheduled its foreign debt on eight separate occasions through 1885. Repeated delays in remittances for interest, drawn-out negotiations for the resumption of payments, and failed efforts to obtain interest on arrears frustrated bondholders in London for decades. At the end of 1885, nine out of sixteen Latin American governments that had borrowed overseas were again in default on their loans, which collectively comprised 44 percent of the total foreign debt of Latin American governments. Of *all* foreign government loans in default in London in the 1880s, some 86 percent were Spanish American.[24] Given this record of serial default, these countries paid dearly on the occasions when they were able to borrow again.[25] While Spanish American public borrowing abroad became synonymous with default, the Brazilian Empire adhered to its obligations even when rocked by political upheaval, economic downturns, and financial crises. It was a feat that even many U.S. state governments in the nineteenth century failed to accomplish.[26]

It was not just in London that the Empire proved to be unusually successful. It also gained access to an ever-increasing amount of long-term *domestic* capital. This was the second feature of its borrowing that makes Brazil an especially interesting case. The government borrowed repeatedly at home in an era when most other Latin American governments were regularly in default. Brazil thus avoided the strongest form of what modern experts in international finance have labeled original sin.[27] Most of the home bonds were denominated in domestic paper currency and after 1838 offered no guarantee of repayment of principal. Investors nonetheless sopped them up. The individual financiers, private banking houses, and commercial lenders that made up the primary market for government bonds served as an important source of long-term state finance. In Brazil the government issued debt in a local market for the bonds that increasingly resembled that of far more advanced economies.

A third feature of interest is the way in which Brazilian creditworthiness came undone some sixty-five years after the first London loan. After the overthrow of the constitutional monarchy in 1889, the republican government faced serious problems raising new loans in London. What is surprising about the onset of difficulties in the 1890s is that many countries that borrowed and successfully serviced their public debt for a lengthy interval of time appreciably reduce their propensity to suffer debt crises. And they especially reduce the chance of defaulting at low levels of debt.[28] Brazil had the singular misfortune of sinking into "debt intolerance" after having avoided it for so long. In 1898 the government defaulted on the London debt.[29] Though it returned to the international capital market several times in the early twentieth century, it defaulted again in 1914, and after 1931 the country fell squarely among governments that were cut off from lending by virtue of having repeatedly failed to honor the terms of their foreign loans. It was this stark reversal of fiscal fortune after the overthrow of the constitutional monarchy that paved the way for Brazil to join the club of nations classified as serial defaulters.

The fourth area of interest involves precisely the linkages between creditworthiness and capital markets. Starting in the sixteenth century, nations whose governments committed to honor sovereign debt also defined an array of financial property rights that resulted in the florescence of financial markets.[30] Imperial Brazil's profile as a quality borrower should have made it a candidate for just such a broad-based financial revolution. That it did not helps shed light on the conditions that must be met for such a linkage to be forged. Despite the demand for both short-term and long-term government debt, a financial revolution in banking and in stock and bond markets proved to be elusive. Imperial Brazil, rather tragically, missed out on the most important positive externality associated with credible public borrowing.

FRAMEWORK, QUESTIONS, AND HYPOTHESES

This book's central concern—how Imperial Brazil achieved the singular feat of becoming a credible borrower while failing to achieve broader financial development—involves several distinct but related parts. The study breaks the topic down by addressing four main questions: Precisely how was the state able to borrow repeatedly during the Imperial era? What specific roles did domestic and foreign capital markets play in the government's borrowing? What accounted for shifts in the government's default risk after it had secured access to loans? And finally, what was the relationship between the political institutions that supported sovereign borrowing and the obstacles to private financial development? The approach followed in answering these questions is that of a case study that works across the boundary between social science and history. Case studies necessarily pose challenges to any attempt to generalize their findings. Yet in providing particular insights they shed new light on issues of broader applicability. The historical investigation of a single case over the better part of a century avoids a number of the pitfalls of cross-country analysis over a relatively short time interval.[31] The book weds modern political-economic theory and method to archival materials and published primary sources in order to emphasize historical specificities, while keeping the more general problem of financial development in close view. It is directed to two main audiences. The first consists of specialists in political economy who work on problems of sovereign debt, financial development, and political institutions. The second is historians. Because the interests of these audiences can be distinct, the fit of the book cannot be congruent with both at every point in the text. Readers with a background in political economy, for example, need not tarry in chapter 2 for the discussion of the ruler's commitment problem. Similarly, historians of Imperial Brazil require no introduction to its political institutions. The book strives to make the history relevant to social scientists, while making an explicit political economy approach relevant and useful to historians.

Assessing the Empire's experience with sovereign borrowing and its relation to financial underdevelopment requires a theory. Social scientists and historians have increasingly invoked institutional factors to help explain important economic outcomes.[32] This book takes Imperial Brazil's political institutions seriously by specifying them as explicitly as possible where relevant and demonstrating how they shaped outcomes by structuring the strategic interaction among purposive agents in the economy and polity. As a point of departure for the rest of the book, chapter 2 presents a model of the political economics of sovereign borrowing. It establishes the conditions under which a ruler will seek to borrow and under which capitalists will agree to lend, despite having no access to third-party enforcement of the debt contract. The model underpins the inquiry of chapters 3 through 5 in particular. It highlights how particular institutional arrangements permit higher levels of borrowing at lower cost—stylized conditions that correspond remarkably well to the Imperial state's own institutions and to its own experience in the capital markets. The most visible of these institutions was the division of fiscal authority between the executive and the legislative branch defined by the Constitution of 1824. The parliament uniquely possessed the authority to change taxes, approve or modify spending, and authorize new borrowing. The lower house—the chamber of deputies—was preeminent in formulating fiscal policy and held a control right over revenues and expenditures. The chamber had the power to ensure there were sufficient funds available to service the debt. The constitutional enshrinement of fiscal authority was a core part of the political penalty for default. Any attempt by the emperor or the executive to unilaterally default on the debt risked provoking a profound constitutional crisis by usurping parliament.

Chapter 2 also establishes the contours of Brazil's public finances from independence in 1822 to the fall of the constitutional monarchy in 1889. It tests the hypothesis that the Empire's fiscal policy was sustainable. While the government ran intermittent deficits, it offset them with surpluses that were large enough to enable it to sustain its debt. Whenever the debt increased, so did the fiscal surplus required to avoid default. Because increases to the debt, along with increases to the budget surplus, both required action by parliament, it can be inferred that borrowing and repayment were conscious political choices.

The hypothesis that Imperial Brazil was unusually successful in both foreign and domestic capital markets is tested in chapters 3 and 4 by reference to the trajectory and terms of its borrowing.[33] While the chapters focus on different markets, they deploy comparable tools and measures to assess changes in creditworthiness. The Empire's foreign debt garnered attention from contemporaries and modern scholars alike.[34] Chapter 3 details the rise of its external borrowing—almost all of which was British in origin—after independence. To make the argument that the state attained the credibility required to convince foreign lenders that it would abide by its contractual obligation to repay, the chapter presents estimates of the amounts owed as well as original estimates of the ex ante cost of borrowing implied by its loan contracts with London bankers. Chapter 4 considers an analogous appraisal of the domestic debt. The hypothesis that the Empire was excessively reliant on foreign lending is rejected. For much of the Imperial era the bulk of Brazil's debt was *domestic* in origin.[35] The volume of domestic borrowing increased more rapidly than the foreign debt, and the cost of new domestic borrowing fell dramatically, especially from the early 1830s to the 1850s. Overall the government enjoyed increasingly favorable terms on its loans in both markets.

Chapter 5 identifies changes in the government's creditworthiness by reference to the default premium on Brazilian bonds traded in London and Rio de Janeiro. By locating persistent shifts using weekly data on bond yields it identifies key turning points in the evolution of the Empire's risk premium. It considers and rejects the hypothesis that Brazil's reputation for repayment was the chief determinant of the decline in country risk. In most instances durable changes in the pricing of Brazilian credit risk in the bond markets were related to domestic political events and foreign policy shocks, especially war. These created political and fiscal stresses that altered bondholders' expectations of the government's willingness to pay. Investors faced such episodes with trepidation and viewed their successful resolution with relief, repricing sovereign risk accordingly.

Financial development is a requirement for, rather than a mere handmaiden of, modern economic growth.[36] The specific form that financial development takes—either through securities markets or through banking—turns out to be less important than achieving at least one of them. That Brazil's financial revolution was ultimately inglorious resulted from its failure to spark the growth of banking and equities markets. Chapters 6 and 7 focus on the capital market with emphasis on the country's financial center in Rio de Janeiro.[37] Chapter 6 draws on original indicators of joint-stock company formation in Rio de Janeiro, along with the history of legislative changes bearing on capital markets, to test the hypothesis that the state's regulatory action stifled private financial development through the early 1880s. Corporate chartering tended to decline in periods when the state's fiscal needs increased, suggesting that government used its discretionary powers in granting charters as a form of fiscal repression. Restrictions on incorporation were especially damaging in branches of business where capital requirements were high.[38]

Chapter 7 focuses on the evolution of commercial banking in Rio de Janeiro. Commercial banking was the sector where regulatory restrictions and barriers to entry were most visible. The few banks that did obtain limited liability joint-stock status became incumbents in what was a fundamentally closed banking system through 1882. Brazil's political centralism directly contributed to limits on the number and size of corporations by restricting entry of firms using the corporate form. Political barriers to entry particularly benefited incumbent banks, limiting competition while offering the prospect of high returns for owners of the banks' equity. The very barriers that afforded these banks a chance to garner economic rents gave them an incentive to oppose entry by potential rivals. Barriers to bank entry were not wholly arbitrary. On the contrary, political-financial cronyism was common in Rio's main commercial banks. Connections between banks and politicians afforded political support to the legal restrictions on bank entry.

In 1889 the Republic fundamentally altered the principal characteristics of the political institutions—as well as the commitment to repay debt—established under the constitutional monarchy. Chapter 8 summarizes the key discontinuities. These were evident in the political-institutional changes wrought by the overthrow of the constitutional monarchy and also in the evolution of Brazil's capital markets. Following the replacement of the monarchy by a military government (which then segued to the oligarchic Republic), sovereign creditworthiness in the 1890s along with fiscal and monetary policy more generally began to founder. Bankers in London and Paris cut off existing lines of credit. The new regime quickly ran into great difficulty in securing new long-term loans in London. Brazil defaulted on its foreign debt in 1898, turning to its London creditors to reschedule its obligations. Over the same period private finance in Brazil lurched along, supporting both the expansion of industry and the growth of the two main stock exchanges, in Rio de Janeiro and São Paulo.

The inversion after 1889 of the trajectories of public and private finance endured until well into the twentieth century. The Republic's pairing of diminished sovereign creditworthiness with an expansion of the market for business finance was no less aberrant than the Empire's success with sovereign borrowing and dismal performance in private-sector financial development. The sequence of changes in Brazil was quite different from that observed in the relatively high-income economies of the North Atlantic. Considering the relationship between politics and finance solely in light of the experiences of advanced economies can do as much to obscure as to illuminate the factors that explain the expansion of capital markets and the political economy of growth. There have been few studies of states that got sovereign borrowing right while getting private financial regulation wrong. This book helps to remedy that omission, leveraging the distinctiveness of the Brazilian case to reconsider the relationship between credible sovereign borrowing and financial development.

CHAPTER TWO

Sovereign Borrowing and Imperial Debt Policy

THE GOVERNMENT OF Imperial Brazil borrowed repeatedly by credibly committing to repay its lenders. Yet the country paradoxically remained mired in financial underdevelopment. This puzzle is addressed in the chapters that follow. This chapter lays the groundwork for the investigation. The first section draws from theoretical work on sovereign debt to derive conditions under which lending and repayment occur and to establish a framework of analysis. Three fundamental hypotheses emerge from the model summarized here (and detailed in appendix I). The second section details the Empire's political-fiscal institutions and provides evidence to support the proposition that those institutions made it possible to borrow. The third section gives an overview of public finance and presents an econometric test of the hypothesis that Brazil's parliament acted to make debt sustainable. The final section presents some implications for subsequent chapters.

LOANS, DEFAULT, AND COMMITMENT

Sovereign debt subordinates economics to politics. Governments may borrow in the market, but political factors are paramount in determining whether governments repay. The market matters only in setting the opportunity cost of capital. The institutions that govern debt policy are of central importance in determining whether a government can borrow.

The amount of credit the state commands depends on the likelihood of repayment. This section details the framework used to investigate sovereign borrowing and financial development. It also highlights four main points. The first is that there are conditions under which government borrowing is desirable. This insight is a standard result in economics but clashes with conventional wisdom on Latin America, where many countries have suffered recurrent debt crises.[1] The second point is that sovereign borrowers are prone to default. Default risk limits access to loans. Reducing default risk to the point that borrowing becomes feasible required a credible commitment to repay. The third point is that solutions to this commitment problem have a fundamentally political character. When the state's creditors (or their representatives) can control the ruler's financial actions, loans are easier and cheaper for the ruler to secure. The fourth point is that successfully committing to repay may promote broader financial development that supports the expansion of the real sector of the economy. The conditions under which this occurs are quite particular, as the Brazilian case will reveal.

Governments borrow to spend money they do not have at their immediate disposal. Debt is desirable when the benefit of public borrowing exceeds its own costs and the costs of alternative actions. Borrowing allows government to bring resources from the future into the present. The purposes of this borrowing can range from the mundane (short-term deficit finance), to the visionary (infrastructure projects with large, long-term payoffs), to the least productive yet most urgent (suppressing internal rebellion or defending against invasion). A sharp fiscal downturn does not make the state insolvent, but in the near term its "liquidity" is limited. By borrowing, a government can sustain much of its activity. Alternatives to borrowing may be prohibitively expensive in either pecuniary or political terms. Sharp increases in taxes create efficiency-degrading distortions; covering a deficit in hard times by abruptly raising tax rates imposes a deadweight loss to the economy at the wrong moment. Sudden cuts to spending can reduce the provision of essential public goods. The use of loans to smooth taxes and the consumption of the public sector may in many instances be better than the costs of the alternatives.

If a government's need to borrow is clear, its ability to borrow is more puzzling. Capitalists lend only in expectation of future repayment with interest. To repay, the government must first command resources that are sufficient to settle the loan. It also must be willing to use those resources for repayment instead of diverting them to other uses. Theoretical work identifies strong incentives for rulers to repudiate debt.[2] The appeal of diverting the money originally promised to creditors makes debt policy inconsistent. The government's optimal choice when it first borrows is no longer optimal when it comes time to return capital with interest.[3] The precepts of efficient public finance require that debt be repaid by taxes on the least elastic portion of the tax base. This turns out to be nothing other than the money that was already borrowed—the ruler "taxes" the money borrowed and defaults on the lenders. Sovereign immunity protected defaulting rulers from legal claims by creditors until well into the twentieth century. The equilibrium in such a setting is not default but an absence of lending if potential lenders exercise foresight.[4] A government's discretionary authority redounds to its own detriment. The incentive to default persists even if the money required to repay is available. Risk of default poses a major obstacle to sovereign borrowing. Fiscal crisis is neither a necessary nor sufficient condition for default. It is rare that either the government or the nation is so severely limited by resource constraints that it becomes truly insolvent.[5]

Historically, defaults are only weakly associated with economic downturns. Fully one-third of defaults since 1820 occurred in good economic times. Many governments sustained debt service in the face of adverse economic shocks.[6] This suggests that a government's ability to repay has less bearing on the risk of default than previously thought. There is no doubt that adverse shocks increase the interest rate that governments must pay to borrow.[7] That default is not an automatic response to downturns highlights the role of political factors. Pressure to free up resources for other purposes becomes especially acute in hard times. Fiscal contraction raises the ruler's political cost of debt repayment, reducing the willingness to repay. That default occurs because the *political* burden of debt is too high means that the ability to repay is not the sole or even the principal issue influencing the ruler's decision. Government default is inherently political because it is rooted in ex post opportunism and the sovereign character of the debtor. The incentive to repay, even when resources are available, is weak in the absence of mechanisms to compel repayment.

Risk of default leaves a government underfunded relative to its ability to service debt. If a government can persuade lenders they will be repaid, it can take loans up to the ceiling set by the strength of its commitment. The more credible its commitment to fully repay, the more it can borrow even in hard times. Commitment is neither cheap nor easy to establish. It is thought that a borrower that values future access to capital will repay even in hard times in order to establish a good reputation and thereby obtain future loans.[8] Yet the threat of exclusion from credit markets is often insufficient to deter default.[9] Only if the number of financiers is sufficiently small, and they are able to act collectively, will the threat of credit market exclusion support lending to the sovereign.[10] If the ruler can circumvent the credit embargo by offering preferential terms on existing debt or new loans and thereby entice some financiers to continue lending, it will undermine the penalty.[11] Creditors left to punish default in an uncoordinated fashion are ineffective. The ruler treats each lender's loan as marginal; the value of the marginal loan is very low, or even zero, making default attractive.[12]

A penalty stronger than that of an uncoordinated (and ineffective) credit embargo seems necessary to sustain lending to a sovereign state.[13] For the borrower's promise to return capital to the lender to be credible, the penalty devised for default must be strong enough to compel repayment.[14] Credibility might require nonmarket sanction mechanisms that are overtly political or even coercive. Political models of sovereign creditworthiness are less common than economic models, but several have identified ways in which political penalties support borrowing.[15] Particular institutional arrangements can facilitate the political representation of creditor interests in ways that made default very costly and nearly impossible. Italian city-states implemented a number of institutional changes that enhanced the credibility of promises to repay debt.[16] The rise of the Dutch Republic involved similar innovations that fostered the first revolution in public finance.[17] The most celebrated case is that of England in the wake of the Glorious Revolution.[18] There, the assignment of control over both taxes and the purse to a standing legislature, along with the political salience of creditors, created a penalty that deterred default.

Several controversies have arisen over the role of institutions that establish creditworthiness by limiting the ruler's authority. Objections have emerged on historical, theoretical, and empirical grounds, mainly in the context of arguments related to the British case. Several studies have cast doubt on institution-based commitment as either a necessary or even sufficient condition for improving the state's credit. One strand of critique argues that it was the rise of more unified tax systems that made higher levels of borrowing possible and more affordable.[19] Another strand argues that risk premia on government debt did not decline in response to institutional changes.[20] Several studies have questioned whether financial property rights more generally were improved by commitment because neither the interest rate implied by returns on private assets nor rates charged by bankers in London fell in the immediate aftermath of institutional changes.[21]

Other findings mitigate a number of these criticisms. A focus on interest rates as the sole indicator of the fiscal impact of institutional changes may be misplaced. James Robinson has pointed out that institutional reforms that enhance the government's commitment to repay may show up not as a reduction in borrowing costs but as an increase in the credit ceiling and the volume of lending.[22] If one were to assign primacy to borrowing costs as an index of creditworthiness, it now appears the rates paid by the British government fell to a much greater extent with the Glorious Revolution than existing critiques suggest.[23] Research that considers the impact of tax capacity jointly with institutional changes finds that states with fragmented tax regimes could nonetheless reduce the risk premia on their loans by establishing a parliament with fiscal authority.[24]

A ruler willing to submit to a stronger penalty for default will gain access to capital only if lenders can commit to applying the penalty in case of default. Creditors confront their own problem of time inconsistency.[25] Imposing ex post the penalty that was announced ex ante may be too costly. If creditors cannot effectively penalize default the ruler will be rationed too tightly; debt is capped at a level less than the supposed true cost the ruler could be made to pay if he defaulted.[26] An alternative to a large but difficult-to-implement penalty is to give creditors control over the very decision to default or repay. This authority could include the power to redirect fiscal resources to debt service in case of shortfalls. The assignment of fiscal authority to creditors (or their representatives) strengthens the default penalty by reducing its dependence on ex post collective action by creditors. Embedding fiscal authority within institutional arrangements makes it costly for the ruler to reverse unilaterally. This transforms the default penalty from an ineffective credit embargo (or the sterile output loss of economic models) to a political crisis. A constitutional government with separation of powers, with its array of checks and balances and the legislative branch's control of fiscal matters, serves as the classic example of such an arrangement.

The consequences of credibly committing to repay may not be limited to simply securing loans. Scholars working in historical political economy have proposed a far more blood-stirring prospect: the institutions that credibly commit the government to honor debt are indispensable not just for borrowing but also for the development of vibrant financial markets more generally. Financial property rights let credit markets develop unhindered by fear of sequestration. Firms can more affordably raise capital, and a key cost of doing business declines.[27] Taken together these propositions imply that getting the political institutions right makes it possible to get the economic institutions right—which in the case of sovereign borrowing improves the creditworthiness of the state, while benefiting the financial sector. The institutional changes in the political arena that provide secure rights in financial property support investment and economic growth.[28] The emergence of markets for corporate equity and debt, the increase in mortgage lending to agricultural enterprises, the growth of banking, and an overall expansion of credit are the central components of successful financial development. Investigators have singled out sound public finance as a prerequisite for the financial development required for modern economic growth.[29] The literature on economic performance finds that financial development has profoundly beneficial consequences for the real sector of the economy.[30]

The points sketched thus far suggest a model of sovereign borrowing in which creditors have the authority to both monitor the Treasury and exert fiscal control. It generates the hypotheses used in the chapters that follow to analyze the Empire's ability to borrow. The model's chief predictions are well established.[31] If penalties for default are so strong that the ruler honors debt in every circumstance, then lenders do not charge a risk premium over the risk-free interest rate. If the penalty for default is too weak, lenders do not extend loans, and the ruler is excluded from the credit market. Penalties that deter default only up to a certain level of indebtedness require the ruler to pay a risk premium to compensate lenders for the risk of default. A ruler that submits to a default penalty in this range can borrow but is rationed credit. Stronger penalties result in a higher debt ceiling and permit larger amounts of borrowing. These results are intuitive and follow directly.

Extending the model to incorporate monitoring and fiscal control by creditors shows how these features reduce borrowing costs, increase the amount loaned, and make the penalty for default a political one. Details on the model and its derivation are presented in appendix I. By way of overview, a ruler seeking to make its promise to repay credible can institute a mechanism to allow lenders or their political agents to monitor fiscal matters related to debt. To make its commitment stronger still, the ruler can give up fiscal authority to lenders or their agents, giving them control over the stream of resources from which debt will be repaid. Embedding these authorities in political institutions, the expectations of which are shared by the ruler and political elites, can make them durable. Violations of these institutional rules are then costly because of the political and constitutional crisis they provoke. The assignment of monitoring and fiscal authority to lenders thus provides an ex ante solution to the ex post problem of how to make the penalty for default credible.

A noteworthy corollary is that monitoring and fiscal authority need not be complete, but their scope and extent matter. Adverse fiscal shocks are less likely to provoke default and proportionally less injurious to borrowing when the degree of fiscal authority assigned to lenders is greater. In the limit, when the fiscal authority held by creditors is complete, service on the debt will continue in all but the most extreme downturns.

Investigators have highlighted some ways by which the linkages between the commitment to repay sovereign loans and broader financial development may operate. Protections for government creditors can contribute to protections for wealth more generally.[32] The result is increased saving and investment. Where the authorization to pool capital to undertake business had been exclusively a royal prerogative, the creation of a standing parliament with fiscal authority could pave the way to reduced restrictions on organizational forms of the firm and broader access to capital. If legislators can capture some of the benefits of new business, whether legitimately or not, they have incentives to support access to corporate charters. The regulatory apparatus becomes more responsive to the goals of entrepreneur constituents and investors, increases the supply of charters, and leads to higher levels of business investment and finance.[33] In the case of Imperial Brazil, however, this hypothesis is rejected. The commitment to repay rooted in a parliament with fiscal authority did not lead to broader financial development.

POLITICAL INSTITUTIONS AND COMMITMENT
IN IMPERIAL BRAZIL

The model just described corresponds to fundamental features of the political institutions that governed fiscal practice in Imperial Brazil. This section fleshes out those features to show how Brazil underwent a revolution in public finance. The Constitution of 1824 enshrined the right of the state's creditors to be repaid. Claims on the Treasury by the state's lenders were as inviolable as rights in other kinds of property; repayment was an explicit civil and political right of Brazilians.[34] As a contemporary analyst noted, "The state's creditors, because they entrusted their capital, or because they served [the needs of the state], have the right to receive their property or wealth."[35] The enforcement of rights required tangible political mechanisms. The model given here emphasized three features that support sovereign borrowing: default penalties, monitoring, and fiscal control. Each of these corresponds to institutional features adopted after independence. The arrangement that the constitution embodied tied the monarch's hands in the areas of taxing, spending, and borrowing by assigning those authorities to a parliament. The shift in fiscal sovereignty in the 1820s from the crown to the new parliament created a fiscal control right.[36] Parliament could meet any attempt to default extraconstitutionally by denying new taxes to the cabinet and the emperor. Political penalties were also available should the executive branch default without parliamentary authorization. One such penalty was criminal prosecution of the finance minister by the chamber of deputies, under the law making ministers responsible for their advice to the crown and their actions on its behalf.[37] Refusal by a cabinet minister to execute laws to service the debt was understood to be a prosecutable offense.[38] Unilateral default by the emperor could generate political deadlock, constitutional crisis, and even risk his removal. The forced abdication of Pedro I in 1831 made clear that the emperor was not immune to sanctions if enough groups found that he had transgressed the basic limits on his authority.

On fiscal questions the attributes of the two houses of parliament differed greatly. Under the constitution the approval of the annual budget was a parliamentary responsibility.[39] Most budgetary authority was concentrated in the chamber of deputies.[40] Proposals for new taxes and their deliberation were reserved first for consideration by the chamber. Similarly, the chamber had precedence in setting expenditures. Spending plans proposed by the cabinet required deliberation and approval in the chamber of deputies first. The senate could propose amendments to reduce outlays, tax rates, or the duration of tax provisions that had already passed the chamber. But it could not amend a bill to increase a tax, extend the period of time the tax would apply, broaden its scope, or increase expenditures.[41]

Because the chamber of deputies was elected, it was the most responsive among the constitutionally defined veto entities to the interests of creditor constituents. This helped to align the interests of the officeholders with those of debt holders. Should the majority support a proposal to default, the deputies in the lower house would be vulnerable to electoral sanctions from the constituents who were most adversely impacted by the pecuniary implications of default—namely, Brazil's merchants and planters. The political standing of the state's domestic creditors made support for default in the elected chamber politically costly. Representative (if oligarchic) government and divided fiscal sovereignty internalized the political costs of default at multiple levels.

To better see the central role of the chamber of deputies in fiscal decisions, consider two paths to default under the constitution. Active default required that either the cabinet or a deputy propose default and that a majority of deputies support it. Passive default required a chamber majority to exclude debt service from the budget or for the chamber to fail to pass a budget at all. In the latter case, no institutional rule defined a budgetary reversion point by which debt service automatically continued until a new budget was passed. Debt repayment required deliberation and support by the chamber each year.

The claim here that there was a political-institutional basis for credible commitment has several testable implications. If a majority of deputies favored repaying the debt, it would use its veto power to block any active proposal to default. If the chamber majority sought to prevent passive default, it would include interest to bondholders in each annual budget. A third implication is that if a majority opposed the financial proposals of the executive, it would contest them. Finally, if the chamber majority wanted to ensure repayment of the debt, it would create mechanisms for monitoring and fiscal control for the part of each year that parliament was not in session.

The hypothesis that the chamber could effectively block active attempts to default is tested by reference to a unique episode in 1831.[42] With the opening of the legislative session, Finance Minister José Inácio Borges dutifully reported the fiscal problems of the Empire to the chamber, calling the external debt that had accumulated during the reign of Pedro I a "financial embarrassment."[43] On 4 June 1831 he proposed to suspend external debt service.[44] The bill found both supporters and opponents on the floor of the chamber. Deputy Cunha Mattos mustered opposition to the bill, arguing that external default had major implications for property owners in general. He cast doubt on whether the cabinet could be trusted to honor the state's obligations, including those to Brazilian citizens: "[The proposal] has caused a widespread shudder in the city of Rio. The people, capitalists, merchants and those with commercial interests, and finally those who value the preservation of property, will all be frightened if they believe that, in front of the whole world, we are going to declare bankruptcy . . . shares of the [domestic] public debt have been offered at will, and no one wants to buy them. . . . their owners deeply perturbed by fear that there is no way the interest on them will be paid."[45] For Cunha Mattos and other opponents, the prospect of a selective default against bondholders in London put the credibility of all government obligations in doubt.

Leaders who supported external default inadvertently stoked the fears of domestic creditors. In arguing that foreign creditors had been unjustly favored by the terms of Brazil's borrowing, the nativist deputy Bernardo de Vasconcelos claimed that English merchants and capitalists held much of the domestic debt.[46] This had the unintended effect of threatening all holders of the domestic bonds with repudiation. Politically, default on external bonds held in London was one thing; default on domestic bonds held in Brazil was another issue altogether. Near the end of the floor debate on the proposal, Deputy Montezuma sought to reject default quickly because the very proposal would inevitably register in the financial market simply by having been considered at all: "The capitalists will say: 'we do not believe in these speeches, the finance minister is right, the public credit is failed.'"[47] Less than a week after the finance minister proposed default, the bill failed on the floor of the chamber by a vote of more than two to one. The chamber's defeat of the proposed moratorium sent a clear message to capital markets on both sides of the Atlantic. The debate and outcome revealed that the interests of domestic creditors and foreign bondholders were not at odds but aligned—they had a common objective in seeing that the state honored its obligations. That the elected representatives of domestic creditors wielded the influence required to make sure that the government did repay owed to the veto authority assigned to the chamber under the constitution.

The chamber could also block new borrowing when it did not agree with the cabinet's goals. The cabinet had no authority to raise funds in the capital market without parliamentary sanction. By design the power to approve new borrowing was "an attribute that belongs to the general assembly; if it were not, it is evident that the government, if it wanted to evade the legislature's authority to fix expenditures and receipts, would be able to compromise the public credit, alienate state revenues, dictate the present and the future, and undermine legislative authority; it would institute absolutism, complete control over fortune and social well-being."[48] When cabinet proposals to borrow came in times of special urgency or from cabinets with an especially strong chamber majority, they were more likely to pass than in ordinary times. Yet such circumstances were no guarantee of success. Opponents could hold up authorization for new loans in order to score political points on other issues. In 1836 the finance minister sought to issue debt to raise 2 million milréis in order to pacify the provinces of Pará and Rio Grande do Sul, which were in revolt. Two prominent opposition leaders, Deputies Miguel Calmon du Pin de Almeida and Bernardo de Vasconcelos, opposed the loan. They used the floor debate to criticize the cabinet for inadequately leading the armed forces and failing to repress the revolts.[49] The bill ultimately passed because of the threat to the integrity of the Empire that the revolts posed.[50] But the cabinet was considerably weakened in the process of defending its proposal, leaving government only a few weeks later. Majority status was also no guarantee that a cabinet would secure support for its financial policies. In the late 1870s an overwhelmingly Liberal chamber ousted its own finance minister, Silveira Martins, after a series of blunders involving a new loan and a large emission of paper currency.[51] To push him out, the majority halted deliberation of other questions and raised a motion to deny confidence in the cabinet. The minister soon departed.[52] It was an example of how the chamber could place the executive branch in check on financial policy and even strip the cabinet of a finance minister whose actions did not have backing on the floor.

The hypothesis that the chamber majority prevented passive default by allocating tax revenues to debt service is tested by reference to spending bills authorized by the chamber. Table 2.1 reports the laws that provided for annual interest on the debt, from the first national budget passed in 1828 after parliamentary recognition of the public debt to the last budget passed under the Empire.[53] Every budget included provisions to pay interest on the external and domestic debt. Budgets were not, however, always passed in time for the start of the new fiscal year. The reversion policy in the absence of a budget was to default on the debt. This never happened because the chamber majority always ensured that the debt would continue to be serviced by passing *prorrogativas*. These measures either extended the previous budget until a new one was voted or voted a more limited bill addressing solely debt service. In at least nineteen fiscal years between 1826 and 1889, prorrogativas were employed for a portion or even all of the fiscal year.[54] That the chamber majority, irrespective of party, ensured that debt was always serviced reveals that political support in the chamber for repayment was consistently strong.

The hypothesis that monitoring by creditors was an important component of the commitment to repay is tested by reference to institutional innovations undertaken by the chamber of deputies. The chamber's capacity to monitor and control fiscal activity while parliament was in session was straightforward. Discussion of the new budget required that the chamber review and approve the previous year's spending.[55] In addition to this annual requirement, from 1830 on the chamber could establish an audit commission at any time.[56] Parliament did not, however, operate on a year-round basis. Regular sessions ran only four months; in some years the emperor extended the session or convened a special session. From the first legislature in 1826 through the last in 1889, the chamber of deputies was in session a little more than 40 percent of the time.[57] This meant that nearly 60 percent of the time deputies could not monitor the Treasury, nor could parliament directly intervene to remedy shortfalls on

Table 2.1

Budget Laws Passed by Parliament for Service on the External and Internal Debt, 1828–89

FISCAL YEAR	NUMBER OF LAW	DATE OF LAW	FISCAL YEAR	NUMBER OF LAW	DATE OF LAW
1829	—	8 October 1828	1861/62	1,114	27 September 1860
1830/31	—	—	1862/63	1,149	21 September 1861
1831/32	—	15 December 1830	1863/64	1,177	9 September 1862
1832/33	—	15 November 1831	1864/65	1,198	16 April 1864
1833/34	—	24 October 1832	1865/66	1,245	28 June 1865
1834/35	58	8 October 1833	1866/67	1,292	15 June 1866
1835/36	38	3 October 1834	1867/68	1,507	26 September 1867
1836/37	99	31 October 1835	1868/69	1,507	26 September 1867
1837/38	70	22 October 1836	1869/70	1,587	28 June 1869
1838/39	106	11 October 1837	1870/71	1,764	28 June 1870
1839/40	60	20 October 1838	1871/72	1,836	27 September 1870
1840/41	108	26 October 1840	1872/73	2,091	11 January 1873
1841/42	164	26 September 1840	1873/74	2,302	28 June 1873
1842/43	243	30 November 1841	1873/74	2,348	25 August 1873
1843/44	317	21 October 1843	1874/75	2,348	25 August 1873
1844/45	347	21 October 1843	1875/76	2,585	3 July 1875
1845/46	369	18 September 1845	1875/76	2,640	22 September 1875
1846/47	396	2 September 1846	1876/77	2,670	20 October 1875
1847/48	396	2 September 1846	1877/78	2,707	31 May 1877
1848/49	478	24 September 1847	1877/78	2,792	20 October 1877
1849/50	514	28 October 1848	1878/79	2,792	20 October 1877
1850/51	555	15 June 1850	1879/80	2,940	31 October 1879
1851/52	586	6 September 1850	1880/81	2,940	31 October 1879
1852/53	628	17 September 1851	1881/82	3,017	5 November 1880
1853/54	668	11 September 1852	1882/83	3,141	30 October 1882
1854/55	719	28 September 1853	1883/84	3,141	30 October 1882
1855/56	779	6 September 1854	1884/85	3,230	3 September 1884
1856/57	840	15 September 1855	1885/86	3,271	28 September 1885
1857/58	884	1 October 1856	1886/87	3,277	25 June 1886
1858/59	939	26 September 1857	1886/87	3,334	16 October 1886
1859/60	1,040	14 September 1859	1888	3,349	20 October 1887
1860/61	1,041	14 September 1859			

Source: Collecção das Leis do Império do Brazil, various years.

Note: Before 1830 and after 1887 the fiscal year corresponded with the calendar year. In several instances a single budget law would address two fiscal years (e.g., 1877/78 and 1878/79). In other instances a single year would have two budget laws, a result of *prorrogativas* (e.g., 1877/78). The budget for 1829 encompassed the province of Rio de Janeiro and the *côrte* district only. No final budget for 1831 was located, although the finance minister did propose a budget to the chamber, covering the first calendar semester of 1830 and the new fiscal year that began on 1 July. The proposal included debt service; *RMF 1829*, 3a Parte, "Orçamento Geral," Documento E, p. 2. Sources do not report passage of the budget by parliament. The budget adopted for 1831/32 was the first for the entire nation.

debt service. The chamber of deputies took several measures to address these limitations on their control.

To make sure that unanticipated budget shortfalls between parliamentary sessions did not disrupt debt service, the chamber delegated authority to the cabinet to align resources with budgeted outlays. Starting in 1833 the budget law permitted the cabinet to shift surpluses across categories within the budgets of each of the ministries.[58] In 1848 the parliament further authorized the cabinet to spend beyond the budget by use of *créditos suplementares* and *créditos extraordinários*. Supplemental credits were created when tax receipts were not sufficient for the budgeted outlay. Extraordinary credits were for urgent necessities not anticipated in the budget, such as the outbreak of war. The chamber made this authority a standing one in 1850.[59] In 1862 the chamber limited supplemental credits to only those expenditures that by their nature tended to vary after the budget passed into law. Shifting surpluses from one part of the budget to cover shortfalls in another ministry required discussion by the full cabinet and was not permitted any earlier than the ninth month of the fiscal year.[60]

In using its expenditure authority, the cabinet could not disregard the parliament's fundamental preferences. The chamber created a requirement, ex post, for the cabinet to stand (or fall) on the basis of its intersession spending. The annual report from the finance minister of the previous year's accounts, which required chamber review and approval before a new budget could be crafted, included the additional credits that had been used by the cabinet. If the majority did not support the additional expenditure, the cabinet could be censured and the minister of finance subjected to prosecution under the law of ministerial responsibility. It was a requirement that had teeth. In 1875 the finance minister and president of the cabinet, the visconde do Rio Branco, sought approval for supplementary and extraordinary expenditures of some 15 million milréis beyond what parliament had authorized.[61] Dissident deputies within Rio Branco's own party demurred. Budget deliberations, including a cabinet proposal for new borrowing, effectively came to a halt. The chamber ensured, however, that debt service would continue to be paid.[62] Only when the cabinet agreed to step down did the chamber majority sanction the past spending, pass the new budget, and authorize new borrowing.[63]

Solving the problem of how to monitor the Treasury between parliamentary sessions the chamber took a straightforward approach. Article 15, section 14 of the constitution charged parliament with debt management. So in 1827 the parliament created a committee of major bondholders, gave them access to the Treasury's accounts on a continuing basis, and placed them face to face with the finance minister every two weeks. The law conceived by the chamber required that five *capitalistas nacionais* who were "most qualified for the duty and who held the largest amounts of apólices" be appointed to manage the operations of the section of the finance ministry that handled debt repayment.[64] The Junta Administrativa da Caixa de Amortização, as the committee was called, oversaw the disbursement of interest to domestic apólice holders and payments to loan agents in London to service the external debt. The members of the junta reviewed the caixa's accounts at its meetings and certified them quarterly.[65] These accounts were made public, providing information to creditors about the transfers from the Treasury for interest payments.[66]

Table 2.2 presents the composition of the junta from 1828, when it was first established, through the end of the Empire in 1889. Its members were a cross-section of the uppermost ranks of the merchant-finance elite of the First Reign, the Regency, and the Second Reign. Fourteen would receive titles of nobility from the emperor. Nine received their first titles only after having begun their junta service. The five who were already ennobled were elevated in rank thereafter. Early members tended to be major merchants or slave traders. Joaquim José Pereira de Faro was a Portuguese-born merchant who founded two insurance companies and created two large coffee *fazendas* in the Paraiba valley.[67] Ignácio [Ignace] Ratton was a prominent financier in Rio, "of council" to the emperor, a founder of the Banco Comercial in 1838, and the president of the powerful commercial association from 1840 to 1846.[68] Joaquim Antônio Ferreira, the "master of a great fortune," was the single largest slave importer to Rio de Janeiro between 1812 and 1830.[69] Francisco José da Rocha (second barão de Itamaraty) was a "major capitalist and property owner" who matriculated with the board of trade as an international merchant at a remarkably young age, built the sumptuous Itamaraty palace, and was a member of a prominent slave-trading clan.[70]

Table 2.2

Members of the Junta Administrativa da Caixa de Amortização, 1828–89

NAME	TITLE	PERIOD SERVED ON THE JUNTA
Joaquim José Pereira de Faro	Barão do Rio Bonito [1st]	1828–43
Ignácio [Ignace] Ratton	none	1828–47
Pedro José Bernardes	none	1828–31
Joaquim Antônio Ferreira	Barão de Guaratiba [1st]	1828–59
José Francisco de Mesquita	Barão de Bomfim	1828–73
Henrique José de Araújo	none	1832–40
José Ferreira dos Santos	none	1840–46
Manoel Lopes Pereira Bahia	Barão de Merity	1843–60
João José de Araújo Gomes	Barão de Alegrete [1st]	1847–62
Francisco José Bernardes	none	1848–63
José Antônio Moreira	Barão de Ipanema [1st]	1859–69
Francisco José da Rocha [filho]	Barão de Itamaraty [2nd]	1860–83
José Joaquim de Lima e Silva Sobrinho	Visconde de Tocantins	1862–89
José Lopes Pereira Bahia	none	1864–69
Militão Máximo de Sousa	Barão de Andarahy [1st]	1870–88
Cândido José Rodrigues Torres	Barão de Itamby	1870–77
Jerônimo José de Mesquita	Barão de Mesquita [1st]	1874–86
Joaquim Antônio de Araújo e Silva	Barão do Cattete	1878–89
Antônio Clemente Pinto Neto	Visconde de São Clemente	1884–86
Antônio de Araújo Aragão Bulcão	Barão de São Francisco [3d]	1888–89
João Baptista da Fonseca	none	1888–89

Sources: Reconstitution of the junta's members relies on city almanacs for Rio de Janeiro; Pedro Plancher-Seignot, *Almanak Imperial do Commércio e da Corporações Civis e Militares do Império do Brasil* (Rio de Janeiro: Casa de P. Plancher-Seignot, 1829), 157; Emilio Seignot-Plancher, *Almanak Nacional do Commércio do Império do Brasil* (Rio de Janeiro: Typographia Imperial, 1832), 154; Sebastião Fabregas Surigue, *Almanak Geral do Império do Brasil* (Rio de Janeiro: Typographia Commercial Fluminense, 1838), 128; Viuva Ogier e Filho, *Folhinha Commercial, ou Pequeno Almanak do Rio de Janeiro* (Rio de Janeiro: Typographia dos Editores Viuva Ogier e Filho, 1843), 125; and for 1850–89, *Almanak Administrativo, Mercantil e Industrial da Côrte e da Capital da Província do Rio de Janeiro [Almanak Laemmert]* (Rio de Janeiro: Eduardo e Henrique Laemmert, 1843–89). Through 1869 these are supplemented by Biblioteca Nacional, Setor de Manuscritos, I-34, 20, 015, "Notas contendo a relação dos membros nomeados para a Junta da Caixa de Amortização," n.d.

After the legal slave trade from Africa to Brazil was outlawed in 1831 and the opportunities to legitimately build wealth as a *negreiro* had ended, the leading state creditors were mainly financiers. Manoel Lopes Pereira Bahia started out as a retail merchant, but the connections he forged in high finance and foreign commerce were strong; he was a brother-in-law of the second barão de Itamaraty, and by the time of his appointment he was the father-in-law of Miguel Calmon du Pin e Almeida, visconde (and ultimately marquês) de Abrantes.[71] Pereira Bahia's son was named to a seat on the junta four years after his father's death, as was his daughter's second husband, Joaquim Antônio de Araújo e Silva.[72] Cândido José Rodrigues Torres was a merchant, capitalist, and the brother of Joaquim José Rodrigues Torres (visconde de Itaboraí), one of the most important statesmen of the era and a founder of the "party of order," as the Conservatives were originally known.[73] Antônio Clemente Pinto Neto was a grandson of the slave-trading merchant barão de Nova Friburgo and became a prominent planter and coffee factor as well as a founding member of the main coffee brokers' interest group in the last decade of the Empire.[74] José Joaquim de Lima e Silva Sobrinho was a longtime merchant and financier; he served as vice president and, later, president of the Banco do Brasil and was president of the commercial association for more than two decades. He was the brother of Luís Alves de Lima Silva (duque de Caxias), Conservative stalwart, army general, and commander during the war against Paraguay.[75]

By virtue of their position as the biggest individual creditors of the government, the members of the junta were able to monitor the debt service department in the Treasury and thereby safeguard their own substantial financial interests. But in doing so they also represented the community of bondholders in general. Their involvement reduced information costs for the state's creditors and the members of parliament. This arrangement, somewhat counterintuitively, made leading bondholders the guardians of the state's own credit.

THE PUBLIC FINANCES OF THE EMPIRE: AN OVERVIEW

It is possible to characterize Brazil's public finances between 1824 and 1889 on the basis of original time series data on the stock of debt, revenues, expenditures, and debt service payments. Several features are noteworthy. Brazil did not often run primary deficits, but when it did they could be quite large. Borrowing was indispensable. Although the net stock of debt did not increase much between 1830 and 1850, market access allowed Brazil to retire old loans with new borrowing. It also allowed the finance ministry to convert short-term unfunded obligations into lower-cost, long-term securitized debt. A remarkable share of the funded debt was domestic in origin by midcentury. Debt-servicing requirements were large enough that default would not have been surprising. Instead of defaulting the parliament responded to increases in debt by programming primary surpluses into the budget. The state's fiscal reaction function accommodated new borrowing by raising taxes and cutting outlays in order to service new debt. This made the debt and the Empire's fiscal policy sustainable, as one might infer from the absence of default over sixty-five years of borrowing. Each of these points warrants elaboration.

The largest outlays over the course of the Imperial era were military in nature, followed by debt service payments. The combined shares of the army, navy, and finance ministries never fell below 50 percent of total spending from 1830 through 1889. Brazil was not unusual in this regard. In Britain, by way of comparison, nearly 90 percent of central government outlays up to the mid–nineteenth century involved current spending on the military and service on the debt, most of which had accumulated as a result of earlier military spending.[76] In Brazil the early conflict in the Cisplatine and the blockade of Buenos Aires in the 1820s, "civil commotion" up through the 1840s, the war with Paraguay in the 1860s, and public relief expenditures in drought-stricken regions in the late 1870s and 1880s all made large demands on revenues.[77]

To cover these costs the central government taxed. Many of the taxes at independence were holdovers from the late colonial era.[78] Most revenues, however, derived from duties on foreign trade, which had become the largest category of receipts after the opening of the ports in 1808. Again, Brazil was not unusual. Import duties were critical to the revenue of the United States in the nineteenth century.[79] In Brazil the share of indirect taxes, consisting almost entirely of import and export duties, rose sharply from the early 1830s, peaking at 90 percent of ordinary revenues in 1841.[80] It declined thereafter but never fell below 70 percent of the government's annual resources. Import duties and related charges were the largest component of indirect taxes. Tariff revenues fluctuated dramatically in the late 1820s and then climbed steeply during the 1830s,

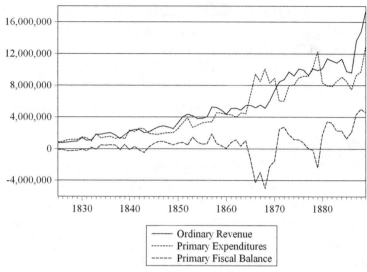

FIGURE 2.1 Ordinary revenues, primary expenditures, and the primary balance, 1825–89 (figures in pounds sterling at 1889 prices)

rising to a peak of 75 percent of revenues in 1841. Thereafter the share of import duties fell steadily but always remained well in excess of half of the central government's receipts. Export taxes accounted for far less, typically between 10 and 20 percent of revenues.

Widely used revenue and expenditure data assembled by contemporaries suggest that the Imperial state ran chronic deficits after 1822.[81] This impression is erroneous. *Total* expenditures did commonly outstrip receipts; in only eleven of sixty-eight years was there a gross fiscal surplus. Modern public finance, however, focuses not on total expenditures but on *primary* expenditures, which exclude payments to service the debt. More often than not Brazil ran a primary fiscal surplus. Figure 2.1 presents ordinary revenues, primary expenditures, and the primary balance (expressed in pounds sterling). Negative balances indicate a primary deficit, while positive balances reveal years of fiscal surplus. The Empire's budget was only occasionally in deficit.[82] The key exceptions were the years up to 1832, a few years at the end of the 1830s and the beginning of the 1840s, the war years from 1864 to 1870, and briefly again in the late 1870s. Of the four periods in which Brazil ran primary deficits, the first corresponded to the campaign against Buenos Aires and the political turmoil of the late First Reign, while the second occurred in the midst of the war of secession in the province of Rio Grande do Sul. The third directly corresponds to the war against Paraguay. The last period coincides with the devastating drought in the northeast, during which the central government spent heavily on projects and relief. The size of the pre-1850 deficits pales in comparison with those of the 1860s and 1870s.

Deficits were recurrent but transitory because fundamental fiscal health proved to be strong. On average, revenues grew more quickly than outlays. Real revenue expanded at an annual rate of 4.3 percent; real primary expenditures grew at only 4.1 percent. Had the year-to-year revenues and outlays hewed closely to these trend rates of growth, Brazil would have enjoyed a consistent and growing primary surplus and the Imperial state would not have had to borrow at all for deficits. There were, however, large year-to-year departures from trend in expenditures; it was mainly the volatility of outlays that made borrowing necessary.

Brazil also borrowed to shift its pre-independence debt to a funded basis. The colonial state had a long record of borrowing and failing to repay. The decade and a half after 1808 in which the crown governed the Portuguese empire from Rio de Janeiro added greatly to this debt. Most royal borrowing was unfunded and rarely amortized. A few small loans were raised between 1808 and 1821 from the local merchant community for purposes ranging from establishing a gunpowder factory to supporting Swiss immigration.[83] To create a new source of lending, Prince Regent João VI created the first Banco do Brasil in 1808, conceding to it a lucrative monopoly over the issue of banknotes. In return, the Royal Treasury drew on the bank at its pleasure. In order to finance military expenditures the government repeatedly raised the cap on the issue of notes by the bank, which the Treasury then borrowed. With João VI's return to Portugal in 1821, he declared the debt of the local Treasury to the bank to be public rather than royal, saddling his Brazilian subjects with the burden.[84] During the progression toward independence the following year, Pedro, as prince regent, forced a loan that added to the inherited debt.[85]

Thus, much like the United States, independent Brazil was born indebted. In 1822 debt was already at least 12.3 million U.S. dollars, or around 2.5 million British pounds sterling.[86] It grew quickly: by 1831 the

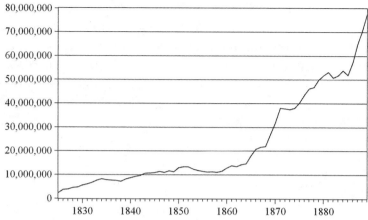

FIGURE 2.2 Real total funded debt, 1825–89 (figures in pounds sterling at 1889 prices)

foreign debt alone was more than 5 million pounds sterling, the funded domestic debt was 18 million milréis, and there were some 38.5 million milréis in *unfunded* obligations, including new arrears on top of the existing debt to the Banco do Brasil.[87] Increasingly, however, the portion of the debt placed on a funded basis grew. Figure 2.2 portrays the trajectory of the annual aggregate real stock of funded debt from 1825 to 1889. Excluded from the figure are unfunded obligations and dividend guarantees (which were contingent liabilities) to railroads and other subsidized firms. It also excludes debt issued by provincial governments. By 1889 every province except Ceará had its own funded debt.[88] In 1889 the total debt of Brazil's provincial governments was 73.5 million milréis, around 10 percent of the central government's own funded obligations.[89] The most remarkable feature underpinning the figure was the growth of domestic borrowing; by the early 1850s the share of debt that had been raised abroad fell below 50 percent for the first time. The Imperial government mobilized domestic savings in a way that was unrivaled elsewhere in Latin America in the nineteenth century. In the early 1870s the share of total debt that was domestically issued in Brazil was double that of Chile and of Mexico, three times that of Venezuela, and more than ten times that of Peru.[90]

Despite rebellions, external war, financial panics, and trade downturns, Imperial Brazil tolerated its debt burden well. Debt tolerance varies greatly across countries. In the latter twentieth century, for example, as many as 20 percent of defaults in middle-income countries occurred when the external debt ratio was 40 percent of GDP or less.[91] Poorer countries were even less tolerant of their debt burdens. For highly debt-intolerant states a debt greater than 20 percent of GDP sharply raises the likelihood of default. National income estimates are notoriously fragile for nineteenth-century Brazil, but for the early 1870s one can state with confidence that its debt came to around 40 percent of GDP.[92] This was less than the levels at which debt inhibits economic growth in advanced economies.[93] It was nonetheless easily within the range at which lower-income countries exhibit elevated rates of default. Yet Brazil always repaid. Evidence on the debt-service ratio (interest and amortization as a share of revenues) tells a similar story. Annual debt payments ran as high as half of ordinary revenues in the late 1830s and never less than the 20 percent figure of the 1850s. Brazil's average debt-service ratio was nearly as high as that of eighteenth-century Britain and France.[94] Yet the ratios are at best a rough guide to outcomes: France defaulted and Britain did not. That Brazil did not default highlights the parliament's willingness to supply the taxes required to make interest payments, despite the relatively high budgetary cost of doing so.

Modern work on sovereign debt identifies a key sustainability condition: so long as the debt does not grow more quickly than the net present value of fiscal resources available for repayment, it is sustainable.[95] Violations of this intertemporal budget constraint cause the debt to explode in size. The rate of increase in per capita income was low in nineteenth-century Brazil, such that growing out of the debt was not an option.[96] Government would have had to run surpluses chiefly through the careful management of outlays for fiscal policy to have been sustainable. That the Imperial government never defaulted might be taken prima facie as evidence of fiscal sustainability. This need not necessarily have been the case; an unsustainable fiscal policy may not have resulted in default until later. The republican government of the 1890s faced considerable difficulty with credit, and its apologists faulted the fiscal practices of the Empire. These concerns direct attention to a testable hypothesis: the Imperial government avoided defaulting not only because the chamber voted to provide money to service the debt but also because it systematically increased fiscal surpluses in response to higher levels of debt.

Three econometric tests of the hypothesis that the Empire's fiscal policy was sustainable are used here. The results of all three suggest that the ensemble of taxes, expenditures, and borrowing undertaken by the government was fully sustainable between 1824 and 1889. The first test is straightforward. If the data series for the government's overall fiscal balance (including interest payments on the debt) is stationary, then fiscal policy was sustainable. Stationarity requires the mean and the variance of the series to remain constant over time. Most of the unit root tests applied to the deficit data reject a unit root in the total fiscal deficit, pointing to sustainability.[97]

The second test is whether the primary fiscal balance (exclusive of interest payments) responds to changes in the debt. Both variables are expressed as ratios to the level of exports.[98] A sufficient condition for sustainability is for the government to increase its primary balance in response to increases in debt.[99] How to conduct the econometric test for this relationship depends on the nature of the data series. Unit root tests show that the annual debt series is nonstationary. The nature of the data for the primary balance is less clear because unit-root tests returned ambiguous results. The approach then is to consider the possibility that the primary balance could be either stationary or nonstationary. Assuming first that the primary balance has a unit root, a sufficient condition for sustainability is that the primary balance and the debt are cointegrated with a cointegrating vector of $[1, -r]$, where r is the rate of interest on the debt.[100] Cointegration is a long-run statistical relationship between variables in which they never drift too far apart. The estimates in panel A of table 2.3 show that the deficit and debt were cointegrated, which is sufficient to establish that fiscal policy was sustainable. Additionally the results imply an average annual cost of capital to the Treasury of 7.9 percent per year. This is consistent with the ex ante interest rates on Brazil's borrowing in London and Rio between 1825 and 1889.[101] The error-correction estimates in panel A further show that short-run deviations from the long-run equilibrium were corrected by way of changes in the primary balance (as one might predict) rather than changes in the debt.

The third test is that for the scenario in which the primary balance data are assumed to be stationary. Because the debt data are nonstationary, all variables are transformed by taking first differences. The response of the primary balance to increases in the debt is assessed using ordinary least-squares regression on the differenced variables. Under a sustainable fiscal policy the coefficient on the debt variable should be positive. Two additional variables control for cyclical influences on the primary balance; both use definitions originating with Barro's work on tax smoothing and employed by other scholars since.[102] GVAR is a measure of the cyclical component of government outlays:

$$GVAR = \frac{g - g^*}{x}$$

where g is the level of government expenditures in a given year, g^* is the trend value of g, and x is the value of exports. Government expenditures above the trend cause the variable to take on a positive value and should be negatively related to the primary balance. YVAR is a business cycle indicator that includes a measure of temporary falls in output:

$$YVAR = \left(1 - \frac{x}{x^*}\right)\left(\frac{g^*}{x}\right)$$

where x is the value of exports in a given year and x^* is the trend of the series. Whenever exports are above the trend, the variable takes on a negative value.

Panel B in table 2.3 presents the results of the regression. The coefficients for the cyclical variables take on the expected signs and values. Although the interest rate implied by the coefficient on debt is higher than what was typically the case in the Imperial era, the positive response of the primary balance to changes in the debt is nonetheless sufficient to demonstrate sustainability. Panels A and B together imply that government increased its required budget surplus by some 8 to 11 pounds sterling on average for each additional 100 pounds of debt.

From these results one can infer that parliament's annual provision of interest and its willingness to increase the amounts allocated for debt service as the debt grew made Brazil's debt sustainable. The chamber of deputies crafted taxes and expenditures under an implicit rule that internalized the intertemporal budget constraint. This responsiveness was visible, by way of illustration, in the new taxes approved by parliament in response to the tremendous increase in spending during the war against Paraguay. These included a personal tax and a tax on salaries of public employees (*vencimentos*) in 1867, a new stamp tax, a property transmission

Table 2.3

Econometric Tests of Fiscal Sustainability, 1825–89

Panel A. Cointegration of the primary fiscal balance and the debt

COINTEGRATING EQUATION

Primary Balance (–1)	1.000
Debt (–1)	–0.079
	(0.033)
	[–2.355]
Constant	0.119

ERROR CORRECTION	D (PRIMARY BALANCE)	D (DEBT)
Cointegrating Equation	–0.393	–0.583
	(0.099)	(0.360)
	[–3.968]	[–1.618]
D(Primary Balance(–1))	–0.053	–0.503
	(0.120)	(0.438)
	[–0.445]	[–1.147]
D(Debt(–1))	–0.058	–0.440
	(0.033)	(0.123)
	[–1.718]	[–3.577]
Constant	0.005	0.0481
	(0.010)	(0.038)
	[0.568]	[1.259]
Adjusted R-squared	0.209	0.169

Panel B. Determinants of the primary balance
Dependent variable: D(Primary Balance)

VARIABLE	COEFFICIENT	STANDARD ERROR	t-STATISTIC
Constant	0.0002	0.004	0.052
D(Debt)	0.109	0.042	2.550
D(GVAR)	–0.904	0.105	–8.599
D(YVAR)	–1.047	0.256	–4.089

Adjusted R-squared	0.73
F-statistic	56.6
Durbin-Watson statistic	2.21

Note: In both panels Primary Balance is the fiscal deficit or surplus (excluding debt service payments) divided by the value of exports, and Debt is the end-of-fiscal-year stock of total debt divided by exports. In panel A, standard errors are reported in parentheses, while t-statistics are reported in brackets. In panel B, GVAR is a variable for the cyclical component of government spending, and YVAR is a variable for the business cycle, as defined in the text. The regression is on the variables in first differences, and all coefficients are significant at the 1 percent level.

tax, and a tax on industries and professions, all introduced in 1869.[103] The political-fiscal reaction function revealed by the econometrics makes clear that policy makers systematically responded to higher levels of debt by programming fiscal surpluses sufficient to service those debts.

CONCLUSION

The principal features of the Empire's political-fiscal institutions made its commitment to repay debt credible. These included the authority of the chamber of deputies to monitor the executive's actions on debt service, the chamber's control right over fiscal matters, the political standing of the state's domestic creditors, and a political penalty should the executive unilaterally default. Together these features predict that the government would honor its debt to bondholders by vetoing proposals to default, funding debt service in the budget, and running a primary surplus large enough to pay interest. These hypotheses about the central role of parliamentary fiscal authority in making the commitment to repay credible are supported in this chapter by several qualitative tests and by econometric estimates of the government's fiscal response to debt.

CHAPTER THREE

Tropical Credibility on Lombard Street

WHEN THE GOVERNMENT of Imperial Brazil needed money that it could not affordably borrow at home, it looked abroad. For the first three decades after independence, the bonds that Brazil issued in London were the largest component of the Imperial government's funded debt. The government took so many new loans after 1850 that by 1865 Senator Francisco Gê Acaiaba de Montezuma (visconde de Jequitinhonha) mocked the frequency and ease with which the Empire could borrow in London: "Lombard Street! Lombard Street! The English capitalists don't stop providing us with money, as much as we like, and when we like."[1] By the 1870s informed observers assessed Brazil to be as creditworthy as the federal government of the United States. And although it could not rival the reliability of Britain as a debtor, the Empire was considered less risky than the governments of Portugal or Austria and considerably more creditworthy than Italy, Peru, Spain, Mexico, and Greece, among other states.[2]

Given the importance of the London loans, an assessment of the terms of Brazil's foreign borrowing is warranted. The first section presents estimates of the contribution of external borrowing to Brazil's fiscal resources. The second section describes how the London borrowing was done. Section three details the loans taken between 1824 and the overthrow of the monarchy. It tests the hypothesis from the model in chapter 2 that Brazil's political-fiscal institutions would allow the government to access loans in the capital market. The fourth section reports estimates of the government's cost of capital on its loans and the risk premium it paid to borrow. These are used to test a further implication: borrowing costs declined as the market increasingly viewed Brazil's fiscal institutions to be effective and durable. Section five presents measures of the probability of default on each loan. Because the risk premium is a direct function of the default probability, the two measures offer views of the same phenomenon from different angles. The conclusion highlights some of the broader implications of the Empire's experience with external borrowing. The chapter's findings can be summarized in the following terms. By most measures the Imperial state's forays into the London market were a success, if not always a bargain. The fiscal authority defined by the Constitution of 1824 conferred on the government a baseline level of credibility in the capital market. Compared with the difficulties the Portuguese crown had encountered since at least 1796, independent Brazil's market access was a notable achievement. While the evidence makes clear that the government was often at its external credit limit in the 1830s and 1840s, after 1850 it could borrow repeatedly and take on more debt. While borrowing costs increased at moments of political and fiscal stress, they declined on average over the Imperial era. Estimates of the probability of default confirm the insights provided by the other measures of creditworthiness. The government's loan maturities were long, with redemption dates that were decades off into the future. British lenders never placed the government on a short leash.

The institutional and political factors that made the Brazilian state's commitment to repay credible were not a one-off matter. The evolution of the quantitative indicators of creditworthiness was uneven until the early 1850s. War in the River Plate region in the 1820s, the suspension of service in 1828 on the Portuguese loan that Brazil had assumed in 1825, the suspension of regular amortization of its own loans, delayed remittances to loan contractors in the 1830s, and waves of internal instability from the late 1820s through the late 1840s meant that the first half of the century was one in which creditors were uncertain whether the political and fiscal institutions of the Empire could assure repayment. Nonetheless, the rejection by the chamber of deputies of the cabinet's proposed external default in 1831, the resumption of service on the Portuguese loan in 1834, and the resumption of amortization of the foreign debt in 1851 were all actions that signaled to foreign lenders that the Empire indeed took its overseas financial obligations seriously. The definitive consolidation of the Imperial state under the Second Reign, with the defeat of the last of the regional revolts in 1848 and the efficacy of the cabinet of the conciliação in the 1850s, further bolstered the government's standing in the London market. The improvement in creditworthiness thereafter was unambiguous. Over most of the Second Reign, Brazil was able to borrow ever larger amounts in London while paying a progressively lower premium for default risk.

BENEFITS AND COSTS: EXTERNAL BORROWING AND FISCAL RESOURCES

Borrowing abroad involved an array of potential advantages and disadvantages. Because sovereign bonds had to be serviced in hard currency, the stability of the exchange rate became a core concern of the Treasury. Brazil's monetary policies influenced not only the local price level but also the sterling value of the milréis. Any increase in the money supply beyond what was required to sustain transactions in the real sector could weaken the milréis and raise the local cost of external debt service. Large amounts of foreign currency debt are also associated with serial default. Excessive amounts of liabilities denominated in foreign currency magnify the vulnerability of the public and private sectors of the economy to external economic shocks. Trade policy also played a role. Persistent growth in imports unaccompanied by an expansion of exports could depreciate the milréis and raise the cost of external debt service. The act of borrowing abroad itself had an impact on trade and the exchange rate. While domestic borrowing could potentially crowd out private sector investment, foreign borrowing potentially lowered the real value of exports by raising their price in the world market. There were also perceived threats to sovereignty embedded in foreign borrowing. The overseas merchant bankers that handled Brazil's loans were not shy about urging specific financial policies on the cabinet in Rio de Janeiro. Bondholders in London organized in response to defaults in Spanish America and elsewhere, creating pressure groups that sought the involvement of the British government on the behalf of creditors.

Yet despite this array of potential costs, foreign borrowing had a clear upside as well. By tapping a capital market beyond the country's borders, the Imperial government greatly broadened the available supply of loans. Borrowing abroad helped mitigate the crowding out of private investment that excessive domestic borrowing might create. Raising money overseas through the issue of bonds denominated in pounds sterling partitioned the market for public debt into foreign and domestic components. This partition afforded the government a mix of flexibility and credibility in its debt policy. Secondary markets for sovereign bonds in London grew quickly in the early nineteenth century, providing liquidity that made these securities attractive to investors.

Gauging the contribution of external borrowing to the government's resources requires data on loan proceeds by fiscal year. The estimates constructed here rely on the provisions detailed in the original loan contracts in London. In instances where the money raised took the form of a single payment, the loan's proceeds are assigned to the fiscal year in which the contract was signed. In cases where the loan contractors raised money via public subscription, the money came in installments, sometimes spread out over more than a year. For loans that straddled two or more fiscal years, the value of the proceeds are allocated using the dates that each installment was credited to the Treasury.[3]

The results show the contribution of external credit. Figure 3.1 expresses the cash raised as a percentage of the government's ordinary revenues each year. The most striking feature of the graph is the outsized importance of the 1824 and 1825 loans. The money they raised tripled the government's resources for fiscal year 1825 and doubled them for fiscal year 1826. The amounts raised from later loans were even larger in absolute terms, and as a percentage of the ordinary revenues they ran in the double digits. London borrowing boosted the government's purchasing power beyond its revenue constraint by nearly 12 percent per year when averaged over the whole period. Because money from new borrowing came in roughly one out of every three years, the typical increment to revenues was closer to 34 percent in the years when borrowing took place. On two occasions in the 1860s the increase in fiscal resources that loans made possible far outstripped this figure. One was the 1863 loan (which was raised in fiscal year 1864). It settled a number of pre-1850 debts and converted a large amount of short-term Treasury bills to a funded, long-term basis. The other outlier was fiscal year 1866, when most of the pro-

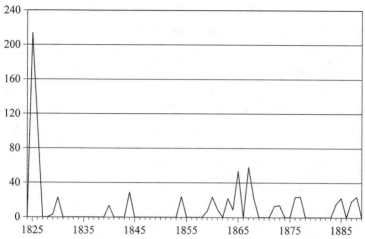

FIGURE 3.1 Additions to ordinary revenues from foreign-funded borrowing, 1824–89 (as a percentage of ordinary revenues)

ceeds from the large 1865 loan to help pay for military operations against Paraguay were received.

BORROWING ON LOMBARD STREET

Brazil's external borrowing was part of a larger process of growing capital outflows from Europe, mainly from Britain, in the nineteenth century.[4] In the 1820s the number of governments issuing bonds through merchant bankers in London grew rapidly. This upswing in borrowing was driven in good part by the demand for funds in newly independent Latin American nations.[5] Low yields on the British national debt left many investors looking for more lucrative opportunities.[6] The new debt issues of largely unproven borrowers in Latin America found an especially favorable reception.[7] The securities of Latin American governments were so popular among investors that a specialized exchange for foreign funds was created in London in 1823.[8] This initial wave of sovereign borrowing soon foundered. Financial panic in London in 1825 took down several banks involved in lending to foreign states.[9] Almost all of the early confidence in the securities of the new Latin American nations turned out to be misplaced. Panic was followed by disaster for many bondholders: every Spanish American government that had borrowed in London had defaulted before the decade ended.[10] Only the investors in Brazilian bonds continued to receive their interest payments.

Access by sovereign borrowers to the London capital market depended on merchant bankers. Many began as accepting houses that specialized in bills of exchange. Most of the London firms that structured sovereign bond issues already had, by 1820, foreign trade, currency exchange, and overseas remittances among their principal lines of business.[11] Merchant banks took deposits, actively traded in securities, discounted bills, advanced short-term credit, maintained correspondents, branches, or partner firms in other countries, and were connected to key London stockbrokers. Such firms played a central role in the government borrowing of the 1820s.

The principal intermediating functions performed by merchant banks involved pricing the new bond issue and drumming up investors. The success of any given bond issue was not guaranteed. Once the issue price had been set, the borrowing state could still be vulnerable to downturns in the bond market. The value added by merchant bankers in structuring the loans had several sources. One was the bank's ability to underwrite the loan by taking it "firm," contracting to provide a set amount of money raised through the sale of the government's bonds.[12] Loan contractors could function as market makers, buying bonds to directly shore up the price. Trusted brokers arranged large requests for shares. This hastened full subscription—allowing the loan to be formally listed on the exchange—and helped boost the bond's market price so that it would equal that in the contract.[13]

Because the identity of loan contractors could matter for the terms under which a government borrowed, states intent on entering the market had to consider the standing of their prospective contractor.[14] In London, the Brazilian government borrowed most frequently, but not exclusively, through the Rothschilds, first through Nathan Mayer Rothschild in the 1820s and then, from the 1850s on, through the N. M. Rothschild & Sons firm.[15] Of eighteen bond issues made in Europe by the Imperial state, the London Rothschilds handled fourteen wholly or in part. While other European merchant banks came and went, the Rothschilds' durability and standing were nearly unmatched. The firm accounted for fully one-fourth of all foreign securities issued in London, with the bulk of their Latin American issues done on behalf of the Brazilian government.[16]

The Rothschild firm used its correspondents in Rio de Janeiro and other ports to keep tabs on commercial, political, and fiscal conditions in Brazil even before independence.[17] Early monitoring was an investment on the part of the merchant bank that later enabled it to perform due diligence on behalf of bond investors. Nathan M. Rothschild avoided states that were poor credit risks. His willingness to handle Brazil's 1825 loan, for example, was clearly welcomed by the markets because it signaled quality on the part of the borrower. One contemporary observer noted that the involvement of the "eminent capitalist" in the new loan left "little cause to doubt that the Government securities of Brazil will, under his auspices, bear as high quotations in the money-market as those of any of the continental States."[18] The consistent focus on the creditworthiness of actual and potential clients meant that the loans Rothschild chose to handle were presumed to be good risks for investors.[19] This remained true more than a half century later: for Brazil's 1883 loan the press noted that "the honoured name of Rothschild, which has been singularly absent in all recent financial operations, was sufficient to guarantee the issue a favorable reception."[20] For the borrowing government there were clear benefits from working with a bank that had developed a good reputation, had an established clientele eager to subscribe loans, and had the ability to support bond prices during the critical period when installment payments were being made by investors.

Irrespective of the identity of the merchant bank handling any particular one of Brazil's loans, the process of borrowing was generally the same. Once credit operations were authorized by parliament and a loan approved by the finance minister, the terms were negotiated between a merchant bank and the Brazilian envoy to the Court of St. James. The ambassador took his instructions from the minister of finance in Rio de Janeiro. The contracts that emerged from these negotiations detailed the fees Brazil would pay to the bank for structuring the loan. The loans almost always had an initial discount to their par, or face value.[21] The contracts further specified the bond's coupon rate.[22] Money raised with the loan usually came in installments paid by the subscribers, with a discount conceded to investors for any early installments. It was also possible, although less usual, for a merchant bank to directly take up an entire bond issue, dispensing its own funds to the government in exchange for the bonds and bypassing the initial public subscription entirely.[23]

In return for the sum raised on the loan, the government contracted to punctually pay dividends, amortization, and fees. Contracts also specified the sources of funding for the loan's service. The issuing bank, in return for the contracted fee, handled coupon payments to bondholders and administered each loan's sinking fund. In nearly every instance when bonds were trading below par, amortization of the loan occurred through purchase in the secondary market by the issuing bank on behalf of the government. When bonds traded above par they were amortized through a lottery drawing conducted by the bank and redeemed at face value. Retired bonds continued to earn interest, which accrued to the sinking fund and was used to retire additional bonds. This mechanism was intended to make the loans self-liquidate and to preserve the seniority of earlier loans.

The government in Rio de Janeiro was not wedded to any particular loan contractor before the 1850s, and turnover among its financial agents in London in the 1830s and 1840s was frequent. Table 3.1 reports the identities of the merchant bankers that handled each of the Imperial government's loans. Of the eighteen distinct issues, two were shared by more than one firm. When the multimerchant syndicate that won the contract for the 1824 loan declined its option in 1825 to raise funds beyond the initial 1 million pounds, Nathan M. Rothschild stepped in to handle the balance of the loan. Two new loans taken simultaneously in 1829 were, in effect, a single issue put together by Rothschild and the syndicate of the merchant banking houses that had originated the 1824 and 1825 loans. New borrowing in 1839 and 1843 utilized yet other merchant bankers in London.[24] Samuel & Phillips in London, formerly of Rio de Janeiro, handled the 1839 loan. The firm was tied by blood relation to Samuel, Phillips & Cia. in Rio de Janeiro, who were regular correspondents of Nathan M. Rothschild.[25] Isaac Goldsmid, another prominent London merchant banker, structured the 1843 loan.

N. M. Rothschild & Sons handled Brazil's return to the London market in 1852 and in 1855 became the official overseas financial agent of the Brazilian government. Foreign bond issues were arranged exclusively via the London Rothschilds through the end of the Imperial era. As the

Treasury's financial agent, the London Rothschilds handled interest payments in Europe on the bonds of Brazil's National Loan of 1879.[26] Despite the firm's role in placing Brazil's debt, it did not ultimately hold large amounts of the bonds in its own portfolio. Brazil's sterling bonds (the overall volume of which was appreciable in the London market) accounted for only 2.4 percent of the London Rothschilds' total holdings in 1886.[27]

Table 3.1 also shows that the principal owed by the government on each loan almost always exceeded the sum raised, reflecting initial issue discounts and the loan intermediary's fees. For example, raising 1.21 million pounds in cash in 1860 required the issue of 1.373 million pounds' worth of bonds. The discount raised the effective yield to initial investors in the bonds beyond the published coupon rate, an approach that made new bonds particularly appealing. Issuance fees collected by the bank (analogous to points and origination fees on present-day loans) were built into the loan. These were usually paid to the intermediary in an additional increment of bonds. The advantage accruing to the government from paying its fees in its own bonds was that it did not have to front cash for the costs of issuing the loan.

ORIGINS AND PURPOSES OF BRAZIL'S FOREIGN LOANS

Table 3.1 summarizes the terms under which the Imperial state borrowed abroad. The declared purposes of the loans varied, from straightforward deficit financing to specific infrastructural uses. Of the eighteen loans, fourteen had little if any conceivable developmental purpose, conventionally defined. Excluded from the table is the Portuguese loan of 1823, which Brazil assumed in 1825. None of the funds raised by the loan went to the Brazilian Treasury; Brazil took over the loan as part of the diplomatic arrangement with Portugal and Britain to recognize Brazilian independence. In a number of instances, portions of new loans zeroed out the remaining balances from earlier borrowing. For example, the 1852 loan retired the Portuguese loan, while the loan of 1863 served partly to redeem the remaining balances on the loans of 1824, 1825, and 1843.[28] Refinancing of this kind proved necessary for a couple of reasons. On some of the early loans there were appreciable balances to be paid off at maturity, a result of the failure to amortize in the 1830s and 1840s. Some of the later loans had, by design, balances due at maturity. These balloon payments, in present-day parlance, were often covered with new borrowing.

Table 3.1

Brazilian External Borrowing, 1824–89

LOAN	PLACE OF ISSUE	PRINCIPAL PURPOSE OF LOAN	BANK	ISSUE PRICE	COUPON RATE	AMOUNT RAISED (IN POUNDS)	AMOUNT ISSUED	MATURITY (YEARS)
1824	London	Deficit and floating debt	Bazett, et al.	75	5	1,000,000	1,333,300	30
1825	London	Deficit and floating debt	Nathan Mayer Rothschild	85	5	2,000,000	2,352,000	30
1829	London	Loan interest	Nathan Mayer Rothschild	52	5	200,000	384,600	30
1829	London	Loan interest	Wilson & Co.	52	5	199,940	384,500	30
1839	London	Deficit and floating debt	Samuel & Phillips	76	5	312,500	411,200	30
1843	London	Portugal (Convention of 1842)	Goldsmid, et al.	85	5	622,702	732,000	20
1852	London	Retire 1823 Portuguese loan	N. M. Rothschild & Sons	95	4.5	954,250	1,040,000	30
1854	London	Extend maturity of 1824 loan	N. M. Rothschild & Sons	100	5	3,173,000	3,173,000	10
1858	London	Buyout of Dom Pedro II railroad	N. M. Rothschild & Sons	95.5	4.5	1,425,000	1,523,500	20
1859	London	Retire 1829 loan	N. M. Rothschild & Sons	100	5	508,000	508,000	30
1860	London	Bailout of private corporations	N. M. Rothschild & Sons	90	4.5	1,210,000	1,373,000	30
1863	London	Retire 1824 loan/1843 loan/redeem Treasury bills	N. M. Rothschild & Sons	88	4.5	3,300,000	3,855,300	30
1865	London & Amsterdam	War finance	N. M. Rothschild & Sons	74	5	5,000,000	6,963,600	37
1871	London	Redeem Treasury bills/finance railroad extensions	N. M. Rothschild & Sons	89	5	3,000,000	3,459,000	37
1875	London	Railroad construction and railroad dividend guarantees	N. M. Rothschild & Sons	96.5	5	5,000,000	5,301,200	30
1883	London	Railroads/public works/central sugar mills	N. M. Rothschild & Sons	89	4.5	4,000,000	4,599,600	38
1886	London	Redeem Treasury bills/cover deficit	N. M. Rothschild & Sons	95	5	6,000,000	6,431,000	38
1888	London	"Abolition"	N. M. Rothschild & Sons	97	4.5	6,000,000	6,297,300	38
1889	London	Conversion loan	N. M. Rothschild & Sons	90	4	17,440,300	19,837,000	56

Note: Excludes the Portuguese loan of 1823.

While taking a new loan to retire an older one did not increase the government's net foreign indebtedness, it did reveal successful ongoing access to credit markets. This access facilitated a variety of other financial operations by the Treasury. Brazil's domestic short-term debt was at times converted to a long-term, funded basis abroad, as in the cases of the loans of 1863, 1871, and 1886. Developmental borrowing by the state, while not frequent early on, increased in the 1870s and 1880s. The government occasionally pursued new loans to cover outlays on railroad extensions. Loans in 1871, 1875, and 1883 went partly for new infrastructure investment. In using loan proceeds to pay for projects that remedied market failures, the state helped to overcome deficiencies in the provision of social overhead capital. Such borrowing created economic benefits that went beyond those arising from the mere smoothing of tax revenues.[29] Conversely, when the proceeds of foreign borrowing were used to bail out investors in failing companies, as was the case with the loan of 1860, it generated additional costs.

An examination of each instance of new borrowing reveals the range of circumstances under which the government took loans in London. Brazil's borrowing can be roughly divided into pre-1850 and post-1850 periods. The first period was marked by serious challenges. During the First Reign and Regency, difficulties in raising tax revenues, problems making timely remittances to loan contractors, and political instability cast doubt on the viability of the new political institutions. Brazil was a risky bet. Spanish American defaults in the 1820s no doubt had an adverse contagion effect on Brazil's bonds in London. The lack of a truly national budget during the 1820s meant that government officials spent on activities that were national in scope but for which tax revenues were largely limited to Rio de Janeiro.[30] At independence the service on the inherited debts from the colonial era and on those of the United Kingdom of Portugal, Brazil, and the Algarves, together with current expenditures, already outweighed anticipated revenues. This shortfall compelled Brazil's first foray into the London capital market, where it arranged for a 3 million pounds sterling loan. The ostensible purpose of the loan was to repay debt to the first Banco do Brasil, retire inconvertible paper currency, and pay indemnities to the Portuguese should a purely diplomatic settlement regarding the recognition of Brazilian independence prove impossible.[31] The first tranche of bonds, raising 1 million pounds, was issued through the merchant banking syndicate of Bazett, Farquhar & Co., Fletcher, Alexander, & Co., and Thomas Wilson & Co., with dividends payable in London, Hamburg, Paris, and Amsterdam.[32] In an arrangement reminiscent of the Portuguese loan of 1796, the provincial treasuries (Juntas da Fazenda) of Rio de Janeiro, Bahia, Pernambuco, and Maranhão were tasked in the contract for the service on the loan, obligated to contribute 60 thousand pounds each per year.[33] The loan was issued at a steep discount: 75 pounds cash for a bond worth 100 pounds at redemption. Rothschild underwrote the remainder of the loan in 1825.[34] This second tranche provided the Imperial government with an additional 2 million pounds, under improved terms. Beyond mortgaging the customs revenues, the loan agreement earmarked remittances of diamonds for coupon payments.[35] Rather than reduce its unfunded obligations at home, which by one estimate came to 20 million milréis (some 4 million pounds sterling at the time), the government spent much of the money from the loans on military operations, first in 1824 to defeat the northeastern rebels fighting to create a regional republic and then later against Buenos Aires in the struggle over Montevideo and the Cisplatine.[36]

In 1825 Brazil's net external indebtedness jumped by nearly 50 percent. No pecuniary benefit accompanied the newly elevated debt burden. No sooner had Brazil garnered the rest of the loan it originally sought in 1824 than it took on the first of several foreign and domestic loans it needed to indemnify Portugal for independence. Full recognition of Brazil by Great Britain hinged on Portuguese acceptance of its former colony's independence. This in turn rested in large part on settling claims held by the Portuguese government and loyalists against Pedro I and the Rio government. Portugal sought compensation for damages in several categories: warships that Brazil seized and kept, unfunded and funded debts, and a debt to the Bank of Portugal. The first and most onerous component of the indemnity was the 1.4 million pound Portuguese loan of 1823. This loan, which the Empire assumed under the secret convention of the treaty of 1825, quickly increased the debt burden.[37] It would lead to the sole instance of default on interest during the Imperial era. Though it was clearly an odious reparation, Brazil did not repudiate the loan. Instead, it merely withheld payments of interest to the bondholders during the succession struggle in Portugal, beginning in 1828. The attempted usurpation of the Portuguese throne by the regent

Dom Miguel prompted Brazil's minister in London, the visconde de Itabayana, to halt the service on the loan.[38] Although the faction of the political elite in Rio de Janeiro most closely tied to Pedro strongly opposed
Miguel's revolt, at issue for the government was whether Brazil would
be credited for interest payments made on the bonds, depending on which
side emerged victorious in Portugal. The emperor's Council of State directly took up the question, opining that it should not be serviced on behalf of either party to the struggle. Rather, the council resolved that
interest should accumulate and be deposited with the Bank of England,
held until such time as the dispute had been resolved.[39] Regular interest
payments on the loan resumed in 1835 after the resolution of the crisis.[40]

A loan in 1829 did not bring any funds to Brazil. The revenue shortfall in Rio was so severe that the government feared it would not be able
to meet interest payments in London. The cabinet in Rio quickly sought
to undertake new borrowing. Finance Minister Miguel Calmon du Pin e
Almeida (later marquês de Abrantes) queried the Council of State on
whether the loan authorized in the budget for the following year should
be secured at home or abroad. The council voted by a majority to raise
the loan within the Empire.[41] Finding the domestic market unfavorable,
the minister returned to the council in December, urgently seeking
approval to borrow in London to cover the deficit for 1828. In an extraordinary session the council approved the request, as did the emperor. While
credit operations had been authorized by parliament in the budget, the
guidelines for the loan's terms were not. The 1829 loan was the only borrowing undertaken after the creation of parliament that did not carry
explicit legislative sanction for its terms.[42] To supply the needed funds,
Rothschild teamed with Thomas Wilson & Co., one of the contractors of
the 1824 loan, to structure two identical new bond issues.[43] The sole purpose of the loan was to cover interest payments on the 1824–25 loans and
to securitize existing advances already made by the contractors.[44] In the
wake of the defaults of the late 1820s, there was little enthusiasm in the
market for a new bond from South America and even less enthusiasm
for a loan designed solely to pay interest. The discount on the loan was
huge, in the range found on bonds of the Spanish American governments
that had already defaulted. The exchange would not formally list the new
loan because issuing new bonds to cover interest on existing debt was not
recognized by the exchange as legitimate. That Brazil had suspended

service on the Portuguese loan also obstructed listing on the exchange.[45] The contractors took all of the bonds themselves. When they later appeared in the secondary market they still traded at a discount relative to Brazil's own bonds from the loans of 1824–25.[46] The very need for the loan in 1829 showed how the costs of the Rio de la Plata campaign had pushed the Imperial government's finances to its debt ceiling. The loan became a political cudgel in the running disputes between Pedro and the chamber of deputies. Only in 1833 did parliament belatedly approve the loan's terms.[47]

During the turbulent years of the Regency in 1831–40, Brazil pursued very little borrowing abroad. Instead, to meet expected shortfalls in interest remittances and to avoid default, there were numerous advances that the Brazilian minister in London leveraged from the original loan contractors and the Treasury's financial agents. With the instability surrounding Pedro I's abdication in 1831, along with a raft of regional revolts, borrowing turned increasingly inward. The Empire did issue one more loan abroad before 1840. By early 1839 it had become increasingly difficult to raise funds in the domestic market at acceptable rates; apólice prices in Rio fell sharply over the second half of 1838 and in early 1839 were quoted as low as 69.5 percent of par.[48] Political instability was the main culprit, but that was compounded by the panic of 1837 in the United States, which had roiled the Atlantic capital markets, with lingering effects that further raised borrowing costs in Brazil. The government turned to London and took a relatively small loan in 1839 through Samuel & Phillips, which had served as the Treasury's financial agent for nearly a decade.[49] The new loan entered the market at 76, with a 5 percent annual coupon. It was clearly preferable to borrowing in Rio in local currency—London was nearly 200 basis points cheaper, and the funds raised were in sterling. Although the loan may have simply securitized debts already owed to Samuel & Phillips and other merchant bankers, it nonetheless allowed the government to meet various payments in the City without having to remit funds from Brazil.[50]

The old question of Portuguese claims reared its head again in the late 1830s. The government had suspended service on the Portuguese loan from 1828 until 1835. It had also failed to pay the other indemnities. A new agreement between Portugal and Brazil made in 1837 and fully ratified in 1842 led Brazil to borrow once more in London in 1843.[51] In the wake of the defaults by U.S. state governments, the London market was not favorably inclined to make new loans to foreign borrowers.[52] Brazil nonetheless successfully placed bonds through the merchant banking syndicate of Goldsmid, Thompson, and King, which had taken over Brazil's financial agency from Samuel & Phillips at the end of the 1830s.[53] The loan's proceeds finally settled all of Portugal's claims.

A second, and very different, era of borrowing by the Imperial state began after 1850. In late 1851 the visconde de Itaboraí, the finance minister of the Conservative cabinet distinguished by its deft handling of complex problems of diplomacy and foreign affairs, scored a separate, more quiet victory.[54] Under his leadership the government resumed regular amortization on its London loans, supplying the Treasury's financial agents and loan contractors with money earmarked for that purpose.[55] More than a decade later the finance minister observed that the Empire had firmed up its credit considerably by fully adhering to the terms of its loan contracts.[56] From the perspective of bondholders the suspension of amortization in the late 1820s had not been especially burdensome. Yet by failing to retire bonds gradually under the terms of the loan contracts, Brazil unavoidably signaled the market that it might ultimately fail to repay the loan when it came due.

The Empire's new and improved standing was soon apparent. Shortly after it had resumed amortization of its external debt, it paid off the balance of the 1823 Portuguese loan with the proceeds from a new loan in 1852 through N. M. Rothschild & Sons.[57] The terms were the best that Brazil had received up to that point, better than those given to Austria that year (also borrowing through the London Rothschilds) and to Peru the year after.[58] The 1852 loan contract was the last to declare that "his Imperial Majesty specially pledges the revenues derived from the Customs, these being the largest and surest source of all the Revenues of the Empire."[59] Thereafter, the more general clause committing "all the resources of the Empire" sufficed for new borrowing.[60] By 1854 the government's credit was sufficiently strong that it could bypass new borrowing by simply extending the maturity of an existing loan. With the loan of 1824–25 coming due, the finance ministry faced a difficult situation. War broke out in the Crimea in late 1853, and the London loan market tightened. Consultation with the loan contractors and existing payment agents determined that bondholders were not opposed to lengthening the maturity of the original loans, which was preferred over making a new issue to retire the remaining bonds.[61] The extension ran to 1864. In 1855 N. M. Rothschild & Sons contracted to be the Imperial government's sole agent for financial matters in Europe and exclusively handled all of the central government's external bond issues up through the overthrow of the monarchy.[62]

Three new loans hit the market in rapid succession in 1858, 1859, and 1860. Two of these helped finance rising state intervention in the economy, which had been gaining steam since 1852.[63] The government borrowed in 1858 specifically to continue work on the Dom Pedro II railroad, a private sector enterprise that had failed to complete its planned construction.[64] The loan bailed out the company's shareholders; the railroad eventually was placed in the government's hands. The terms of borrowing were once again favorable, better than those on loans to Chile, Sweden, and Turkey that same year.[65] In 1859 a small loan paid off the remaining bonds of the 1829 loans that were set to mature. The government opted to refinance the 1829 debt rather than settle it outright. The financial crisis of 1857 created an unfavorable foreign exchange market, and the Treasury felt it was too expensive to buy the British pounds needed to pay off the debt. The result was a conversion loan that, despite the circumstances, proved more successful than had been expected.[66] In 1860 the government borrowed to bail out yet more businesses in Brazil. The proceeds were earmarked for the Recife and San Francisco Railway Co. (the British-owned line in Pernambuco); the União e Indústria wagon road company, which served the coffee zone in the Paraiba valley; and the Mucury navigation company, an up-country concern.[67] While the loan was taken out for the direct benefit of three private enterprises, the Imperial Treasury served as its guarantor.[68] This made the loan a sovereign issue. There were challenges in placing it, however. It was too close on the heels of the loans of 1858 and 1859. Brazil's risk premium in London had already moved upward in 1859, a partial reversal of the dramatic decline in risk earlier in the decade. And while N. M. Rothschild & Sons processed the bond issue, it did not take it firm. This meant that the bank itself did not underwrite the issue by taking a position in the bonds. The difference this made soon became clear: the bonds were slow to find a market.[69] The amount eventually raised on the 1860 loan was 1.21 million pounds.[70]

For the rest of the 1860s borrowing in London became more expensive than it had been in the 1850s. Funds were available, but the American Civil War roiled capital markets, tightening credit for most sovereign borrowers overseas. Brazil became ensnared in a diplomatic kerfuffle with the British government in a dispute known as the Christie Affair.[71] One might believe that the conjuncture would be particularly unfavorable for new borrowing. Yet business trumped diplomatic discord, and N. M. Rothschild & Sons launched the 1863 loan, unimpeded by the breakdown in relations between the two governments. The loan had three purposes. It retired the remainder of the original 1824 and 1825 bonds.[72] It redeemed the loan of 1843 that was soon coming due, refinancing once again what remained of bonds originally issued to settle old Portuguese claims from independence. And it helped convert short-term debt to a funded basis by using some of its proceeds to retire domestic Treasury bills.[73]

The outbreak of hostilities with Paraguay at the end of 1864 led Brazil to seek another loan in short order. The 1865 loan was by far the largest up to that point, taken out early in the war in anticipation of military expenses. In June 1865 the barão de Penedo, the Brazilian representative in London, arranged to borrow 5 million pounds. The bonds were initially set to enter the market with a 4.5 percent coupon and an issue price of only around 68. Raising the coupon rate to 5 percent pushed the issue price up to 74, resulting in more cash for the Imperial government at only a trivially higher interest rate.[74] The operation was a departure from precedent in two ways. First, it was issued both in London and on the continent in Amsterdam.[75] Second, the contract stipulated that all amortization of bonds had to take place at par; Brazil could not buy shares in the open market at less than their face value in order to meet its contracted sinking fund requirements. Despite the restrictions on amortization, the finance minister in Rio celebrated the direct sale of bonds in continental Europe because it broadened both the primary and secondary markets for the government's securities. Marketing part of the loan in Amsterdam helped alleviate a looming surfeit of Brazilian bonds in London, where the Empire's debt already "weighed heavily on the market."[76] In light of the circumstances the loan was well received; it was well oversubscribed and soon traded at a premium to its issue price.[77]

The 1863 and 1865 loans, despite successful launches under adverse circumstances, generated appreciable political recrimination once their details became known. Both loans carried discounts larger than what Brazil had accepted with its 1860 loan.[78] Yet the terms on the 1863 loan were better than those on loans to Italy, Portugal, Colombia, and the Confederate States of America that same year.[79] In the case of the loan of 1865, the minister of finance rebutted criticism regarding the low price of the issue by blaming general conditions in London.[80] He also pointed to two irrefutable facts: the loan was large relative to Brazil's existing stock of foreign debt, and war loans were not popular among investors. The issue price and coupon rate did not compare especially well with the terms of loans to Italy and Peru in 1865. The more restrictive features, however, such as the requirement to amortize at par, were applied to other sovereign borrowers as well that year.[81]

The Imperial government did not return to the London market until 1871, shortly after its victory over Paraguay.[82] Borrowing soon took off. The motives for the new loan were the conversion of short-term Treasury debt, funding the remaining deficit from the war, and covering new developmental expenditures. A domestic issue of apólices in 1870 failed to fully cover extraordinary expenses for the armed forces at the end of the Paraguayan campaign. Essential extensions to the Dom Pedro II railroad, the "great improvement" project that had been taken over by the government, remained incomplete.[83] The terms of the 1871 loan were among the best obtained by any borrower in the London market in the early 1870s, including loans to France, Spain, Peru, Argentina, and Massachusetts.[84] Brazil borrowed abroad yet again in 1875 in lieu of borrowing at home. Reports on the Rio money market blamed tight credit on heavy borrowing to pay for railroad construction, fueling predictions of a local financial crisis following on the contraction that began in the North Atlantic economies in 1873.[85] Overseas markets caught wind of the government's active interest in a new loan late in 1874. Reports of a loan arranged through the Deutsche-Brasilianische Bank proved erroneous.[86] But in a departure from previous practice the finance minister, visconde do Rio Branco, worked to arrange a loan with Émile Erlanger & Company in Paris. By January the London Rothschilds had outmaneuvered Erlanger and won the contract.[87] The 1875 bonds entered the market at an enviably high price of 96.[88] A cartoon

FIGURE 3.2 "At Last": The Rothschild loan of 1875 (*Semana Illustrada*, 31 January 1875, 5904)

of the era depicts the turn of events (fig. 3.2). In this illustration, the portly Rothschild character has had his belly tapped with a spigot from which money pours. The flow is directed by the visconde do Rio Branco into Brazil's barrel of Danaides, the mythical vessel that can never be filled, which represents the Imperial Treasury. The cartoon portrays the main features of the episode: the Treasury's leaky coffers, the drama of the Erlanger-Rothschild scramble for the loan, and the question of the Rothschilds' fees. The caption reads, "After Erlanger gave out, the fat Rothschild drained off some five million pounds of his own lard to put in our barrel of Danaides, skimming some fat off the lard for himself beforehand, naturally."

The volume of foreign borrowing accelerated appreciably in the 1880s. By 1882 the government was committed to construction expenditures on the railroads it owned, dividend guarantees on private sector railroads,

and subsidies to central sugar mills, among other outlays. With pro-
grammed expenditures expected to outstrip tax revenues, the cabinet
arranged to borrow again. N. M. Rothschild & Sons underwrote 4.6 million pounds worth of 4.5 percent bonds at an initial price of 89, infusing
the government's account in London with nearly 4 million pounds sterling.[89] The loan was quickly oversubscribed and soon traded at a premium.[90] Brazil returned to the London market again in 1886 and borrowed
6 million more pounds.[91] Investors more than doubly subscribed the
issue, and the loan fetched a price even higher than the Rothschilds had
initially indicated would be possible.[92] Under similarly favorable circumstances Brazil borrowed in 1888.[93] The loan's ostensible purpose was to
cover expenses related to the abolition of slavery, although no indemnities
were ever paid to slaveholders, and the money was in fact put to other
uses. But the largest foreign loan by far was the one subscribed in the last
year of the Empire to convert all bonds bearing coupon rates of 5 percent to
new bonds with coupon rates of 4 percent.[94] Using the proceeds of the 1889
loan, the Imperial government successfully and advantageously consolidated much of its foreign debt, reducing its debt-servicing requirements.

The conversion loan was one of the crowning financial achievements
of the Imperial state. Memorialized in a cartoon in the *Revista Illustrada*,
the conversion is depicted as the sacrament of financial penance (fig. 3.3).[95]
The title of the drawing, "The Conversion of the External Debt," was
a triple entendre. Its literal meaning stemmed from the financial operation in London per se. A second meaning derived from the success with
which Finance Minister visconde de Ouro Preto had "converted" the
bondholders into believers in the Empire's creditworthiness, enticing
them to continue to invest in Brazil's sovereign bonds despite the cut
in their coupon rate. A third meaning was a play on the political subtext;
there was a contemporaneous debate over a proposal to legislate the freedom of religion in Brazil. In the picture Ouro Preto is a priest seated in
the confessional. Dressed as a woman, the kneeling penitent (who bore
a striking resemblance to Leopold de Rothschild) represented British
bondholders. The book on the floor, entitled "Protestantism," partially
covers one of Brazil's London bonds. The penitent holds the end of Ouro
Preto's belt, on which the new coupon rate, "quatro por cento," is written.
The finance minister imposes penance and supplies absolution thus:

FIGURE 3.3 "The Conversion of the External Debt"
(*Revista Illustrada*, 12 October 1889, 4)

"My child, we are in a season of penitence and fasting. Because of your
Protestant background I can be even more severe. No matter. Your interest rate will be reduced by only one percent. Instead of five, four. And in
return I absolve you of all of your old sins." The old sins were presum-
ably the way British bankers had structured most of Brazil's loans to bear
a 5 percent coupon over the preceding six and a half decades. Standing
in the background in the doorway of the church is visconde de Figueiredo,
a major Rio de Janeiro banker. The feathered cap he wears customarily
adorned an indigenous figure in the pages of the *Revista,* who as an al-
legory stood for the Empire. Figueiredo's presence at a remove, along with
the headgear, suggest that Brazil's financial class had an interest in the
conversion; the money the operation saved the Treasury each year would
flow in part to new investments and accounts in Rio. The cartoon hailed

an end to the Empire's subservience to British capital on terms established by bankers in London.

The model of chapter 2 is silent on the question of the relationship between creditworthiness and the loan's term. Intuitively, when lenders are more confident of repayment they will extend credit for a longer span of time. Lenders who are more skeptical prefer repayment of the loan earlier rather than later and will put the borrowing government on a short leash by curtailing the loan's term. Loan contracts that specify a long period of repayment imply lender confidence in the state's willingness to repay its debt. None of the London loans had maturities of less than twenty years. Most loans through the early 1860s had thirty-year maturities. Maturities lengthened on average from 1865. The bonds of Ouro Preto's 1889 conversion loan were not scheduled to mature for fifty-six years.

By the end of the Empire, the government had issued bonds in London with a face value of nearly 67 million pounds sterling and had raised nearly 60 million pounds in cash. Because of amortization and the refinancing of old loans with new ones, the size of the debt in terms of the total bonds in circulation at any point in time was considerably less than this total. The structure of the bonded debt at selected intervals between 1825 and 1889, by coupon rate, is presented in table 3.2. Bonds with

Table 3.2

Foreign Funded Debt Outstanding, by Coupon Rate, 1825–89 (thousands)

YEAR	4 PERCENT	4.5 PERCENT	5 PERCENT	TOTAL
1825			5,086.2	5,086.2
1830			5,331.7	5,331.7
1840			5,580.4	5,580.4
1850			6,182.6	6,182.6
1860		3,743.5	3,911.5	7,655.0
1870		5,712.6	7,008.1	12,720.7
1880		2,800.1	13,663.7	16,463.8
1889	19,837.0	10,514.5		30,351.5

Note: Debt is the amount owed given by the face value of bonds in circulation and originally issued overseas, in thousands of current pounds sterling. The figures include Brazil's own bond issues along with the Portuguese loan of 1823 that Brazil assumed in 1825.
Source: See appendix II.

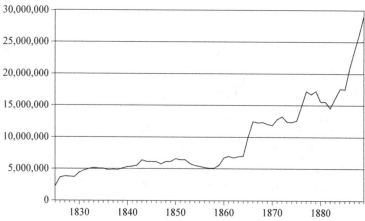

FIGURE 3.4 Real foreign debt, 1825–89 (figures in pounds sterling, adjusted to 1889 values)

4.5 percent and 5 percent coupons predominated until 1889. Figure 3.4 presents the overall stock of foreign debt at the end of each fiscal year. Between 1829 and the early 1860s new loans added only slightly to the net external debt. If one assumes that, because of credit rationing, Brazil's demand for foreign funds exceeded what the market was willing to lend, the foreign credit ceiling can be identified with precision: it equaled the stock of Brazil's foreign debt after each new loan was issued. Increases in the size of the debt would thus indicate an increase in the debt ceiling. Through the late 1850s the market rationed credit that limited Brazil to the debt it had accumulated by 1830. In securing new loans the government could improve the terms of its debt in London but could not increase its net indebtedness. The existence of the lower debt ceiling obviously did not imply exclusion from credit markets. Yet the effect was to limit the growth of external borrowing after 1829 until well into the Second Reign.

Upward shifts in the debt ceiling were apparent in the 1860s, 1870s, and 1880s. The 1860s saw a 65 percent increase in the size of the foreign debt. This expansion was overshadowed by new borrowing between 1880 and 1889, when the stock of foreign debt grew by more than 80 percent. Growth in the demand for credit alone could not explain these increases since it would imply that Brazil had borrowed below its credit ceiling in earlier decades, which was not likely the case. Higher tax revenues after

1850 no doubt played a role in loosening the credit rationing constraint. What had changed drastically by the 1850s were investors' expectations that the institutions that made the debt politically sustainable were both effective and would endure.

MONEY AT INTEREST: THE COST OF CAPITAL

London capitalists rationed credit to the Imperial government in accordance with their appraisal of the likelihood of repayment. Lenders charged a premium for bearing the risk of default. This premium was not fixed but varied with changes in the perception that Brazil would repay. In this regard the market's treatment of Brazil was no different from that accorded other sovereign borrowers. A main implication of the basic model of sovereign borrowing presented in chapter 2 is that a reduction in the probability that the government would respond to an economic or political shock by defaulting reduces the interest rate the government must pay to borrow. The Empire's borrowing costs declined on average, even though it both paid a default premium and borrowed substantially greater amounts over time.

The loan of 1859 exemplifies how the uncertainty about repayment that bondholders faced translated into a premium for risk. The 1829 loan was scheduled to mature after thirty years, requiring complete redemption at par of all of the outstanding bonds. Because the government did not amortize the loan for more than twenty years, some two-thirds of the bonds were still in circulation at the end of 1858.[96] To complicate matters, in December 1858 unusually heavy rains washed out roads, delaying the arrival of the coffee crop in the port of Rio de Janeiro. The resulting fall in exports immediately registered as a depreciation of the milréis in the first months of 1859. Retiring the loan would require a tax increase or a major diversion of revenues from other uses. This was difficult in both practical and political terms. Moreover, repayment had to be in sterling; the impact of such a large operation on the already stressed market for foreign exchange implied additional economic and political costs. Complicating matters further were conditions in London, where the market for foreign loans had been negatively impacted by the war between France and Austria over Lombardy. In Rio two finance ministers sought some way to refinance the bonds.[97] The solution came at the eleventh hour in the form of a new loan that settled the old debt. The upshot is that these sorts of difficulties made repayment uncertain for bondholders and justified the risk premia that London lenders charged.

To chart the evolution of the Empire's borrowing costs, the interest rate on loans in the primary market is calculated here. The government's cost of capital on each loan is taken as the interest rate at which the amount of money raised on the loan was equal to the discounted present value of the future streams of dividends, amortization, and fees that the government agreed to pay. The realized cost of borrowing would differ from this contractual measure to the extent that Brazil delayed amortization or gave discounts to investors who advanced their installments for the loan earlier than required in the contract. But because the ex ante interest rate derives from the loan agreements, it indicates precisely the state's marginal cost of new capital.

In determining the amount of money raised and the value of interest payments, amortization, and fees, several adjustments are warranted. Contracts can accommodate various contingencies, but not all of them. One adjustment involves the loan proceeds. The value of the cash raised from a loan was often less than its listed price. On many loans Brazil received its money from bond investors in installments. The Treasury was obliged to pay full interest on the loan from the date of the contract, even if the loan proceeds were not complete. The finance ministry had to wait a number of months and in some cases as long as a year before all of the proceeds from the loan were received. This delay reduced the real value of the funds raised and raised the interest rate.

The loan of 1871 serves as an example. It was contracted at 89 percent of the bond's face value, to pay a 5 percent coupon each year, divided into two semester payments of 2.5 percent each, with interest accruing from the date of the contract. The contract required bond investors to supply money in five installments: five pounds on subscription, then four more installments by specific dates over the next six months, totaling 89 pounds on a 100-pound bond.[98] The first semester interest payment of 2.5 pounds came due on 1 August, just after the fourth installment and before the bond was fully paid. The flow of installments must be discounted by the coupon rate on the loan to arrive at the effective value of the money raised (details on the discounting for all of the loans are reported in appendix III). The value of the money that had been credited to the Treasury by the first interest payment was only a little more than 65 pounds. This made the first-semester yield 3.85 percent (instead of the 2.81 percent it would have cost Brazil if the loan's full proceeds had been supplied at closing). This was equivalent to an annual yield of 7.7 percent (instead of 5.62 percent on a fully paid bond). By the time the final installment had completed the 89 pounds per bond, the proceeds were worth only 87.6 pounds to the Treasury. The delay of raising the loan by installments, with interest accruing from the contract date, raised the loan's cost. The value of loan proceeds for every loan paid in by installments is adjusted to account for this feature.

A second adjustment involves how loan balances would be paid down. Amortization provisions in the loan contracts required that a fixed portion of the loan be retired each year. Each year interest would be paid on the total value of retired bonds. This money went to a sinking fund that retired even more bonds by purchasing them in the open market. Any bonds that remained in circulation at maturity would be paid at their face value. The method used to meet each year's required amortization depended on the market price of the bonds. If prices were below par, the required increment of bonds to be amortized was purchased in the market by the loan contractors and credited to the Brazilian Treasury. When the prices were above par, the portion of bonds to be retired was "called" by lottery drawing and paid at par. Amortization by repurchase when prices were below par reduced the effective cost of the loan. The principal exception was the 1865 loan, the only one for which the contract stipulated that amortized shares had to be redeemed at par. As a practical matter there were a few other exceptions. One came in 1882 and involved bonds from the 1871 loan. It was more cost effective to retire shares trading above par, paying full market value, than it was to wait until a lottery drawing could be made because the delay would have required the payment of an additional semester of interest to the holders of the bonds selected for retirement.[99]

The government could not presume at the time it borrowed that it would be able to retire its bonds at less than face value. To make the interest rate estimates comparable across loans, all amortization is assumed to occur at par. Given that the cost of capital is estimated on an ex ante basis, strict conformance to the amortization provisions of the contracts is assumed in the calculation, even for pre-1850 loans (which in practice were not regularly amortized until after 1850). Additional retirements of bonds, using the sinking fund, are assumed to occur in accordance with the contract, also at par.

Given the assumptions regarding amortization and the adjustments to the value of loan proceeds, the ex ante cost of capital on a loan is calculated as the internal rate of return that sets the government's future stream of interest payments, amortization, and banking fees just equal to the (appropriately discounted) cash raised from the loan:

$$M = \sum_{t=0}^{T} \left[\frac{D_t + A_t + Fd_t + Fa_t}{(1+i)^t} \right] + \frac{B}{(1+i)^T}$$

where M is the value of the cash Brazil received, D is the interest payment on the total issue in circulation at time t, A is the amount of bonds amortized (including the additional increment each year retired with the sinking fund), Fd is the merchant bank's fee for handling interest payments to bondholders, Fa is the fee on annual amortization purchases, B is any balance outstanding at maturity, T is the terminal period of the loan, and i is the government's ex ante cost of capital.[100] The fees to intermediaries meant that the government paid more each year than bondholders would actually receive.[101]

Table 3.3 and figure 3.5 present the cost of capital for each instance of external borrowing. Changes in borrowing costs over time had two sources: changes in marketwide conditions and changes in country-specific factors. To distinguish these, the yield on Britain's consolidated debt, or consols, is calculated for the week in which each loan was contracted. This gives an estimate of the risk-free return on capital. The risk premium in the last column of table 3.3 is simply the difference between the cost of borrowing and the consol yield that is apparent in figure 3.5.[102] Consol yields varied relatively little during the period under consideration; almost all of the changes in the interest rate come from changes in Brazil's risk premium. The Empire's borrowing costs were relatively high for its first loan, in 1824. For the second loan, in 1825, these costs fell by more than 100 basis points, despite a rash of defaults in the London market. The lower cost on the larger second loan owed partly to the alleviation of Brazil's diplomatic difficulties vis-à-vis Portugal and partly

Table 3.3

The Government's Cost of Capital on New Borrowing in London, by Loan, 1824–89

LOAN	ANNUAL AVERAGE INTEREST RATE (%)	RISK PREMIUM (%)
1824	8.74	5.54
1825	7.64	4.35
1829	13.89	10.41
1839	8.20	4.96
1843	7.58	4.37
1852	5.53	2.43
1854	5.59	2.32
1858	5.64	2.40
1859	5.60	2.44
1860	6.23	3.05
1863	6.44	3.17
1865	8.95	5.57
1871	6.75	3.46
1875	6.11	2.85
1883	6.21	3.30
1886	6.23	3.38
1888	5.29	2.62
1889	5.12	2.47

Note: The annual average interest rate for each new loan is the ex ante cost of capital implied by the terms of the contracts between the Imperial government and the parties who agreed to supply funds. The risk premium is calculated as the difference between the interest rate and the yield on British consols in the week that each loan contract was signed. The Portuguese loan of 1823 is not included; because Brazil received none of the money, a calculation of the rate of return is not possible.

to the involvement of Rothschild. Borrowing costs were at their highest with the interest-covering loans of 1829. Interest rates on subsequent small loans were lower, although they remained at an elevated level into the 1840s—an unsurprising finding given the political instability of the Regency and the early Second Reign. Capital costs fell to unprecedented lows through the 1850s, rose slightly in the early 1860s, and then jumped with heavy new borrowing during the war against Paraguay. They

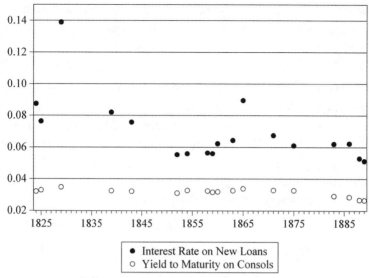

FIGURE 3.5 Cost of the Brazilian government's borrowing in London, 1824–89

resumed their decline after the war, falling off sharply near the end of the 1880s.[103] In an era when British consol yields ranged from 2.45 to 4 percent a year, Brazil's "country risk" was plainly apparent.[104] Nonetheless, what the Imperial government had to pay to borrow declined a good deal, the main exceptions being moments of clear political or fiscal stress.[105] Before 1852 political instability left bondholders uncertain about the survivability of the Empire's political institutions. These concerns were serious—if the government were to wholly collapse, the penalty for default could become irrelevant to policy makers. Chapter 5 delves further into the question of default risk and its change over time through an analysis of the secondary markets for the Empire's bonds. It is nonetheless clear that the default premium on new loans had been greatly reduced by the early 1850s, as the institutional basis for debt repayment proved to be durable.

THE PROBABILITY OF SOVEREIGN DEFAULT

Because the market did not view lending to the Imperial state as an investment without risk, Brazil's sovereign bonds in London paid hundreds of basis points in interest over consols. In the market for new loans investor expectations about the probability of future default are embedded in the issue price. A lower issue price implies a correspondingly higher interest rate for the borrower. Given information on the issue price, loan maturity, and coupon rate, the market's assessment of the probability of default can be quantified. To make comparisons across loans a single default scenario is considered: upon receipt of the loan's initial proceeds, the government repudiates the debt entirely. The probability of repudiation can then be calculated with two assumptions. First, bondholders are risk neutral, so they are indifferent between a certain payoff and the expected value of an equivalent bet. Second, there is a two-point probability distribution over outcomes, which must be either one of two states: either full compliance with the loan contract or full repudiation.[106] Taking the expected value of the bond investment as that of a fair bet, the expected return to the investor from purchasing the bond must have been at least as large as the actual return on British consols. The difference between the two returns provides the basis for estimating the probability assigned by the market to Brazilian default.

The initial price that investors paid for a bond implied a rate of return of at least $(1 + i)$ if the government honored the loan. In the full-repudiation scenario the rate of return is zero, reflecting the total loss of interest and principal. The expected return is the weighted average of these two returns, where weights are the probability of repayment and the probability of default. The investor's expected payoff had to be at least as good as that which it would receive with certainty from investing in consols:[107]

$$pL(1 + i) + (1 - p) L(0) \geq L(1 + r)$$

where $(1 + i)$ is the expected rate of return to the bond purchaser who buys the bond at issue and holds it to maturity, zero is the return under default, p is the probability of repayment, $(1-p)$ is the probability of default, and r is the consol yield. Simplifying the expression, the probability of default is

$$(1 - p) = \left[\frac{i - r}{1 + i} \right].$$

Consider for the purpose of illustration the loan of 1858. N. M. Rothschild & Sons sold bonds for 95.5 pounds in cash on each. The government agreed to pay the bondholder 2.25 pounds sterling per semester and to then redeem the bond for 100 pounds after thirty years.[108] The rate of return to an investor who purchased the bond at issue and held it until maturity would be 1.0507, or an average annual return on principal of 5.07 percent, so long as Brazil honored the loan.[109] At the time of issue the same investor had the option of instead purchasing a consol, which provided a yield of 3.096 percent per year. Because the expected return on the bond must have been at least as much as the investor could have earned on a consol, the implied probability of repudiation is

$$(1-p) = \left(\frac{0.0507 - 0.03096}{1.0507} \right)$$

or 1.9 percent.

This measure is necessarily biased by the assumptions required for its computation. If default was expected to take a form other than repudiation, the probability of default would be greater than that of the dire case here.[110] The direction of changes in the default probability over time would remain the same, however. As long as the type of default scenario is held constant across loans, the calculation provides a consistent indicator of changes in the market's assessment of default risk.

The ex ante rates of return for a buy-and-hold bond investor are estimated for each loan, along with the probabilities of repudiation, and are reported in table 3.4 and shown in figure 3.6. The results are telling. The market's perception of the risk of default was at its highest in 1829, when the government resorted to new loans just to cover interest on its existing debt. Repudiation risk exceeded 7 percent (and the risk of a milder interest-only default was fully 65 percent). By the time the government borrowed again in London, a decade later, the probability of default had declined and continued to fall into the 1850s. The loan at the start of the war with Paraguay exhibited an elevated probability of default, rising to a level not seen since 1839. The probability of repudiation fell again after the war, declining by the end of the Imperial era to a level not seen since the 1850s. The market's assessment of the likelihood of default adjusted

Table 3.4

Implied Probabilities of Repudiation on New Loans at Issue, 1824–89

LOAN	EXPECTED YIELD TO MATURITY	CONSOL YIELD	PROBABILITY OF REPUDIATION
1824	7.62	3.20	4.3
1825	6.75	3.29	3.3
1829	11.39	3.48	7.6
1839	7.31	3.24	3.9
1843	6.71	3.21	3.4
1852	5.04	3.10	1.9
1854	5.41	3.27	2.1
1858	5.07	3.24	1.8
1859	5.27	3.16	2.0
1860	5.53	3.18	2.3
1863	6.23	3.25	2.9
1865	7.54	3.38	4.0
1871	6.15	3.28	2.8
1875	5.66	3.26	2.3
1883	5.62	2.91	2.6
1886	5.80	2.85	2.9
1888	4.96	2.67	2.2
1889	4.88	2.65	2.2

Note: All figures are percentages. The expected yield is for a hypothetical investor who subscribed to the loan at issue and held the bond until maturity. Consol yield is the yield to maturity on standard reference consols in the week that each loan contract was signed. The repudiation probability is that implied by the expected yield and consol rate at the time of contracting the loan, calculated in the manner discussed in the text.

in accordance with changing expectations regarding the political costs in Brazil of debt service. The tendency over the course of the Empire was for the probability of default to decline.

CONCLUSION

The desirability of borrowing in London was clear, given that it was impossible to meet all the state's financial needs from the domestic market alone. Foreign loans were the single most important component of Brazil's funded debt until the 1850s. Money raised in London helped cover

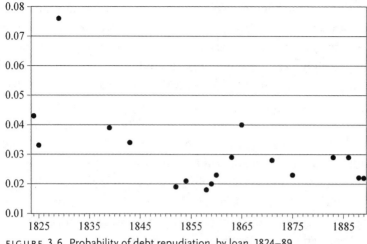

FIGURE 3.6 Probability of debt repudiation, by loan, 1824–89

critical shortfalls in resources needed in the early decades after independence, when the effectiveness of state building was most in doubt. The credibility of the Imperial state's commitment to honor its financial obligations allowed it to borrow substantial sums abroad. Loans took the form of bonds issued through various merchant banks and contractors in London. Most went through the banking house of N. M. Rothschild & Sons. No other Latin American government was able to borrow as consistently, under such favorable terms, and without default.

Servicing the foreign debt nonetheless presented a serious challenge during the First Reign and Regency. Throughout the 1830s and 1840s Brazil failed to follow through on the contracted amortization on its London loans. The Imperial state's willingness to pay was further called into doubt when it suspended all service on the Portuguese loan of 1823. In the 1820s and 1830s the government sometimes resorted to short-term advances from its London bankers in order to make its interest payments on time. Yet on no occasion did its overseas bondholders fail to receive interest on debt issued by the Imperial government. After midcentury, as Brazil resumed full amortization of its external loans, the government repeatedly returned to the London capital market and successfully raised funds. Repeated defaults in Spanish America meant those states paid high interest rates when they were allowed to reenter the London capital market. The association of high risk premia and ostensibly hot Spanish American countries led otherwise keen observers to advance preposterous explanations for the pattern of default: "The connection between a temperate climate and pecuniary thrift, and between a hot climate and pecuniary recklessness, is very clearly demonstrated."[111] Brazil's "pecuniary thrift" was a relatively rare instance of an emerging market in the tropics whose government repaid its debt. The reputation the Empire acquired as a stalwart debtor in the London market had a firm underpinning in its fiscal and political institutions.

All of Brazil's London borrowing was in pounds sterling. This choice had several implications. Lenders preferred repayment in their own money. If a loan was denominated in the borrower's currency, the value of the bonds and the interest payments could be eroded by the borrowers' monetary policy, even if the borrower otherwise faithfully adhered to the loan contract.[112] To avoid the higher interest rates that would be required to borrow in their own currency, governments can index their debt to offset changes in the purchasing power of the money in which the debt is denominated. For an open economy with a floating exchange rate, the value of the debt is most directly indexed by denominating it in a hard currency. Combining nominal and indexed debt can strengthen the commitment to repay.[113] A government that issues both types of debt has less incentive to inflate away the nominal component because it would make the indexed debt more expensive to repay.[114]

Yet modern macroeconomics also identifies a key trade-off for a government that must index its debt in order to borrow. While it may reduce the interest rate on loans, it also magnifies the debtor's exposure to external crisis. Adverse shocks like drops in trade, abrupt shifts in lender sentiment, "sudden stops" in capital inflows, a war, and so forth can alter the perceived benefits and costs of repayment.[115] Historically, higher levels of foreign currency debt are associated with debt intolerance and a higher propensity to default.[116] Persistently high ratios of indexed debt to nominal debt in many countries—both in the nineteenth century and today—suggest that there may be few practical alternatives to denominating loans in key external currencies. The Empire's mix of external and domestic debt helps explain why it had only modest inflation, even though it relied mainly on paper currency. The exchange-rate target of 27 pence per milréis was adopted in 1846. Yet the milréis floated most of the time, with no fixed value in gold or sterling.[117] Inflation would weaken the mil-réis and raise the cost of servicing the London debt. The government internalized the cost of any inflationary policy it might pursue.

Despite its foreign borrowing in sterling, Imperial Brazil was neither debt intolerant nor did it become a serial defaulter. It escaped the strongest form of financial original sin. Avoiding overexposure to external debt depended partly on the Empire's striking success at borrowing money at home, in its own currency, for long maturities.

CHAPTER FOUR

Borrowing on Rua Direita

IN EARLY 1828 a syndicate of Rio de Janeiro capitalists consisting of Francisco José da Rocha, Lourenço Antonio do Rego, and José Francisco de Mesquita submitted a bid to the Imperial Treasury for the first issue of bonds authorized by parliament under the national debt law of 1827. Rego was registered with the board of trade as a merchant, while Mesquita (later barão de Bonfim) was an important slaver and creditor of the Treasury who would soon become one of the first debt commissioners on the Junta Administrativa da Caixa de Amortização.[1] The family of Rocha (who was later made second barão de Itamaraty) also had interests in slave trafficking. Rocha would eventually become one of the state's most important creditors, joining the junta some three decades later. Rocha, Rego, and Mesquita invited other individuals to join their venture to compete for the loan to the government.[2] A month later their bid won. "Not wanting to lose even an instant," they quickly informed their "shareholders" that they had taken the 6 percent apólices at 65 percent of face value.[3] They locked in an attractive annual yield of 9.2 percent.

Apólices like those that Rocha, Rego, and Mesquita bought became the mainstay of the domestic public debt. They proved consistently popular among slave traders, banking houses, Brazilian rentiers, foreign merchants in Brazil, and British capitalists. Nathan Mayer Rothschild sought to invest in them from London.[4] By midcentury apólices were common in the portfolios of Brazil's wealth holders.[5] Banks and public companies counted them among their safest assets. The bonds formed part of the landscape not only of public finance and investing but also of the society and the culture as well. Apólices made regular appearances in the literature of the era as a source of fixed income for key figures in prominent nineteenth-century novels. In *Luciola* (1861), a treatment of Rio society by the writer and Conservative politician José de Alencar, the courtesan Lucia directed the other protagonist, Paulo, to use some of Anna's money for taxes and "with the rest buy apólices in [Anna's] name."[6] In Alencar's *Senhora* (1875), the young Aurélia, having received an unexpectedly large inheritance, tries to convince her uncle and tutor of her maturity by telling him that she understood "apólice yields."[7] In Machado de Assis's classic *Dom Casmurro* (1900), Bentinho recounts that upon being widowed in 1857 his mother, Maria da Glória Fernandes Santiago, reallocated her wealth by selling the plantation and the field slaves and buying a dozen buildings in town, slaves to rent out, and "a certain number of apólices."[8]

One of the most striking features of the Brazilian Empire's sovereign borrowing was the success with which it issued debt at home. Regular use of external finance was far less surprising than repeated recourse to loans in Rio. There is little reason to expect the government to enjoy any particular success at borrowing in the home market. Brazil had, at best, only modest rates of saving. Yet even in the early period of heavy reliance on London for loans, domestic sources of funds always accounted for a quarter or more of the total debt. Nearly the entire debt inherited in 1822 was owed to people who were mainly in residence in Brazil. Yet almost none of the pre-1822 debt was funded, and most of it had been "loaned" involuntarily. During the 1820s the pressing need to pay arrears, to settle accounts with Portugal, to cover the costs of the military campaign against Buenos Aires, and to invest in the new apparatus of governance resulted in a remarkable restructuring of this internal debt, one that was as much political as it was financial. By 1830 the government had successfully placed its old floating obligations on a firmly funded basis, no longer borrowed with arbitrary and ad hoc expedients, and regularly drew on internal credit markets through a mix of short-term Treasury bills and long-maturing bonds. Because domestic rather than foreign issues accounted for the most rapidly growing component of the public debt, the bulk of the government's long-term funded debt came to be domestic in origin. The debt was domestic not because of the nationality of the creditors. Merchants from abroad who had taken up residence in Brazil invested in the bonds too.[9] The debt was domestic because it was subscribed and issued locally, and it was denominated mainly in domestic paper currency.[10] Government bonds were not the first securities launched in the Rio capital market (the earliest were equity shares of the first Banco do Brasil). But apólices did become the largest single category of securities in the market soon after their introduction in 1828 and were certainly the most liquid of all securities for the entire Imperial era. Despite the important role of Rio-based foreign merchants as investors in the domestic debt in the 1820s and 1830s, the bulk of domestic bond-holders were Brazilian. If an indicator of external financial dependence is the share of the public debt that was issued abroad, Imperial Brazil emerged by the 1850s as the single Latin American nation with the greatest degree of autonomy in borrowing.

By submitting to a strong penalty for default and ceding a control right over finances to the parliament, the state elicited from Brazil's own relatively underdeveloped capital markets a surprisingly large amount of savings.[11] Among the consequences arising from the creation of this internal debt was the capacity to quickly tap domestic money markets. This made a key difference during the war against Paraguay. Domestic borrowing was especially important to the war effort in the crucial year of 1868. It was then that the volume of Treasury bills in circulation reached their peak, the government took out a National Loan, and then followed up with a massive issue of apólices.[12] Servicing this rapidly expanding debt necessarily required new sources of revenue, which the state obtained by taxing previously unencumbered areas of economic activity. The large increment to long-term domestic debt created during the war, as well as the tax response needed to service this debt, contradicts claims that the conflict failed to stimulate the growth of a "fiscal state."[13]

This chapter documents the central role played by domestic borrowing. The large share of the debt that was domestic distinguished Brazil from the other Latin American borrowers. It also falsifies long-standing claims that the Empire was excessively reliant on external sources of finance. The first section establishes the contribution of domestic sources of public finance. The second section sketches the structure of the government's domestic obligations. The third section focuses on government borrowing via apólices, while the section that follows does the same for the three large National Loans. The fifth section turns to the contours of the primary market for lending, identifying the chief characteristics of the state's lenders. The subsequent section establishes the government's record as a credible borrower by reference to the increasing volume of borrowing, and the seventh section examines the terms of credit. The conclusion addresses some of the implications of Brazil's experience for scholars' understanding of sovereign borrowing more generally.

THE CONTRIBUTION OF DOMESTIC BORROWING
TO PUBLIC FINANCE

The shift from late-colonial ways of borrowing to the use of long-term funded debt was profound. It originated with two main institutional features identified in chapter 2: the Constitution of 1824 and the debt law of 1827. Jointly these defined the fiscal and monitoring authorities of the parliament. This institutional arrangement was indispensable to the emergence and growth of voluntary long-term lending to the state. Loans allowed the government to smooth taxes while meeting expenditure surges. That borrowing in the home market was an important source of funds can be gauged by comparing loan proceeds to ordinary tax revenues. The existence of initial issue discounts on loans (the size of which were not always made explicit in the reports of the finance ministry and which varied over time) means that the face value of the bonds is a poor guide to the amount of money raised. Contemporary accounts show that between 1828 and early 1879, raising 279.7 million milréis required the issue of 6 percent apólices with a face value equal to 320.3 million milréis.[14] The average discount at issue for the period was nearly 13 percent. To estimate the annual proceeds of borrowing the number of bonds issued each year is multiplied by the average initial-issue price. For years in which primary market prices were not available, they were estimated from the secondary market as detailed in appendix II. The proceeds of the three National Loans are then added to give the total domestic funded borrowing by year. Figure 4.1 presents the percentage increase in the

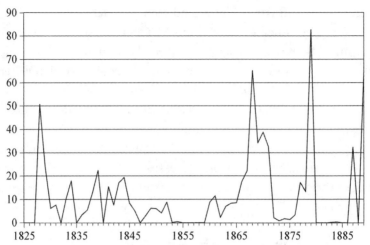

FIGURE 4.1 Additions to ordinary revenues from domestic funded borrowing, 1825–89 (data are by fiscal year)

government's resources each year produced by this borrowing.[15] In roughly one-third of the years between 1827 and 1889, domestic borrowing contributed few or no resources. But in other years the amounts could be astounding. The first issues of apólices in 1828 immediately boosted the Treasury's resources by 50 percent. In the years up to 1852 the funds borrowed in the Rio market added as much as 25 percent to the government's purchasing power. Domestic borrowing then fell off sharply, as the government borrowed quite affordably in London for the rest of the decade.[16] By the 1860s internal borrowing sprang back, adding as much as 10 percent each year to the government's ordinary revenues. Things changed quickly with the onset of war against Paraguay. Ever-larger tranches of new apólices after 1864, combined with the National Loan of 1868, meant that over the course of the war domestic borrowing increased the government's ability to spend by as much as 65 percent beyond its (already rising) ordinary revenues. Heavy borrowing through the wartime years fell off quickly in the 1870s, only to explode again with the drought crisis at the end of the decade. In 1879 the cash raised with apólices and a new fixed-maturity loan nearly doubled the government's normal annual resources. The government's ability to use the capital market to smooth taxes and meet spending needs was remarkable, especially during periods of severe fiscal stress.

SEIGNIORAGE

The government did not altogether abandon nonloan expedients after 1827. The bulk of Brazil's monetary base was paper currency.[17] The Treasury took over the issue of paper money from the first Banco do Brasil when its charter expired in 1829, and it was the sole source of paper money until 1853. The Treasury again monopolized the issue of paper currency from 1866 to 1888. Despite occasional efforts to adhere to gold, the Treasury's currency was not backed by any specie standard. Fiat paper money provided seigniorage revenues that allowed the government to spend beyond what its ordinary revenues and loan proceeds would allow. Figure 4.2 shows the resources the government obtained from seigniorage from 1828 through 1889 as a percentage over its ordinary tax revenues.[18] For years in which the Treasury retired more notes than it issued (implying redemption of paper money in specie or bonds), seigniorage takes on a negative value. Such periods were the exception rather than the rule.

During the First Reign and Regency, seigniorage was more important than borrowing with funded loans. The government of Pedro I repeatedly used the first Banco do Brasil in the 1820s to finance the state. The notes issued by the bank (which passed directly to the Treasury in the form of "loans") added greatly to the unfunded debt under the First Reign. The emperor increasingly relied on this expedient until parlia-

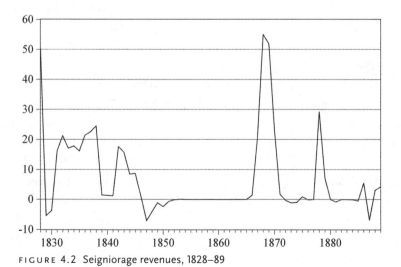

FIGURE 4.2 Seigniorage revenues, 1828–89

ment cut him off under the debt law of 1827. For part of the tumultuous 1830s seigniorage was more important than borrowing. Once the issue of paper money became the purview of the new Banco do Brasil in the early 1850s, there were no new issues by the Treasury until 1866 during the war against Paraguay.

After 1838 seigniorage, like borrowing, tended to come in bursts. Indeed its use tended to coincide with borrowing in the primary market. Seigniorage and home borrowing were substitutes for foreign loans.[19] This coincidence between domestic borrowing and the Treasury's new issues of paper money was mainly a result of the war against Paraguay in the 1860s and the drought relief expenditures in the late 1870s. Covering outlays by issuing paper money was clearly of benefit to the government when spending needs were particularly urgent. Yet excessive issues risked creating price inflation that would erode the real value of debts denominated in milréis at the expense of existing creditors. Heavy use of seigniorage in one period could make it harder to borrow in the future if lenders were skeptical that the value of loan settlement payments would be preserved. This points to another connection between seigniorage and funded borrowing. The National Loans in 1868 and 1879 were distinguished from apólices in that they paid interest in sterling, which insulated bondholders from local inflation. Both were launched near in time to large increases in paper money by the Treasury. Creditors and the government alike understood that recourse to seigniorage undermined the attractiveness of apólices. New borrowing in such instances required an anchor to assure lenders that the value of repayment was secure.

THE STRUCTURE OF THE DOMESTIC DEBT

Apólices, National Loans, and Treasury bills were the main components of the domestic debt. Yet beyond these the Imperial state incurred a variety of other pecuniary obligations. Table 4.1 details the state's debts in 1889, the last year of the constitutional monarchy. The funded debt consisted of long-term loans paying interest and accounted for the bulk of all obligations. The floating debt had interest-bearing and non-interest-bearing components. The noninterest part consisted of paper currency along with old banknotes assumed by the Treasury.[20] The interest-bearing component consisted of private-party deposits of various sorts held by the government, along with short-term Treasury bills.

Table 4.1

Distribution of Central Government Obligations in 1889, by Category

UNFUNDED DEBT	MILRÉIS	SHARE
Paper money	188,863,763	0.192
Treasury bills	28,962,000	0.030
Caixa Econômica	24,534,590	0.025
Diverse deposits	16,295,133	0.017
Cofre de Orphãos	15,340,439	0.016
Emancipation Fund	6,857,143	0.007
Colonization Fund	6,033,022	0.006
Bens Defuntos e Ausentes	4,067,889	0.004
Depósitos Públicos	1,320,251	0.001
Monte de Socorro	919,392	0.001
Dívida Auxiliar	148,765	0.000
Dívida Inscripta	138,318	0.000
Dívida Anterior a 1827	22,177	0.000
SUBTOTAL	293,502,882	0.299
FUNDED DEBT		
Apólices (all coupon rates)	381,655,300	0.389
Foreign debt	252,816,814	0.258
1879 loan	34,232,500	0.035
1868 loan	18,953,500	0.019
SUBTOTAL	687,658,114	0.701
TOTAL	981,160,996	

Notes: Table does not include National Loan of 1889, which was taken in fiscal year 1890.
Foreign debt converted to milréis at the annual average rate of exchange.
Source: RMF 1889, 32–37.

Paper money alone accounted for nearly two-thirds of the floating debt. The most important interest-bearing form of debt in the unfunded category was Treasury bills, which raised money quickly for near-term needs. The use of bills had first been authorized in the late 1820s. Data on the volume in circulation became available only with the law of 1837 that regulated their issue. Until 1845 there were two types. Treasury *bilhetes* paid 6 percent interest on their face value when they matured and were issued at discounts that varied with market conditions. For brief intervals early on the bilhetes comprised the bulk of short-term unfunded debt. By the end of 1845 *letras de tesouro* became the sole short-term debt instrument. Letras differed from bilhetes in that the coupon rate could differ from 6 percent. They were issued under parliamentary sanction in anticipation of revenues to be collected within the current fiscal year. The maximum tenor of Treasury bills increased over time: in 1837 bills could be used for financing for no more than three months and could not be rolled over. Later the limit was raised to six months, and then again to twelve months.[21]

By 1889 Treasury bills accounted for only 3 percent of the total public debt (funded and unfunded). But the quantity of Treasury bills in circulation varied enormously over time. Figure 4.3 presents the face value of the bills in circulation at the end of each month from 1838 through 1889. At times of financial crisis the flight to quality boosted demand for the bills, which were seen as "a popular, because an entirely safe, resort for floating capital, and consequently of no inconvenience to the Treasury, while a great convenience to capitalists."[22] The largest increase in new bills came when the Treasury needed to pay for war. By the time Paraguayan armed forces made their first ground incursion into Brazilian territory at the end of 1864, bills were already being sold in anticipation of high military expenditures.[23] At their peak in 1869 there were nearly 82 million milréis of bills in circulation, almost 40 percent of the total domestic securitized debt (bills, apólices, and National Loan combined).

FIGURE 4.3 Treasury bills in circulation, by month, 1838–89 (current milréis)

Treasury bills served other important purposes as well. Although they were short-term instruments, they nonetheless helped initiate long-term projects. Legislation in 1871 authorized the government to issue some 20 million milréis in bills to help pay to extend the lines of the government-owned Dom Pedro II railroad.[24]

The remaining categories of the unfunded debt did not finance any appreciable outlays and accounted for only a small proportion of the government's overall obligations. One was deposits in the Caixa Econômica, a government-run savings bank and pawnshop that provided simple savings accounts. Because the Treasury administered these deposit accounts their balances were a government obligation.[25] Another was the so-called orphans account consisting of estate funds held in trust. Its purpose was to safeguard the wealth of minor heirs and protect their assets from the "vicissitudes of luck."[26]

Figure 4.4 portrays the evolution of the domestic debt by source. Apólices were the lion's share of the debt at any given moment, usually

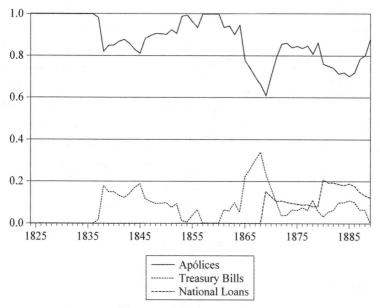

FIGURE 4.4 Sources of domestic debt, by type of loan, 1824–89. Pre-1828 apólices consist of forced loans taken between 1796 and 1822. Apólices from 1828 on include 4 percents, 5 percents, and 6 percents. National Loans are the fixed-exchange rate loans of 1868 and 1879.

more than 80 percent of the total. Notable exceptions came during the war against Paraguay and again in the 1880s. Both periods saw outsized borrowing using Treasury bills and National Loans.

ORIGINS AND USES OF APÓLICES

Before 1828 most of the state's financial obligations were either short term in nature or long term but wholly unfunded. Between 1800 and 1822 there were at least six notable instances of forced and quasi-forced lending. Three were interest-paying loans: one for a gunpowder factory in 1808, another taken from a single Rio merchant firm in 1811, and a third to subsidize Swiss immigration in 1818.[27] Three others were *donativos* (donations), which were little more than capital levies on Rio merchants and bureaucrats. The largest of these was in 1817 to help put down the revolt in Pernambuco. Most of the debt owed to the first Banco do Brasil was the result of repeated forced loans under the guise of seigniorage. The National Loan of 1822 to cover military outlays at independence closed out the era of involuntary lending to the crown.

With the adoption of the Constitution in 1824 loans could be funded only by parliament. Debts accumulated before 1824, as well as those contracted by the emperor before parliament had been seated, were royal rather than public and required parliamentary sanction before they could be repaid. Parliament's assumption of the royal debts in 1827 paved the way for domestic funded borrowing, mainly via the sale of apólices.[28] The national debt law authorized an initial issue of 6 million milréis worth of apólices to consolidate floating debts and to cover the deficit, plus another 6 million milréis in apólices to retire the bank's paper money. It also specified an amortization rate of 1 percent per year of each increment of apólices placed in the market.[29] Subsequent issues of apólices required new legislation from the parliament stating the amount to be issued, the source of revenues for future debt service, and the purpose of the funds raised. The earliest issues, like that discussed at the start of the chapter, typified the pattern of debt placement that would prevail until banks took the lead in the 1860s. A cosmopolitan mix of foreign and domestic merchants in Rio was the primary market for these apólices. In October 1828, for example, the Treasury auctioned 1.2 million milréis of apólices. Three parties tendered offers. One was the partnership of slave traders Rocha, Rego, and Mesquita that had taken the issue earlier in the year. Another was José Buschental, a Rio-based financier originally from Strasbourg, Alsace.[30] The winner, however, was an ad hoc syndicate of Rio-based foreign merchants, March Irmãos & Cia. and Naylor Irmãos & Cia.[31] That the government could borrow through competitive bidding in the primary market rather than through forced loans or donations demonstrated just how far the state's credit had advanced in the six years since the forced National Loan of 1822. This new debt was funded—that is, attached to a portion of the public revenue that the parliament had willingly mortgaged to pay interest—and its management was transparent, monitored by the Junta Administrativa da Caixa de Amortização. Both features helped confer credibility on the state's promise to repay its creditors.

Because apólices were denominated in paper currency they offered no protection against inflation. Interest was paid with cash received by the Caixa de Amortização from the Treasury. Interest was also paid at times in customshouse credits (*assignados da Alfândega*).[32] If the domestic price level increased it would reduce the value of these payments, conferring seigniorage rents on the state and in effect exploiting holders of the domestic debt. This possibility was no secret to the investors, who required a premium to compensate not just for the risk of default but also for the risk of loss in the inflation-adjusted value of their securities. The risk premium on local apólices usually exceeded that on the sterling-denominated bonds Brazil issued in London.[33]

A key weakness in the new market for apólices was its geographic fragmentation. Most were issued in Rio de Janeiro; only a few were marketed through Treasury offices in the provinces. Interest on an apólice was payable only at the office of origination. This restricted the circulation of the new securities within the Empire.[34] Parliament eliminated this restriction in the 1840s with an eye to broadening the ownership of apólices and deepening the market. Thereafter, bondholders could collect interest at any Treasury office that issued apólices (at that time Rio, Bahia, Pernambuco, and Maranhão), irrespective of where the bond originated.[35]

By the end of 1839 the retirement of apólices by either open market operations or lottery drawing formally ceased. Military spending had increased as a result of the war of secession in Rio Grande do Sul, and a large number of bills had to be redeemed. Parliament revised the budget, further increasing military outlays and making sharp cuts in other areas of

spending. The changes made suggest a considerable degree of fiscal desperation: a large issue of paper currency, authorization to seek a new loan
abroad, authorization to borrow by issuing apólices for as little as 80 percent
of face value, authorization to borrow from religious brotherhoods—and
a general halt to the amortization of the debt.[36] The suspension was
sustained by a succession of finance ministers through the 1840s.[37] Had
amortization proceeded as Finance Minister Bernardo Pereira de Vasconcelos had desired in the 1830s, with no new additional issues of bonds, the
internal debt could have been retired by 1848.[38] Any chance of reducing the
domestic debt was obviated not just by the end of amortization, but also
by continuous new borrowing through 1853. In 1839 apólices became, in
effect, perpetual annuities, subject to retirement at the discretion of the
parliament and the finance minister. On the surface, the suspension of
amortization should have elevated the state's credit risk. That Brazil continued to borrow through apólices reveals that the state's willingness to
service the debt was seen as providing adequate compensation.

By the overthrow of the constitutional monarchy in 1889, more
than 380 million milréis of apólices had been issued, only 10 million
of which were retired. Most initially carried a 6 percent annual coupon
rate. Table 4.2 reports the principal purpose of each legislated increment
of 6 percents issued through the 1880s. As in the case of foreign borrowing the funds raised were used for varied purposes.

Apólices served various ends for the Treasury. The government certainly borrowed through apólices when market conditions were more favorable in Rio than in London.[39] Apólices were also used as an expedient
way to settle claims. Restitution for ships and cargoes (prizes, or *prezas*)
seized during the blockade of Buenos Aires and for Portuguese properties sequestered at independence (some taken as a "mere precaution")
relied on apólices, not cash.[40] Payments in large blocks of apólices depressed their price in Rio, as many of the foreign recipients and their
agents sought to quickly convert them to cash.[41] Apólices helped the Treasury retire bills, converting short-term debt to a long-term funded basis.
The Treasury was required to redeem bills by using resources from the
same fiscal year in which they had been issued, which meant it had to
accumulate substantial cash balances in a relatively brief period.[42] Getting creditors to accept higher-yielding apólices in exchange for their
lower-yielding bills could sometimes prove challenging. Treasury bills

Table 4.2

Issues of 6 Percent Bonds (*Apólices*) Authorized by Parliament, 1828–82

PERIODS	PRINCIPAL PURPOSE	AMOUNT ISSUED (IN MILRÉIS)
1828–32	Deficit	13,496,600
1832–34	Indemnities (*Prezas*)	5,974,600
1837	Revolts	1,723,000
1837–38	Deficit	5,861,400
1839	Deficit	1,918,000
1840	Military expenditures	303,400
1841	Deficit	4,105,600
1842–43	Deficit	5,346,600
1842–45	Portuguese claims	2,124,200
1843–44	Royal dowry and trousseau	1,720,000
1843–46	Deficit	1,495,000
1844–45	Deficit	2,344,000
1844–48	Deficit	7,505,400
1846	Deficit	336,000
1851–53	Deficit	5,213,800
1858	Portuguese claims	5,400
1860–62	Swap for shares of Recife and San Francisco Railway Co.	2,466,400
1860–63	Swap for shares of Bahia and San Francisco Railway Co.	186,600
1860–72	Swap for shares of Dom Pedro II railroad	11,328,600
1861–62	Withdraw paper money	2,150,000
1863	Withdraw paper money/Redeem notes and Rio de la Plata indemnities	5,890,400
1864	Takeover of União e Indústria turnpike road	3,161,000
1865	Withdraw of paper money/Royal weddings	1,228,000
1865–72	War against Paraguay	143,894,700
1869	Land purchase	50,000

(Continued)

Table 4.2 *(continued)*

PERIODS	PRINCIPAL PURPOSE	AMOUNT ISSUED (IN MILRÉIS)
1870	Island purchase	1,705,800
1870	Redeem treasury notes	25,000,000
1871	[unknown]	600
1873–76	Dock company investment	2,734,000
1876	Deficit	8,600,000
1877	"Diverse"	30,000,000
1877	Dowry	1,200,000
1879	Consolidation of floating debt	40,000,000
1880–82	Swap for shares of Baturité railroad	606,000
Total issued		339,675,100
Total amortized		10,154,200
Amount in circulation in 1889		329,520,900

Source: RMF 1891, table 6.

dominated the short end of the yield curve, had no ready substitute, and often had superior liquidity.[43]

The state also used apólices to reduce its burden from railroad dividend guarantees.[44] Swaps of apólices for railroad stock put nearly 10 million milréis of new apólices into circulation. But it was the war against Paraguay that generated the single largest increase. Borrowing for the war effort accounted for more than 40 percent of all of the 6 percent apólices issued during the Imperial era. Raising such a large amount over just a few years required that the government boost the yield to investors by placing apólices at lower prices. Despite these considerable amounts of new domestic borrowing during the war, the inflationary emission of paper money still proved necessary to cover expenses, which further worked to push apólice prices down.[45]

Apólices were quoted regularly in Rio's secondary market, and trading was usually active.[46] Despite wartime increases in the interest rate, the general tendency was for yields on the apólices in the secondary market to decline. In the 1870s the government first considered whether to refinance by converting its 6 percent apólices to a 5 percent basis or to simply make all new issues from that point forward bear a 5 percent coupon.[47] By the

Table 4.3

Issues of 5 Percent Bonds (*Apólices*) Authorized by Parliament, 1830–86

PERIODS	PURPOSE	AMOUNT ISSUED (IN MILRÉIS)
1830–83	Fund pre-1827 obligations	2,000,000
1886	Consolidate floating debt	50,000,000
Circulation		52,000,000

Source: RMF 1889, table 9.

early 1880s apólices regularly traded above par. Consistently low yields enticed the government to pursue the conversion. In his report to the parliament, Finance Minister João Lustosa da Cunha Paranaguá (visconde de Paranaguá) pointed out that coupon-rate reductions had already been successfully implemented in Argentina, Spain, Belgium, and France.[48] While he did not press for the immediate conversion of the existing debt, in his view all new borrowing should shift to a 5 percent coupon. In 1886 the government switched to the issue of 5 percent apólices exclusively. As table 4.3 shows, most of the 5 percents appeared in a single operation in 1886 to redeem bills and paper currency.

By that time parliament had already authorized the conversion of the existing 6 percents.[49] With the success of the new 5 percents the cabinet took action in 1886. It was left to Finance Minister Francisco Belisário Soares de Souza to execute the operation. A deputy from a prominent family of planters and politicians (his uncle was the visconde de Uruguai, a senator, councilor of state, and one of the founders of the Conservative party), Belisário, as he was known to contemporaries, had held—alongside the visconde de Tocantins and the visconde de Figueiredo—a directorship of the Banco do Brasil from 1876 to 1880.[50] He married into the Teixeira Leite family, which included other important planters and Paraiba valley financiers, who were major investors in the National Loan of 1868.[51] Belisário kicked off the conversion by directing the Treasury to offer face value for the 6 percent apólices that at the moment were trading at a premium.[52] The market's immediate grasp of the implications brought prices down to par. This left bondholders with two options: swap for new apólices bearing the 5 percent coupon or cash out. Investors seeking the most liquid low-risk yield that was available locally had no alternative.

There was widespread interest in the new bonds.[53] Most holders of 6 percents simply swapped for the new 5 percents. Those who did not redeemed their apólices at par either at Treasury offices in Brazil or in London. Within a year of the announcement nearly all of the bondholders had agreed to participate. Only 2 percent of the apólices were in the hands of holdouts who tried to bring claims against the Imperial government.[54] The conversion, widely heralded as a success for the Treasury and the cabinet, reduced the annual interest outlays on the domestic debt.

ORIGINS AND USES OF NATIONAL LOANS

Beyond its use of apólices the Imperial state borrowed three times on a large scale using loans with a fixed maturity, first in 1868 and again in 1879 and 1889. They were called National Loans because they were marketed directly to a broader investing public rather than to just a handful of participants in the primary market. The National Loan of 1868 was a war loan, while that of 1879 helped fund expenditures for relief projects in the drought-afflicted northeast. The 1889 loan was part of the banking reform of the late Empire and was intended to provide banks with the required means for backing their own notes.[55]

Table 4.4 summarizes the terms of these issues. All of the loans were denominated in milréis yet promised interest and repayment of principal at a fixed rate of foreign exchange. While the loans were raised internally, their pegged values to external currencies made them more like Brazil's foreign sterling loans in the eyes of bondholders.

The bonds from the 1868 and 1879 loans were lucrative for the initial investors. In 1868 observers in London initially found it difficult to believe that Brazil was borrowing yet again while at war, particularly in the wake of the large London loan in 1865 and the ongoing issue of apólices at home.[56] So it was surprising indeed when the 1868 loan was triply oversubscribed in the Rio market.[57] Investors loaned in paper milréis and in return received interest and principal in gold (or gold equivalent) at a fixed exchange rate that was far more favorable than that prevailing in the wartime currency market.[58] The 1868 bonds were gilt-edged securities in their purest form. The initial buyers of the bonds were able to convert badly depreciated wartime paper money into a stream of future gold payments. Demand for the bonds was high, and they traded at a premium to their issue price for months thereafter.[59]

Table 4.4

National Loans

LOAN	INTEREST COST	PURPOSE	COUPON	AMOUNT RAISED (IN MILRÉIS)	AMOUNT ISSUED	PERIOD (YEARS)
1868	8.84	War finance	6	27,000,000	30,000,000	33
1879	5.71	Cover deficits/retire floating debt	4.5	50,000,000	51,885,000	20
1889	5.12	Subsidy to banking and agricultural lending	4	100,000,000	109,694,000	41

Note: The loans were to be settled in sterling equivalent in accordance with the exchange rate clause in the loan contracts.
Sources: see text.

The introduction of the 1868 loan brought an outpouring of complaints from existing apólice holders.[60] It subordinated existing debt to a new loan by inverting the seniority among the creditors. Because the new loan promised regular amortization its bondholders would be repaid before the owners of apólices, who had seen no redemptions of their bonds since the late 1830s. It smacked of preferential treatment for the new lenders. This was then compounded by a large new issue of paper currency authorized by parliament in the amount of 40 million milréis. Apólice holders were fully exposed to the resulting price inflation, while investors in the National Loan were protected from currency depreciation by the loan's exchange rate clause.

As favorable as the terms of the 1868 loan were for investors in the new bonds, there was a limit to how high they could rise. While prices initially ran well above the face value in the secondary market, the bonds were callable, and the first round of amortization at par put pressure on the price.[61] The gold clause came to matter less over time as the milréis recovered. When the loan first hit the market in October 1868, the exchange rate stood at 19 1/2 pence per milréis, near its wartime low.[62] A 6 percent dividend in gold on a 1,000-milréis bond paid a bondholder 6.75 pounds in gold or sterling. Raising that much at the market rate of exchange cost the Treasury 83 milréis instead of the 60 milréis that the government would have paid out on an apólice with the same coupon rate. The stronger postwar milréis brought the government's cost of service on the loan down a good deal.[63] With the victory over Paraguay, the cost to the Treasury of a 6 percent coupon payment fell to nearly 6 pounds sterling by the early 1870s.

A little more than a decade later, in June of 1879, the parliament authorized a new National Loan in the form of bearer bonds. Interest was payable in Brazil, Lisbon, London, and Paris.[64] While similar in its terms to the loan of 1868, it carried a lower coupon rate and fetched a higher price. Interest and principal were fixed in sterling rather than gold, with the government having the option of paying dividends in either the pound (which was legal tender in Brazil) or the equivalent in paper currency at the market rate of exchange. The milréis was stronger than it had been for the National Loan in 1868, but not by much, averaging a bit more than 22 pence in 1879. The new loan was tremendously successful among bond investors. On a 50-million milréis issue, the Treasury received orders for the new bonds in excess of 123 million milréis.[65] The offer prices had only a modest discount, and the bulk of the issue went out the door at 96 percent.[66] Of the nearly 50 million milréis raised, more than 37 million were received in cash, another 10.5 million in rediscounted Treasury bills, and some 2 million milréis in exchange drafts on Europe.[67] As in 1868, investors bought the bonds with local currency and were repaid in sterling or its equivalent, protecting them against any future weakness in the milréis.[68] In early 1880 shares of the 1879 loan were already being used for remittances to Europe, and "the whole amount is said to have been subscribed for at Rio, with a view, no doubt, on the part of many of the holders to its eventual transfer to the European market."[69] In London the bonds traded only privately at first.[70] Soon they were formally listed on the exchange. Their attractiveness in Europe stemmed from the exchange clause.[71] As one of the many favorably inclined observers put it, "The interest on this Loan can never be paid in depreciated paper, for such a proceeding would be at once a breach of faith and an act of insolvency, to which a State like Brazil, high in credit and proud of its position, could never descend."[72]

The third National Loan came in the aftermath of abolition in 1888. In the 1880s mortgage financing for Paraiba valley coffee growers dried up. Mortgage default rates jumped. Crop yields were falling, as was the price of coffee, damaging the planters' balance sheets. Growing political pressure to abolish slavery further reduced the value of assets that planters could pledge as collateral for credit. In response a succession of Conservative finance ministers used Treasury balances to extend low-cost credit to banks so that the banks could in turn extend subsidized credit to planters. The initial effort was so popular that the government expanded the *auxílios a lavoura* (aid to farming) policy, and the Liberal cabinet that came to power in June 1889 continued the program. To boost the banking sector the Ouro Preto cabinet borrowed through a National Loan in 1889. The key innovation with the new loan was that its proceeds were denominated in the same currencies in which it was to be settled: gold or sterling.[73] This was possible because the milréis had recovered to the point where it was fully convertible to pounds. Interest on the loan was payable at the Caixa de Amortização in Rio de Janeiro; the Treasury offices in Bahia, Pernambuco, Pará, Maranhão, Rio Grande do Sul, and São Paulo; and at agencies in London, Paris, Lisbon, Porto, Berlin, Amsterdam, and New York. The loan was not only the largest domestic debt operation of the Imperial era; at 11.25 million pounds sterling it raised more new money than any loan contracted under the Empire, domestic or foreign. It also had the longest maturity of any National Loan, at forty-one years. It did not, however, remain in the market for very long. Late in 1890 the republican government redeemed most of the bonds that remained in circulation, paying with specie that had been deposited by banks with the Treasury as backing for their banknotes.[74] The bonds took the place of the gold as backing for the notes.

THE MARKETS FOR GOVERNMENT DEBT

Demand for the government's bonds involved two interconnected tiers of investors. Lenders who purchased bonds at issue comprised the primary market. The secondary market consisted of those who purchased the bonds once they began trading. The primary market was the merchant and financial community in Rio. Concentrated downtown, especially on Rua Direita (present-day Rua Primeiro de Março) and the cross streets of Rua do Ouvidor and Rua da Alfândega, the city's private bankers, trading firms, coffee factors, foreign merchants, and early on, slave traders made up the primary market for the government's bonds. The district was home as well to Brazil's sole organized securities exchange. That the government's loans were securitized as bonds facilitated the expansion of the secondary market, in which a large number of traders could price and exchange risk. The liquidity afforded by the secondary market supported in turn the vibrancy of the primary market and redounded to the benefit of the government's borrowing.

Little changed in the primary market between 1828 and 1852. While competitive, the market was also concentrated. A mix of Rio-based foreign trading houses, brokers, and Luso-Brazilian merchants took most of the Treasury's new issues. The state's dependence on these individual merchant lenders was recurrent. The one difference was the gradual eclipse of the great slave traders as major lenders, with the shift of the slave trade from a legal to "contraband" basis in 1831. Even in times of fiscal stress the state found local capitalists willing to lend. In 1838, as Samuel & Phillips, Brazil's financial agent in London, and the original London loan contractors became increasingly frustrated with delayed remittances and leveraged advances, merchants and dealers in Rio lined up to take positions in new issues of bonds. Over the course of March and April several firms and brokers took nearly 1.4 million milréis of new apólices.[75] João José de Araújo Gomes (later barão de Alegrete), already a top domestic creditor who would soon be appointed to the junta as one of the Empire's major apólice holders, added a modest 42 thousand milréis worth to his portfolio. José Ignacio Tavares took 50 thousand, as did another merchant, Antônio Joaquim de Silva Tibre. João Miers loaned 84 thousand milréis, and the firm Souto, Dovey & Benjamin took at least 133 thousand. Edward Johnston alone took nearly a third of the bonds issued over the two-month interval, some 443 thousand milréis. Johnston, a broker-dealer who also discounted commercial paper, went on to establish a partnership in Rio in 1842, later opening a branch office in Liverpool, and became a partner in the firm of Johnston, Napier & Co. in Bahia.[76]

Concentration in the primary market was high. A half dozen Rio merchants absorbed more than 60 percent of the new issue over a period of a couple of months. Of the apólices next issued in 1843 and 1844, three firms took up fully one-third: Edward Johnston & Company, Samuel, Phillips & Cia., and José Antonio Moreira.[77] In 1845–46, Moreira and Samuel Phillips & Cia. took some 2 million milréis more of new bonds, about 80 percent of the year's issue.[78] This pattern was the norm for the era. A small group of broker-dealers consistently provided the bulk of the lending in the primary market.

Commercial banks made their first appearance in the primary market for the government's loans in the 1850s. Consortia of merchants and brokers had long joined forces to invest in new bonds. As loans became larger they were harder to place. To be sure, in the 1850s the city had Brazil's most important private banking houses, which variously performed the functions of broker-dealers, discounters, accepting houses, and merchant bankers. These included Gomes & Filhos, Oliveira & Bello, Montenegro, Lima & Cia., Fortinho e Moniz, A. J. A. Souto, and Bahia Irmãos & Cia. But with the exception of the Banco Commercial the financial landscape had been largely devoid of joint-stock banks. By the early 1860s the downtown district, by then already home to the new Banco do Brasil, had the Brazilian and Portuguese Bank and the London and Brazilian Bank. This growing commercial banking sector played an increasingly important role in placing new bonds, as individual merchants, private banks, and local syndicates could no longer summon sufficient resources to handle the size of the loans. Accessing a primary market that was deep enough to accommodate large new issues of bonds required that the Treasury work with multiple dealers. Syndication on the part of lenders certainly helped spread the risk on new loans. But it was the creation of larger banks and the increased liquidity after the end of the slave trade that contributed to an increasingly competitive demand for bonds at a much larger volume. The involvement of Rio joint-stock banks in the 1850s prefigured their expanding role in state debt in the 1860s and 1870s.

Traditional broker-dealers remained active in the primary loan market and even handled large tranches of debt. In 1851 the Treasury sold more than 3 million milréis worth of 6 percent apólices to the partnership of Gomes & Paiva.[79] The firm contracted to pay 860 milréis for each share issued at 1 thousand milréis, which meant they received the apólices at the midpoint of the previous year's range of prices.[80] In 1852 Gomes & Paiva again took 6 percents, below par.[81] They got a bargain, since in April the government revealed that it had sold 1 million milréis in apólices to the Banco Commercial *above* par.[82] The Banco Commercial was also the key player in the government's 1853 swap of apólices for some of its own sterling bonds in London.[83] Because broker-dealers had ample experience placing the bonds with clients, the larger banks often partnered with them in bidding on new issues. The new Banco do Brasil became the most important bank in this regard. While it had rivals, it increasingly took larger positions in new issues of debt. When domestic borrowing heated up again in the 1860s, the bank took by itself an issue of 2 million milréis of 6 percents.[84] Even as borrowing became more dependent on the involvement of large banks, the primary market for new issues remained reasonably competitive. To retire a block of Treasury bills in 1863 the Finance Ministry entertained three separate bids on new apólices: one from the Rio securities broker-dealer Henrique [Henry] Nathan on behalf of the private bankers Montenegro, Lima & Cia.; another from the Rio-based London and Brazilian Bank; and a third from the Banco do Brasil, which had partnered with Gomes & Filhos. The Banco do Brasil and Gomes & Filhos team won, taking more than 5 million milréis worth of apólices in three separate tranches with no commission, on the condition that the Treasury refrain from placing additional apólices during 1864.[85] The bank's initiative was handsomely rewarded. Apólice prices rose to face value within a month and remained well above the issue price of 90.5 percent through most of 1864.[86]

By 1868 wartime borrowing made the placement of new debt at favorable terms noticeably difficult. Complicating matters further was the loss of many local banking firms in the crisis of 1864. So the finance ministry structured its first National Loan, which drew on nearly every player: large commercial banks, the nouveau riche of the coffee trade, long-established merchants and dealers, and private individuals. The loan was oversubscribed in Rio at a rate of almost four orders for each bond sold; nearly thirteen hundred parties tendered offers.[87] Bond investors ran the gamut from people with no prominence in business who bought a couple of shares to the city's major banks, which took up thousands of new bonds. By now, however, the most important subscribers by far were the big banks. The Banco do Brasil alone took on the largest single piece of the loan, at nearly 5,000 shares. The Banco Rural e Hypothecário and the English Bank of Rio de Janeiro each took nearly 1,000 bonds, while the Rio-based London and Brazilian Bank took a small position with fewer than 250 shares. Of the thirty largest positions taken by noninstitutional lenders, the broker-dealers and large-scale merchants assumed no fewer than half. A large stake went to Finnie Brothers & Company, a merchant and brokerage firm that had been active in Rio since at least the 1820s.[88]

Among the individual investors one family, the Teixeira Leites, stood out. They were a clan of lenders, coffee factors, and planters in Vassouras, in the heart of the coffee-rich Paraiba valley. Francisco José Teixeira Leite and Joaquim José Teixeira Leite, originally from Minas Gerais, were scions of the first barão de Itambé, himself a financier and likely one of the wealthiest men of the coffee zone during his lifetime. Joaquim took 357 shares of the National Loan, while his wife, Anna Esmeria, took 179 bonds and his daughter Eufrásia took another 179 shares. Joaquim's brother Francisco (who less than three years later was made barão de Vassouras) bought the bonds as well. Francisco had been head of the Vassouras branch of the Banco Commercial e Agrícola in 1859 before it closed (yet another brother, João Evangelista, had been president of the main branch in Rio), and in 1873 he would be a key investor in the new Banco Industrial e Mercantil.[89]

Together the various members of the family bought almost 1,000 shares of the 1868 bonds, a collective stake in the loan that was nearly as large as that of any of the Rio banks, save that of the Banco do Brasil. Manuel Gomes de Carvalho (barão do Rio Negro), a Paraiba valley planter and financier who specialized in discounting commercial paper and trading in apólices, took hundreds of bonds of the 1868 loan as well. His wife was a Teixeira Leite, and his brother was the second barão do Amparo, who also invested in the loan. These two men, coffee barons both, were sons of the first barão do Amparo and brothers of the visconde da Barra Mansa, all of whom were *fazendeiros* around Vassouras and Barra Mansa.[90] The Teixeira Leites, like many of the upper-crust families of the province's interior, were broadly connected by marriage to other prominent clans and their descendants, particularly those who were important figures in the Conservative party.[91] Indeed, the major financier in Rio who was *not* related to other prominent financiers and statesmen was the exception rather than the rule. This was no atomistic primary market of transient, anonymous investors. These were people who mattered in how the Empire was governed, how its policies were crafted, and how business was done.

The size of the new issues run through Rio's banking during the war was without precedent. In 1869 both the Banco Rural e Hypothecário and the Banco do Brasil took extraordinarily large positions, the former buying some 20 million milréis worth of new apólices, while the latter took

25 million in December. In late 1870, at the end of the war, the government again issued 25 million milréis in apólices through several banks.[92] The large sizes of the loans and the reliance on banks persisted after the war's end. In June 1876 the government borrowed by placing 5 million milréis of apólices through the Banco Rural e Hypothecário, initially concealing the issue from the public to try to prop up prices in the market.[93] Then in January 1877 the Banco do Brasil agreed to take 30 million milréis for only 3 percent less than face value.[94] It was a strong play by the bank. By paying only 970 milréis for a bond already trading in the market at 1,010 milréis, the bank stood to gain an instantaneous return.[95] Yet the bank was soon outdone. In January 1879 a whopping 40 million milréis in apólices hit the market under contract with the Banco Rural e Hypothecário and, as brokers, Alexandre Wagner, José Luiz Cardoso de Salles (the barão de Irapuá), and Francisco Figueiredo (who six months later would be ennobled as visconde by Pedro II, bypassing the rank of barão altogether).[96] An agreement between the Treasury and the lenders stipulated that no new apólices would be placed for more than a year to help support the price. Thus when the government needed to borrow again for drought relief only six months later, it launched a new National Loan. The local concentration of lenders that had been typical up to that point remained evident; more than 98 percent of the bonds for the 1879 loan went to subscribers in Rio, with the lion's share landing in the commercial banks. The broad investing public that "national" implied played little to no role this time around. The Banco do Brasil by itself took more than 50 percent of the bonds, while the New London and Brazilian Bank, Banco Commercial, and Banco Industrial e Mercantil all took positions. A few banks in the provinces, along with Portuguese banks, invested as well.[97]

By the 1880s the shift toward the predominance of banks in lending to the state was largely complete. When the government paved the way for its 1886 domestic debt conversion with a public subscription for new apólices bearing a 5 percent coupon, it was run through the Banco do Brasil. The bank explicitly signed on to underwrite the loan agreeing to take any unsubscribed apólices at the end of the offer period.[98] It contracted with the government to place 50 million milréis of apólices for a fee of 0.5 percent on the initial subscription. Buyers could purchase the new securities with currency, Treasury bills, or banknotes.[99] The apólices entered the market under "unexpectedly favorable conditions," and the issue was well oversubscribed by the end of the first day of its offering.[100] The Banco Industrial e Mercantil took 1 thousand apólices, and the Banco do Brasil's own mortgage department subscribed nearly 2 thousand bonds. But it was the Banco Rural e Hypothecário that stunned the market, purchasing 26 thousand shares, more than half of the issue. Several private investors stood out as well. Joaquim Gomes Leite de Carvalho (second barão do Amparo), the prominent Vassouras capitalist and property owner who had invested in the National Loan of 1868, bought one thousand of the new apólices, while the visconde de Figueiredo—a director of the Banco do Brasil in the 1880s and a major shareholder in the Banco Internacional do Brasil, the Banco del Credere, and the Banco União do Crédito—personally took one-fifth of the entire loan.[101] The crowning achievement in the government's partnership with big banks in issuing debt came just ten weeks before the overthrow of the constitutional monarchy. The Treasury ran the National Loan of 1889 through four major banks: the Banco Commercial do Rio de Janeiro, the Banco Rural e Hypothecário, the Banco do Brasil, and the Banco Internacional do Brazil.[102] Demand for the new bonds outstripped the amount offered by four to one.[103]

Just where all of these bonds ended up once they passed through the primary market depended on preferences toward risk, return, and liquidity. Apólice holders included private individuals, foreign nationals residing in Brazil, merchants, private banks, and a variety of organizations. In the 1830s this latter group included a large number of religious lay brotherhoods, the Santa Casa da Misericórdia (Holy House of Mercy) of various towns, along with the first Banco Commercial. In 1838 the private Caixa Econômica alone held almost 70 percent of the apólices owned by all organizations.[104] With the appearance of joint stock companies in the 1850s, businesses held a larger portion of apólices, which allowed otherwise idle cash to earn a relatively secure return.[105] Of the commercial firms that kept apólices in their own portfolios after midcentury the Banco do Brasil's holdings were probably the biggest. The most the bank ever had on its books was in 1877, the year it took the entire new issue of some 30 million milréis of apólices. Even then, the apólices the bank owned were only around 10 percent of the total in circulation.[106] By a wide margin most of the domestic public debt ended up in the hands of individuals, whether they were merchants, business owners, planters, or rentiers.

THE VOLUME OF DOMESTIC BORROWING

A main testable implication of the model of credit rationing presented in chapter 2 is that a ruler can borrow more, and more affordably, by submitting to a stronger default penalty. In Brazil the political arrangements of the 1820s that vested parliament with control rights over finances provided the foundation for the default penalty. Given that this mechanism was rooted in domestic political interests, one might predict a strong positive effect on the supply of loans from the home market. This prediction is borne out by the evolving structure of the Empire's debt. In the decades after independence domestic borrowing emerged as an increasingly important component of the state's funded obligations. The growing ease with which successive cabinets engaged in new borrowing at home over sixty years was economically remarkable, but also exhibited a clear political-institutional logic.

Figure 4.5 shows the real stock of domestic debt (both long-term and short-term borrowing) from fiscal year 1829 through 1889.[107] The apólice

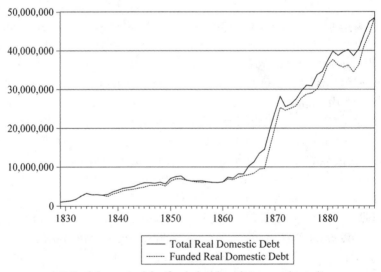

FIGURE 4.5 Real domestic debt (funded and total) in pounds sterling, 1829–89. Funded debt is sum of bonds originally issued in Brazil and in circulation at end of each fiscal year. Total debt is the sum of funded debt and the Treasury bills. Both series are converted to sterling at the average annual market rate of exchange and deflated to constant 1889 values by the British wholesale price index.

debt is converted to sterling using the annual average exchange rate, while debt taken under the National Loans is directly expressed in sterling on the basis of the loans' exchange rate clauses. The sum is then placed on a constant price basis in sterling using the British wholesale price index. Three phases in the trajectory of domestic borrowing are evident. The first, to 1852, was one of gradual expansion, reliant on individual merchants in Rio for loan placement. In the second phase borrowing tapered off until the early 1860s. The government found favorable borrowing conditions in London from 1852 on, so it took its loans there. In Rio de Janeiro the government sought to channel the available private savings (which had increased as a result of the end of the slave trade) to favored businesses. One of these was the Banco do Brasil, which the government had created as a privileged bank of issue. The other was the Dom Pedro II railroad, which would dramatically lower the cost of bringing coffee down from the Paraiba valley. Both projects required high levels of capital investment, and one way to help provide it was for the government to limit its local borrowing. The third phase began with the war against Paraguay; domestic debt exhibited a large, nearly discontinuous jump, increasing by more than 150 percent in just a few years. The debt stock continued to grow after the war at a reduced pace, but then once again ran up quickly with the new internal loans of the 1880s. Capping the decade, and the Imperial era, was the 100-million-milréis National Loan of 1889. The sheer size of the operation had no precedent in Brazil. Figure 4.6 gives a sense of contemporary views of the loan. It depicts the finance minister (visconde de Ouro Preto) reclining on bags filled with money. It was a caricature but no exaggeration: the Treasury simply piled up cash from the operation. Domestically issued debt attained the highest level of the Imperial era in the wake of the loan, with a total of 464 million milréis in circulation (more than 50 million pounds sterling at the prevailing rate of exchange).[108]

The model predicts that domestic capitalists should be willing to supply the government with credit so long as they wield an effective penalty for default. The especially large increase in domestic lending after the 1850s is nonetheless puzzling. Rising demand for loans by the finance ministry cannot by itself explain the increase in the debt stock over the longer term, unless Brazil consistently borrowed below its debt ceiling. But if lenders rationed credit to the state, the higher levels of debt imply an

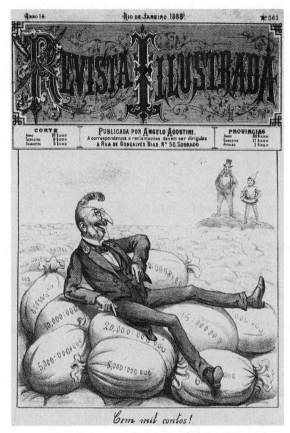

FIGURE 4.6 Caricature of Minister of Finance Visconde
de Ouro Preto reclining on the proceeds of the National
Loan of 1889: "Cem mil contos!" (One hundred million
milréis!) The youthful observer in the background
represents the *Revista*, and the man on the left is visconde
do Figueiredo, a major financier and investor in the Banco
Internacional, one of the four banks involved in issuing the
loan. (*Revista Illustrada*, 31 August 1889)

increase in the supply of loans. To be sure, the growth of tax revenues increased the state's ability to repay. But loan supply depended on the willingness to repay. A stronger penalty would shift the rationing constraint,
raising the credit ceiling, and allow higher levels of borrowing.[109]

Several factors contributed to the increase in the debt ceiling after
midcentury. By the 1850s the demonstrated resilience of the Empire's
political institutions, especially during the tumultuous 1830s and 1840s,

boosted lenders' confidence in the government's willingness to repay in hard times. Another factor was taxes. Revenues increased over time, and the fiscal extraction rate (given by the ratio of tax revenues to total trade) shot up between 1865 and 1870. The creation of new taxes during the war showed that the state had the political capacity required to extract more resources. The higher extraction rate was tantamount to a decline in the political cost of taxation. Such a decline would shift the supply curve for loans in the same direction as an increase in the default penalty. Higher taxes, and a higher extraction rate, signaled not only an ability to repay additional debt but also a willingness to raise the revenues that would make default less likely.

A third factor that increased the supply of credit to the state was the fundamental change in the structure of the primary market. The fact that there were fewer but bigger entities supplying capital, combined with the fact that most of them were politically well connected, could only strengthen the penalty for default.[110] The creation of the Banco do Brasil in the early 1850s was motivated precisely by the state's need to manage its obligations. Policy makers were aware that pooling so much of the capital of the merchant class could help loosen credit restrictions on the state itself. When government borrowing in Rio resumed in earnest in the 1860s the Banco do Brasil, along with the other commercial banks that the government allowed to incorporate, had transformed the primary market for the state's debt instruments. There were not many commercial banks, but in placing loans the Imperial state relied heavily on them. In 1886–87, by way of example, the Banco do Brasil discounted a total of 46 million milréis in Treasury bills by purchasing and holding them to maturity. The bank thus served as the market for roughly 90 percent of the peak amount of Treasury bills in circulation that year.[111] The new structure of the financial sector after the 1850s and the demonstrated ability to impose new taxes in the 1860s enabled borrowing at substantially higher levels over time.

THE TERMS OF DOMESTIC BORROWING: BOND PRICES
AND THE COST OF CAPITAL

Unlike the post-1855 relationship between the Imperial government and N. M. Rothschild & Sons in London, no Brazilian bank could claim exclusivity in handling domestic borrowing. Transactions costs in Rio differed from those in London. In Rio, the finance ministry usually floated new apólices directly to broker-dealers, in most instances without paying overt fees to issue. There were no fees on interest and amortization either, since these were handled by the Treasury's own offices. This did not mean that issuing debt at home was costless. On the contrary, costs, including compensation to the dealer for the risk that he might be stuck with bonds that he could not sell at a profit, were built into the initial discount. In nearly every instance new apólices entered that market at less than the prevailing price. This discount raised the effective yield to dealers as well as the government's cost of capital above the current yield on otherwise identical securities. Primary market prices varied with the lenders' perceptions of the government's creditworthiness. The first apólices in 1828 entered the primary market at only 65 percent of par.[112] The government issued so many apólices so quickly in 1828 that by the end of the year it became difficult to find new takers.[113] The average issue price from 1828 through 1835 ended up being only 63.4 percent of the securities' face values. Apólices placed near the end of 1833 dropped sharply in price, fetching only 53 percent for the Treasury.[114] Prices improved in the second half of the decade, despite a surge of regional revolts around Brazil. Between the end of 1836 and April 1839 the Treasury issued nearly 8 million milréis in new 6 percent apólices, at an average price of 75.3 percent of par. One batch went out at a remarkable 89.5 percent.[115] From April 1843 through March 1844, new apólices commanded between 69 percent and 100 percent of face value.[116] The average issue price over the same twelve-month period was 76.8 percent of par.

Guaranteeing a high issue price often involved concessions to lenders by the finance ministry. In February 1848 the government placed 6 percents at full face value—under the condition of not issuing any more apólices that year.[117] An issue in 1876 for 5 million milréis was initially concealed from the public altogether in order to avoid an adverse impact on the market price. By the time news of the issue broke, it had little if any negative impact on price because "existing home stocks have not been affected by it more than is usually the case when new bonds jostle old in a limited market."[118] Large issues of new apólices taken by banks in 1877 and 1879 employed similar clauses designed to protect lenders from loss in return for giving the Treasury the best possible terms.[119]

Primary dealers often made good profits, even without special concessions. In 1851 the 6 percents brought in 860 milréis each for the Treasury. The initial discount stemmed from expectations that the Imperial government would soon have to borrow again to help finance its campaign in the Rio de la Plata. To the good fortune of the bankers who took the issue, within five months the risk of a wider conflict had diminished, and the market price on apólices approached 920 milréis. A year after issue the market price had risen to 98 percent of par and was poised to rise further in 1852 with the defeat of Rosas in Argentina. In 1851 Brazil also issued a small parcel of apólices in payment against long-standing Portuguese claims.[120] As stipulated in the agreement between the two countries, the Treasury issued these at a heavy discount, being credited with only 73 percent of the par value. Given the prevailing market prices, the recipients of these shares were enviably positioned to turn a handsome and instantaneous profit.

Improvements in the government's standing in credit markets during the early 1850s were reflected in the conditions attached to new borrowing. In late 1851 and 1852 the government was able to issue 6 percents in a higher price range, between 940 milréis and 1,015 milréis—a considerable improvement.[121] The placement of new bonds above par was without precedent in Rio. High bond prices persisted until 1860, when expectations of a large new issue to exchange for shares of Dom Pedro II railroad stock brought prices back down to par.[122] By 1862 the government could command only 93 percent for new 6 percents.[123] The next year, despite considerable competition among banks to take the loan, new apólices raised only 90.5 percent for the Treasury.[124] The heavy borrowing near the end of the war against Paraguay was conducted at a price of 91.5 percent. Given the large existing stock of debt, the terms on the new bonds "exceeded the most flattering expectations."[125] Apólice prices recovered through the 1870s; large issues in 1876 and the massive issue made in 1879 both raised full face value for the Treasury.[126] The National Loan of 1889 was offered at 90 percent of par because of its low coupon rate, but strong demand pushed the price above 91 before fees, with more than a third of the bonds being subscribed at 91.5 or higher.[127]

The finance ministry undertook debt swaps of several types. In March 1853 the government used 6 percent apólices to retire an increment of its own London bonds worth some 23,200 pounds sterling in a rare direct swap of domestic bonds for external debt.[128] More common, as noted earlier, were the swaps of long-term debt for short-term debt. In early 1877 the Treasury made the large new issue at 97 percent of the par.[129] The price was below the prevailing market rate, providing for a nearly instantaneous profit. But the bond investors' gain was not necessarily the government's loss. The Banco do Brasil took all of the bonds, paying in Treasury bills. The Treasury was able to defer the full cost of the bills' redemption, converting short-term debt into long-term debt.

Evidence on initial-issue prices of apólices and the bonds of the National Loans makes it possible to calculate the government's interest rate on domestic borrowing. Rates reveal two fundamental indicators of creditworthiness: the state's marginal cost of capital and the domestic market's appraisal of default risk. As with the London loans the risk premium is taken as the difference between the borrowing rate and the yield on consols. Estimates of the risk premium provide insights into contemporary views on creditworthiness that would otherwise not be available to modern investigators. Higher risk premia indicate greater pessimism on the part of lenders regarding the prospects of repayment.

From 1828 to 1879 the government's average take on new issues of 6 percents came to 87.3 percent of face value, implying an average annual borrowing cost in the range of 7 percent per year.[130] In the 62 fiscal years after domestic funded borrowing began, the Treasury took loans through apólices in 47 of them. The ex ante interest rate on this borrowing can be calculated for 32 years in which the primary market prices of new apólices are available. Interest rates are calculated under two scenarios to accommodate the different approaches to amortization employed by the government. Estimate A is calculated on the assumption that at the time of borrowing the market expected that loans would be amortized in accordance with the sinking fund provision of the law that established the public debt. The 1827 law directed the Caixa de Amortização to retire each year 1 percent of each tranche of apólices plus an additional increment purchased using the interest on apólices that had already been redeemed. By this sinking fund provision each new issue would self-liquidate over a period of 33.4 years.[131] Using this contracted maturity, the cost of borrowing in the domestic market is calculated in the same way that the cost of new borrowing in London was derived in chapter 3. The state's ex ante cost of borrowing is given by the internal rate of return, i_A in the expression:

$$PV = \sum_{t=0}^{T} \left[\frac{(D_t + S_t)}{(1+i_A)^t} \right]$$

where cash raised from borrowing is the present value (PV), the annual outlay on interest is D, and the annual outlay on amortization via the sinking fund is S.[132] The internal rate of return (i) sets the amount raised on the issue to equal the stream of future interest payments and amortization.

Estimate B is calculated under the assumption that the apólices would *not* be amortized. This scenario prevailed after 1838, when amortization was suspended (and may have been expected by bond investors all along). Under this scenario, S is zero, T is infinity, and the cost of new borrowing equals the current yield at issue.[133] Estimates A and B differ by the cost of amortization.

Capital costs are calculated for both scenarios on every tranche of 6 percent apólices between 1828 and 1880 for which initial issue prices are available, as well as the major issue of 5 percents in 1886.[134] Several adjustments were warranted. Before 1851 the Treasury issued a substantial number of apólices as payment to settle claims by the Portuguese and debts dating from independence. By the terms of the settlement agreements the bonds went to claimants at a fixed discount (the effective price was usually 73 percent), with the Treasury debited for the full face value of the bonds. These particular bonds did not involve borrowing at market rates. Over the interval in which most such claims were settled (namely, the 1840s), borrowing occurred at prices ranging from a low of 70 to a high of 90. In calculating the interest rate, the bonds issued under indemnity arrangements are excluded so as not to bias the estimate of the government's cost of capital.

Figure 4.7 presents estimates A and B of the ex ante cost of new debt issues in Rio.[135] Either estimate is sufficient to indicate the general timing and direction of changes. The two estimates can be linked to make a single series by taking into account the timing of parliament's suspension of amortization. Estimate A, which is higher because of amortization,

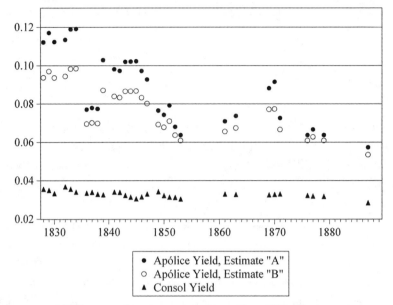

FIGURE 4.7 The cost of new borrowing with apólices, 1828–87

is used through 1838, and estimate B is used thereafter. The composite series presented in figure 4.8 is a consistent indicator of the state's cost of borrowing on the most important component of domestic debt over almost the entire Imperial era.

Figure 4.8 plots as well the interest rates for the National Loans of 1868, 1879, and 1889. The loans differed from apólices by virtue of their fixed maturity and the fact that they were settled in specie or its equivalent.[136] For these loans the Treasury's ex ante cost of borrowing depended on the future course of the exchange rate. And because the value of the milréis varied so much, the cost of debt service was uncertain. The National Loan of 1868 was the most extreme case of the three. Because the loan was taken near the wartime nadir of the milréis, the sterling equivalent of the money raised in Rio was only some 68 percent of the loan's face value—a huge discount. If the future value of the milréis was expected to remain as low as that of 1868 (about 13 milréis per pound sterling), the implied cost of capital in 1868 was quite high, in excess of 12 percent per year. If the loan were instead repaid at the target exchange rate of 27 pence per milréis (closer to 9 milréis per pound), the cost would

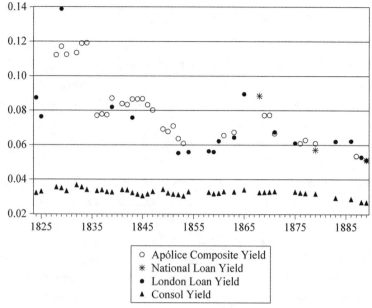

FIGURE 4.8 The cost of new long-term borrowing (all sources), 1824–89 (borrowing costs in London and consol yields are from chapter 3; borrowing costs for National Loans and apólices are calculated as detailed in text)

have been much less, around 7.5 percent per year. The Treasury clearly counted on a stronger exchange rate once the war was won. A reasonable estimate of the expected future exchange rate at the time of borrowing is the rate that actually prevailed from 1870 (when victory was clear) through the end of the constitutional monarchy in 1889: about 10 milréis per pound on average. At that rate the ex ante cost of the loan was closer to 8.8 percent, which is the figure used here. For the loans of 1879 and 1889 the milréis was stronger than it was in 1868, so the impact of the exchange rate on the expected costs of the later loans was less, and no adjustment is warranted.

The cost of Brazil's domestic loans exhibited a clear tendency to decline over the Imperial era despite increases in the stock of debt. Interest rates on apólices peaked with the political instability around the end of the First Reign and during the early Regency in the 1830s. New borrowing from 1828 through 1834 cost more than 11 percent a year. One might suspect that the steep decline thereafter is a statistical artifact of the shift in the series from estimate A to estimate B after 1838, save for the fact that borrowing costs computed *with* the amortization provision had already plummeted by 1836 (see fig. 4.7). By either measure the rate of interest on new loans jumped back up in the late 1830s and stayed there until the second half of the 1840s. Political turmoil and its implications for lenders' views of the viability of the institutions on which repayment depended are plainly visible in these shifts in borrowing costs. Instability at the end of the First Reign and in the early Regency raised costs, as did the cascade of uprisings and revolts that reached their greatest intensity from 1839 through 1845. Lower borrowing costs, which persisted into the early 1850s, followed the end of the decade-long war against the *farrapo* secessionists in the south. The interest rate began to rise slightly in the early 1860s as a result of some of the largest new bond issues since 1842. The sharp increase in the amount of borrowing during the war against Paraguay (see fig. 4.5) had as its counterpart elevated rates of interest (see fig. 4.7). Although information on wartime borrowing costs does not exist for every year, the most expensive of the large wartime domestic loans seems to have been the National Loan of 1868.[137] Though the postwar debt remained quite large in comparison with prewar levels, domestic borrowing costs came down quickly after Brazil's victory over Paraguay. Interest rates stayed at levels comparable with the rates of the early 1850s, despite nearly uninterrupted increases in the size of the debt. The National Loan of 1889 was the most affordable, costing a scant 5.12 percent in annual interest and principal.

Figure 4.8 plots the interest rate on Brazilian loans in London (taken from fig. 3.5). Borrowing costs in Rio were usually somewhat higher than in London because of the risk to domestic lenders that the government might weaken the milréis. Yet inflation expectations on the part of domestic lenders could not have been very high. By 1889 the milréis had achieved parity with the pound, making the interest rates on the National Loan in Rio de Janeiro and the conversion loan in London nearly identical. Figure 4.8 further suggests that the Finance Ministry was a shrewd customer in the capital markets, taking conditions in both London and Rio into account when deciding where to place new debt issues. The result was a structure of borrowing costs that could exhibit slightly different levels depending on which currency denominated the loan but with similar trends over time. Remarkably, Brazil's expanding domestic debt market allowed the state to borrow affordably and flexibly at home.

The persistent spread between the interest rate on apólices and the yield on consols shows that the domestic market always believed there was a Brazil-specific risk of default. This probability can be estimated from the cost of capital and the return on the risk-free alternative.[138] The relevant rate is that an initial investor in apólices expected to receive and the return that could be had if the investor bought consols instead. As in chapter 3 the calculation assumes for the sake of clarity that lenders expected the government to honor its debt with probability p or to repudiate with probability $(1-p)$. The rate of return under repayment is that for a hypothetical lender who acquired the bond at issue and received semester interest payments for the life of the bond. In the case of pre-1839 loans the investors received their capital when the bond matured. For loans in 1839 and after, the expected return excludes the return of capital but includes perpetual interest payments. The price paid for a new apólice implied a rate of return of at least $(1+i)$ if the loan was honored and zero if it was repudiated. For a risk-neutral investor the expected payoff from the apólice had to be at least as good as that from investing in consols.

Following the setup in chapter 3, the probability of repudiation at issue is the ratio of the spread to the return to the bondholder when the government repays:

$$(1-p) = \left[\frac{i-r}{1+i}\right].$$

With data on the apólice internal rate of return i from figure 4.7 and on the contemporaneous consol yield, the calculation of repudiation risk is straightforward. Figure 4.9 plots the probability of repudiation on new issues of apólices from 1828 through 1889. Both the level of the probability and its evolution over time are noteworthy. In the market's assessment the chance of outright repudiation of any new domestic loan was always less than 7 percent, even when the risk premium was at its highest in the early 1830s. There was some doubt, though not much, that Brazil would honor its domestic debt. The probability of repudiation at the height of the war against Paraguay (corresponding to a scenario in which Brazil suffered catastrophic defeat or otherwise viewed repayment of a new loan as impossible) was less than 5 percent, despite the elevated debt burden.

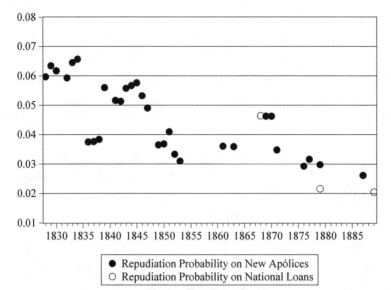

FIGURE 4.9 Probability of repudiation on domestic borrowing, 1828–89
(open circles represent apólices and filled circles represent National Loans;
probability of repudiation calculated as described in the text)

As the most severe form of default, repudiation might also have
been the least likely. When partial defaults are considered, their probability increases sharply. Consider a hypothetical scenario in which
interest would never be paid, but the principal was returned to the
bondholder at maturity after thirty-three years. For the apólices sold in
1832, the market's assessment of the probability of default jumps from
less than 8 percent to fully 30 percent. The softer the form of default
considered, the more it was seen as likely by the market. For the purposes of illustrating changes over time, the specifics of the default scenario do not matter. As long as it is held constant over all of the loans,
the direction and relative size of changes in the default risk remain the
same. Elevated probabilities of default in the late 1820s and early 1830s
had fallen by half in the early 1850s; the likelihood of default during
the war against Paraguay was less than 70 percent, as large as it was
some forty years earlier, when the debt was much smaller. Creditors
increasingly viewed the prospect of repayment favorably, despite rising
debt levels.

CONCLUSION

Imperial Brazil constitutes a rare case in which a government with a fiat currency did not have to rely mainly on foreign loans to meet its borrowing needs. From 1828 it regularly issued bonds that promised repayment with interest in paper money. By 1839 these bonds were converted to perpetuals, like British consols, with no deadline for the return of principal but a promise to always pay interest. Perhaps the strongest evidence for the hypothesis that political penalties for default sustained public borrowing at home was the growth of the domestic long-term funded debt. The amount of debt that was domestic in origin indicated the potential of the home capital market to mobilize savings. More important, it indicated the government's commitment to repay. Indeed, by the middle of the nineteenth century most of Brazil's debt stock was domestic, and increasingly new borrowing would be from the domestic market.

In Eichengreen and Hausmann's original definition of financial original sin, governments that could not borrow abroad in their own currency also had difficulty issuing long-term debt at home.[139] Brazil's ability to borrow in the domestic market in its own currency from the late 1820s onward is thus surprising. Domestic borrowing was beneficial in several ways. Local currency debt (nominal debt) affords governments a cushion against adverse shocks. Fiscal shocks that appear too suddenly to solve with new loans or that are simply too large can be partly covered through monetary policy—at least until revenues recover or the state's noninterest spending can be reduced. The capacity to pursue an independent monetary policy lets the state determine the real cost of debt repayment (and the real return to bondholders). Such flexibility is desirable in downturns. Yet only rarely were developing economies in the nineteenth century able to avail themselves of this option.[140] When fiscal pressure grew extreme, the adjustment mechanism tended to include default. Even in a successful case like that of Imperial Brazil there was a trade-off. Borrowing in the home currency cost more because lenders required compensation for the risk of value-eroding price inflation. The premium the government paid to borrow locally was the cost of the insurance that allowed it to inflate away a portion of the debt if faced with a fiscal shortfall.

The Empire performed this balancing act well. The government engaged in inflationary finance in hard times, as was the case during the

1820s, the late 1830s, and again during the war against Paraguay. Yet recourse to seigniorage revenues was neither extreme nor frequent. Brazil's mixed debt structure disciplined any monetary excesses. After the 1830s domestic wealth holders viewed a major permanent decline in the milréis as unlikely; parliament was constrained in its use of seigniorage by the cost of servicing the external debt in pounds sterling.

Brazil's ability to borrow in a market in which lenders tendered competing offers was about as far removed as one could imagine from the model of forced lending that prevailed through 1822. The Imperial state repeatedly drew on varied sources of long-term funded domestic credit, from the late 1820s until the very eve of the overthrow of the constitutional monarchy in 1889.[141] Using perpetual annuities in the form of apólices, and fixed-maturity loans, the government covered deficits, bailed out selected private firms, invested in infrastructure, and fought and won wars. That it punctually paid interest provided ex post confirmation of the ex ante creditworthiness embedded in its political-fiscal institutions. The extent of its long-term domestic borrowing was exceptional. Brazil was a rare instance of a peripheral economy that successfully raised a major portion of its debt at home.

CHAPTER FIVE

Turning Points

DEFAULT RISK ON TWO SIDES OF THE ATLANTIC

GOVERNMENT BONDS REPRESENTED sovereign promises to repay with interest the money that the government had borrowed. Using them to borrow made the original sovereign promise divisible and transferable. Investors traded the Brazilian Empire's bonds in the secondary markets of London and Rio de Janeiro. When pricing bonds, traders took into account the characteristics of the loan (coupon rate, value at maturity, time to maturity), the market rate of interest, and their own forecast about whether the government would honor its promise to repay. Because markets aggregate all available information regarding a state's ability and willingness to service its debt, bond prices and yields reflected what was known about creditworthiness and risk at any given time. Bond investors sorted nineteenth-century governments "according to their credit in the money markets of the world, as measured by the rate of interest which their stock can be purchased to pay." Market prices conveyed information about sovereign risk that was rapidly updated: "bad security requires high interest, carried out in the most perfect manner in the adjustment of prices, by the daily and hourly judgments of the Stock Exchange of the world."[1] Bond investors charged additional interest for "bad security" in the form of a risk premium. The risk premium is readily indicated by the difference between the yield on a government's bonds and the return on relatively risk-free alternatives.[2] The size of this premium depended directly on bondholders' appraisals of the probability of default and follows from the model presented in chapter 2. A debtor state's risk of default is not fixed. Events or information that changes the market's view of the likelihood of default appears as changes in the bonds' yield. Changes in the risk premium provide insights about political and financial events that may otherwise not be available.[3]

This chapter focuses on the evolution of Brazil's credit risk between 1824 and 1889. Interest rates on the Empire's bonds revealed more about Brazil-specific default risk than they did about the underlying supply of capital in Rio de Janeiro and London. The overall decline in the risk premium in markets on both sides of the Atlantic suggests that the Imperial state was viewed as an increasingly reliable borrower over the course of the nineteenth century. Yet borrowing costs did not decline uniformly; the risk premium even increased substantially over several intervals of time. Where new political institutions made sovereign promises to repay more credible, one would expect a permanent fall in the risk premium. That the risk premium might persist (or even rise) has led some investigators to question the validity of institutional determinants of creditworthiness.[4] Increases in the risk premium are, however, less damaging to the institutional argument than they may initially seem. In the best-studied case, that of Britain's Glorious Revolution, the default risk on long-term borrowing before the revolution was so high that the market would not supply the loans. Long-term borrowing costs were, in effect, infinitely high. Within a few years the government could borrow long at a far more affordable 8.5 percent.[5] The claim that "institutional reforms are not rewarded by financial markets" fails to take into account the extraordinary shift from an unobservably expensive rate on a type of loan that was beyond the government's credit ceiling to a much lower rate on a type of loan that became available with the establishment of credibility.[6] Institutional arrangements that reduce *opportunistic* default do not necessarily provide an ironclad guarantee of repayment and do not eliminate all default risk. As such, increases in the risk premium after credit has been extended to the state do not conflict with the model of credible borrowing outlined in chapter 2. Any event perceived by the market as increasing the political cost of servicing the state's debt will raise the risk premium, even if the underpinning institutions that support repayment are unchanged.

Markets considered far more than just economic or financial fundamentals in assessing creditworthiness. Variability in the risk premium was clear from the estimated costs of new borrowing reported in chapters 3 and 4. Because loans were taken only intermittently, the yield on existing bonds in the secondary market provides additional information on default risk over the intervals of time during which there was no new borrowing.[7] Each successive price observation conveys updated information about the expectation of default. When the bonds are traded with sufficient frequency, changes in credit risk can be assessed on a relatively continuous basis. Weekly data make it possible to assess sovereign credit risk on both sides of the Atlantic from the 1820s through 1889. This allows a more precise characterization of the evolution of sovereign risk over time and gives special attention to events associated with major shifts in default risk.

This chapter has three goals. The first is to identify changes in Brazil's sovereign risk that represented durable shifts, along with their timing and magnitude. Since Brazil partitioned its domestic and foreign debts, the risk premia on bonds in both markets are considered. The second goal is to locate the proximate causes of such shifts in contemporaneous events. The third is to assess the degree to which structural breaks in the risk premium help explain its overall decline between 1824 and 1889. The principal findings run in the following terms. There were four major shifts in sovereign credit risk in each of the two markets where Brazil placed its debt. Because the markets were distinct, investors in the two markets did not necessarily view the risk of default in the same way. Only in 1852 did any of these shifts coincide. The other three major breaks in credit risk in the Rio de Janeiro bond market all came before 1852. In the London market they all came after 1852. Most of the shifts in the Rio risk premium were associated in some way with internal conflict. Major shifts in Brazil's London risk usually involved the question of external war in the Rio de la Plata. In London, bond investors behaved as if their greatest concern was war involving Brazil and its southern neighbors. In Rio, bond investors appeared to be worried more about war *inside* Brazil.

The different emphases in the two markets may not have depended solely on the types of conflict. They may have been a result of the dissimilar attributes of the bond issues in each market. Bond investors had two concerns: that interest payments arrive on time and that payments hold their value. In Brazil the government could erode the value of the sovereign promise that domestic bonds represented and reduce its own cost of servicing them by resorting to inflation. Apólice holders might be confident of punctuality of payment yet ultimately uncertain about the real value of the interest they would receive. Internal conflict raised apprehensions not only about the heightened risk of default but also about the specter that the government's use of seigniorage would create inflation and reduce the real value of coupon payments. London bondholders faced no inflation risk because Brazil paid interest there in sterling. What London bondholders worried about was whether interest would be paid at all. The London market perceived external conflict as particularly threatening.

The first section details the construction of original measures of sovereign bond yields and risk premia in the London market. The second section introduces the method for detecting structural breaks, or "regime shifts," in the risk premium data. It applies this method to search systematically for durable changes in the risk premium series and relates them to key events. The third and fourth sections construct measures of yields and risk premia on bonds issued in the Rio de Janeiro market and apply the same estimation framework to locate major structural shifts in sovereign risk within Brazil. Section five considers debtor reputation as a competing explanation for the overall decline in Brazil's risk premium. The final section addresses several implications of the chapter's findings.

MEASURING BRAZILIAN SOVEREIGN RISK

Government bond yields make it possible to measure the risk premium, which can then be used to identify critical turning points in a state's creditworthiness.[8] Candidates for such changes must possess two properties: they should be quantitatively appreciable and they should be durable. Small changes from day to day or week to week within a data series that covers decades may be little more than trading "noise."[9] The method used here identifies persistent structural breaks in the risk premium. Just how long a shift in the risk premium must persist in order to be considered durable depends on the time span covered by the data, their frequency of observation, and the maximum number of breaks chosen by the investigator. This choice involves some intrinsic trade-offs; the approach here is to use a minimum interval of about three and a half years between possible break points.

Sovereign bonds were those that the government issued in London in pounds sterling. The sovereignty of the borrower limited the scope of action that creditors could take in case of default. The option value of default by the sovereign issuer was a form of insurance, a contingency to be exercised should the political cost of repayment rise to unacceptable levels. Because the Imperial government never entirely retired its external debt and never defaulted, its bonds traded nearly continuously in London after the first loan was issued in late 1824.[10] The market prices of the bonds included both market risk and Brazil-specific risk; bond prices could rise or fall for reasons that had nothing to do with Brazil per se, a point that contemporaries understood well.[11] Drawing on the basic model of chapter 2 and appendix I, the yield on the bond is a rate of interest:

$$i = \frac{(1+r)}{p} - 1$$

where $(1+r)$ is the risk-free rate of return, and p is the probability that the government will repay the loan. If the probability of repayment is less than one, i exceeds r. By subtracting the risk-free component from the yield, the risk premium or spread (s) over the risk-free yield can be isolated and decomposed into two components:

$$s = (i - r) = \frac{(1-p)}{p}(1+r)$$

where the first term on the right-hand side is the odds of default (the probability of default divided by the probability of repayment), and the second term is the risk-free rate of return available to investors. Investigators conventionally use changes in the spread to indicate changes in the market's assessment of default risk. Intuitively, the spread decreases in the probability of repayment, p, and increases in the probability of default $(1-p)$.[12]

The investment in the London market that came closest to being risk free was the British state's consols. Most consols paid a fixed amount in sterling for perpetuity or until the government called them to be settled. The default risk on consols was nearly zero by the early nineteenth century.[13] London was the world's financial center, and long-term changes in consol prices reflected fundamental shifts in the relative scarcity of capital. Because the Empire's bonds in London promised interest and the repayment of principal in pounds sterling, they were free of Brazilian currency risk. All sterling bonds in London carried the same currency risk (which was the risk that the Bank of England would not maintain the value of the pound). Changes in the risk premium reflected the market's appraisal of changes in the likelihood that Brazil would either fail to pay interest or fail to redeem the bond as promised.

The risk premium series is constructed in three steps. First, weekly Brazilian bond prices are converted to yields-to-maturity that are adjusted for the frequency of coupon payment.[14] More than three thousand observations of weekly prices for Brazilian bonds in London from 1825 to 1891 were collected from three sources: the *Times* of London, the *Course of the Exchange*, and the *Economist*.[15] The breadth of coverage by these sources differed a good deal at various points in time. All three were scrutinized for the entire period of publication up through 1891 to determine which provided the best coverage at any given moment. The task of creating a continuous series of yields was complicated by the fact that no single Brazilian loan traded over the entire period. Ideally, the bond prices used would come from one loan that circulated during the entire period. This ideal cannot be met in practice. The yield series is constructed from subseries of yields for bonds from nine loans. The span of each subseries was selected to avoid using observations too close to the maturity date, at which point the prices of bonds converge on the redemption value of the bond. Before the bonds used in one subseries matured, the base is shifted to the bonds of a newer loan. (Table A.II.1 presents details on loans that comprise the nine subseries, with an accompanying discussion in appendix II.) The changing base of the series, from bonds of one coupon rate to another and from one maturity to another, is a source of concern because it could generate breaks as an artifact. To ensure that this is not the case, the dates of the structural breaks estimated below are compared with the beginning dates of each subseries.

The use here of the yield to maturity to derive the risk premium differs from the approach of most other historical studies, which usually employ the current yield. The current yield is the bond's coupon rate divided by its market price. The current yield would be the superlative measure only if bondholders were concerned solely with their yield in the current semester or year. For an investor looking beyond the current semester, the bond's eventual maturity date—and the accompanying implied capital gain or loss—figured into the evaluation. The yield to

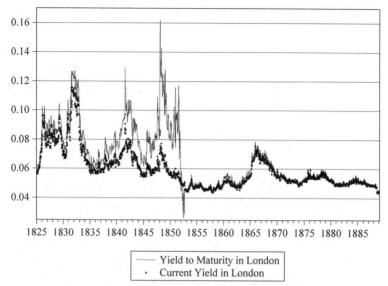

FIGURE 5.1 Yield to maturity and current yield on Brazilian bonds in London, 1825–89

maturity is complicated, and its precise computation by investors at the time was unlikely.[16] But precision was not a requirement for investors to grasp that bonds had a redemption date that impacted their value and thus its yield. Bond prices could fall and then trade below both the purchase price and the par value for a considerable time, so even short-term investors could find themselves in a buy-and-hold situation. Figure 5.1 presents the yield to maturity series for Brazil's London bonds and plots the more commonly used current yield. It is clear that the yield to maturity differed markedly from the current yield before 1852. The Empire's bonds in the first half of the century traded below par, often at a large discount. Moreover, the volatilities of the two yield measures differed, with the changes in the yield to maturity exhibiting greater amplitude. Once volatility declined in 1852, the yields became quite similar in level.

The second step in deriving Brazil's London risk premium is to calculate the British consol yield. Weekly consol prices come from the same sources as those used to obtain prices for Brazil's London bonds. Until April 1881 the data are for 3 percent consols, which paid interest twice yearly. In April 1881 the market value of the 3 percents exceeded par for the first time, increasing the likelihood that the bonds would be called.

This makes them less than ideal as a measure of the long-run rate of interest from that point on. From April 1881 the consol yield series is based instead on New Gladstones, which were 2.5 percent consols first issued in 1853. On both subseries of consols the yield to maturity is that for a perpetual annuity.[17] Beginning in 1884 the reference consol for the series changed again, shifting to the New Childers.[18] The main difference involved the frequency of the dividend payment, which shifted from a semester to a quarterly basis.[19]

The frequency of the consol price observations, like that of the Brazilian bond prices, was weekly, with one difference. Until 1862 the Exchequer's books were closed on consol trades in the weeks between the announcement of the ex-dividend date and the actual payment of interest. The *Course of the Exchange* did not usually report prices during the weeks when the books were closed. Other sources, especially the *Times*, sometimes did report forward prices for trades that would be settled once the Exchequer reopened the books. Whenever available, the forward price quotations were used for observations during the closings. Where gaps in the series remained, the last consol price available was used until regular trading resumed.

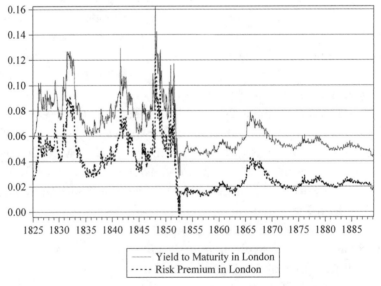

FIGURE 5.2 Yield to maturity and risk premium on Brazilian bonds in London, 1825–89

Table 5.1

Descriptive Statistics, Brazil Sovereign Risk Series, 1825–91

SERIES	OBSERVATIONS	MEAN	STANDARD DEVIATION	MINIMUM	MAXIMUM
Original yield to maturity	3,394	0.06663	0.0196	0.0264	0.1623
Interpolated yield to maturity	3,470	0.06627	0.0195	0.0264	0.1623
Original risk premium	3,388	0.03449	0.0182	−0.0038	0.1245
Interpolated risk premium	3,470	0.03409	0.0182	−0.0038	0.1245

To complete the risk premium series, the consol yield is subtracted from the yield to maturity on the London bonds. The resulting risk premium series is presented in figure 5.2, with descriptive statistics in table 5.1. Three features stand out. First, except for a brief and highly exceptional interval in the early 1850s, Brazil's London bonds were always riskier than British consols. Second, the Empire's default risk declined tremendously in 1852. Third is the shift from high volatility in the pre-1852 period to much reduced volatility after 1852. From the perspective of the London market, Brazilian sovereign risk before 1852, both in its level and volatility, looks like it came from a different country than the one that borrowed after 1852.[20]

SHIFTING RISKS

Durable shifts in the mean of the risk premium series reflect fundamental changes in politics and public finance that affect the market's assessment of Brazilian creditworthiness. Several techniques for distinguishing such shifts from random variation and short-term fluctuations exist.[21] The Bai-Perron approach tests for the existence of statistically significant shifts in the risk premium.[22] The advantage of the approach is that it locates breaks in the series without imposing any prior expectations on their existence or timing and can simultaneously locate multiple breaks when they are present.

Two conditions must first be met. The first is that the risk premium series must be stationary; that is, it does not exhibit a unit root.[23] Non-stationary data greatly increase the likelihood of finding statistically spurious breaks.[24] Most of the standard unit root and stationarity tests reject a unit root in the London risk premium. A Zivot-Andrews test that allows for an endogenously selected break rejects the null hypothesis of a unit root at 1 percent (with the break coming in the last week of October 1851).[25] As the preponderance of the results points to the stationarity of the series, the Bai-Perron approach can be implemented. The second requirement is to define the minimum interval over which a change in the mean must persist in order to have been generated by a break. There is a trade-off between the minimum interval length and the maximum number of breaks that can be detected. Minimum intervals that are too short can pick up small shifts in risk that do not last very long, whereas long intervals risk missing breaks. The choice here is the shortest interval allowed by the length of data series that also allows for as many as nine breaks. This comes out to be 173 weeks, slightly less than 3.5 years between potential break points.[26]

Table 5.2 presents the estimates from the structural-break regression on the risk premium. The hypothesis that there is no break in the series is rejected.[27] While the procedure allows for as many as nine breaks, the results of three separate tests reveal only four breaks across nearly seven decades.[28] The parameter estimates reported in the table are those of the sequential test and are readily interpretable in terms of basis points of the bond's yield (where 1 percent equals 100 basis points). None of the breaks come before 1852. The spike in yield that is so obvious in 1831 does not register as a break, which is a result of the requirement that there be a major change in the mean and that the change persist for more than three years. Despite the fact that the data observations are weekly, none of the breaks is estimated with particularly high precision, and the confidence intervals are wide.[29] The table reports the 90 percent confidence intervals for each break, expressed as the dates of the starting week and ending week. Even then, the smallest confidence interval of any of the four break points spans more than a year. This is partly owing to the magnitude of the breaks, which in percentage terms are large. Because a number of events with the potential to shift the mean level of risk could

Table 5.2

Break Points in the Risk Premium Series for Brazilian Sovereign Bonds
in London, 1825–91

BREAK WEEKS (T_i)	BOUNDARY MONTHS FOR 90% CONFIDENCE INTERVAL		PROPORTIONAL CHANGE IN RISK PREMIUM
26 February 1852	26 February 1852	17 August 1854	−70.6%
1 September 1859	7 November 1857	5 March 1860	+26.7%
15 September 1864	14 August 1863	26 September 1864	+73.7%
10 December 1869	6 August 1869	27 October 1871	−33.3%

PARAMETER	β_i	CORRECTED STANDARD ERRORS
β_1	0.051	0.0037***
β_2	0.015	0.0006***
β_3	0.019	0.0006***
β_4	0.033	0.0022***
β_5	0.022	0.0006***

$R^2 = 0.67$ Number of breaks selected by:

$F(5, 3,465) = 1,412.3$ supF(L+1/L) test=4

$n = 3,470$ Sequential procedure=4

*** significant at 1% level Repartition procedure=4

Note: The parameters are the average risk premium for each segment of the series. The Bai-Perron UD max and WD max tests (not reported) support the existence of breaks versus the null hypothesis of no breaks. With a 5 percent trimming on the series, the minimum interval length between breaks is 173 weeks, while the maximum number of structural breaks allowed is nine. The number of breaks selected by the sequential procedure is four, which are those reported here.

transpire in a yearlong (or longer) window of time, the interpretation of the breaks in terms of events gives heavier weight to events close to the break dates. Even then it is not possible in most cases to isolate a single event that in and of itself accounts for the market's movement.[30]

The first break in the series comes in February 1852. It kicked off a large decline in the government's risk premium and the overall cost of borrowing (visible in the primary market, as discussed in chapter 3). Risk fell a full 70 percent, from an average level of 5.1 percent over the period from 1825 to 1852, to only 1.5 percent thereafter—or just 150 basis points on top of consol yields. This was a remarkable reduction in the market's expectation that Brazil might default. The confidence interval around the break runs from the week of the break itself to August 1854.[31] Two events that bridge weeks just before and after the start of the confidence interval warrant mention. First, between November 1851 and March 1852 the Imperial government resumed the regular amortization of its London bonds for the first time in more than twenty years. The announcement that bonds from the 1824, 1829, and 1839 loans would begin to be retired via open market purchase came in May 1852; shipments of gold from Brazil to London for amortization also fall within the confidence interval of the break.[32] The remittances specifically earmarked for the sinking fund bolstered confidence that the Empire was willing not only to pay interest but also to pay down the principal. A second factor that likely helped improve bondholder sentiment was the repression of slave traders. Under growing British pressure by 1850, the Brazilian cabinet began to crack down on the openly practiced "contraband" trade in slaves from Africa. The police shut down the major facilities for offloading and auctioning slaves along the *fluminense* coastline by 1851. Brazil's enforcement efforts reduced diplomatic tension with the British government over the slave trade issue.

Two other important events occurred well within the confidence interval of the break. In 1852 Brazil arranged new borrowing in London, its first credit operation in the City in nearly ten years. It was also the first issue run through the Rothschild house since 1829. The loan's purpose was to pay off the Portuguese debt that Brazil took on in 1825. Definitively settling the only external obligation on which Brazil had ever suspended interest was another positive signal. Successful reentry into the primary market for loans no doubt increased confidence in Brazilian bonds, as did underwriting by Rothschild. It is not clear how widespread the knowledge of the new loan was in London. While the *Times* seems to have carried no mention of it, the decree authorizing the contracting of the loan was issued in Rio in March, the preliminary contract between Brazil's minister in London and the Rothschilds was signed in July, the general instrument of borrowing was signed in London in September, and the final loan contract was notarized in London in November.[33]

While all of these events no doubt figured into the market's change in sentiment, it is likely that the most important event was war or, rather, its culmination. The strategic situation in the Rio de la Plata had occupied the Brazilian government since independence. In late 1851 the ongoing conflict between the Empire and Juan Manuel de Rosas, the governor of Buenos Aires, led to an increased buildup of Brazilian forces, which was highlighted in reports in London in January 1852.[34] Then, in the same week as the structural break in the risk series, came news of a major advance against the forces of Rosas by units led by Justo José Urquiza and supported by Brazil. This was followed just two weeks later by notice of the military defeat of Rosas in the battle of Caseros.[35] The Brazilian government had invested considerable diplomatic resources in helping build the anti-Rosas coalition. It had also sent ground and naval forces to participate directly in the fighting. The withdrawal of Brazil's ground forces from Argentine territory and of most of its naval presence from surrounding waters by August 1852 punctuated the end of the conflict and falls squarely within the confidence interval around the break.[36] The defeat of Rosas put an early end to a potentially costly war for Brazil in the Rio de la Plata region. The Empire emerged from the conflict victorious, politically preeminent in the south, and fiscally intact.

The second break in the risk premium appears in the first week of September 1859. Of the four London breaks it has the widest confidence interval. The break partly reverted the previous decline in risk, but only by about 40 basis points—quantitatively the least important of the shifts detected. A number of key events transpired in the period delimited by the confidence interval (running from late November 1857 to March 1860). New borrowing in London inside this window (in 1858) increased the stock of debt and raised overall debt service requirements, which might have raised the risk premium. The Empire reduced its tariff rates in 1857 with the repeal of the famous Alves Branco tariff of 1844 and further reduced the rates later in 1857 and again in 1858.[37] If the market expected revenues to suffer a decline with the reduction in the tariff, it would require a larger risk premium. That revenues did not fall suggests that the reduced tariff would not by itself account for a durable shift in credit risk. The transatlantic commercial crisis that began in New York in 1857 and quickly hit Rio and London begins at the very start of the confidence window for the break. A month before the break, the cabinet led by the visconde de Abaeté was replaced by the emperor with one led by barão de Uruguaiana.[38] Both cabinets were Conservative, so the issue was not partisan. Banking policy was the most salient question of the moment. Around the week of the break news arrived from Rio of a bill to require banks to begin redeeming their notes in gold a few years hence, and "the prospects of the measure becoming law had already led to a severe financial crisis in all the chief cities of the empire."[39]

One key factor driving the shift in the risk premium was no doubt a renewed risk of conflict in the Rio de la Plata. The end of 1858 brought with it the signing of a collective defense treaty between the Urquiza regime in Argentina and the governments of Uruguay and Brazil. The agreement was seen as increasing the risk of conflict because Urquiza was faced with a "threatened revolution" in Buenos Aires and might call on allies for military assistance under the new treaty. News of the treaty appeared in London in early 1859 in the form of reports from Uruguay that indicated anxiety: "If this be true it will cause some dissatisfaction here, as the opinion is general that this country should steer clear of any compromise that might lead to a war."[40] The week of the break brought news that Brazil had given "undisguised countenance" to Urquiza's campaign against the "peace and independence of Buenos Aires" and reported further military buildup with Brazilian support.[41]

The third break in the level of default risk came in September 1864. It is associated with a diplomatic crisis between Brazil and its rivals to the south, the government of Paraguay and the ruling Blanco party of Uruguay. Pronouncements from all sides created a growing anticipation of war.[42] The conflict in the region was multilayered and had both international and factional aspects. Brazilian landowners in Uruguay had grievances against that country's government, Paraguay's leader held pretensions of wielding regional influence, and the Buenos Aires government was suspicious of the intentions of both Brazil and Paraguay. In June the emperor's speech at the opening of parliament noted that in Uruguay "the rights and legitimate interests of our countrymen residing there continue to be violated" and that Brazil was sending a special mission to obtain "satisfaction for our claims." The speech was soon reported in London. In August the Imperial government issued an ultimatum to the Uruguayan government to desist from enacting anti-Brazilian measures.[43] The Paraguayan president, Francisco Solano López, soon broke off diplomatic relations with Brazil, declaring that any move by Brazil into Uruguay would be viewed as an act of war. In the same week as the structural break, the market received news of the worsening conflict inside Argentina and also of a rumor of the advance of some two thousand Brazilian troops across the Uruguayan border.[44] The news was premature, as the invasion did not happen until October; in early November reports from late September arrived in London with an assessment that Paraguay was on a near certain path to war with Brazil.[45] The market was not surprised: it anticipated with considerable precision the onset of a major conflict and in addition expected that it would be expensive for Brazil. The mean of the risk premium series jumped by more than 70 percent. The nature of the events most closely associated with the upswing can readily be disentangled from other events within the confidence window by virtue of the break's sign. The most noteworthy political event should have moved the risk premium in the other direction, had it been the actual source of the break. The Progressista cabinet of Francisco José Furtado (sandwiched as it was between two other Progressista cabinets) came to power at the end of August 1864.[46] Its program included the goal of balancing expenditures and revenues, which should have reduced default risk. The looming war overwhelmed promises of fiscal discipline in the eyes of the market.

The final break in the risk premium series comes in December 1869.[47] Over the preceding months there were regular reports of the ongoing advance of the Brazilian army and the progressive weakening of the Paraguayan forces. On Christmas Eve papers arrived in London carrying news from mid-November informing that Solano López had "abandoned his forces and fled towards the north, his present whereabouts being unknown."[48] The break in the risk premium that week brought the level of risk back down nearly to the prewar level. The timing makes sense, but such a steep decline was surprising given the huge run-up in every component of the Empire's debt since the beginning of the war five years earlier. The confidence interval around the break encompasses the last major military engagement of the war in 1869 at Campo Grande/Acosta Ñú, the death of Solano López at the hands of Brazilian forces in

March 1870, the acceptance by a vanquished Paraguay of the validity of the Triple Alliance Treaty in June, and the establishment of the new constitution and the Brazil-dominated Paraguayan government in November 1870.[49] While the interval also includes the debate in Brazil's parliament over the Free Birth law and its ultimate passage (the first step toward abolishing slavery), there was no particular feature of the emancipation measure that would have necessarily cut the Empire's risk premium by one-third.[50]

A long list of events of a political and fiscal nature that one might think would be of importance do not show up as durable shifts in the Empire's London risk premium by the criteria employed here. These would include, most obviously, the pre-1850 revolts, the political crisis of the First Reign, the Additional Act of 1834, elevated diplomatic and naval pressure by the British to suppress the slave trade in the mid-1840s, and the abolitionist movement of the 1880s. This does not mean these events were unimportant in terms of their impact on sovereign risk, just that if they were important, they did not have a durable effect on the level of default risk perceived by British investors. On the basis of the risk premium data used here, the expected consequences of conflict in the Rio de la Plata trumped all else in driving durable changes to Brazil's default risk in London. Britain's diplomats had long viewed the potential for conflict in the River Plate as the most consequential of Brazil's foreign policy considerations.[51]

Expectations of war (or peace) mattered because war, more than any other factor, could dramatically drive up the government's bills. This was just as true for Brazil as it was for any European country at the time.[52] War implied an increasing demand for loans, rising debt service costs, and greater fiscal strain due to the tug-of-war between current military spending and the requirement to service existing debt. These would be sufficient to elevate the risk premia in terms of the model of sovereign borrowing of chapter 2. The structural break results also confirm what is suggested by visual inspection of figure 5.3. Though a baseline level of credibility that permitted the government to issue long-term debt had been established by the Constitution of 1824, it did not imply an irreversible decline in default risk, and creditworthiness proved quite variable over time.

FIGURE 5.3 Risk premium regimes in London, 1825–89

GOVERNMENT BOND YIELDS AND RISK PREMIA IN RIO DE JANEIRO

The approach taken to estimating breaks in the London risk premium data can be applied to the Empire's domestic debt as well. For the domestic bonds the analysis relies on weekly measures of the yield to maturity on apólices that paid an annual 6 percent coupon in domestic currency.[53] Apólices at 6 percent were first issued in Rio de Janeiro in early 1828, and secondary market quotations of their price became available in the second half of 1829. Prices are available nearly continuously until the conversion in 1884. Prices for the converted bonds run beyond the end of the monarchy in 1889. The long series of data points makes the 6 percent apólice (and its 5 percent successor) the superlative security to use in constructing the domestic yield series. From 1829 through the beginning of 1850 prices come from the *Jornal do Commércio* and a few other Rio newspapers. With the adoption of the commercial code in 1850, apólice prices were recorded in the official quotations of the Rio stock exchange, which is the main source for the series for the rest of the period of interest.[54] Apólices were quoted only when there were transactions or when the brokers had shares on offer. Of the 3,231 weeks spanned by the period

Table 5.3

Descriptive Statistics for Rio de Janeiro Apólice Yield and Risk Premium
Series, 1829–91

SERIES	OBSERVATIONS	MEAN	STANDARD DEVIATION	MINIMUM	MAXIMUM
Original yield to maturity	2,823	0.06978	0.01768	0.04904	0.17114
Interpolated yield	3,231	0.06899	0.01721	0.04904	0.17114
Interpolated risk premium	3,231	0.03707	0.01604	0.01660	0.13543

considered, there were 2,823 observations of apólice prices; prices are missing for some 12.6 percent of the weeks. To maintain the continuity of the data series, values for these missing observations were interpolated by using a cubic spline function. The basic statistical properties of the original and interpolated series are quite similar, as seen in table 5.3.

Bond prices and the coupon rate provide the basis for calculating the yield. Though apólices created under the National Debt law of 1827 were supposed to be retired at a rate of 1 percent a year, they were perpetuities for all intents and purposes. Because the apólice price at any point in time was the net present value of the future stream of coupon payments into infinity, the yield to maturity equals the current yield.[55] The current yield is adjusted for the twice-yearly interest payments.[56] As in the case of Brazil's London bonds, the consol yield is taken to represent the risk-free alternative investment. Consols did not trade in Brazil, yet Brazilian banking institutions, resident international merchants, correspondent brokers, and wealthy individuals all had access to the London market. The major Rio investors, who in many cases were market makers, could always earn the consol yield by using merchants to place their money in London. This made consols the risk-free alternative investment even in Rio de Janeiro.

While both apólices and consols had very long maturities, they differed in the currency in which they paid dividends and hence exhibited different inflation risks. No measure of actual or expected inflation exists for Imperial Brazil at a weekly frequency, so no adjustment to the yield for inflation is possible. The risk premium for apólices thus has a different basis than that for Brazil's London bonds. Netting out the consol yield from the apólice yield leaves, as the residual, pure default risk combined with inflation risk to give a measure of overall sovereign risk. Changes in the risk premium reflected the local market's appraisal of changes in the likelihood that the Imperial state would either fail to pay interest or use inflation to erode the real cost of domestic debt service to the Treasury and hence the real value of the dividends. Figure 5.4 graphs the yield and the risk premium. The first feature that is clear from the figure is that both declined over time. In general the increases in yields from 1829 on were intermittent, nonpermanent, and a fairly predictable response to unpredictable events. Indeed, the sharpest changes in Rio yields came with the political instability at the end of the First Reign.[57] Yields increased sharply right after the abdication of Pedro I but dropped precipitously soon afterward. The successful emplacement of the Regency did not threaten the core institutions of the constitutional monarchy, mitigating any perception that political instability might result in the repudiation of the domestic debt. Yields again increased by some 200

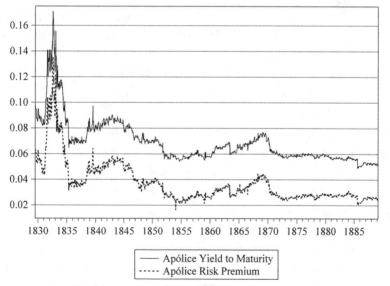

FIGURE 5.4 Yield to maturity and risk premium on 6 percent apólices in Rio, 1829–89

basis points from 1835 to 1844, as a well-known series of local uprisings and revolts erupted in various parts of Brazil. The decline from the mid-1840s appears to be related to the pacification of the longest-running secessionist revolt, in Brazil's far south. It may also have been an illusory effect of the new tariffs in 1844, despite the fact that revenues did not dramatically increase. That year did bring a reduction in the government's noninterest expenditures, creating a primary fiscal surplus that would persist until the outbreak of war with Paraguay in the 1860s.

Rio yields hovered below 6 percent for much of the 1850s during the government of the Conciliation. They rose gradually thereafter, yet even at the height of the war against Paraguay in the 1860s the risk premium was less than the levels seen in the early 1840s. Hefty new issues of debt by the government, both at home and overseas, did not stop yields from falling again below 6 percent, where they stayed for most of the 1870s and 1880s. The conversion of apólices in April 1886 from bonds with a 6 percent coupon to a 5 percent basis had only a slight impact on yields when it was implemented.

A comparison of figures 5.2 and 5.4 shows that yields in Rio moved higher than those in London during the politically turbulent era of the late 1820s and early 1830s. These differences in yields had nothing to do with the lower coupon rates on the London loans; this was simply priced into the bond, adjusting the yield accordingly. The differences instead had to do with the currencies in which the securities were denominated. The value of interest payments that were due in sterling was in doubt only if exchange rate depreciation was so severe that it caused Brazil to default. The value of interest payments on apólices was less certain, since it was vulnerable to local inflation. Yields in Rio actually turned lower than those on London bonds in the late 1840s, as the milréis ended a slide against the pound sterling. This momentary reversal of yields was not typical; investors charged on average around 30 basis points more to hold apólices than they did sterling bonds.

SHIFTING RISKS IN RIO DE JANEIRO

The estimation of shifts in the local risk premium proceeds in three steps. The first ascertains the stationarity of the apólice risk premium series.[58] The second tests the null hypothesis of a constant mean of the

Table 5.4

Break Points in the Risk Premium Series for Apólices in Rio de Janeiro, 1829–91

BREAK WEEKS (T_i)	BOUNDARY MONTHS FOR 90% CONFIDENCE INTERVAL		PROPORTIONAL CHANGE IN RISK PREMIUM
20 November 1834	20 November 1834	23 September 1836	−48.7%
31 August 1838	8 September 1836	31 May 1839	+28.2%
16 August 1847	3 August 1847	2 February 1849	−26%
5 January 1852	11 August 1843	8 January 1852	−21.6%

PARAMETER	β_i	CORRECTED STANDARD ERRORS
β_1	0.076	0.0075***
β_2	0.039	0.0019***
β_3	0.050	0.0017***
β_4	0.037	0.0006***
β_5	0.029	0.0013***

$R^2 = 0.77$
$F (5, 3,226) = 2,164$
$n = 3,231$
*** significant at 1% level

Number of breaks selected by:
supF test = 4
Sequential procedure = 4
Repartition procedure = 4

Note: The parameters are the average risk premium for each segment of the series. The Bai-Perron UD max and WD max tests (not reported) reject the hypothesis of no breaks. With a trimming value of 5 percent, the minimum interval length between breaks is 161 weeks, and the maximum allowed number of structural breaks is nine. The number of breaks selected by the sequential procedure is four.

risk premium series against the alternative of one or more structural breaks. Step three estimates the number and location of any breaks through the sequential procedure.[59] Table 5.4 presents the estimates, showing four shifts in the Rio risk premium series. These came in November 1834, August 1838, August 1847, and January 1852. The risk premia regimes implied by these breaks are displayed in figure 5.5. Unlike the London risk premium, for which all of the breaks occurred in 1852 or later, in Rio de Janeiro all of the breaks came in 1852 or before.[60]

The first two breaks came in the decade of the Regency (1831–40), already highlighted as an era of political turmoil and sharp, short-term

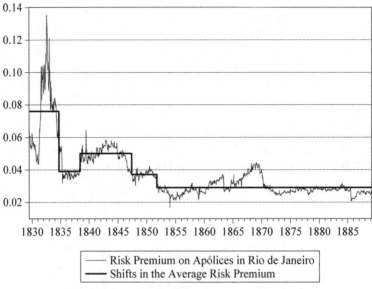

FIGURE 5.5

FIGURE 5.5 Risk premium regimes in Rio de Janeiro, 1829–89

changes in domestic bond yields. The first break in late November 1834 saw the risk premium decline by nearly half. It was the week that news of the death of the former emperor Pedro I arrived in Rio from Europe.[61] Pedro's death brought an end to concern that conflict might erupt between restorationists seeking his return and the nativists, who had pressed him to abdicate. It is straightforward to ascribe the break to the political consequences of Pedro's death. A number of other events could have worked in the same direction. One was the Cabanos war, or *Cabanada,* in the northeastern provinces of Pernambuco and Alagoas, which had been under way since 1832. It was Conservative and restorationist; news of Pedro's death took the wind from the movement's sails. By December 1834 the rebels were critically short on men, arms, and resources, and the uprising ended with the capture of its leaders.[62] Coming three months before the break (outside the 90 percent confidence interval but inside the 95 percent interval) was arguably the single most important post-1820s institutional reform of the Imperial era.[63] In August 1834 the parliament approved the constitutional amendment known as the Additional Act, which created a new set of authorities for provincial governments. The reform was a step in the direction of political decentralization, which had long been the goal of regional elites outside of Rio as well as of many liberal political leaders. The reform mattered as much for what it did not do as for what it did. Most important, the act's relatively limited scope of change revealed the embrace by the enfranchised elite of the core political arrangements embodied in the Constitution of 1824. Because the act was adopted during the Regency there was no influence from the throne over parliament's deliberations and decisions. The passage of the act reaffirmed the political viability of the Empire's institutions and in particular the sovereignty of the parliament, which was fundamental to the commitment to repay debt.

Events of a more transitory character further reinforced the perceptions that the Rio government was strong enough to deal with centrifugal forces in the provinces. The outbreak of the *Cabanagem* revolt in the province of Pará in 1835 falls within the confidence interval on the break. The revolt by its very nature would suggest greater risk of default, not less.[64] But the interval includes the decisive retaking of the provincial capital, Belém, by government forces. In early May 1836 the regent noted in his speech at the opening of parliament that "Belém would be retaken shortly," and the rest of the news from May and June was generally positive regarding the successes of the legalist forces on the battlefield.[65] Although the revolt ran for several years, the threat it posed was much reduced (if not necessarily any less bloody). The month of May in 1836 effectively marked the victory against what the British press had labeled a revolt by "indians" but which in fact was more socially and ideologically complex, having class, racial, and political dimensions.[66] After the recapture of Belém, the revolt posed little threat either to central authority or to the state's fiscal health. The start of the separatist revolt in Rio Grande do Sul, the *farroupilha,* in September 1835 is also within the confidence interval. This revolt, however, was not resolved for a decade and if anything would be expected to raise the risk premium, not lower it, as the data here show.[67]

The second break, at the end of August 1838, kicked off the only durable increase in the Rio risk premium. It came in the wake of the *Sabinada,* a violent months-long revolt in Bahia.[68] Less than a year later, in December 1838, came the *Balaiada* revolt in the northern province of

Maranhão, where local Liberals fought against local Conservatives as well as against the *regresso* cabinet in Rio that was working to roll back the main provisions of the Additional Act. It was a year-and-a-half-long struggle that would involve slaves as well as local property owners. In between these two revolts was a steady stream of updates on the ongoing fighting in Rio Grande do Sul, little of which could be characterized as encouraging for supporters of the central government. Barman has noted that by August 1839 the outlook for Brazil was widely seen as poor; British diplomats thought the political end of the Empire was near.[69] The bond market dated the start of the downturn about one year earlier but otherwise was in agreement with the assessment. By September yields had spiked sharply, signaling a major burst of pessimism within a period of already elevated default risk. Local bonds revisited depths not seen since 1834.

The third shift in risk, in August 1847, has a broad confidence interval that accommodates the Praieira revolt, considered "Pernambuco's 1848."[70] Liberals in Recife revolted against changes implemented locally following the appointment of a Conservative cabinet. The revolt unfolded against a backdrop of anti-Portuguese sentiment and a long history of provincial opposition to centralized rule from Rio de Janeiro. It was the last major regional revolt of the Imperial era. It began in November 1848, but news from the region had been worrisome for months, with reports from Recife of growing political tensions. The bond market may well have anticipated the conflict to come.[71] Though the revolt came after the estimated break point, it falls inside the confidence interval. Given that the risk premium declined rather than increased, what really registered in the Rio market was not the threat the revolt posed to the central government but the defeat of the rebels in early 1849—the average risk premium fell by 26 percent.

The final break in the series came in January 1852. The average default premium fell to its lowest level up to that point in time, less than 300 points over consol yields. The break corresponded to the nearly simultaneous break in the London risk series. The turning point for the Rio bond market came just before the military defeat of the Argentine forces in the battle of Monte Caseros and only a little more than a month after Brazil formally joined with Uruguay and several Argentine provinces in the effort to defeat Rosas.[72] The confidence interval on the estimate, however, runs all the way back to late 1843. As with the break in

London, it cannot be ruled out that several other events played a role in the decline in risk.[73] It is noteworthy that the Empire's strategic success in 1852 in the Rio de la Plata had depended on holding together its alliance with Uruguay and rebels in Argentina's provinces. The coalition had been forged by the special minister for the region, the Conservative Honório Hermeto Carneiro Leão. Carneiro Leão was soon ennobled as visconde do Paraná, and his achievement paved the way for his appointment the next year as president of the cabinet of the conciliação. The bipartisan council of ministers that he assembled would govern during an era in which default risk would be the lowest of any period during the history of the Empire.

REPUTATION AND RISK

The analysis of the preceding sections tested the hypothesis that the Empire's risk premium shifted in response to political and diplomatic events and their fiscal implications. This section considers a competing hypothesis: that the changes in Brazil's risk premium stemmed mainly from its evolving reputation as an increasingly reliable debtor. Borrower reputation figures prominently in one strand of the literature on sovereign creditworthiness.[74] States with histories of repeated default are considered poor credit risks and must pay a higher premium when they can borrow.[75] A government may choose to invest in a good reputation by always repaying its debts, even in very bad times. It does so in the hope that it can maintain access to the capital market in the future.[76]

Brazil has been cast as a case that proves the reputation hypothesis. Tomz argued that Brazil, like any unproven borrower, paid a high risk premium until it had established a solid record of servicing its debt. With regular, consistent interest payments to bondholders the interest rate Brazil was charged fell.[77] Brazil's record of debt service over the Imperial era thus engendered a good reputation that ostensibly accounts for the decline in its risk premium on the London market.

There are two limitations to the reputational argument as applied to the Empire. The first is its reliance on "ocular" regression techniques, based mainly on a graph of the data. The second is that it treats deviations from the downward trend of the risk premium (corresponding to the abdication of Pedro I in 1831, the so-called civil war of 1835–45, and so on) as temporary interruptions rather than considering the possibility of fundamental shifts in the mean. Whether the Empire's record of interest payments can explain the decline in the risk premium is assessed using a two-part econometric test. The first part tests for the predicted relationship between the risk premium and an index of interest payments to bondholders. This provides a statistical foundation for the putative reputational effect. The second part then tests whether the reputational model can improve on, or reject outright, the structural breaks model of shifts in Brazil's risk premium.

The first specification in table 5.5 presents the results of the regression of the risk premium on the variable for debtor reputation defined by Tomz—the length of time of uninterrupted interest payments.[78] The parameter estimate is negative as expected. The risk premium predicted by this reputational model fell from 5.3 percent in 1825 (or 530 basis points above consols) by more than two-thirds (to 1.5 percent) by late 1889. Note that the reputational model of sovereign creditworthiness does not predict any discontinuous changes in the risk premium, only a continuous decline so long as Brazil continued to pay interest. Yet this is at odds with the results of Table 5.2, which identify multiple persistent discontinuous shifts in the market's appraisal of default risk. Because neither of these models is nested within the other, the question of which should be favored cannot be resolved by classical hypothesis testing on subsets of parameters.

To see if one model predominates requires a non-nested hypothesis test.[79] It uses the fitted (predicted) risk premium from each of the models as an independent variable in the other. The approach is best illustrated in steps. By using the parameters of the reputational model one can calculate the predicted value of the risk premium each week. If the coefficient on this predicted risk premium is statistically significant when it is included in the structural breaks model, the reputational model dominates the structural breaks model. Otherwise, the structural breaks model cannot be rejected as an explanation of changes in the Empire's default risk. Analogously, if the fitted value of the risk premium from the structural breaks model is significant when added to the reputation model, the structural breaks model rejects the reputational model. It is also possible that neither model dominates the other, or that both models do.

Table 5.5

Test for Reputational Effect in the London Risk Premium

VARIABLE	PAYMENT HISTORY MODEL	STRUCTURAL BREAK MODEL	STRUCTURAL BREAKS + PREDICTED RISK	PAYMENT HISTORY + PREDICTED RISK
C	0.0533***	0.0513***	0.072***	−0.0048
	(0.005)	(0.004)		(0.005)
Payment history	−0.000011***			−0.00000137
	(0.0000018)			(0.0000014)
DBP2		−0.0361***	−0.0406***	
		(0.0035)	(0.0141)	
DBP3		−0.0323***	−0.0385***	
		(0.0035)	(0.0126)	
DBP4		−0.0181***	−0.0257***	
		(0.0039)	(0.0115)	
DBP5		−0.0289***	−0.04***	
		(0.0036)	(0.0083)	
Predicted risk (payment history)			−0.455	
			(0.3963)	
Predicted risk (breaks)				1.072***
				(0.1087)
F-statistic	2,076	1,768	1,467	3,572
Adjusted R-squared	0.37	0.67	0.68	0.67

Note: *** significant at 1% level. All specifications use ordinary least squares regression with HAC standard errors (in parentheses). The third specification includes the risk premium predicted by the payment history model as an independent variable. The fourth specification includes the risk premium predicted by the structural breaks model.

Specification 2 of table 5.5 regresses the risk premium on dummy variables for each distinct risk regime defined by the breaks in table 5.2. This provides a baseline result for the structural breaks model that is analogous to specification 1. The results of this estimation are equivalent to those of table 5.2.[80] To test whether Brazil's reputation for repayment can reject this break point model, the third specification adds as an independent variable the risk premium predicted by the payment history. If the reputation for repayment was important to creditors in determining how much to charge Brazil for default risk, the parameter estimate on the fitted risk premium should be positive and statistically significant. As the table shows, the reputational model does not dominate the structural breaks model.

The specification in the final column of the table reverses the direction of the test. A fitted risk premium is first generated from the structural breaks model. It is then added as an independent variable in the regression for the reputational model. The coefficient on the fitted risk premium is positive and statistically significant. Moreover, the reputational effect originally indicated by the payment history variable loses all statistical significance. Taking the two tests together, one can reject the hypothesis that a reputation for making regular interest payments was the main determinant of changes in Brazil's risk premium between 1825 and 1889.[81] While a reputational effect on the risk premium is seemingly visible in the graph of the data and intuitively plausible, it does not pass the statistical tests that would give it the force of a finding. The Empire's risk premium shifted when the market reassessed the likelihood that the government would default. The market's outlook depended not on past performance but on events in Brazil and their implications for future repayment.

CONCLUSION

The focus of this chapter has been the size and timing of changes in the risk premium on Brazil's bonds in Rio de Janeiro and London. The evolution of the Empire's risk premium for the period 1824–89 shows that ongoing access to long-term credit at home and abroad came at a fluctuating price. Some movements in risk were more durable than others. The overall decline in interest rates on Brazil's bonds was not smooth. Visual inspection of the data reveals a risk premium that fell substantially over time but also exhibited discontinuous shifts. Identifying the sources of changes in credit risk required an empirical strategy to establish which of the changes persisted and which were simply short-term responses to news or events. It also required an analytical framework in which the risk premium could shift in either direction in response to changes in bond-holders' appraisals of the likelihood of default. Reliance on the framework provided by the model of chapter 2 allows for increases as well as declines in the risk premium.

A limitation of the data on borrowing costs in the primary markets in chapters 3 and 4 is that observations of the risk premium are available only when the government took out new loans. Original evidence on weekly measures of risk in the secondary markets of London and Rio made it possible in this chapter to identify changes in credit risk on a continuous basis. Domestic bond yields ran as high as 16 percent a year and as low as 6 percent. The yield on sterling bonds varied nearly as much, between 13 percent and 4 percent per year. Little of the movement in yields over time came from changes in the underpinning risk-free cost of capital; nearly all yield changes derived from changes in the Brazil-specific risk premium. The risk premium on the Empire's bonds varied far more than actual (or even perceived) institutional changes alone could account for. Credit risk in London ran from a negligibly small level to nearly 12.5 percent. The average tended toward the lower end of the range, at around 340 basis points above consols. In Rio, the risk premium never went below 1.6 percent and was 13.5 percent at its peak. The average was slightly higher than in London, at around 370 points above consols.

The results of the structural break tests established probable dates of persistent changes in the market's perception of the government's creditworthiness. The timing of the break points helps to identify market-moving events, even though isolating a single unique cause for each break was not possible. The large reduction in risk in 1852, for example, probably had more than one cause. Irrespective of the precise channels through which events shifted the risk premium, bond markets in London and Rio registered key turning points. The focus of the bondholders was not, however, always the same in the two markets. Recurrent political instability under the Regency and early in the Second Reign created more durable shifts in perceptions of default risk in Rio than in London. Conflicts with external rivals garnered greater concern from bondholders in London. Turning points, critically, were not unidirectional. When events suggested to the market that the state's willingness or ability to service its debts might have diminished, the risk premia in London and Rio rose accordingly. While Brazil's reputation for steady repayment grew, markets looked forward rather than backward when pricing default risk.

The level of default risk in both bond markets dropped to historically low levels in the early 1850s. During the war against Paraguay, the risk premium on London bonds briefly flirted with levels not seen since the 1840s. Yet overall, risk after midcentury never again came near the peaks seen during the 1830s, despite the fact that the Empire carried a much larger debt load in the later period. The decline in the risk premium should have held ramifications for the economy as a whole. In particular, one would expect that the slide in the state's borrowing costs would have resonated in the broader capital market. It did not, however, reduce the interest rates for businesses or planters. This divergence between the government's relatively privileged line of credit and the obstacles to finance encountered by private entrepreneurs seeking access to financing indicates a fundamental disconnect in the market for capital.

CHAPTER SIX

Controlling Capital

INSTITUTIONAL OBSTACLES TO INCORPORATION

IN 1853 IRINEU Evangelista de Souza lost his bank in Rio de Janeiro, but not because it had failed. In fact, it was a profitable, dividend-paying concern. Souza had secured a charter just two years before to organize his Banco do Commércio e Indústria do Brasil, colloquially known as the Banco do Brasil.[1] He set it up as a joint-stock corporation (*sociedade anônima*) under the Empire's new commercial code.[2] Souza knew the code well because he had helped write it.[3] The bank ceased to exist because the finance minister found it convenient to force its merger with another bank to create one that the government could control and that would serve the state's own financial needs as well as those of commerce. How Souza's bank came into being and how he lost control of it highlight the way in which arbitrary political decisions made it difficult for entrepreneurs to incorporate and raise capital in Imperial Brazil. That the state was an obstacle to mobilizing capital is surprising. Political institutions that support credible sovereign borrowing are strongly associated with the growth of capital markets and business finance. In Brazil the effect of those political institutions on financial development was the opposite of what one would expect on the basis of the Dutch, British, and United States experiences.

There was nothing unusual about Souza's bank, except that it was large and had an authorized capital twice that of its sole rival, the Banco Commercial. Both banks financed local commerce, in part by issuing promissory notes of very short duration called *vales*—designed to be re-deemed after five days, enough time to settle local transactions. In prac-tice the vales were widely used and remained in circulation for much longer. At the start of 1851 the discount rate on high-quality commercial paper in Rio was in the range of 7 to 7.5 percent per year. Souza's entry into the market and the vales his bank issued helped reduce short-term interest rates. By the end of the year the rate had fallen some 250 basis points, fluctuating between 4.5 and 5 percent a year.[4] In 1852 the two banks issued even more vales, keeping the rate at 4.5 percent. Increas-ingly, however, vales found their way into more speculative deals and investments. Discount rates began to rise, but in early 1853 they held steady at 5.5 percent. When too many of the new investments delivered unfa-vorable returns, the holders of vales began to exchange them for cash.

The prospect of a flood of note redemptions caused both Souza's bank and the Banco Comercial to halt most discounting. By the end of March the short-term interest rate had shot up to 8 percent. The local market seized up. In June the rate hit 10 percent. Even bills of the highest quality were difficult to place. To jump-start credit, Finance Minister (and chief of the cabinet) Joaquim José Rodrigues Torres, a founder of the Conservative party, advanced Treasury bills to both banks.[5] Yet he was no great sup-porter of either of them. He did not see them as an effective solution to the monetary problems that had become intractable through the 1840s. And he was critical of the risks posed by their speculative lending, declaring to parliament that "while beneficial, banks can also cause great perturbation in the economic order if they do not adhere to rules and safeguards."[6]

Rodrigues Torres wanted a high degree of control over the banks in order to compel a solution to instability in the credit market. He also wanted to put banking capital to work on behalf of state finance. Achiev-ing control spelled the end of the bank Souza had created. The minister forced the fusion of the two banks by creating a new Banco do Brasil, whose shareholders would enjoy a lucrative monopoly over the issue of banknotes. In return for its monopoly the bank had to use part of its capi-tal to retire old notes remaining from the long-defunct first Banco do Brasil. Those notes were an obligation of the Treasury; by having the bank exchange them, the Treasury did not have to pay their holders. The govern-ment did not control the bank outright, but its influence was very strong. While shareholders would elect its directors, Rodrigues Torres reserved for the cabinet sole authority to select the bank's president and vice president. After outlining his plan in his speech to parliament in May 1853, he introduced it as a bill in the senate. Among the bill's co-sponsors was the marquês do Paraná, whom Souza had positioned as president of his own bank. Paraná would preside over the famous cabinet of the conciliação that came to government later in the year and found the appeal of a government-controlled bank to be irresistible. The proposal for the new bank passed both houses of parliament and became law in early July. Parliament, anticipating that the two existing banks fold into the new one, went even further, authorizing the banks to issue notes (rather than the short-duration vales) to further aid the merchants and firms that had grown accustomed to discounting their bills at only 4.5 percent before the crisis.[7]

Souza and his board were left with little choice. Under the article of the commercial code that required government approval of incorporation, dissolution was called for whenever a corporation no longer served its original "social purpose."[8] Rodrigues Torres's proposal left the existing banks in a weak position. They would not be able to compete against a bank with a monopoly over notes. And in turn they would no longer serve the public need that had justified their charter, leaving them vulnerable to dissolution. A week after passage of the law, the board of Souza's bank, having received the government's invitation to join the new bank, communicated to its shareholders that fusion was "inevitable."[9] Souza and his shareholders should have been able to control the new board, given that his bank contributed more equity to the deal. They did not. His rivals, the directors of the Banco Comercial, were as well connected as he was and had been in business longer. Despite bringing more capital to the merger, the elections for the new board left Souza without a majority.[10] Souza's injury was compounded when Rodrigues Torres selected a loyal and subservient midlevel Conservative politician and government functionary—not a financier—as the first president of the new super bank. Souza resigned his seat and ultimately liquidated his position. Rodrigues Torres, in one of his last acts before the new cabinet came to power in September, approved the final statutes of the new Banco do Brasil, clearing the way to call up its capital.[11] The next year the emperor ennobled Souza with the title of barão de Mauá and made Rodrigues Torres the visconde de Itaboraí.

Mauá had experienced firsthand one of the vulnerabilities of raising capital to conduct business in Imperial Brazil. He would soon encounter another. He immediately set out to organize a new bank so that he could implement his original vision of branching out all over Brazil. To try to keep the new bank from being hijacked by the cabinet, he sought a different organizational basis under the law, one he hoped would reduce his exposure to government intervention while making it easier to expand into the provinces. Modeled on the French Banque Lafitte, the new Banco Mauá, MacGregor & Cia. drew its investments from partners instead of from shareholders. To transcend the limits on size that accompanied the partnership form of business, Mauá chose to make his bank a *sociedade em comandita por acções*—a partnership but with tradable equity shares, much like common stock. For the bank's controlling partners, including Mauá, there was no limit to their personal financial liability in case of failure. The liability of the nonmanaging partners, around 180 equity investors, was limited to their capital. Mauá exploited what appeared to be a key loophole in the commercial code of 1850. Unlike the French code under which the Banque Lafitte operated, Brazil's code did not specifically allow limited liability partnerships with tradable shares. But it also did not prohibit them. Mauá went so far as to gain informal approval by discussing his plan with the new finance minister and the former president of Mauá's former bank, the marquês do Paraná.

Once again Mauá's interests did not align with those of the government. In the senate Rodrigues Torres attacked Mauá's bank soon after its organization, criticizing the use of the comandita form with tradable shares. Nonplussed, Mauá called up the full capital of the firm, intending to deliver a fait accompli via the market. In parliament and within the cabinet, opposition grew. The worry was that the Banco do Brasil, which the government needed to succeed in order to retire the old banknotes from circulation, would be weakened by competition for both capital and business from the new Banco Mauá, MacGregor & Cia. From within the cabinet Minister of Justice José Tomás Nabuco de Araújo delivered the blow. His decree retroactively banned firms organized as partnerships from issuing tradable shares and ordered the cancellation of all existing partnership deeds with such features. Mauá complied, and his bank survived the change in organizational form forced on it.[12] But it did so only as an unwieldy partnership without tradable equity, which limited Mauá's ability to expand the business as he had envisioned.[13]

Mauá's travails highlight how restrictions on the organizational forms that entrepreneurs could select disrupted investment and business. Because the cabinet's measure applied not just to Mauá but also across the board, Brazil missed out on the potential benefits of having a secondary market for shares of partnerships. In isolation it might seem a small matter. Yet in a setting where government policy already made it very difficult to create and sustain joint-stock companies, a partnership with tradable shares would have constituted a valuable alternative form of the firm for pooling capital. Mobilizing capital for small business faced few institutional obstacles in Imperial Brazil. Mobilizing capital for big business, however, depended wholly on government favor.

Despite its success as a sovereign borrower, the Empire exhibited persistently inefficient financial intermediation. Until the 1880s the government restricted the use of the corporate form to raise capital, while denying access to substitutes, such as tradable share partnerships. Before 1850 there was no general provision for the granting of limited liability to investors in businesses. Joint-stock companies were rare, created on an exceptional basis and then only with cabinet approval. The adoption of Brazil's first commercial code, in 1850, made limited liability and joint-stock status synonymous in the form of the sociedade anônima. It was not a form of business available to everyone. The code vested the government with the authority both to approve charters and to cancel them. Entrepreneurs seeking to use the joint-stock form had to gain approval of the cabinet to incorporate. If a firm further sought a government concession or privilege (such as opening a business in more than one province), the act of incorporation required the approval of both the cabinet and the parliament.

In 1860 the notorious *lei dos entraves,* or law of impediments, made it even more difficult to incorporate, especially for banks. All requests for incorporation had to pass muster with the emperor's Council of State, in addition to securing parliamentary or cabinet approval or both. Petitions for a corporate charter could be considered only after the entire plan of the business, including its sources of capital, had been arranged. The section of Empire of the Council assessed the public and private utility of the proposed company. Lists of subscribers (mustered in advance) in proposed companies—by name and amount—were scrutinized by the councilors, along with the more mundane administrative features of petitions.[14] In 1875 one contemporary critic, Henrique Milet, declared that the 1860 law was "the most perfect instrument ever invented to kill the spirit of association and individual initiative."[15] Only in 1882 did parliament remove these restrictions, finally making incorporation for many types of firms broadly available through simple registration. Even then the old restrictive procedures remained in place for foreign-owned firms, businesses commercializing foodstuffs, and banks that sought to issue notes.

Brazil was not alone in laboring under excessive restrictions on incorporation. France had similar strictures in place until 1867. Yet French entrepreneurs also enjoyed access to other forms of the firm that allowed both limited liability for investors and the right to issue tradable shares. These limited liability partnerships with equity shares (the *société en commandite par actions*), made possible by a revision to France's commercial code of 1807, became a common way to pool capital through midcentury.[16] In Brazil, however, obstacles to incorporation were far more costly precisely because the government explicitly banned the French-style partnerships with shares. The difficulty of obtaining a corporate charter in Brazil did not mean that incorporation was impossible. Even under a relatively closed regime of incorporation such as the one that operated between 1860 and 1882, the government granted charters. Restrictions meant that the ability to incorporate depended on discretionary and even arbitrary decisions by the state.

Control over the use of the corporate form, and the broader access to capital that it provided, served three purposes. Government could ration access to the corporate form to channel capital to projects that met political goals. There was a public finance motive for restricting incorporation as well. By limiting incorporation, government could tilt private savings toward its own use. Restricting the opportunities for investors in stocks and corporate bonds could help push money into shares of government debt. Finally, restrictions on incorporation limited entry by new firms with high capital requirements. Barriers to entry protected the market share of incumbent firms. This was especially visible in the case of commercial banks, turning the entire sector into an oligopoly. The implication of these restrictions on adopting the joint-stock limited liability form of the company was the same irrespective of motive. Businesses for which the required level of investment was relatively large were effectively barred from raising capital if they could not sell shares to investors.

One claim that emerges from the literature on sovereign debt and financial development is that the benefits of credibly committing to repay debt can spill over to the private sector. In relatively high-income economies, the new property rights in financial assets that resulted from the credible commitment to honor sovereign debt did contribute to the process of financial development.[17] A consequence of assigning fiscal control to the legislative branch was that government's capacity to expropriate or hold up wealth holders, including owners of financial assets, was reduced. The crown (or executive branch) would lose its monopoly control of corporate chartering and business regulation, sharing authority with the legislative branch. Because legislatures proved more responsive to the needs of entrepreneurs than absolutist monarchs, accommodation replaced arbitrary decisions regarding the organizational forms of enterprise.[18] Incorporation was a matter for the parliament to deal with in the political marketplace and became more accessible to entrepreneurs.

In light of the experiences of the United Kingdom and the United States, one might reasonably expect Brazil's credible commitment to repay public debt to foster the growth of financial intermediation in the form of equity markets, bank lending, markets for corporate debt, or some combination of these. Yet in Imperial Brazil the shift of financial authority to the parliament provided no particular boost to the opportunities for incorporation by private firms. Despite an impressive improvement of sovereign creditworthiness after independence, no broad-based financial revolution ever transpired under the Empire.

The extent and durability of restrictions on incorporation in Imperial Brazil were surprising. They are the subject of this chapter, which tests the hypothesis that restrictions on incorporation limited the use of the corporate form to raise capital. Previous historians have addressed how particular changes in commercial law from the 1850s on made incorporation more or less feasible.[19] The treatment here models the role of restrictions on corporate entry more generally, marshals new evidence on the timing of changes in corporate chartering, provides statistical tests of the regulatory hypothesis, and considers fiscal motives for financial repression.

The principal findings that emerge from the assessment of the legal and quantitative evidence on corporate formation run along the following lines. First, incorporation was rare until the establishment of general procedures under the commercial code of 1850. After a decade of accelerated rates of corporate formation, changes to the code in 1860 made the corporate form far less accessible. Incorporation was only partly liberalized with the reform of the commercial code at the end of 1882. Over the entire Imperial era regulatory restrictions undermined the financing of large firms by limiting the organizational form that entrepreneurs could adopt. In several sectors the selective award of corporate charters after midcentury gave Brazil a few firms that were local behemoths. The favored status and dominance of these firms derived as much from political considerations as from business prospects. Tightened requirements between 1860 and 1883 did not end incorporation but gave policy makers considerable leeway to bluntly repress chartering and push capital toward apólices and bonds of the National Loans. Second, reducing the regulatory obstacles to joint-stock company formation made a difference. The 1850s saw higher annual rates of incorporation than did the two decades after 1860. While the regulatory changes of the early 1890s are often singled out as the main cause of the increase of Brazil's joint-stock firms, the legal conditions were already in place by 1883, and the expansion was already under way by the latter part of the decade.[20] This more favorable regulatory environment for corporations was visible in the increase in chartering activity during the 1880s and in the growth in the total stock of capital embodied by corporate equity shares listed on the Rio de Janeiro stock exchange. The final insight is that the persistence of such restrictions through 1882 makes it clear that the creation of credible government debt in the 1820s did not automatically foster a regulatory regime that facilitated entrepreneurs' access to capital. Simply put, there was no financial revolution in Imperial Brazil. The adoption of political institutions that made sovereign debt credible was much less glorious in this regard than it was in Britain.

The rest of this chapter proceeds in five sections. The first summarizes the organizational forms of the firm available to entrepreneurs in Imperial Brazil. The second details the changes in the Empire's corporate law, provides an overview of the types of firms that operated in Brazil, and presents an analytic chronology of commercial legislation. The third section presents a model of the entrepreneur's choice of organizational form when seeking a corporate charter is costly and entrepreneurs face expropriation risk. The fourth section offers quantitative indicators of firm formation (for both corporations and partnerships) and relates changes in them to the timing of regulatory changes. The results are consistent with the predictions provided by the model. The last section concludes.

THE FIRM AND ITS LEGAL FORMS IN THE EMPIRE

The ability to access capital markets in which tradable shares could be issued and exchanged is an important part of financial development. So is the ability to access loans. Effective financial intermediation could be provided by either banks or securities markets.[21] What mattered for the finance of business was whether political and institutional conditions facilitated the development of at least one of these two modes of finance. Had the corporate form—or its closest substitute, the joint-stock partnership—been freely available under the Empire, more firms would have been able to tap securities markets for capital. Access to equity and debt financing with shares that are securitized matters for two reasons. The existence of a primary market makes it possible for firms to obtain initial funds for capital investment both by issuing stocks and by borrowing with bonds. Securities markets further make it possible for individuals and organizations to trade shares of the firm's equity and debt. This secondary market is a critical source of liquidity that further bolsters the primary market for initial issues of new stocks and bonds.

This is not to argue that a higher degree of financial development in the nineteenth century would have *necessarily* transformed Brazil into a high-income economy. Countries required far more than just banks and securities markets to attain elevated levels of output per capita. Nonetheless, every investigation to date reveals that improved financial intermediation is among the factors that impel modern, sustained economic growth. In Brazil artisans and even small manufactories encountered strong local and even regional demand for their goods in the nineteenth century. Improvements to the mechanisms of financial intermediation would have unambiguously elevated gross domestic product.[22] For some enterprises the very viability of the firm was inextricably tied to the availability of finance that could come only through the corporate form.

Railroads, large commercial banks, shipping firms, and public utilities were businesses in which restrictions on size implied by the partnership form led many entrepreneurs to organize their firms as corporations. Open access to incorporation can thus be seen as an important ingredient in financial development.

The most common and most basic form of the business firm available to Brazilians under the Empire was the sole proprietorship. Proprietorships had a number of distinguishing characteristics. In a proprietorship the firm's business was generally not separate from that of the individual proprietor. Although anyone who made commerce the principal source of his or her livelihood was required to register with the board of trade, many small-scale proprietorships likely never bothered to do so. A business failure left the proprietor personally liable for the firm's debts and restricted the owner's ability to legally undertake new business until they had been fully discharged. This limited the size of proprietorships but otherwise was not necessarily a disadvantage. By sharpening the penalty for nonperformance, full liability for debts enhanced the creditworthiness of the proprietor.

Beyond the sole proprietorship various forms of business partnerships were available to entrepreneurs in Brazil. Legally, the partnership had an identity partly separate from that of the individual partners. Some partners enjoyed limits on their liability. Managing partners, however, did not. Claims against the partnership were claims on the personal assets of at least one of its partners and perhaps all of them, depending on the specific form the partnership took. The Empire's commercial code of 1850 allowed four types of partnerships.[23] A simple partnership, the *sociedade em nome coletivo,* was one in which all partners contributed to the firm's equity and each partner was fully liable for the firm's obligations. Alternatively, *sociedades em comandita* involved at least "one active" partner and at least one nonmanaging partner. All partners contributed equity, but only the active partners carried full liability for the firm's debts. Service partnerships, *sociedade de capital e indústria,* had an equity partner with unlimited liability and a partner who contributed skills or labor. Less common was the fourth type of partnership, the *sociedade em conta de participação,* which brought together an active partner and a hidden partner. The active partner took on liabilities solely in their name. After 1882 there was a fifth type of partnership, the *sociedade com acções.* It could divide the capital of the partnership into equity shares, which could then trade in the secondary market, like shares of joint-stock companies.[24] The capital paid in by limited partners comprised the tradable equity shares, and limited partners were responsible for debts only up to the amount of their contracted capital.[25] Active partners remained fully liable for the firm's debts.

As accommodating as Brazil's 1850 commercial code was with respect to partnerships, corporations were a different matter altogether. If all types of business were equally profitable, irrespective of organizational form, then there would be no reason to observe the existence of both partnerships and corporations. In practice, certain activities could be undertaken profitably only if they were organized as corporations. Non-state-owned railroads in Brazil, for example, were in nearly every case corporations with tradable equity. The scale and capital intensity of a railroad enterprise required more capital than could be reasonably assembled in a partnership. The Brazilian corporation was a limited liability joint-stock firm, known as a sociedade anônima. The Empire had no general legal provision for incorporation until 1850. A few firms had operated as joint-stock firms (some apparently without limited liability) before the adoption of the commercial code in 1850. Firms could secure limited liability status as corporations only through a government charter.[26]

The corporate form of the firm escaped several limitations faced by partnerships. One was the problem of untimely dissolution. The exit of a partner required the legal dissolution and reconstitution of the partnership if the firm was to continue. This was costly because it made the firm operate under constant uncertainty about its capital and its organizational integrity as a business entity. Potential turnover of partners kept partnerships small; the greater the number of partners, the more frequent the disruptions from partners departing would be. The corporation provided an organizational form that obviated this problem of untimely dissolution. Unlike partnerships, the corporation was a distinct legal entity, separate from the individual legal identities of its owners. The exit or death of an owner did not force the reorganization, liquidation, or re-registration of the corporation. Any stake in the corporation could simply be sold in the secondary market. Additionally, investors in corporations shared in all profits and losses, much as they did in a general partnership. But unlike a general partnership, all corporate investors enjoyed limited liability and were responsible for the firm's debts only up to the capital they had agreed to subscribe.

The advantages of the corporate form to entrepreneurs were not absolute. For any business in which the cost of shirking was especially important, the partnership form might be preferred. Where there is a high likelihood of exploitation of small-stakes shareholders by more senior owners, investors also may prefer a partnership.[27] Yet in almost all instances one of the corporation's principal advantages relative to a partnership was that it could raise capital from a large number of investors, many of whom might commit only a modest amount of money. For partnerships, raising the same capital would potentially imply a prohibitively large number of partners.

In Brazil, the importance of the corporate form in transcending the limits to scale can be gleaned from the record for a period in which evidence on the sizes of new firms is available. Over the interval 1850 to 1865 the mean size of joint-stock firms newly chartered in Rio de Janeiro was 3.3 million milréis per firm (based on the amount of capital they were authorized to raise in the market). The mean capital of partnerships registered in Rio over the same period was only 109.1 thousand milréis per firm, a thirty-fold difference in capitalization.[28] This gap in size was persistent. In the mid-1880s the typical new joint-stock firm had an authorized equity that was nearly thirty times that of the typical partnerships in the coffee trade (which were usually better capitalized than partnerships in other branches of business).[29] This difference between corporations and partnerships reveals the one area in which the corporate form conferred an indisputable advantage: size.

EVOLUTION OF CORPORATE LAW UNDER THE EMPIRE

Countries with a long civil law tradition ostensibly have weak investor protections and less financial development. This question has dominated comparative assessments of corporate law and economic performance.[30] Although Brazil was a civil law country, it exhibited legal constraints on entrepreneurs seeking to adopt the limited liability form that went well beyond the problem posed by weak shareholder rights. Weak shareholder rights were simply not the main obstacle to incorporation. The rights of the shareholders corporations were well defined and fully transparent once the commercial code of 1850 was implemented. The main obstacle to incorporation was the difficulty in obtaining a corporate charter in the first place. The challenge to entrepreneurs in Brazil can be summarily illustrated by a cursory comparison with Britain. The fundamental difference between the regulation of the corporate form in England (the canonical common law case) and in Brazil was a simple one: in England, after 1844 anyone could start a corporation and register it, while in Brazil nobody could start one without previous authorization of the government. In England, William Gladstone's Companies Act of 1844 made the formation of a joint-stock company a simple and inexpensive administrative procedure. Further, limited liability for companies became widely available in 1855.[31] In Brazil, there was no established procedure for creating limited liability joint-stock companies at all until the end of 1849. With the adoption of the code of 1850 the granting of corporate charters came at the discretion of the government. The ability to access capital by creating tradable equity shares was controlled by politicians, who implemented the very model that the British had just abandoned.

Business restrictions in Brazil had deep roots. The commercial code of 1850 offered numerous advantages over the hodgepodge of medieval and early modern regulations the country had inherited from Portugal. In the wake of independence, all Portuguese regulations that were not explicitly overturned by new legislation remained in effect. A bewildering array of provisions from past laws thus governed business until 1850. These derived from the Portuguese Filipine Ordinances of 1603, themselves based on Manueline Ordinances of 1514, which in turn drew on Afonsine Ordinances of 1480. Further, there were specific colonial regulations applicable to Brazil that addressed issues of commerce in the colony.[32] The chief legal innovation of the Pombaline reforms was the adoption of the "Law of Good Reason."[33] Under the law parties could draw on the commercial regulations of all Christian nations in business affairs. Brazilian commercial law at independence thus had multiple components: edicts of the Portuguese crown; regulations specifically for the colony (including the years after the arrival of the royal court from Portugal in 1808); decrees that had governed business matters in the United Kingdom of Portugal and Brazil from 1815 to 1822; and, in the absence of other provisions, the Law of Good Reason. By the early nineteenth century Brazilian commercial jurisprudence could be that of any one of a number of other nations. Up to midcentury the commercial code of

France, and later those of Portugal and Spain, increasingly constituted the rough legal foundations of Brazilian business.

It was left to the Imperial government to create specific statutes to replace the more archaic ones in effect. The chamber of deputies began work on a commercial code in the 1830s, but none was adopted during that decade or the next. A few joint-stock companies organized, though without limited liability. The delay in creating a mechanism by which firms could incorporate generated legal uncertainty for entrepreneurs and gave the emperor's cabinets wide discretionary authority over incorporation.[34] Only in 1849 was the first general provision governing the establishment of joint-stock companies with limited liability implemented by cabinet decree, anticipating the passage of the commercial code by parliament the next year.[35] Under the 1849 law, limited liability status required approval either from the cabinet (in the case of firms near Rio) or from provincial presidents, who were appointed by and responsible to the cabinet. Unless and until the designated authority granted limited liability, a firm could not organize and issue shares as a corporation.

Barriers to incorporation in Brazil were not the result of excessive stockholder liability provisions. The commercial code of 1850, the more restrictive companies' law passed in 1860, and the liberalizing legislation of 1882 all limited shareholder liability.[36] Limited liability was just that—limited. It did not imply an absence of liability. From 1850 onward shareholders in joint-stock firms were liable for the value of their shares. What investors stood to lose in case of failure was strictly limited to the equity stake they had taken on. The 1882 law that finally made incorporation an administrative procedure carried an additional safeguard against the creation of unviable firms for speculative purposes. It specified that, if the company failed, shareholders would be liable for the amounts they had originally agreed to pay in when they subscribed their shares, even if the firm's directors had not yet called all of the capital. If any shares had already been traded before they were fully paid in, their original owner remained liable for the subscribed amount for five years.[37] This provision allowed firms to get off the ground with a minimal amount of capital, yet at the same time incentivized investors to fully realize their subscribed capital in a timely manner. The remaining provisions of the law discouraged the formation of fictitious companies with shares that might be rapidly "flipped" by speculators and unscrupulous organizers.[38]

With the adoption of its commercial code in 1850, Brazil embarked on three decades of corporate legal evolution that can only be described as underwhelming from the perspective of entrepreneurs. Article 298 of the code made it possible to establish a joint-stock company. The code was transparent, yet clarity in the law was not incompatible with excessive stringency. Article 295 of the code carried over the 1849 provision that limited liability firms could organize only with cabinet approval. Moreover, for any firm seeking a government concession or privilege, the approval by the cabinet of limited liability status depended further on the approval of the parliament as a whole.

Legislation in 1860 made it even more difficult to obtain a corporate charter for many types of firms. The new law was especially onerous for banks because it shifted part of the authority for the granting of limited liability for financial firms to the emperor's handpicked Council of State.[39] Though the law of impediments mainly targeted banks, it also applied to companies seeking to build a railroad or canal in more than one province.[40] Authority over the granting of incorporation and limited liability to the types of firms that stood to confer the greatest economic benefits rested with the council, not just with the cabinet and parliament. For more than two decades after 1860, the sections of Treasury and Empire of the Council of State busied themselves scrutinizing the statutes of every proposed banking company, many railroads, and numerous other proposed companies that sought a privilege or concession.[41] By rationing access to the corporate form, the law rationed access to the capital market.

The excessive restrictiveness of the 1860 addition to the commercial code was widely noted by contemporaries. Even cabinet ministers occasionally acknowledged the negative impact of the law on corporate formation. In his annual report to the parliament in 1868, Minister of Agriculture Miguel Pinto de Sousa Dantas wrote that "*sociedades anônimas* continue to be ruled by the law of 1860 . . . in my view prejudicially for the spirit of association."[42] There were several attempts in parliament to loosen the restrictions of the law of 1860.[43] When the surge of new corporations that began with the end of the Paraguayan war dropped off in the second half of the 1870s, worried politicians who favored fewer restrictions finally took action. In 1879 a measure proposed by Minister of Justice Lafayette Rodrigues Pereira to allow broad access to incorporation passed the Liberal-controlled chamber of deputies but stalled in the senate.[44] Finally, at the end of 1882, pushed along by a Liberal cabinet and aided by Lafayette in his capacity as Imperial senator, the senate amended and passed the measure, eliminating the more arbitrary and politicized forms of scrutiny of charter requests and moving Brazil in the direction of the model provided by the English Companies Act.[45]

By the beginning of 1883 most aspirants to joint-stock status could establish their companies with limited liability through an administrative registry and without further government interference. Three important exceptions (in addition to long-standing limits on banks of issue) to the newly liberalized regulations survived intact, however. These included any proposals to establish corporations created with foreign capital, any companies commercializing foodstuffs, and joint-stock financial firms that engaged specifically in mortgage lending (*sociedades de crédito real*), all of which continued to require government approval.[46] A separate provision of the reformed commercial code allowed partnerships with unlimited liability and tradable shares, like those permitted in France until 1857. Nearly thirty years after Mauá's attempt to sell shares in his partnership-based bank, the government finally allowed entrepreneurs the flexibility to do so. There is no indication that many (if any) partnerships in Brazil took this form. The contemporaneous liberalization of incorporation can be safely presumed to have satisfied demand for an organizational form in which entrepreneurs could raise funds with tradable shares.

REGULATORY REGIMES AND THE CHOICE OF FORM

The cost of politicized restrictions on incorporation had two elements. Some firms never got off the ground at all. Other firms had to take a less-preferred organizational form. Several factors of a political and regulatory nature could push an entrepreneur to choose a partnership (or not invest at all) when the corporate form was too costly to arrange. A simple model of the entrepreneur's choice of the form of the firm is presented in appendix I. It focuses on three elements: the entrepreneur's cost of securing a corporate charter, the probability of charter approval by the regulatory authority, and risk of expropriation. The model highlights a key point: even where the corporate form is both privately efficient and increases the social surplus, the entrepreneur will refrain from incorporation if expropriation risk is too large, if the cost of seeking a corporate charter is too high, or if the probability of a charter petition being approved is too low. All of these costs were salient for entrepreneurs in Imperial Brazil. Changes in the law on incorporation can be interpreted in terms of changes in key parameters of this model.

Consider an entrepreneur who is organizing a firm and who needs capital. The entrepreneur can create the firm with partners by a simple act of registration. Or he can create the firm as a joint-stock company with a charter from the government. The entrepreneur's choice depends on the relative benefits and costs of the two organizational forms. As Lamoreaux and Rosenthal have demonstrated, neither organizational form is intrinsically superior in every circumstance.[47] The choice of form involves trade-offs for the entrepreneur. Under the corporate form the entrepreneur's liability is limited, usually to no more than his own equity stake. This can raise the corporation's borrowing costs relative to those of a proprietorship or partnership. At the same time, partnerships may be unattractive because of the costs of untimely dissolution when a partner leaves or dies. Corporations do not entail this problem in that an owner who seeks to exit the corporation can simply liquidate her or his position in the secondary market without disrupting the firm. The separation of ownership from control in corporations, however, may make them less attractive than partnerships in some economic activities. Indeed, the shirking and monitoring costs seen as intrinsic to partnerships may even be magnified, not reduced, in a corporation. Yet once all of these trade-offs are reckoned with, there are some activities that require capital beyond amounts that partners could provide. This difference is particularly large for activities in which the minimum efficient scale is large relative to the market. In such cases incorporation is desirable.

Assume that for a subset of activities the profitability from incorporation exceeds the profitability of partnerships. Two conditions could create such a differential. If the elasticity of the total return with respect to capital is sufficiently large, then the corporate form of the business would have a higher total return than the partnership because the scale of the activity under the corporation is higher.[48] The second channel is one in which the productivity of capital is greater for the corporation than it is for the partnership, even if the amount of capital the entrepreneur can pool is the same under both forms. If both effects are present, then the gains from incorporation are compounded.

In the absence of political and regulatory obstacles the entrepreneur's choice would be simple: if the expected profitability of incorporation exceeded that of the partnership, the entrepreneur would incorporate. However, under the restrictive regime an entrepreneur had to take into account not only the internal benefits and costs of incorporating but also factors external to the firm. These included the costs of seeking a corporate charter, the probability that the government would approve the charter, and the likelihood that government would honor the charter once the entrepreneur had invested. These costs were all plainly apparent in Brazil until 1883. Under the best of circumstances petitioning for charters required costly political lobbying. Petitions for charters could be denied on minor technical grounds after a lengthy delay. The terms of approved charters might not be those that organizers sought, making the project less attractive to investors and undermining the entrepreneur's business plan. Many political decision makers, like Rodrigues Torres, viewed joint-stock companies as an exceptional form of business, of public interest as well as private, and thus subject to intervention whenever government saw fit. Mauá's experience in 1853 is a case in point.

To see the impact of the restrictions in a simplified setting, consider an entrepreneur who seeks to create a new business in an activity that is best undertaken using the corporate form, because it offers a higher total return to capital than would the partnership form of the firm. For the sake of exposition, there are two investment options: business, which produces an uncertain entrepreneurial return, and shares of government debt, which yield a relatively stable market return. The entrepreneur can always earn the market return on his wealth by investing in public debt. Any wealth that is not invested in the business is allocated to apólices. The profit-maximizing amount of capital invested in the business increases in the elasticity of the return with respect to capital, in the probability that the government will honor the charter, and in the productivity of capital. If charter petition costs are too high or the probability of approval too low or the risk of ex post expropriation too high, the entrepreneur eschews incorporation.[49] In that case the partnership is chosen so long as the expected return exceeds that of the outside option, which is apólices. If the amount of capital that can be raised under the partnership is too small for the business to be viable, then the entrepreneur does not invest and holds wealth only in apólices.

Several illustrative cases are worth detailing. The first sets an efficiency benchmark in which petitions to incorporate are approved with certainty at only a trivial cost and there is no risk of ex post expropriation. Assuming the return of the activity undertaken as a corporation exceeds that of the partnership, the entrepreneur will choose to incorporate. At the other extreme is the case in which there is no chance the government will approve the corporation. The entrepreneur will not waste money on a petition and will move directly to creating a partnership (so long as there are expected profits from doing so), even when a corporation would otherwise be the preferred form of the firm. If the expected profitability of the activity organized as a partnership is too low, the entrepreneur does not undertake the enterprise at all and instead invests all wealth in public debt. This scenario is costly to the economy; it impels the entrepreneur to create the business through the wrong organizational form or to refrain from the undertaking altogether.[50] Two intermediate cases are relevant as well. In the first there is a cost to petitioning and there is also expropriation risk, but a charter will be automatically granted. In such a case the petition cost must be low enough and the return differential large enough for the entrepreneur to incorporate. Otherwise the entrepreneur prefers the partnership. Finally, the most general scenario is one in which there is some probability of a petition being approved, a cost to petitioning, some risk of expropriation, and a productivity differential between the corporation and the proprietorship. The entrepreneur's choice depends on the overall configuration of parameter. If all the costs of incorporating, taken together, are sufficiently large, the entrepreneur will not petition for a charter. Restrictions on incorporation result in a level of business investment that is lower than it would be with open incorporation, and more of the entrepreneur's wealth is allocated to public debt.

CAPITAL FORMATION AND JOINT-STOCK COMPANIES:
DIMENSIONS AND TIMING

On the basis of this framework several hypotheses regarding the impact of the changes in the regulations governing incorporation can be formed. If government restrictions on incorporation impacted entrepreneurs' choices of organizational form, then changes in those restrictions should be visible in the changes in the number and types of firms created over time. The entrepreneur's condition for incorporation was less likely to be met with restrictions that either increased the cost of seeking a charter or presented a sufficiently high risk of expropriation. Such restrictions were broadly relevant until 1883. Before the adoption of the commercial code in 1850 the threshold for incorporation was difficult for entrepreneurs to meet. After 1850 the condition became easier to satisfy simply because the commercial code at least defined the process by which a charter could be pursued. While this process was still political, it was nonetheless more accessible. Newly tightened restrictions imposed in 1860 reduced the probability of a petition being approved and likely raised the cost of petitioning. This regulatory change can be predicted to have pushed entrepreneurs toward forming partnerships and away from incorporation. The reform of December 1882 that made incorporation a simple act of registration for most firms meant that petitions were approved with certainty. It reduced the cost of securing a charter for most types of business and very likely reduced expropriation risk by depoliticizing the process of incorporation.

The empirical analysis consists of three partial tests of the hypothesis that changes in government restrictions on incorporation resulted in changes in the number or form of new firms selected by entrepreneurs. The first test is relatively exploratory in nature, using annual time-series evidence on the number of corporate charters granted in order to identify shifts in chartering activity. The second test uses data for Rio de Janeiro from 1850 through 1865 on both the creation of partnerships with partially limited liability (comanditas) and the formation of new corporations. The advantage of these data is that they exclude sole proprietorships and common partnerships. This restricts the cases considered to those firms created by entrepreneurs who sought to both pool capital and obtain limitations on investor liability. Changes in the rate of creation of the two types of firms permit inferences about the impact of regulatory change in 1860. The third test charts changes in the capitalization of joint-stock corporations listed on the Rio stock exchange from the 1850s through the 1880s. A prediction of the model is that regulatory changes impact the choice of organizational form as well as the amount of capital invested in business. The third test takes this dimension into account.

The first test locates durable changes in the number of new corporate charters over time. Shifts that coincide with changes in regulations on incorporation would support the view that regulations mattered in entrepreneurs' choices of the organizational form. Shifts at other points in time do not necessarily run against the hypothesis; other factors and events could independently impact the supply of and demand for charters. Without analogous data on the creation of comandita partnerships as the alternative to incorporation, the test necessarily remains a partial one. The focus is on charters to firms originating within Brazil.[51] The charters were culled from all executive decrees related to business regulation, including reforms of statutes, authorization of local branches of foreign firms, increases in the authorized capital of existing firms, and mergers.[52] The annual charter series runs from 1808 up through 1900. There is some concern that the series may understate the number of charters in the 1890s, as state governments under the Republic took on an important role in business regulation. However, truncating the series to a shorter period (say, to 1889) risks missing any break in the late 1880s. The data are well suited to the Bai-Perron approach to identifying break points.[53] There are five breaks in the series: in 1850, 1871, and 1887 chartering activity shifted durably upward, while 1877 and 1892 were years marking the onset of persistently lower levels of chartering.[54] Table 6.1 reports the econometric results and the break years.

The timing of the shifts is noteworthy for two reasons. First, some of them correspond to changes in the laws regulating incorporation. Second, they make clear that legal changes per se were not the only factors that could impact corporate chartering. The sharp positive break in 1850 in particular corresponds to the creation of the commercial code. As restrictive as it was, it nonetheless liberalized the policy on incorporation. Brazil went from having no clear mechanism for chartering to having one that was similar to that of Britain under the Bubble Act. The commercial code was a definite improvement over the status quo, which over a period of more than four decades had resulted in the issuance of only a handful of charters. One might expect that the more restrictive regulatory regime that began in 1860 would reduce the volume of corporate charters. Yet 1860 does not register as a break point. The new and tighter restrictions did not prohibit incorporation outright. Rather, they assigned additional discretionary control to the government over which firms would get charters.

A burst of new chartering activity in the early 1870s, which occurred under the more restrictive legislation, suggests how government

Table 6.1

Break Points in the Issue of New Corporate Charters, 1808–1900

BREAKS (T_i)	BOUNDARY YEARS FOR 90% CONFIDENCE INTERVAL	
1850	1850	1850
1871	1870	1874
1877	1876	1877
1887	1870	1887
1892	1892	1901

PARAMETER	β_i	CORRECTED STANDARD ERRORS
β_1	0.26	0.09***
β_2	11.3	2.81***
β_3	36.3	3.33***
β_4	9.45	2.47***
β_5	56.5	25.80***
β_6	4.0	0.66***

R-squared$=0.62$

$F(6, 87)=23.6$

$n=93$

*** significant at 1% level

Note: The charters are those for firms originating in Brazil and exclude those foreign firms seeking to establish operations in Brazil. The parameter estimates give the average number of newly chartered firms for each segment of the series. Both the UD max and WD max tests (not reported) support the existence of breaks against the null of no breaks. The 5 percent trimming parameter limits the minimum interval between breaks to four years. The five breaks selected under the Bayesian Information Criterion are reported.

discretion over chartering worked. Government subsidies to certain firms, especially railroads, resulted in an increase in charters even under less-than-favorable procedures for incorporation. The sharp upward shift in charters in 1871 was also clearly linked to victory over Paraguay. The end of the war, combined with an increase in coffee export earnings, may well have spurred expectations of profit in new business opportunities. But the supply of charters mattered as well. The shift highlighted how limited access to incorporation during the 1860s had served as a form of financial repression to help fund the war. The model above showed that if incorporation is sufficiently unattractive (because of either high chartering costs or high expropriation risk), entrepreneurs channel a larger share of their wealth into low-risk assets. Low-risk assets were the securities that had been issued in ever larger amounts during the war, namely, apólices, bonds of the National Loan of 1868, and Treasury bills. The government had not tapped the London market between 1865 and the end of the war, and as a result it needed to increasingly draw on domestic savings to absorb its growing issues of bonds and bills. By limiting the supply of new corporate charters it could, in effect, force an increment of private savings into its coffers. The timing of the increase in chartering strongly suggests that precisely such a phenomenon had taken hold in the late 1860s. The end of the war in 1870 reduced the growth in the government's demand for new funds at home, eased its reentry into the London capital market, and lessened the need to squeeze more savings out of Brazilians. As a result, the government looked more favorably on incorporation. Once this initial postwar burst in chartering was over and the government needed to boost its borrowing again for drought relief, chartering tightened up, as reflected in a downward shift around 1877.

The liberalization of incorporation in 1882 does not appear as a break in the chartering data. Scrutiny of the data reveals that chartering activity picked up in the two years immediately preceding the new law and fell off right after it. This pattern is less mysterious than it might seem. It is consistent with the continued use of discretionary authority to cherry-pick projects rather than with a ban on incorporation altogether. By 1882 political momentum to liberalize incorporation had been building for years. The uptick in charters around 1880 may have reflected this shift in political sentiment. The legal liberalization of incorporation at the end of 1882 was as much a lagging indicator of the new policy preferences as anything else.

If the absence of a shift in the chartering data in 1882 rules out an immediate impact from the law, it does not mean the law was irrelevant. One episode in particular makes this especially manifest. In 1888 there was a massive increase in the money supply and credit, as the cabinet promoted the creation of banks with the right to issue currency.

Grafted onto the liberalization of incorporation after 1882, this sharp increase in liquidity resulted in a similarly sharp increase in incorporation. Entrepreneurs both gained access to cheap credit and leveraged the ready availability of the limited liability form of the firm. Easy credit alone would have no doubt raised investment. That the expansion took place in a setting where entrepreneurs could freely choose the organizational form of their business made more capital-intensive undertakings feasible. The number of corporations in Rio de Janeiro more than doubled in a year. The resulting boom bridged the end of the Empire in 1889 and the first years of the Republic. If this boom was magnified by the Republican reforms in 1890 that reduced the liability of investors in firms that had not fully paid in their capital, it was also well under way before the constitutional monarchy was overthrown. The negative break in chartering in 1892 is consistent with the deflating bubble that ended the *encilhamento* stock boom. The firms that were speculatively organized after the reform of 1890 with only part of their capital paid in made for a house of cards. Once liquidity dried up, the demand for new corporate charters fell back to levels consistent with the pre-bubble run-up.

The second test considers whether the more restrictive incorporation procedures adopted in 1860 impelled some entrepreneurs to select comandita partnerships rather than corporations. The impact of the 1860 law, at least in the short term, can be detected in the contrast between two measures of firm formation. The first is presented in figure 6.1, which reports the capital of joint-stock companies newly authorized each year from 1851 through November 1865 (at current prices). From 1851 through 1860 the government authorized annually on average an additional 11.4 million milréis of domestic joint-stock capital. From 1861 through 1865, in the wake of the adoption of the law of impediments, new government authorizations of capital fell to an average of only 2.7 million milréis per year. One might be tempted to believe that a few large corporations created in the 1850s might bias the magnitude of this shift. Yet the pre-1860 data purposely exclude the two largest firms of the decade, the Banco do Brasil and the Dom Pedro II railroad. This elision biases the test against finding a change between the two periods. Had these two firms been included, the pre-1860 averages would have been much larger and the decline after 1860 even more precipitous.

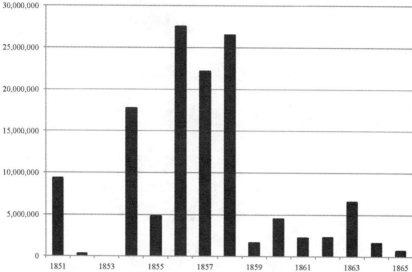

FIGURE 6.1 Newly authorized joint-stock companies, 1851–65 (milréis). These figures exclude both the Banco do Brasil, which incorporated in 1854, and the Estrada de Ferro Dom Pedro II, which incorporated in 1856. Both were high-capital firms (30 million and 38 million milréis, respectively), the creation of which depended heavily on government subsidy or privilege. Including them would increase the pre-1861 figures by a good deal, further strengthening the argument in the text. (Calculated from figures in Brazil, Ministério da Justiça, *Relatório* [Rio de Janeiro, 1866], appendix I)

The closest alternative to the corporation was the sociedade em comandita. The limitations that a partnership placed on firm size have already been noted. The pace of creation of comandita partnerships after the law of impediments in 1860 can be contrasted with the falloff in the formation of corporations. There was no change to the intrinsic attractiveness of comandita partnerships in 1860. Yet, as figure 6.2 shows, the average rate of formation of comandita partnerships accelerated following the new restrictions on incorporation. Considering the evidence in figures 6.1 and 6.2 together, the rate of investment in new corporations fell at the same time that the number of new limited liability partnerships increased. The inference to be drawn is clear: the 1860 law likely caused at least some entrepreneurs to select the partnership form, as Mauá ultimately did. In terms of the model, the increased regulatory scrutiny requiring that charters for many types of firms not only be approved by the cabinet and parliament but also be reviewed by the Council of State either

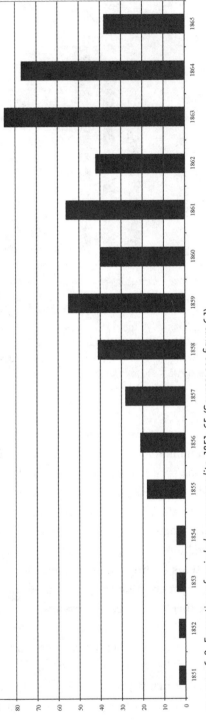

FIGURE 6.2 Formation of *sociedades em comandita*, 1851–65 (Source: see figure 6.1)

reduced the probability that a charter would be granted or raised the cost of seeking a charter or both.

The third test focuses on the timing of changes in capital formation by corporations that listed on the exchange in Rio de Janeiro between 1851 and 1888. Like the first test, it does not address limited liability partnerships because there is no comparable evidence on the amount of capital formed in the latter over the same period. It also necessarily excludes joint-stock firms that did not list on the Rio exchange. Yet two considerations recommend this measure as a partial test. First, an increase in the number of new firms listed would indicate a more general increase in the total capital in corporations in Rio de Janeiro. Second, there could be effects from the shift to a less restrictive incorporation regime that are not visible in the number of corporations. The model predicts that the amount of capital allocated by entrepreneurs and investors to business investment depends in part on the perceived risk of expropriation. If investors reduce their assessments of the probability of expropriation, the total amount of capital in existing joint-stock firms could increase. Perceptions of expropriation risk were likely influenced by the type of incorporation regime. Indeed, the very politicization of business entry that underpinned the regime of restrictive incorporation could have caused investors to view the risk of expropriation as being high. Liberalization of incorporation would then imply a relative depoliticization of business investment and could signal investors that expropriation would be viewed as illegitimate and hence less likely.

Together these effects direct attention to changes in the total paid-in capital of companies listed on the Rio exchange. Table 6.2 presents estimates of the paid-in capital of limited liability joint-stock firms at various intervals from 1851, right after the adoption of the commercial code, to 1888.[55] The estimates have been built up on a firm-by-firm basis from stock listings in the contemporary commercial press.[56] These are left in their nominal (current price) form. Entrepreneurs' investment decisions did not revolve around considerations of the firm's capital in constant prices (i.e., a decrease in the real value of the firm's paid-in capital did not occasion new investment to make up for the "loss"). In the absence of stockbroker yearbooks there is some uncertainty regarding how complete the tally of companies is for Rio in 1851. Up to 1850 at least five surviving firms in Rio had already taken on the joint-stock form. The value

Table 6.2

Paid-In Equity Capital of Domestic Joint-Stock Companies
Traded on the Rio de Janeiro Stock Exchange, 1851–88

YEAR	PAID-IN CAPITAL (IN MILRÉIS)
1851	3,840,000
1855	39,925,000
1860	86,691,916
1865	81,117,164
1870	71,390,337
1875	162,191,740
1880	143,877,251
1885	251,704,160
1888	250,202,942*

* This figure does not include 62.4 million milréis of debenture shares
that had been issued mainly between 1881 and 1888.
Note: Figures include British-based freestanding companies that operated
in Brazil and whose shares occasionally traded on the exchange.
Sources: See text.

of the paid-in capital for these firms is available in the late 1840s only for
the Banco Commercial. Four of these five companies later registered as
sociedades anônimas with the board of commerce within the first year
of the new commercial code. The registry recorded the companies' authorized levels of capital but not how much had initially been paid in. In
addition to the four existing firms, seven others registered in the first year
after the adoption of the code. Of those seven firms, it is possible to estimate the amounts paid in for five.[57] The estimated paid-in capital for all
of the joint-stock firms known to have issued shares by 1851 comes to
around 3.8 million milréis.[58]

The 1850s was truly a boom decade in the Rio capital and money markets, and the growth of listed firms on the exchange reflects this. Between 1851 and 1860 sociedades anônimas were permitted to organize
relatively freely so long as they could secure a charter. The expansion depended on several factors. The end of the transatlantic slave trade, as
noted, figured into the boom as well: "As a consequence of the complete
repression of the trade in Africans, capital previously employed in illicit

transactions flowed into the market, from which resulted a decline of 3.5 percent to 4 percent per year in discounts, and an extraordinary increase in the prices of shares of all companies."[59] The expressive growth in corporations from 1851 to 1855 increased the capital formed by more than an order of magnitude, rising to nearly 40 million milréis, paid in to thirty-three firms.[60] From 1855 through 1860 the value of joint-stock capital more than doubled again. With the 1860 law things stalled. Between 1861 and 1865 there was no increase in the paid-in equity of Rio corporations; on the contrary, capital fell, as several companies failed and there was little new entry.

The slowdown in capital formation in new corporations that followed the 1860 law was no doubt exacerbated through 1870 by a local financial crisis in 1864 and then especially by Brazil's war against Paraguay. The nominal value of paid-in corporate equity in Rio actually declined even further between 1865 and 1870, to only 71 million milréis. The end of the war, however, saw a dramatic turnaround in the Rio stock market. Money invested in corporations more than doubled over the short interval of five years. This record of increase was not accompanied by any major legal or regulatory changes. Three factors help explain the rapid expansion. First, on the heels of the victory over Paraguay, the government reduced a good deal of its floating internal debt by undertaking new foreign borrowing. This released local funds previously invested in short-term Treasury bills for investment in private sector activities.[61] Second, the victory reduced the need to limit charters as part of a strategy of financial repression, as argued above. Third, specific market interventions by the state at times accelerated the pace of incorporation dramatically, but in a highly directed manner. Major investments, many subsidized by government, appeared in the first half of the 1870s, with new corporations for railroads, streetcars, urban lighting, and shipping.[62] The rapid increase in joint-stock capital in the immediate postwar years was not sustained, however, in the period 1875–80.

The 1882 reform of the commercial code was the most important step taken toward liberalization of the incorporation in Brazil since 1850. The econometric analysis did not find a sudden increase in chartering activity. The law's impact was no doubt more gradual. Although several scholars have highlighted the significance of the 1882 law, others have dismissed the importance of the reform.[63] There are several reasons why one would not observe an immediate increase in new corporations. One is that the reform came in the midst of a significant economic downturn. At the end of 1882, business in Rio de Janeiro was still in a slump because of the fall in the price of coffee from the late 1870s. One would expect an increase in new firms only with a cyclical recovery. The large upward shift in 1887 (see table 6.1) is consistent with this scenario.[64] Additionally, the liberalization in 1882 signaled to the market that Brazil had shifted to a regime in which expropriation risk was reduced in a broader sense (by reducing government's discretionary authority over private-sector investment decisions). One would expect to see an increase in the amount of capital formed in corporations. The large increase in the capital of the companies on the exchange in the 1880s is consistent with this prediction. From 1880 to 1885 paid-in capital increased by 75 percent. Moreover, corporate debt became an appreciable component of finance for the first time. Debt took the form of debentures that paid a fixed coupon. These had first appeared in the Rio market in 1878, and their issue was formally sanctioned under the law of 1882. The creation of new debenture debt provided an additional 62 million milréis in capital for joint-stock firms in Rio by 1888.

Finally, there was a tremendous increase both in new firms on the exchange and in capitalization in late 1888 and in 1889.[65] The banking reform undertaken by the cabinet of the visconde de Ouro Preto led to a credit boom that juiced the market. But the institutional conditions in which the boom began were the result of the liberalization of 1882. One inference that can be drawn from the timing and extent of these changes is that corporations in Imperial Brazil labored not only under regulatory limits on entry but also under credit constraints arising from the Empire's small, concentrated banking sector. Fixing the first problem helped make solutions to the second problem possible, which then redounded to growth of finance in general.

CONCLUSION

The Brazilian state gave entrepreneurs no general legal basis for incorporation before 1850. Once it did establish mechanisms for incorporation, it reserved for the cabinet the authority to determine if a firm would be permitted to raise funds by issuing shares and to operate with limited liability. The impediments law of 1860 expanded discretionary political authority over incorporation for many types of firms. Despite a secular decline in the costs of public borrowing, capital remained difficult to obtain in the private sector. Legislators and cabinet ministers from the Liberal party sought to reduce the restrictiveness of these laws in the late 1860s and 1870s. The levers of business regulation were firmly in the hands of politicians, not the market, for six decades after independence. The passage of the companies' law at the end of 1882 simply came too late to repair the economic record of the Empire. In Brazil the very form of the firm that in the United States accounted for a growing share of industrial output was beyond the reach of entrepreneurs who did not enjoy political favor. The result was financial underdevelopment.

Most arguments about the relationship between sovereign commitment and successful financial development draw heavily on the experiences of North Atlantic economies. Drawing on the British historical experience, North and Weingast argued that political institutions that credibly commit the sovereign to repay debt also promote financial development. Imperial Brazil sharply diverged from this ideal. There was little hint of broader financial development more than a half century after the adoption of political institutions that committed the government to honor its debt. The very political institutions that worked so effectively to enhance sovereign creditworthiness fostered restrictive regulations that undermined the ability of firms and entrepreneurs to flexibly choose the best organizational form for their businesses. In the absence of a corporate charter, it was simply impossible to raise appreciable amounts of capital through the market. Financial development was not a reflexive response to improved government creditworthiness. The connection between public finance and private capital market development depended on specific institutional details and political circumstances. Why legal restrictions on incorporation were not lifted before 1882 is a question of the Empire's political history that remains to be more fully explored. But the apparent contradiction between a state that committed to a property right for its bondholders, yet at the same time hindered the mobilization of capital for new enterprises, becomes more intelligible when one considers the public finance implications of the government's discretionary authority over incorporation. At moments when the government's demand for funds increased or when it was at its external credit ceiling, restrictions on capital's ability to find entrepreneurial uses helped to shake loose new domestic credit for the state. Restricted access to the corporate form served as a rudimentary and blunt form of financial repression. Up to 1850, when internal political instability posed a recurrent threat to the state, obstacles to incorporation meant that domestic wealth holders seeking additional investment opportunities steered part of their money to government debt. The decline in borrowing costs and renewed access to the London loan market at midcentury alleviated the state's credit constraint, coinciding with a new and more liberal regime of incorporation under the 1850 commercial code. Greater discretionary authority over incorporation after 1860 proved useful during the war, when the Treasury hit its credit limit in London and the government's demand for local funds spiked. The government's return to the London market in 1871 provided new access to credit at nearly the same moment that numerous new railroads needed to use the corporate form to raise their initial capital. Loosening restrictions on incorporation in the early 1870s required no changes in the law. This permissiveness did not last. Lower levels of corporate chartering activity in the late 1870s coincided with heavy government borrowing in response to the severe northeastern drought. The continued improvement in the government's credit at home and abroad in the 1880s, with lower borrowing costs and a rapidly increasing volume of loans, once again coincided with less restrictive incorporation.

The rough correlation between changes in the Treasury's demand for new funds and changes in access to the corporate form suggests a public finance motive for the state's policy. Nonetheless, the barrier to entry created by restrictions on the corporate form was not without support in the market; it conferred highly valued benefits on incumbent firms. Financial repression in this form was consistent with the state's fiscal needs. It was also consistent with rent-seeking behavior by privileged companies. The coincidence of restrictive incorporation in the financial sector on the one hand and the privileged standing of selected firms on the other can be illustrated by turning to the role of insiders in commercial banking.

CHAPTER SEVEN

Concentration and Cronyism

COMMERCIAL BANKING IN RIO DE JANEIRO

DESPITE THE DECLINE in the government's own borrowing costs over the nineteenth century, Brazil's planters and entrepreneurs continued to pay high, even exorbitant, rates of interest to borrow. By the mid- to late 1870s the best rates were those charged to coffee planters in Rio de Janeiro, around 8 percent a year.[1] This average was depressed by loans from the Banco do Brasil. The bank's low rates were not typical—it screened for high-quality borrowers, reducing its risk. Rates for coffee planters in the Paraiba valley who had to borrow from merchants and other nonbank lenders were higher, between 8.8 and 11 percent per year. Outside of the core coffee zone, borrowing was even more expensive. In 1873 the Banco Mercantil da Bahia noted that farmers in the province were paying 12 percent interest a year for their loans, most of which were short term in nature.[2] Borrowers in Espírito Santo and Rio Grande do Sul similarly paid 10 to 12 percent interest. Interest rates were as high as 24 percent in Rio Grande do Norte, São Paulo, and Minas Gerais. In Pernambuco rates were even higher than in Bahia, nearly 30 percent a year. In some places it was even worse. In the province of Paraiba the cost to borrow ran as high as 72 percent a year.[3] Interest rates at that level, for all intents and purposes, rationed farmers out of the credit market. Almost no one could pay that much and remain in business. The government obtained money locally for as little as 5.7 percent. But for borrowers in the private sector capital was not cheap.

One feature that was common to many of the countries that had early revolutions in both public and private finance was the development of commercial banking. Commercial banks engaged in short-term lending and the discounting of bills. Banks complemented the securities markets that financed the longer-term capital requirements of firms.[4] One might expect banks to help fill the financing void in Imperial Brazil, where the institutional environment disfavored access to equity investment via limited liability incorporation. Yet more than six decades after independence, Brazil's banking sector remained small and concentrated. The few commercial banks that operated during the Imperial era were wholly inadequate for the purpose of financing modern economic growth. Barriers to entry in commercial banking compounded the debilitating consequences of restrictions on incorporation.

One possible explanation for the small size of the banking sector—and the one that is stressed here—is the role of political barriers to entry. An alternative view is that such barriers were not decisive. In this view low demand for financial services limited the number of banks. Since Brazil had a simple economic structure, other intermediaries, such as coffee factors and merchants, could satisfy much of the real sector's financial needs. The dearth of banking was a result, not a cause, of underdevelopment. The problem with this view is that Brazilian agriculture required more credit than could be supplied by just a few banks. The scale of the coffee sector alone was huge. Planting was a multiyear investment problem that required short-term credit as well as longer-term loans. Because the basic labor costs for an appreciable share of the workforce were fully capitalized as the prices of slaves, the need to finance labor acquisition would have further raised loan demand. Foreign trade, which grew larger decade over decade, also required sources of credit. Yet the banking sector was persistently small, and interest rates were remarkably high. Given that the basic services that commercial banks supplied were used intensively, it is unlikely that a lack of demand for banking services explains the small size of the commercial banking sector. Instead, institutional features, underpinned by fiscal needs and particular political interests, helped to restrict entry and kept the number of joint-stock banks low.

All of the restrictions that banks faced in Brazil were the result of the nearly total concentration of authority in the hands of the central government. Extreme administrative, regulatory, and political centralization heavily limited the accountability of policy makers to the broader class of citizens with commercial interests. The retention of authority over bank entry at the highest level could be useful in some respects but highly detrimental in others. For example, the government's delegation of monetary authority to the new Banco do Brasil was designed to increase credit while helping to provide a stable currency. Yet the 1860 law requiring full gold backing for banknotes effectively eliminated banks of issue other than the Banco do Brasil. The cabinet subsequently required meticulous review of every petition to create a company. Conducted by the emperor's Council of State, the review made the process of obtaining a bank charter more arbitrary and inefficient. Appointed for life, the councilors had no electoral connection to entrepreneurs, and a negative opinion from them virtually guaranteed that the project would not receive legislative sanction. More generally, the limited political accountability of policy makers to constituents in need of banking services is known to stymie financial development, precisely because it tends to restrict entry of new banks into the market.[5]

Ironically, the same political centralization that allowed the state to extract taxes effectively and to politically commit to service its debt also accounts for an array of formal and informal barriers to bank entry. The result was commercial bank concentration, market power, high interest rates for borrowers, and high bank profits. Worse still, the rent-seeking opportunity this institutional arrangement created meant that the restrictions on entry took on a self-enforcing quality. Groups that were already well established in banking had incentives to support entry barriers on firms that would become competitive rivals. In Rio de Janeiro the wealthy, well-connected individuals involved in commercial banking were, in effect, privileged incumbents in a setting in which aspiring banks could be refused entry by being denied limited liability incorporation. The prevailing restrictions on bank creation reduced the level of competition and allowed existing banks the opportunity to garner economic rents— profits beyond those that could be secured in a competitive market—on their lending activities.

There is no evidence that these banks organized an overt lobby or interest group to steer policy toward barring new entry. Rather, incumbent banks individually secured their position by appointing prominent politicians as bank directors (or by otherwise establishing close ties with statesmen), often when they were still sitting officeholders in the national government. This particular form of political-financial cronyism reinforced the institutional obstacles to entry in banking. Limits on entry kept the bulk of banking assets concentrated among relatively few banks and allowed incumbent banks to generate higher returns, on average, to their investors than a more competitive environment would have permitted. The resulting underdevelopment of credit markets meant that Brazilians taking loans, whether from banks or private parties, faced high borrowing costs.

This chapter assesses the evolution of joint-stock commercial banking in Rio de Janeiro. The findings occupy five sections. The first highlights general issues in the relationship between banking and financial development and sketches the principal activities of Rio's joint-stock commercial banks. The second turns to the role of government in banking. Section three presents original indicators of financial underdevelopment, using evidence from private loan contracts and the structure of the banking sector. Section four examines the direct connections between bankers and politicians to illustrate the nature of financial cronyism. Section five tests the hypothesis that the largest bank in a highly concentrated market had persistently high profits. A sixth section considers the reforms of the late 1880s in light of the Empire's decades-long restrictions on banking, while the final section concludes.

WHAT BANKS DID

In the nineteenth century banks had several ways to create credit. One was to lend the money pooled by equity investors directly to borrowers. A second was to make loans using a portion of deposits. A third was to make loans by issuing banknotes, if permitted to do so by government. In varying degrees banks in Imperial Brazil did all of these things. Lending most often took the form of the bank discounting commercial paper, which involved the purchase of short-term loans held by other creditors, often merchants or retailers, and then holding the note until it matured. Long-term loans by Rio banks were so rare as to be nearly nonexistent early on, appearing only with the creation of specialized mortgage banking in the late 1860s. Even the rapid expansion of the banking sector from late 1889 into the early 1890s was not accompanied by a sudden shift to long-term bank lending. Deposit banking was similarly modest.[6] Lending by issuing banknotes was sporadic. With the exception of the periods 1808–29, 1853–66, and 1889 only the Treasury issued currency that was legal tender.

The joint-stock banks in Rio de Janeiro were of two types: commercial and mortgage. Initially, commercial banks issued notes, even when they were not chartered as banks of issue. These notes took the form of *vales*, which under the law were valid for only a brief period. During periods of limited liquidity vales often remained in circulation beyond the legal limit. Before 1866 a few commercial banks also garnered the privilege of issuing longer-term banknotes. The Banco do Brasil began in 1853 with a monopoly of note issue. Other banks, including the Banco Commercial & Agrícola and the Banco Rural & Hypothecário in Rio de Janeiro, along with the Banco de Pernambuco, Banco do Maranhão, and the Banco da Bahia, issued notes through a series of cabinet decrees in 1857 and 1858.[7] The government blocked new issues of notes in 1860, and in 1862 restored the Banco do Brasil's monopoly of issue, until the Treasury reclaimed the sole right to issue currency in 1866 during the war against Paraguay.

The most common line of business in commercial banking involved several different forms of short-term finance. The array of banking services in the 1880s was fairly typical of the period that began in the early 1850s. The second Banco Commercial was organized in 1866 and resembled a high-end pawnshop in certain respects. It advertised itself as a bank that "discounts Treasury bills, and those bills of banks and the market; makes loans against apólices, the stocks of banks and companies, gold, silver, and diamonds, goods, and commercial bills; and provides mortgage loans for urban buildings in this city." The English Bank of Rio de Janeiro listed services involving nearly every financial instrument and brokerage transaction imaginable under the commercial code. These included the "discount [of drafts]; pays interest on current deposits; emission of special credit on money deposited or guaranty; emission of credit on the principal markets of Europe; transfers funds in foreign markets; contracts and purchases of foreign exchange; purchase and sale of precious metals," along with "the purchase and sale of any securities, including apólices, shares of banks and companies, etc., and accepts the collection of drafts, reception and payment of interests and dividends, and money transfers, at reasonable commissions, etc., etc."[8]

Mortgage banking was less common than short-term lending against collateral and the discount of commercial paper. Dedicated mortgage lending was first introduced in 1866 with the creation of the mortgage account within the Banco do Brasil.[9] With the exception of the Banco do Brasil, the banks specializing in mortgages were barred from engaging in other types of lending and commercial banking operations. The few mortgage banks in existence provided long-term financing, but only for the most creditworthy members of the planter class and urban property owners. The Banco de Crédito Real do Brazil made "mortgage loans on urban and rural properties," while the Banco Predial "made loans in mortgage bonds, for mortgages on rural and urban properties," for periods from ten to thirty years.[10]

GOVERNMENT AND BANKING

The special importance of banks in financial development has long occupied the interest of scholarly investigators. While there may still be no consensus on the strict necessity of banking for financial development, there is little disagreement about what banks can contribute.[11] The potential of banks to boost financial development rests with their ability to mobilize savings and allocate credit, matching savers and borrowers in a way that properly accounts for risk. To the extent that banks could mobilize capital more effectively by being larger, joint-stock banks had particularly high potential. By creating a joint-stock bank, a potentially large number of investors could pool capital, which then could be used to grant loans to entrepreneurs and other borrowers. For relatively backward economies, Gerschenkron famously stressed the role banks could play as substitutes for both securities markets and self-financing on the part of industrial entrepreneurs.[12] Universal banking of the type found in Germany, by way of example, did partly substitute in a direct fashion for securities markets, providing long-term lending to companies.[13]

Still, bank credit need not take the form of long-term loans, and long-term lending was not a necessary condition for banks to play an important financial role. Even the seemingly modest contributions by banks engaged principally in short-term lending served a valuable function for merchants, planters, and entrepreneurs. Irrespective of the size or duration of loans, banks contributed to efficiency by screening borrowers for quality, in terms of their likelihood of repayment. Repayment of private sector loans depended on the viability of the project the entrepreneur undertook. Banks performed a valuable risk management function, taking care to preserve the capital of equity shareholders by lending prudently. It was the banks' risk management role that made them an important source of productivity in financial intermediation. While banking varied in its relative importance to overall finance across countries and over time, in every case where banks were permitted to operate, and operated in a legitimate fashion, they proved to be valuable financial intermediaries.

The Empire's dearth of joint-stock commercial banks was one of several obstacles to long-term lending. Property rights complicated long-term mortgage lending. Debtor rights under the law were strong, which exacerbated credit rationing. Foreclosure on a farm in the case of nonperformance involved a legal process of forced adjudication, potentially costing the creditor more than the collateral pledged against the debt was worth.[14] This in turn made it difficult for borrowers to collateralize assets (especially land), left lenders vulnerable to ex post opportunism on the part of the borrowers, and undermined long-term agricultural lending.[15] Unless a borrower obtained a loan from the specialized mortgage-lending department of the Banco do Brasil or one of the few other mortgage lenders, long-term borrowing secured by real property was nearly impossible to obtain. Even if a borrower was able to gain access to shorter-term credit they still encountered high interest rates. For example, in 1873 the Banco Mercantil da Bahia expressed an interest in engaging in rural mortgage lending, noting that farmers in the province were paying as much as 12 percent interest a year for their loans, most of which were short term in nature.[16]

The main problem was that the only way to incorporate as a joint-stock bank was to first obtain permission to do so from the central government. Brazilian policy toward banking was similar to that found during the period 1844–57 in England, when commercial bank entry was restricted by law. Yet these thirteen years in England were an interregnum in an era of growing liberality that allowed commercial bank entry on a large scale.[17] In Brazil, by contrast, the sorts of restrictions that prevailed in England for less than a decade and a half characterized most of the nineteenth century. There was a public finance logic underpinning the government's heavy control of joint-stock banking. This does not mean that the government was opposed to banking. It needed at least some banks to facilitate its domestic borrowing. The pre-independence creation of the first Banco do Brasil is the country's earliest example. Between 1809 and 1829 the government's reliance on the bank to finance public expenditures left Brazil with an inconvertible currency and a hefty portion of its early public debt.[18]

After the expiration of the first Banco do Brasil's charter, a handful of commercial banks, including one in Rio de Janeiro, the Banco Commercial, were permitted to operate.[19] Lending to government by the new Banco do Brasil in the 1850s was conditioned on profit-generating privileges for the bank. The very basis of the new bank's existence in the 1850s was an exchange of favors between the bank's investors and the government.[20] The bank agreed to help the government retire old paper currency, replacing it with the bank's own notes that were backed by gold. Replacement of the old notes was to take place at a rate of 2 million milréis per year, until a total of 10 million milréis had been retired, thereby providing an interest-free loan to the government.[21] In return the government conferred on the bank a monopoly of banknote issue, with the Treasury giving up the right to issue any additional paper currency. Such privileges necessarily implied government-imposed limitations on entry by rivals for at least some of the bank's activities. Many policy makers viewed banks, especially those issuing notes, as sources of potential instability in money markets and markets for foreign exchange.[22] The periodic appearance of commercial crises in Rio served for contemporary critics as evidence of the excessive risk to stable money markets that banks of issue posed. Because public-sector domestic borrowing and the Treasury's cost of external debt service depended in part on favorable conditions in these same money markets, financial crises and exchange-rate fluctuations implied costs to the government. Taken together, these factors meant that most policy makers were generally predisposed to exercise heavy controls on entry by large banks.

The institutions that governed the creation of Brazil's joint-stock commercial banks were the provisions of the body of commercial law discussed in chapter 6. Government regulation of bank entry passed through four distinct phases under the Empire, phases that corresponded to the broader restrictions on incorporation. The first phase was characterized by very low entry, since there was no standing legal provision for joint-stock bank formation before 1850. A few joint-stock banks began operation in the 1830s, but they did not enjoy limited liability. The second phase began with the adoption of the first commercial code in 1850, which permitted the formation of limited liability joint-stock banks under restrictive terms (see chapter 6) and assigned the authority to grant bank charters to the parliament and cabinet. The third phase, beginning in 1860 and continuing through 1882, was more restrictive still, since joint-stock banks required the approval not only of the parliament and cabinet but also of the emperor's Council of State. The fourth phase saw a reduction of restrictions after 1882, but even then any bank seeking to issue notes required high-level government approval to operate.

Before 1850 the only basis for creating a joint-stock bank was by specific government decree. On an exceptional basis several banks, usually one in each of the major port cities involved in overseas commerce, were permitted the joint-stock form in the late 1830s.[23] The adoption of the commercial code in 1850 established the first general provision for joint-stock banks. Like other sociedades anônimas, however, banks could organize only with the approval of the cabinet. The even more restrictive law of 1860 retained this provision and added to it one by which banks could issue notes only if they adhered to convertibility in gold at a ratio of one to one.[24] Moreover, under the 1860 law, approval from the parliament, not just the cabinet, was required to create any bank that issued notes, vales, or any similar sort of monetary instrument that could substitute for currency.[25]

Though the reform of 1882 made incorporation a simple administrative procedure, the government's role in bank entry was not eliminated. The 1882 law maintained the restrictive provisions of the law of 1860 in specifically limiting entry by note-issuing banks. These continued to require parliamentary approval.[26] The 1882 law also maintained tight control over mortgage-lending banks (bancos de crédito real), which were potentially important sources of long-term credit.[27] The last major changes in banking regulations under the Empire came nearly at the end, from November 1888 to July 1889. In an effort to shore up political support for the constitutional monarchy in the wake of slavery's abolition, the government implemented several reforms that sharply boosted the role of banking in private sector finance. The first was a provision to permit multiple banks of issue for the first time since 1862.[28] The second was a large subsidy program to encourage banks to engage in mortgage lending to rural producers, concentrated heavily in coffee-growing regions where the wealth of planters had been most adversely impacted by the abolition of slavery.[29]

From its creation until late 1889, the Banco do Brasil enjoyed special status in one way or another. There were limits on its influence and role, however. When it did have the privilege of issuing notes it only rarely maintained strict convertibility in gold. To support its issue of currency, the bank maintained a reserve of gold and Treasury bills and could choose at its discretion which of the two it used to redeem its own notes. The decree authorizing the bank permitted it to issue notes on its reserves at a generous ratio of 2:1. At various points between 1854 and 1866 the bank was allowed to issue at the even higher rate of 3:1, depending on the tightness of the Rio money market. At these ratios the value of the privilege to issue was high, even when the issue required backing in gold.[30] The war with Paraguay led the government to reclaim its power to issue currency in 1866, which it then monopolized until late 1888. The reworking of the Banco do Brasil's statutes with the government in 1866 led to the creation of the special mortgage section with its own capital account, from which the bank would make long-term loans, mainly to planters in the coffee zone.

The bank did not have an exclusive arrangement with the government to handle public debt accounts. It almost captured the lion's share of the government's domestic debt servicing operations in the late 1870s. The barão de Cotegipe, in his capacity as finance minister, proposed in 1877 a new internal debt-servicing arrangement to reduce the cost of staffing the Caixa de Amortização and to place the logistics of debt service on a footing similar to that found in England. Under this arrangement the Banco do Brasil would have been responsible for retiring each year a portion of the banknotes in circulation with its own resources. In return it would have handled the annual retirement of a portion of the apólices in circulation and then used the interest paid by the government on the retired apólices to take more banknotes out of circulation.[31] A similar proposal appeared a couple of years later when the future visconde de Ouro Preto did his first stint as finance minister.[32] Neither proposal was ever implemented. The Treasury did open a deposit account in the Banco do Brasil by 1879, where it parked its surpluses. The bank also undertook foreign exchange operations on behalf of the Treasury, to which the finance minister attributed part of the improvement in the sterling value of the milréis in 1879.[33]

No bank enjoyed continuous direct subsidy from the government. It was privilege that boosted the fortunate banks. Mortgage banks, for example, were uniquely permitted to issue so-called mortgage bonds to help finance their long-term lending. These bonds did not securitize actual mortgages. On the contrary, they were the currency in which loans were extended. Borrowers then had to sell them in the market at a discount to raise cash.[34] Although the typical mortgage came due after just a few years, the banks issuing the mortgage bonds borrowed even longer and as a result did not have to fully commit their own equity to engage in lending. Exceptional government support of banks was apparent, to varying degrees, during the three crises that rocked Rio's financial sector in 1857, 1864, and 1875. The 1875 crisis involved by far the greatest degree of government assistance. The first great depression began in 1873 but took nearly two years to register an impact on the financial markets in Brazil. In 1875 several private banking houses, along with the Banco Nacional, became insolvent and suspended withdrawals by depositors and payments to creditors.[35] The Banco Nacional, along with Mauá's large private bank, were both liquidated as a result of the crisis.[36] These two failures did not mean, however, that the government pursued a policy of benign neglect. It had more pressing concerns, especially with respect to the condition of the Banco do Brasil. The government's response to the crisis took several forms. First the Banco do Brasil and then the government issued advances to financial institutions that were seen as salvageable. Over a period of four months the government extended a total of fifteen loans to three banks for slightly more than 16 million milréis. The bank repaid these loans gradually over the next nine months.[37] The three banks that received the support in turn extended new credit to clients, limiting the numbers of failures by other firms.

The Imperial government needed banks to help meet its own needs. It was not heavily dependent on commercial banks as a final market for its bonds. But the finance ministry still found banks quite invaluable for subscribing new issues, allowing the government to more easily place its short-term bills and long-term bonds in the market. Indeed, the banks' role in issuing new debt was more crucial than the role they played as holders of government bonds. Relatively few of the commercial and discount banks that reported their operations for 1873 listed bonds of the National Loans or apólices in their portfolios. The chief exception was the Banco do Brasil, which, between its combined commercial and mortgage sections, held nearly 22 million milréis of 6 percent apólices and almost 2.5 million milréis of the National Loan of 1868. With total assets of 90.5 million milréis, government securities accounted for more than a quarter of the bank's portfolio. The apólices corresponded to nearly two-thirds of all 6 percent apólices in the hands of establishments and organizations, but only around 8.5 percent of all 6 percents in circulation. The portion of the National Loan that the bank held in 1873 was nearly identical, at 8.6 percent of the bonds outstanding. Of twenty-six other banking establishments throughout Brazil, only four reported holding Imperial bonds: the Banco Nacional in Rio (around 1 million milréis in apólices), Banco de Campos (31 thousand milréis), Banco Mercantil da Bahia (822 thousand milréis), and the Caixa de Economias da Bahia (33 thousand milréis). All told, these accounted for less than 2 million milréis of all government-issued securities in circulation. Among the twenty-six banks were four foreign-owned banks—the New London and Brazilian Bank, the English Bank of Rio de Janeiro, the Banque Brésilienne-Française, and the Deutsch Brasilianische Bank—none of which enumerated apólices in their portfolios.[38] The large domestically owned commercial banks also structured and placed a number of issues for provincial governments. The Banco Commercial of Rio, for example, supplied loans for the province of Sergipe, while the Banco do Commércio similarly loaned money to the provincial government of Minas Gerais.[39]

MARKET CONCENTRATION AND BORROWING COSTS

Two basic tests are sufficient to illustrate the very limited extent of private financial development in Imperial Brazil. The first derives from original research findings on private sector lending in Rio de Janeiro, using loan contracts recorded in Rio's notary offices.[40] If the institutions that credibly committed the state to debt repayment improved private finance in the way that North and Weingast argued, one would expect private borrowing rates to fall in Brazil in the same way government borrowing costs did. Yet over the course of the nineteenth century interest rates for private loans in Rio de Janeiro remained high. They declined in the late 1860s but convergence on the government's borrowing costs was so slow as to be negligible.

Figure 7.1 presents the average annual rate of interest on private lending contracts recorded in the city from 1835, when usury limits were removed, to 1889. Interest rates on these loans were considerably higher than those on government bonds. The average spread between private market interest rates and the government's cost of capital was some 580 basis points.[41] Changes in private borrowing costs were not wholly divorced from the state's cost of capital, even if their respective levels were quite different. Private rates on borrowing from 1835 through 1843 generally followed the upward trend of apólice yields and then similarly declined through the early 1850s. Mortgage interest rates rose between 1855 and 1860 along with apólice yields and then fell slightly. The most striking divergence between the two series came during the war against Paraguay, when apólice yields jumped while mortgage rates extended and even accelerated their prewar decline.[42] One would not expect mortgage interest rates to fall in the midst of a major war. But the decline came right after the Banco do Brasil established its mortgage-lending section, which consistently charged lower interest rates than other banks. Even then average mortgage interest rates were persistently higher than the government's cost of capital. By 1885, when yields on long-term government debt were well below 6 percent in both Rio de Janeiro and London, average mortgage interest rates in Rio de Janeiro were still at 10 percent.

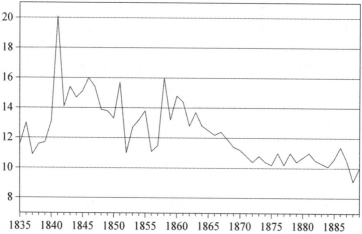

FIGURE 7.1 Average interest rates on private lending, Rio de Janeiro, 1835–89

The second indicator of financial underdevelopment was the high degree of market concentration of commercial banks in what was otherwise a reasonably competitive activity. Private banking houses and merchant lenders were relatively numerous in Rio. The main barrier to entry in private banking was simply having some money to lend. Table 7.1 provides an overview of the commercial banking sector in the city from 1855 to 1888.[43] Several features shown in the table stand out. The first is the slow rate of new entry. New banks appeared on the scene only occasionally. And not all of them survived. The 1850s was a transitional decade, one in which the near monopoly held by the original Banco Commercial was eroded with the entry of Mauá's Banco do Brasil in 1851. Monopoly was then briefly restored by the government-mandated fusion of the two banks into the third Banco do Brasil in 1853. The appearance of two other sizeable commercial banks, along with Mauá's new transatlantic banking partnership, increased competition somewhat during the decade. The 1860s witnessed the creation of only one domestic commercial bank but saw the arrival of two new British banks, which were freestanding companies organized in London. Four new domestic banks and two more foreign banks appeared on the scene in the 1870s. The crisis of 1875 resulted in the demise of three of the joint-stock banks, along with Mauá's partnership bank. Thanks partly to the newly reformed companies law at the end of 1882, the 1880s saw another uptick in entry, though none of the new banks were large by local standards. Overall, foreign firms played a relatively minor role in Rio commercial banking. From a peak of nearly 30 percent of joint-stock commercial banking assets in 1865, the relative position of foreign banks fell to less than 10 percent of assets by 1885. Throughout the Second Reign the vast bulk of Rio's commercial banking assets came from domestic sources.

Despite the overall expansion of banking assets, which was strongest in the 1880s, the commercial banking sector remained relatively small and highly concentrated through the later decades of the Empire. Table 7.1 reports the share of total banking assets held by each bank. The assets of the banking sector grew more than sixfold between 1855 and 1889. The magnitude of this increase seems large, until one considers that the level of joint-stock banking assets in existence at the start of the period was very low. The sector grew from only three commercial banks in 1855 to some fifteen by the eve of the banking reform of

Table 7.1

Share of Commercial Banking Assets, by Bank, Rio de Janeiro, 1855–88

BANK	1855	1860	1865	1870	1875	1880	1885	1888
Banco do Brasil	0.6	0.558	0.590	0.511	0.375	0.512	0.434	0.387
Banco Rural e Hypothecário	0.273	0.145	0.117	0.188	0.083	0.081	0.077	0.064
Banco Comercial e Agrícola		0.187						
Banco Comercial do Rio de Janeiro				0.135	0.156	0.103	0.118	0.125
Banco Nacional de Depósitos e Descontos					0.118			
Banco Industrial e Mercantil					0.097	0.041	0.032	0.026
Banco Predial					0.020	0.040	0.053	0.044
Banco do Comércio					0.051	0.052	0.047	0.061
Banco Auxiliar							0.003	0.004
Banco de Crédito Real do Brasil							0.079	0.093
Banco de Crédito Real de São Paulo							0.044	—
Banco União do Crédito							0.010	0.012
Banco União dos Lavradores						0.009	0.000	0.000
Banco del Credere								0.016
Banco Internacional do Brasil								0.085
Mauá, Macgregor e Cia.*	0.127	0.110	0.040					
London and Brazilian Bank*			0.141	0.050	0.054	0.086	0.056	0.036
Brazilian and Portuguese Bank*			0.112	0.116	0.045	0.075	0.046	0.031
Brasilianische Bank fur Deutschland*								0.017
Real total assets (millions of milréis)	94.0	136.5	186.7	190.6	249.0	314.6	494.5	603.1

* Foreign-owned bank or foreign-partnered bank.

Note: Two foreign joint-stock banks were so short-lived that they do not appear in the table: the Banque Brésilienne Française (1872–75) and the Deutsch Brasilianische Bank (1873–75). The Banco de Crédito Real de São Paulo was a mortgage bank in São Paulo with offices in Rio de Janeiro.

Sources: Most of the asset figures come from balance sheets in the semester and annual reports of banks. For years in which no published report to shareholders has survived, end-of-year balance sheets are taken from the *Jornal do Commércio* and the *Diário Official do Império*. For additional information on the data, see appendix II.

24 November 1888. Over the same interval five other banks had failed. The most salient feature of the evolution of commercial banking sketched in table 7.1 is the persistent leadership of the Banco do Brasil, the dominance of which continued well after the loss of its note-issuing authority in 1866. Most joint-stock banks remained small by comparison over the Second Reign. By 1888, when the bank's share had shrunk to less than 40 percent of total Rio commercial bank assets, the next largest bank still had only one-third of the assets of the Banco do Brasil.

The large share of banking assets held by one firm and the small number of banks overall meant there was a persistently high degree of concentration of commercial banking. High concentration did not indicate merely the low overall level of banking development. It further suggests a potentially large degree of pricing power and screening of lenders by the banks operating in the market for loans. The most common measure of the degree of market concentration used by investigators is the Herfindahl index, which takes into account each firm's market share of activity. The version of the index employed here is the sum of the squared shares of total banking assets accounted for by each bank, for a given year:[44]

$$H_t = \sum S_{it}^2.$$

Two qualifications are warranted when interpreting this measure of concentration. The first is that contemporary statements of banking assets are intrinsically inaccurate, as a result of the leeway banks enjoyed in their ability to place certain items on their balance sheets. The asset statements frequently include a number of categories that may have been exaggerated in value. This was particularly the case with unissued equity shares, which some banks carried on their balance sheets for years on end. Gross banking assets are thus at best a rough indicator of the size of the bank's activities. Under the assumption that the risk of accounting distortions was roughly equal across banks, the measure of concentration is unbiased.

The second caveat is that the validity of the concentration index as an indicator of potential market power varies with the manner in which the market is defined. A market with only one active firm but a strong competitive fringe of potential entrants is contestable. The market's Herfindahl index indicates pure monopoly, yet because rivals can readily contest the firm's position, it prices its output as if the market was more competitive. Though commercial banks in Rio de Janeiro faced relatively little threat of much entry by other large joint-stock banks, precisely because of the restriction imposed by law, they certainly confronted a competitive fringe of lenders. These consisted of private banking houses, coffee factors, merchants, and even private parties. It is doubtful, however, that these other lenders were competing for the same customers or loans. Commercial banks lent money at lower rates of interest, on average, than private banks because commercial banks had greater resources to lend and were also able to screen their borrowers meticulously. Dealing principally with high-quality customers put commercial banks in competition with each other, but given that there were so few of them, the market could hardly be characterized as fully competitive.

Conventional standards for assessing market concentration define a Herfindahl index between 0.15 and 0.25 as revealing a moderately concentrated market and any measure in excess of 0.25 as highly concentrated.[45] Figure 7.2 presents the Herfindahl indices for the joint-stock commercial banking sector in Rio de Janeiro from 1855 through 1888. At every point in time Rio banking exhibited substantial opportunities to exercise market power. In 1850 there was only one joint-stock bank in Rio de

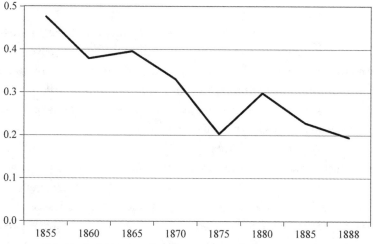

FIGURE 7.2 Herfindahl index of market concentration among commercial banks, Rio de Janeiro, 1855–88

Janeiro—the concentration ratio was one. It took relatively little entry to reduce the ratio; by 1855 it had fallen below 0.5. From these extreme levels early on to the reduced ratio of 0.2 in the 1870s and 1880s, concentration persisted. Though it clearly declined as new banks were allowed to enter the market, the very large share of all joint-stock bank assets controlled by the Banco do Brasil and the relatively small number of banks overall kept market concentration high.[46]

CONNECTIONS AND CRONYISM: BANKERS, BUSINESSMEN, AND POLITICIANS

Brazil's propensity to a small, concentrated banking sector stemmed logically from the political centralization that restricted the possibility of provincial initiatives in joint-stock banking and made possible repressive laws on entry that applied nationwide. Because the central government monopolized the authority to approve joint-stock banks, provincial governments could not craft their own banking policies. The banks chartered by the central government faced little competition. And the incumbent banks themselves had an obvious interest in limiting entry as well. One strategy for protecting a bank from rivals was to secure its influence in the policy-making arena by including influential men on the board of directors. Directorships of Rio's commercial banks exhibited two especially important types of connections. One was a tie among highly prominent individuals within the commercial and financial community. Yet this approach to limit entry went beyond simply recruiting well-connected business figures as directors. In effect, it involved a more direct form of cronyism, as current officeholders in the national government served on bank boards while still involved in the elaboration of policies and legislation. Sitting officeholders rarely occupied the bulk of the directors' seats in banks. The majority of bank directors were, as one would expect, key investors and major financial figures, many having built on successful careers as merchants. But politicians nonetheless appeared as bank directors in Rio with regularity. In addition to appointing political officeholders as directors, many banks were tied to prominent policy makers via other business linkages, by kinship, and through friendship. The direct ties identified here are meant to be illustrative and are no doubt understated measures of the extent to which political-financial connections in Rio's lending banks had influence on the possibility of entry.

The community of corporate directors in Rio de Janeiro, especially in finance, was not especially large. Multifaceted ties within the broader commercial community marked the directorship of the Banco do Brasil from the outset.[47] Of the bank's fifteen original directors, two held the title of *conselheiro,* and at least nine were registered with the board of commerce under various categories: "capitalists," consignment brokers, factors (commission agents), freight forwarders and expediters, or otherwise generically as merchants. A number of the directors came directly from the two banks that were fused into the Banco do Brasil. Among these was Mauá, who also was the president and organizing force behind numerous other companies, including the Petrópolis railroad, a streetcar company, an iron foundry, the Amazonas Navigation Company, and the Central Colonization Company.[48] Another director coming from the original Banco Commercial was José Carlos Mayrink, who would later serve as president of the new Banco Commercial at its founding in 1866. He was the father of Francisco de Paula Mayrink, who would become one of late-nineteenth-century Brazil's most prominent businessmen.[49] João Francisco Emery had been president of the Banco Commercial and was also director of the Phenix Fluminense insurance firm. The directors Balthazar de Abreu e Souza and Joaquim José do Santos Junior had similarly been officers of the first Banco Commercial, and the latter was a director of the Argos Fluminense insurance company.

These sorts of business connections were not limited to the directors of the Banco do Brasil. Interlocking ties among the boards of directors of other banks and companies were common. Themistocles Petrocochino, one of the founding directors of the Banco Nacional, was registered as a merchant, had also been a director of the Banco do Brasil, and was a founding director of the Macaé-Campos railroad.[50] Another director of the Macaé-Campos railroad, Manoel Alves de Souza Pinto, was a founding director of the Banco Industrial e Mercantil.[51] The president of the Banco do Commércio (established in 1874) was Henrique Corrêa Moreira, who was also president of the Integridade insurance company.[52] The Banco Commercial e Agrícola had as one of its founding directors in 1858 Francisco de Assis Vieira Bueno, an attorney by training who in 1865 became the president of the Banco do Brasil.[53]

It is in no way unexpected that successful merchants and financiers were involved as founding directors of Rio's banks. And it would be surprising to not find multiple connections among bankers and other businesses. What is more revealing, in terms of safeguarding the privileged position of joint-stock banks in the market, are the banks' indirect and direct political ties. Officeholders figured prominently on corporate boards of banks (and often of companies as well). Serving as a bank director was no obstacle to holding public office. The blatant conflict between the private and public interest of such connections was not a concern in Brazil's electoral laws. Several examples serve to illustrate the cronyism between banks and politicians. The most politically well-connected bank was, unsurprisingly, the Banco do Brasil. Under its statutes and the law, the government named the bank's president during the period in which the bank enjoyed the power to issue currency. The first president of the newly merged bank in 1854 was João Duarte Lisboa Serra. Given the government's role as overseer of the bank, it seems straightforward that Serra was also a politician and sitting officeholder, a member of the chamber of deputies representing the province of Maranhão. In the early 1860s the bank's president was Cândido Baptista de Oliveira, an Imperial senator and member of the emperor's Council of State who had served twice in the cabinet, including once as finance minister.[54] The last president while the bank still held the privilege of issuing notes in 1866 was no less than an Imperial senator, Francisco Gê Acaiaba de Montezuma (visconde de Jequitinhonha), who had previously served in two cabinets.[55] Yet the ties between the bank and politicians were not simply a result of the government imposing loyalists on the bank. Theóphilo Ottoni, a prominent Liberal politician and businessman who later would become a senator, was one of the bank's founding directors in 1853, elected by its shareholders. He had helped lead the failed Liberal revolution of 1842 against the Conservative government. Thirteen of the sixty-one directors, or 21 percent, of the bank whose signatures appeared on the bank's notes between 1853 and 1866 ultimately held or would hold a position in the chamber of deputies, the senate, cabinet, or Council of State, and some of them in more than one of these.[56]

Direct political connections persisted well after the government relinquished its authority to appoint the bank's president in 1866. The first elected president of the newly unfettered Banco do Brasil was Francisco de Sales Torres Homem, twice a finance minister, four times a deputy, and ultimately an Imperial senator.[57] In the late 1860s and early 1870s

José Joaquim de Lima e Silva Sobrinho (visconde de Tocantins) presided over the bank's board. He was a four-time deputy from the province of Rio de Janeiro and the brother of the prominent Conservative and army general duque de Caxias, the battlefield nemesis of Ottoni back in 1842.[58] The visconde de Tocantins was a key player in the formal mechanism of public debt management, having first been appointed to the administrative board of the Caixa de Amortização in 1863. José Machado Coelho de Castro, a politician who had served as a substitute deputy from the province of Rio de Janeiro in the late 1850s, was president of the bank for several terms in the 1870s and 1880s.[59]

The composition of the boards of directors of other banks shows that the participation of political officeholders was in no way limited to the Banco do Brasil. The first president of the Banco Nacional was none other than the visconde de Prados, Camilo Maria Ferreira Armond, who had been a deputy from Minas Gerais in the 1840s, and who in 1879 would be named to the emperor's Council of State.[60] The Banco Nacional held nearly 12 percent of Rio's joint-stock bank assets in 1875, a share exceeded only by the Banco do Brasil and the Banco Commercial. From 1875 until the bank liquidated in 1878, its president was João Lins Vieira Cansanção de Sinimbú (visconde de Sinimbú), a senator from Alagoas who ultimately served in three cabinets, including a stint as the cabinet's president from 1878 to 1880.[61] The Banco do Commércio, which accounted for about 5 percent of the commercial banking assets in the 1880s, was not just tied in politically. Politicians representing the province of Minas Gerais in the chamber of deputies ran the bank. Its president in 1886 was Manoel José Soares, a registered merchant who was a sitting deputy from 1882 to 1888 and an Imperial senator thereafter. One of the bank's other two directors was Antônio Cândido da Cruz Machado, the visconde de Serro Frio, a Conservative senator from Minas Gerais.[62] Other bank directors who were well connected politically became officeholders only after having established themselves first as financiers. One example was Francisco de Paula Mayrink, the president of the Banco de Crédito Real do Brazil and of other companies in the 1880s and 1890s. Having gotten his start at the Banco Commercial when his father was one of its directors, he worked his way up in high finance. Tied to the Liberal party under the Empire, he became a congressman after the advent of the Republic and held numerous positions as an officer in joint-stock companies.[63]

The connections afforded by politician-directors were vital in look-ing out for the bank's interests, but alone were not sufficient to salvage a bank that had made unsound lending decisions. In Rio's financial melt-down of 1875 the Banco Nacional, presided over by none other than Sinimbú, failed to recover from the crisis. Later, while he was serving as prime minister, Brazilian courts attempted to hold Sinimbú responsible for the bank's failure. His cabinet commanded a majority in the cham-ber of deputies, which dutifully absolved him of culpability in early 1879.[64] As strong as the Banco Nacional's political links were, they did not enable it to defy the laws of financial gravity, and it definitively closed its doors in 1878. But the bank, as a result of its close ties to prominent politicians, had nonetheless enjoyed considerable government assistance in its time of trouble.

BANK CONCENTRATION AND PROFITS

The high degree of concentration in Rio commercial banking—Herfindahl indices were continually above 0.18 up through 1888, and a single bank always commanded more than one-third of the city's joint-stock banking assets—generates an obvious hypothesis: bank profits should have been high. Otherwise, barriers to entry, the political influ-ence of directors, and the like would have been largely purposeless from the perspective of the bank's equity holders. At first blush it is clear that bank profits could not be high at every moment. Selected banks did fail in Rio, including some well-connected ones like the Banco Nacional. Even a normally profitable bank can become insolvent when it finds itself overleveraged in the midst of a major liquidity crisis. The hypoth-esis that bank profits were high, on average, proves challenging to test comprehensively. Many banks published their balance sheets in only a summary fashion and without income and loss statements. Unless the balance sheets included indications of net income, it was not possible to compute rates of return. The Banco do Brasil did publish information suf-ficient to provide a test. Given its size and privileges, it likely outper-formed the other banks. Yet the concentrated character of the sector in general should have boosted the profits of most other banks as well.

Figure 7.3 presents annual estimates of the return on equity for the Banco do Brasil. Equity is defined here as the original funds raised from purchasers of the bank's common stock, which comprised the bank's

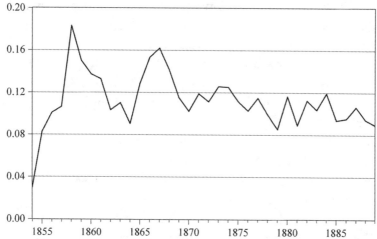

FIGURE 7.3 Return on shareholder equity, Banco do Brasil, 1854–89. Return on equity is measured as the bank's net operating revenues plus net change to all reserve funds, divided by the shareholder equity (paid-in stock plus retained earnings). (Banco do Brasil, *Relatório*, annual issues, 1854–89)

capital. As a concept of profit, the return on equity focuses on the net earnings appropriated by the bank's stockholders in the form of dividends summed with changes in the bank's retained earnings, on which the stockholders had a claim. Profit is thus measured as the ratio of the bank's gross return on all its assets each year, less its operating costs, divided by the paid-in capital. The Banco do Brasil never once operated at a loss. On the contrary, the return on equity invested had risen by 1858 to 10 percent and rarely fell below that level through 1889. Annual rates of return on the original amounts invested in the bank's shares typically hovered in a band from 10 to 15 percent. The bank was quite clearly a profitable enterprise. High profits, which persisted even after the bank lost the authority to issue notes, are consistent with the hypothesis that banking concentration in Rio de Janeiro created economic rents to the banks' shareholders. Those persons fortunate enough to have acquired the bank's shares when they were first issued enjoyed the fruits of the restrictions on entry that reduced bank competition. In the case of the Banco do Brasil, later investors in those shares enjoyed reliably large, steady returns.

High profits on the bank's stock were not just a result of its market power. They reflected its political influence as well. Government assistance to distressed coffee planters was assistance to the bank as well. The Banco do Brasil's mortgage department had concentrated its lending in plantation districts from the very creation of its mortgage portfolio in the late 1860s. In 1880 the bank held mortgages in the province of Rio de Janeiro on 346 fazendas, the collateral of which included nearly 19,000 slaves. All of the mortgaged fazendas were in coffee-producing districts—none were in the sugar-producing municipality of Campos, for example. In Minas Gerais there were 136 mortgages against plantations with more than 5,000 slaves, while in São Paulo there were more than 200 mortgages against some 8,671 slaves. Even Espírito Santo had a dozen plantations mortgaged with the bank, with more than 600 slaves in total. Of some 30 million milréis in outstanding mortgage debt held that year by the bank, more than 93 percent was on plantations with slaves.[65]

Access to credit from the Banco do Brasil was highly desired. In the Paraiba valley, over more than a decade of falling coffee prices from 1873 to 1884, the average interest rate on loans from the Banco do Brasil was 300 basis points less than rates on loans from other banks, and 400 to 500 basis points cheaper than loans from coffee factors and merchants.[66] By the early 1880s many of the planters who owed the bank money faced increasing difficulties, despite interest rates that were relatively favorable. Coffee prices had fallen over a period in which slaves had become more expensive. With the abolition movement gaining steam, the Banco do Brasil's presidents perennially commented on the growing uncertainty attached to rural mortgage lending. By 1885, of 620 long-term rural mortgage loans, barely half (314) were performing. Of the loans in default 59 were behind by only one payment—in most instances this meant six months overdue. But for nearly one-fourth of the encumbered fazendeiros repayment was probably hopeless—they were behind four or more payments on their loans.[67] Things were even worse in the short-term rural loans. Of 89 short-term mortgages, more than half, 48, were behind one or more payments. Because of this severe underperformance of the mortgage portfolio, the bank froze its rural lending and began to gradually liquidate the portfolio. The high delinquency rate persisted. In 1887 just under 50 percent of the rural loans outstanding were one or more payments behind.[68]

The dire contraction of credit available to the planter class led the government to pass legislation in 1885 authorizing the Treasury to aid banks and boost credit by lending cash (ostensibly at 6 percent interest) against the banks' apólice holdings.[69] Between January and June 1887 the

Banco do Brasil drew 10 million milréis from the Treasury under the law. In December it went back for 2 million more milréis of credit, an operation it repeated two more times in early 1888.[70] That the Treasury borrowed cheaply in London and passed along the savings to private debtors through Brazilian banks could be seen as a shrewd use of the state's creditworthiness. The problem is that these loans suffered from an insider bias: they all went to the Banco do Brasil, and then disproportionately to bail out the planter class. Figure 7.4 depicts the informed cynicism of contemporaries: a group of groveling but well-fed planters on their knees crowd around the finance minister, who pours a ration of cash into their open mouths while standing atop a bench that represents the Banco do Brasil. The caption was quite literal: "Thanks to the goodwill of the government the planter class is going to get into millions [of milréis] at low interest and at long maturity. Ah! Lucky devils!"[71]

FIGURE 7.4 Minister of finance feeding cash to the coffee planters, 1888 (*Revista Illustrada*, 4 August 1888, 5)

The deep concern of the Banco do Brasil's directors about the bank's own fortunes, as its borrower base was increasingly distressed and its loans underperformed, would be wholly understandable, save for one fact. The bank's annual return on shareholders' equity never fell below 9.5 percent throughout the entire period of supposed trouble, and the average over the period remained in the double digits. Low-cost money from the Treasury may or may not have been passed on by the bank to credit-strapped borrowers in an economically sensible way. But the Treasury's injections most certainly helped the bank's equity owners. Irrespective of coffee prices and the crisis of abolition, the bank's shareholders experienced no interruption in the double-digit payouts to which they had been accustomed for decades.

THE LAST REFORM

The problems of excessive concentration in the banking sector and the undersupply of bank credit persisted through the 1880s. Only in the regime's eleventh hour did the last cabinets to govern under the constitutional monarchy take steps to increase the supply of credit. The abruptness in the shift in emphasis reflected a continuity of political concerns over all else. As late as 1886 the Conservative position, and the orthodox view, articulated by Finance Minister Francisco Belisário Soares de Souza was that the persistent weakness of the milréis relative to the pound sterling was a result of excess paper money in circulation.[72] His solution was to wring the paper currency out of the economy, seeking to reestablish an equilibrium at an acceptable overall price level but with a milréis that was convertible at the official parity. It was hardly the sort of approach that would boost credit locally without the more direct intervention using the resource of the Treasury. A cluster of factors accelerated the return to parity. A turnaround in export prices contributed to the rise in the value of the currency. The government's borrowing in London in 1886 brought loan proceeds in sterling to Brazil, which also boosted the value of the milréis. The favorable interest rates on the government's new borrowing held down the Treasury's debt service requirements, which helped as well.

The abolition of slavery in May 1888 brought matters to a head. Although the planters of the traditional zones of coffee cultivation were no longer as economically central as they had once been, they had long been the core supporter of the monarchy. Abolition without compensation risked a sharp falloff in support for the regime at precisely the moment in which its rivals—republicans, positivists, and Liberal supporters of federalism—gained strength in the parliament and behind the scenes. The same cabinet that secured abolition from the parliament, headed by João Alfredo Correa de Oliveira, envisioned a solution to maintaining support. It would make cheap credit widely available. The approach was two-pronged. One involved outright subsidy from the Treasury, of the type already extended to the Banco do Brasil under the 1885 law.[73] The new "aid to planting" program in 1888 pumped 4.3 million milréis in Treasury funds into banks that agreed to extend loans to planters for terms of up to five years.[74] Most of it went to the Banco do Brasil. The other part of the strategy was to revive banks of issue, with the paper money backed in a way that would limit inflationary pressures. In May 1888 the president of the cabinet assembled a committee, which included the visconde de Ouro Preto, to draft legislation for banks of issue.[75] Six months later the law cleared both houses of parliament, and in January 1889 the cabinet implemented it albeit with fairly restrictive conditions.[76] In particular the requirement that banks issue notes against apólices proved unappealing, and the law had little impact.

By that point the milréis had achieved parity with the pound. Adopting the gold standard would keep the government's borrowing costs down, while also making it possible to increase credit by issuing gold-backed notes. The new cabinet, presided over by Finance Minister visconde de Ouro Preto, expanded both of the programs established under the João Alfredo cabinet. In June 1889, Ouro Preto further boosted the aid-to-planters program. The original contracts from 1888 were with two banks only, the Banco do Brasil and the Banco da Bahia. Ouro Preto expanded the program to some seventeen banks around Brazil, underwriting and supplying funds earmarked for loans to farming in areas where planters were most adversely impacted by abolition. In a series of contracts signed between the government and the banks from June through October 1889, the cabinet committed to provide 87.5 million milréis, interest free, to the banks—nearly a twenty-fold increase over the original program the year before.[77] The banks in turn committed to provide an equal amount of their own funds to the program. The interest earned on the loans underwritten by the government would accrue to the banks.

The Treasury would be in a position to meet its part of the deal by using the savings from the external debt refinancing in London, along with the proceeds of the National Loan it would soon issue in Rio de Janeiro. Many of the banks, however, would have to issue notes as originally envisioned in 1888 to take advantage of the program and fulfill their requirements under the arrangement. What they needed was relief from the requirement that banknotes be fully backed by apólices. Ouro Preto gave it to them shortly after coming to government, removing the restrictions by announcing a decree in July that permitted banks to issue convertible notes in amounts up to three times the value of the bank's capital constituted by specie.[78] The two strands of the aid-to-planters program supported each other. It no doubt benefited planters, although the extent to which the loans went to actual farming activities is not clear. The spillovers from the vast increase in credit were highly visible. The number of companies organized under the permissive incorporation provisions of the 1882 law and listed on the Rio de Janeiro stock exchange more than doubled in 1889.[79]

To use the facility to issue notes afforded by the July decree, the banker and financier visconde de Figueiredo organized a new bank in September. This new Banco Nacional was designed to merge with Figueiredo's existing Banco Internacional. While the new bank was a local concern, it also drew on a large investment from the Banque de Paris et Pays Bas. A couple of weeks later Figueiredo contracted with the Treasury to use the new notes the bank would issue to help retire the Treasury's own currency. In return the Treasury would give the Banco Nacional an equal amount in the new gold-denominated apólices of the 1889 National Loan, paying coupons of 4 percent a year in gold. The Treasury would redeem the apólices at full face value at a rate of 2 percent a year.[80]

In short, for every metallic milréis (or equivalent in English sovereigns or other coin) that Figueiredo's Banco Nacional held in its vault, it could issue three milréis in notes. It could either lend these or exchange them for existing Treasury notes. The Treasury then accepted its own notes from the bank, paying in return three milréis' worth of gold apólices. Each of those in turn generated revenue for the bank from the 4 percent coupon. It was a lucrative arrangement in the short term because the bank received a guaranteed 12 percent on its original investment in coin specie. It was lucrative in the longer term as well since the apólices would be retired and the "principal" paid in gold to the bank, as if it had actually loaned money somehow to the Treasury.

Ten other banks had sought and received permission to issue notes under the July decree. Only the Banco Nacional received a favorable side arrangement to do so, and it was the only one to actually issue the notes. The deal was, in effect, pretty much the same plan used by the cabinet thirty-six years earlier for the Banco do Brasil. Except the terms were even more favorable to the new privileged bank than the one that came before. The entire arrangement between the finance minister and the new bank was caricatured in the *Revista Illustrada* as a variant on the standard

QUADRO BIBLICO

FIGURE 7.5 "Quadro Bíblico" (biblical scene): Brazil being baptized with paper money, 1889. The caption reads, "The baptism of Brazil in the Jordan of paper money and banks of issue. It seems like it does not displease history . . ." (*Revista Illustrada*, 5 October 1889, 8)

depictions of the baptism of Jesus (figure 7.5).[81] In the place of Jesus is the Indian that represents Brazil. The visconde de Figueiredo takes the place of John the Baptist in the scene, baptizing Brazil with paper currency instead of water from the river Jordan. He stands on a bench that represents a bank, a common motif in such caricatures, in this case a bench labeled with his new endeavor, the Banco Nacional. Instead of bearing the usual expression for the "lamb of God," the banner on Figueiredo's staff reads "Agnus Celsi"—a reference to Afonso Celso, the finance minister and visconde de Ouro Preto. The barely discernible head of the dove of the Holy Spirit that descends on Brazil is that of Ouro Preto.

None of the changes undertaken by Ouro Preto in the last six months of the constitutional monarchy could conceivably salvage the Empire's legacy of restrictive banking. The policies resurrecting the authority of banks to issue notes in 1888 and 1889 did not come out of a major institutional shift. They were ad hoc, piecemeal adjustments to the existing commercial code. They were not even really designed to forge a vibrant banking sector with the goal of financial deepening. They originated with cabinets deeply worried about political threats to the very survival of the constitutional monarchy.[82] The Ouro Preto cabinet finally pulled out all the stops financially in hopes of recovering the lost political support of the former slave-owning class (or transcending the problem altogether) by making as much credit as possible available. Nothing about any of the banking reforms in those years guaranteed they would be durable.

CONCLUSIONS

The limits on private financial development in Imperial Brazil followed from the control its political institutions gave politicians over nearly every branch of financial intermediation. The central government's regulatory policies limited entry in commercial banking. A quantitative test of the hypothesis that extreme political and regulatory centralization was a root cause of the underdevelopment of banking requires a counterfactual scenario beyond the reach of existing method and evidence. Consideration of alternative political-institutional arrangements that existed at the time makes it possible to venture a more qualitative assessment. Had the constitution given Brazil's provinces their own authority to charter banks, the country would have had more banks and appreciably greater financial intermediation. Political federalism of this sort elsewhere created a fruitful competition between subnational administrative entities that fostered policies to attract mobile factors of production, including financial capital.[83] In the nineteenth century, state governments in the United States often endeavored to ease shortages of credit and promote finance, chartering appreciable numbers of banks at the state level.[84] It did not matter that many of the early banks were little more than schemes for pooling capital to be employed narrowly in other businesses involving the banks' own directors or that the mechanisms for their chartering in some states were thoroughly corrupt.[85] What did matter was the policy autonomy of state legislatures that empowered them to respond to local needs and facilitate the creation of banks when and where necessary.

In Imperial Brazil provincial presidents had the authority to charter joint-stock banks within their provinces. But presidents were appointed by the cabinet in Rio, whose instructions trumped any local efforts to authorize additional financial intermediaries. As a result, there was never a movement to create banks in Brazil's provinces like that found in the United States under free banking. Imperial Brazil missed out entirely on the financial benefits that a decentralized division of bank chartering authority could have engendered.

Brazil was not an isolated case. Governments in many countries favored the creation of a few privileged banks, in return for loans made to the government. These privileges often entailed restrictions on the entry of rivals who could potentially erode the economic rents of the privileged entity. If the Imperial state was unremarkable in this regard, it nonetheless was one of the few cases in which the political institutions that committed the state to repaying its own debt also limited broader financial development. Twice the government took the lead in organizing a superbank: first in 1808 and again in 1853. On both occasions it did so in order to tap the resources of the merchant community of Rio de Janeiro, awarding privileges to the banks in exchange for help in meeting shortfalls or otherwise solving a problem of public finance. In both instances the institutions governing bank chartering had remarkably low levels of political accountability. By delegating review authority over joint-stock bank formation in 1860 to the Council of State, elected politicians further gave up much of the influence they might have been able to exercise in favor of less restrictive regulation of bank entry. The result was that most Brazilian entrepreneurs faced high interest rates, assuming they could even access a loan.

Given the regulatory setting, political-financial cronyism became a common feature of big banks. A number of Rio's commercial banks placed national political officeholders in directors' seats. Some of these men had backgrounds in the merchant community or as investors, but relatively few seem to have been uniquely qualified to run a bank. Their value to the bank came through the influence they could wield in the policy arena. The curious persistence of high bank concentration and policies that limited entry becomes more intelligible in light of the incentives to cronyism that were created by highly centralized control over banking policy. Institutional barriers to bank entry played a central role in Imperial Brazil's financial backwardness, which in turn had negative consequences for the real sector of the economy. Concentrated banking became a hallmark of Imperial Brazil, as was the commitment to honor the public debt. These two features were not contradictory: they both followed from the logic that emerged from the Empire's highly centralized political institutions.

CHAPTER EIGHT

Fall from Grace

IN THE 1820S, Imperial Brazil credibly committed to honor its debt. The reliability with which the government met its obligations for more than six decades after independence was unique among the nations of Latin America. So, accordingly, was the state's capacity to borrow. It purposively withheld interest for only one brief period, and then only on a debt that had been foisted on Brazil as part of its independence settlement with Portugal. Brazil always made good on its own loans, and its bondholders always received their interest payments. The Empire attained a record of debt service in the nineteenth century that was better than that of several of the United States. It was a strikingly successful case of emerging market sovereign debt on the periphery of the world economy in the nineteenth century.

The political institutions formalized by the Constitution of 1824 established Brazil's commitment to repay loans. The constitution articulated the principle of repayment as a political right, created a counterbalancing set of veto players on questions of fiscal policy, and defined electoral ties between the legislators of the lower house and their propertied constituents. Chapter 2 showed how this array of features embodied mechanisms not only to penalize government default but also to prevent it altogether. Neither new borrowing nor default could take place without the approval of a majority in the chamber of deputies. Deliberations on new taxes had to be initiated within the chamber, and new budgets were implemented only after winning the chamber's approval. In case of an unanticipated deficit, the chamber could prevent default by either shifting expenditures to cover the debt or by raising taxes to obtain the needed funds. In instances when the chamber could not complete a budget in time for the new fiscal year, it passed a more limited bill that committed tax revenues to the continued service on the debt. Individuals, not banks, ultimately held the bulk of the government's domestic bonds. Citizen-bondholders almost certainly had incomes sufficient to participate in elections. If the chamber of deputies were to support default, it would have meant the loss of the backing of an influential component of the electorate. That this mechanism worked was made clear in 1831, when the cabinet proposed a selective external default. Most of the chamber opposed the measure, viewing it as posing a threat to the domestic debt holders. To monitor the actions of the Treasury and the cabinet, the parliament created a standing commission of the leading individual bondholders in Brazil.

Taken together, these features show that the chamber's fiscal authority under the constitution was strong. Transgressions against constitutionally defined authority would likely evoke a damaging response. This meant that political penalties in case of a unilateral default were wholly feasible in Imperial Brazil. The political crisis leading to the abdication of Pedro I in 1831 did not involve the debt or even questions of public finance in any direct fashion. But it showed that violations of fundamental understandings and expectations within the polity could call into question the legitimacy of the executive branch's actions. The perceived unwillingness of the emperor to abide by convention justified a withdrawal of support of an appreciable portion of the elite. The prospect of such penalties helped make credible the government's commitment to honor its debts.

The achievements of the constitutional monarchy in sovereign debt markets were considerable. Committing to repay made it possible to borrow when the government most needed funds. The evidence presented in chapter 3 showed how the Empire borrowed in London at least once per decade and always with long maturities. It could refinance outstanding loan balances by taking new loans at a lower coupon rate. It could even extend the maturity of loans at full face value. In what perhaps was the ultimate test of creditworthiness, the government could borrow a large sum needed to wage war, sharply increasing its stock of debt, at only modest increase in its cost of borrowing. Access to the capital market was not limited to the Empire's London borrowing. Chapter 4 documented the remarkable growth of domestic long-term borrowing. This debt consisted of perpetual apólices and long-maturing bonds. Borrowing repeatedly in Rio de Janeiro with an unbacked currency, the Imperial government succeeded in getting domestic lenders to take on inflation risk. By the early 1850s the value of the domestic portion of the funded debt was larger than the foreign debt. Brazil, more than any other Latin American nation, was able to rely on its domestic market for critical credit needs. The costs of borrowing varied when the markets reappraised the likelihood of default. Chapter 5 showed how revolts and war tended to raise default risk, though the Empire's biggest war did not have nearly the impact that early political instability had on the bond market. The interest rates the Empire paid to borrow generally fell over time. The decline in borrowing costs after the Paraguayan war was such that Brazil ultimately refinanced both its domestic and external debt in the 1880s.

If public finance was one of the Empire's crowning achievements, among its principal deficiencies were the obstacles it erected to private financial development. Imperial Brazil failed to undergo a broad-based financial revolution. In stark contrast to other cases where political institutions supported successful sovereign borrowing, Brazil never completed the virtuous sequence that North and Weingast argued was available to all countries: the creation of institutions that limited the authority of the crown, and the resulting rise of credible public borrowing, followed by the fluorescence of private financial markets. In Imperial Brazil, private financial development at no point kept up with the progress of the public debt. Chapters 6 and 7 demonstrated how interest rates in the private capital market remained stuck at relatively high levels, even when public borrowing costs fell appreciably. Long-term private equity finance was difficult to access because strong legal restrictions on incorporation limited the formation of joint-stock companies for most of the Imperial era. Restrictions were even tighter on banking firms and were further strengthened in 1860. From that point on, forming a limited-liability joint-stock bank required the approval of the cabinet as well as a favorable review on the part of the emperor's Council of State. Because incorporation was not an administrative measure but a political one, entrepreneurs seeking to organize a company and issue equity were subjected to arbitrary limits imposed by the state.

The restrictions on incorporation served two goals. First, they helped the Treasury meet fiscal requirements at critical moments by redirecting capital toward investments in its bonds. Second, they helped channel the funds of the private sector to projects that had large capital requirements and that were political priorities. In the end these consisted of a handful of large banks along with specially selected railroads. The lack of responsiveness to entrepreneurial initiative inherent to this institutional arrangement favored existing banks, as made clear in chapter 7. Cronyism, whereby politicians also served as directors of commercial banks, was not an accidental feature of Brazil's political-financial landscape. In a system in which policy makers had only limited accountability to the broader needs of commerce, political-financial cronyism supported barriers to entry in banking.

Only at the end of 1882 did Imperial policy makers begin to dismantle these restrictions. Business saw little immediate impetus from the reform, given the contemporaneous downturn in coffee export earnings and its negative implications for savings and investment. Experiencing some recovery by mid-decade, business finally turned up. The growth in the number of companies listed on the Rio de Janeiro stock exchange was well under way by 1889, a delayed result of the liberalization of 1882. For most of the Imperial era, however, the institutions that governed the mobilization of capital for both the financial and real sectors stifled business investment. Private financial development simply never fully reflected the Empire's accomplishments in public finance. This divergence would persist, but in an inverted fashion, in the Republic.

By 1889 Brazil had attained a degree of creditworthiness without precedent in the country's history. Its cost of borrowing was cheaper than ever, and the loans were the largest of those it had secured. The risk of default at which the market priced its debt revisited the previous lows of the 1850s. Having achieved convertibility between the milréis and the British pound, the visconde de Ouro Preto kicked off the government's 100-million-milréis National Loan subscription in August in Rio de Janeiro. In September the Brazilian minister in London closed the deal with N. M. Rothschild & Sons to consolidate and refinance nearly 20 million pounds sterling worth of the existing sovereign bonds. These measures had been less visibly preceded in July by the award of a 5-million-pounds sterling line of credit in Europe through the Banque de Paris et Pays Bas, backed by a consortium of Hambro & Son, Baring Brothers, and Brown, Shipley & Co.[1] The credit the bankers offered to the Imperial government was no doubt a prelude to what they hoped would be future business handling Brazil's loans.

On 15 November 1889 an aged general in Rio de Janeiro led local units of the Brazilian army in deposing the emperor and overthrowing the constitutional monarchy.[2] The coup d'état was planned and executed by radical republicans and junior army officers. It initiated a five-year period of what was, in effect, military rule. Within a couple of weeks, as the markets digested news of the overthrow, the prices of Brazil's bonds in London began what would become a fairly steady slide. The spread between the yield on the bonds and that of consols rose, revealing a growth in negative sentiment on Brazil as a debtor.

Evidence from bond prices is not required to infer that the regime change complicated Brazilian borrowing. In December the new military government sought to draw on the line of credit opened in July. There was no reason not to do so. Fundamentals remained strong, as they had been earlier in the year. The overall fiscal deficit was small, and the primary balance was positive. The Treasury had plenty of money to service its existing debt. Exports were up, as was the price of the most important of the export commodities: coffee. Despite all this, the bankers revoked the line of credit. Hambro in London wrote to the bank in Paris that "it was quite with our approval that a telegraphic message was sent to you to the effect that with the change of Government we considered the credit [from July] had lapsed . . . we conclude that you will be of the same opinion and will consequently take the needful steps to prevent any drafts being issued upon us in respect of the lapsed credit."[3] Indeed, there would be no loans on par with what had been made available to the monarchy forthcoming from Europe for the new government. The coup did not create widespread political violence or turmoil, yet the change in regime from a constitutional monarchy to a military-civilian junta had raised the alarm. This provisional government adopted the positivist motto of "Ordem e Progresso" (order and progress) and within a couple of years convened a constituent assembly that crafted a federal constitution. Yet even as the new republican government took form, an attempt to borrow long term in London in 1892 fizzled into a small issue of short-term debt, as N. M. Rothschild & Sons would agree only to issue Treasury bills denominated in sterling. The "Republic of the Sabre" gave way to complete civilian control in 1894. By then it was clear that the confidence of the markets in Brazilian institutions had been damaged.

While few historians identify the coup in 1889 with a major change in the society, there was a shift in control from a central class of national officeholders (and the party organizations that helped make them) to multiple regional elites that commanded the political machinery of the wealthiest states of the country.[4] The change in the form of government would prove beneficial to Brazil in some ways and costly in others. By devolving certain policy-making authorities from the central government to the states, the new system boosted infrastructure and provision of public goods in the wealthy regions. Yet it also exhibited lower rates of political inclusion than the monarchy as well as political dominance of the nation by only a subset of regional elites. The development of the country's credit markets during the first decade of the Republic was tumultuous. But the outcome in private financial markets would be better than it was for public finance.

From the onset of the Republic the requirements that entrepreneurs had to meet to organize joint-stock companies were increasingly weakened by the government. Following the more than doubling of listed companies over the last ten months of the monarchy, the increase of newly organized companies and existing firms going public in 1890 was so large that even close observers had difficulty keeping track. Some three hundred "companies" registered their statutes with the board of trade in Rio de Janeiro—aiming to raise more than 1.3 *billion* milréis in equity capital. The annual business retrospective for the year stressed, "It is difficult if not impossible to offer a summary of everything that happened in our market over the year . . . so many and so diverse in their purpose were the companies organized."[5] Some of them would soon be readily recognizable as large, even successful firms: the Companhia Industrial do Brazil, for example, and the Banco dos Estados Unidos do Brazil. Countless others would never even raise the initial capital required for their shares to trade, irrespective of their pretensions—the Bank of Universal Credit seems to have vanished before it ever appeared. Others that did raise capital did not survive the collapse of the bubble; some of the more spectacular failures were implicated in schemes to defraud investors, such as the Companhia Geral de Estradas de Ferro (a railway holding company), whose directors were either in jail or on the lam before the end of 1892.

While there were some early measures to try to rein in the excesses of the boom, such as increasing the capital requirements for new listings, effective regulatory oversight went largely out the window. The republican government built on Ouro Preto's program of chartering new banks by reducing further the requirements for backing notes. In doing so it grafted an extraordinary monetary expansion onto newly eased requirements for organizing joint-stock companies. By taking the financial reforms of the late Empire to their illogical extreme, the government ensured that there would be a bubble—and a crash. True to type, when the bubble burst, a large number of firms quickly went under. Within a couple of years there were actually fewer actively traded firms on the exchange than there had been back in 1886.[6] As part of this boom-to-bust cycle the banking sector underwent a tremendous expansion, followed by a corresponding contraction.[7]

The stock market speculation that began in 1889 and continued until 1891 had some durable effects on the real sector of the economy, but not many. The number of joint-stock companies traded on the São Paulo stock exchange by 1900 was barely one-third the number in 1891. The Rio de Janeiro stock exchange did better, ending the decade with more paid-in capital than it had at the end of the Empire. The São Paulo stock exchange ultimately experienced tremendous growth—but only after 1905.[8] The collapse of the milréis during the 1890s corralled much of the consumer market for the benefit of domestic manufacturers. Equipment, however, came mainly from abroad. A currency that had fallen by 1898 to less than one-third its 1889 value in sterling became an obstacle to the expansion of industry. It comes as no surprise that real annual manufacturing investment declined by well more than half between 1890 and 1900.[9] Only after the turn of the century did industry embark on a sustained expansion.[10] The use of long-term debt financing by corporations, which began before the end of the Empire, also declined through the 1890s. Save for an uptick in 1898, debenture issues under the Republic did not surpass their late-Imperial levels until 1902.[11] A good number of manufacturers operating in the 1920s did trace their origins to firms that first listed their shares during the early 1890s.[12] These included many of Brazil's cotton textile firms, which increasingly turned to the reinvigorated capital market after 1900.[13] Nonetheless, much of the initial growth in private finance in the 1890s was ephemeral—the nineties was a lost decade. Certain vulnerabilities that first emerged during the decade persisted. Orthodox economic policy adjustments following the Funding Loan of 1898 contributed to a new banking crisis in 1900, one that nearly tore out the very moorings of the domestic financial system. Eight banks in Rio de Janeiro, along with several others around Brazil, either closed their doors due to failure or had to enter into a judicial moratorium in order to come to terms with creditors and to reorganize.[14]

The government's own financial position deteriorated badly over the same interval in which Brazil's private financial markets lurched upward along their turbulent path. The divergent trajectories of public and private finance that characterized much of the Empire inverted under the Republic. The increase in the government's bond yields in London after the emperor's overthrow in 1889 was not abrupt and not large in the beginning. Yet the secondary market for Brazilian debt assessed the change in institutions unfavorably. The primary market for new loans was not so perturbed by the coup at first. The contract signed in London with N. M. Rothschild & Sons in the weeks before the emperor's overthrow—converting a huge share of the external debt to a 4 percent basis—was finalized with the provisional government in April 1890 without any change in its clauses.[15] The long record of successful government borrowing under the Empire contained little to suggest Brazil would run into difficulties in the 1890s.

Problems of a kind Brazil had not experienced since the 1820s soon began to accumulate. These were of three types: a downturn in the markets for Brazil's main export, coffee; fiscal deficits; and high inflation with a deteriorating milréis. The first of these adversely affected Brazil's ability to repay; the second increased the need to borrow; and the third reduced the real cost of servicing the internal debt while making the external debt more expensive. Together these problems weighed on the Treasury and contributed to external default in 1898. None of these problems, however, were without precedent in Brazil: the constitutional monarchy had experienced all of them, at times simultaneously, yet it had never defaulted.

The fall in the price of coffee over the 1890s has been implicated by some investigators in the worsening exchange rate, which in turn increased the cost of servicing the external debt. Yet the evidence suggests that distress in the coffee sector was no more detrimental during the 1890s (either in terms of its impact on coffee export earnings in local currency or earnings in its sterling equivalent) than it had been when coffee prices had hit their previous nadir in the early 1880s.[16] The origins of the declining milréis—and the rising cost of external debt service—ultimately lay outside of Brazil's coffee fields. Fiscal deficits were a more proximate stressor. Between 1889 and 1898 Brazil ran a surplus in only one year. On the revenue side, the central government lost a crucial component of tax receipts to the cause of federalism. State governments captured all of the export taxes under the new regime, allowing them to finance their own sovereign borrowing. Import duties remained the most important overall category of central tax revenues, but the reassignment of export revenues to states clearly did not help the national Treasury. The central government deficit of 1894 was especially large because of military outlays required to suppress revolts against the regime in Rio de Janeiro and Rio Grande do Sul. Deficits in 1896 and 1897 were not as big but were still substantial, increased by the cost of putting down the Canudos rebellion in the backlands of Bahia. The deficit of 1898 was so large that it exceeded ordinary revenues. It stemmed not from a fall in taxes but from a near doubling of outlays. By then the steep decline in the exchange rate mechanically generated larger fiscal deficits, a result of the need to service the external debt and the requirement to pay railroad dividend guarantees in sterling.

The hypothesis that growing distress in servicing the Treasury's external obligations resulted solely from deteriorating fiscal fundamentals seems unlikely when one takes into account the monetary schemes pursued under the Republic. A major problem was the succession of finance ministers who pursued locally inflationary monetary policies, rendering the milréis inconvertible. The most prominent of these was Ruy Barbosa, the renowned jurist and politician of both the Empire and the Republic and the finance minister of the provisional government that took power in the coup.[17] At first blush Barbosa's banking policies varied little from the expansion already put into motion by the last finance minister of the Empire. Ouro Preto's reform had reintroduced banks of issue to boost credit. The provisional government of the Republic went further, giving one bank in each of three banking regions a monopoly of issue. These banks were then allowed to issue notes at a rate of 3:1 against the face value of apólices that they held. The late Imperial banking reform had allowed banks to issue notes against specie at a rate of 3:1. The difference between the two approaches was great, and the consequences of Barbosa's effort to energize banking soon ran out of control. The Empire's hard-earned achievement of restoring convertibility to the milréis at the end of the 1880s went by the wayside.

Barbosa was not the finance minister for very long, but subsequent administrations followed a similar policy. The amount of paper money in circulation ballooned over the decade. In 1895 the portion of the currency that had been issued by banks outstripped that issued by the Treasury. Overall, paper money in circulation more than tripled between the overthrow of the monarchy and the external debt moratorium of 1898. The resulting price inflation drastically reduced the real value of domestic apólices.[18] That the milréis declined continuously against sterling was not unexpected. This created a new challenge: how best to reduce the excess of inconvertible paper money in circulation without provoking (or exacerbating) downturns. Policy makers learned that there was no good way to do so. Twice during the decade—first in 1892 and again with the Funding Loan agreement in 1898—Brazil undertook deflationary monetary policies in the midst of contractions of the real sector.

All of these problems signaled creditors that something was fundamentally amiss. Doubts in London regarding the sustainability of the external debt only grew over the decade. The spread of the yield on Brazil's bonds over consols increased. The average risk premium across the 1890s was nearly double the level that had prevailed between 1870 and 1889.[19] Several institutional disparities between the Empire and the Republic shed light on why the Republic encountered such difficulty raising new debt whereas the constitutional monarchy had often done so with ease. As the postcoup provisional government lingered in power, its leader, General Deodoro da Fonseca, ruled without a legislature and was thus unchecked by any institutional veto player. Policies came directly from the ostensible cabinet, a handpicked advisory council. This situation persisted until 1891. That year the new federal constitution reestablished the legislative branch of the government and vested the new congress with authority over public finances, much like that enjoyed by the old parliament. Deodoro shut down the congress soon after. He was later ousted by the vice president, General Floriano Peixoto, who then reestablished the congress.[20] By this time the center of policy-making authority had shifted decidedly toward the executive branch.[21] The new federal legislature simply did not command in practice the influence over fiscal policy that its Imperial counterpart had demonstrated. By the end of the decade both houses of the congress would receive the executive's budget proposals at the eleventh hour and approve them, in the words of one critic, "without controversy, without study, and without discussion."[22] On fiscal matters Brazil's congress became a rubber-stamping entity.

Against the backdrop of extremely loose monetary policy, growing deficits, and the lack of legislative checks on the executive, the republican government ran into considerable difficulty raising new loans at home and abroad.[23] In 1890, 100 million milréis of the existing 5 percent apólices were converted to 4 percent apólices payable in gold in order to give some protection against rising inflation. The other three-fourths of the 5 percent apólices in circulation continued to receive coupon payments in inconvertible currency. The inflationary turn made most apólices increasingly unattractive to investors. Ironically, in the effort to tame inflation, a financially more orthodox administration succeeded in placing 100 million milréis of new 5 percent apólices in the domestic bond market in 1896 as part of a plan to withdraw paper money from circulation and destroy it.

Brazil was not alone in starting the 1890s in a weaker position in external credit markets. The decade had an inauspicious beginning for Latin American sovereign borrowers in general. There is evidence that the Argentine debt crisis of 1890 led to a reappraisal of default risk in London for the region as a whole.[24] But the increasing spread between the yields on Brazil's bonds and British consols predated the onset of the Argentine crisis by more than six months, beginning soon after the overthrow of the constitutional monarchy in 1889. Then, in the months immediately after the onset of the Argentine crisis, the spread actually shrank some. Changes in Brazil's risk premium were only loosely associated with Argentina's misfortunes. More relevant to Brazil was the rising cost of servicing its existing external debt. Over the decade the milréis had its most severe decline since the war against Paraguay. Monetary policy accounted for much of the downward spiral, while real balance-of-payments issues exacerbated it.[25] To the degree that the fall in the value of the currency resulted from loose monetary policy, the government's actions were self-defeating. The weak milréis played an increasingly central role in the rising burden of foreign debt service.

As conditions for servicing the existing external debt worsened, new borrowing became difficult. The bills issued through Rothschild in 1892 had extremely short maturities of between nine and fifteen months.[26] Brazil's London banker had, in effect, put it on a short leash. It was a remarkable stumble for a country that less than three years before, during the last year of the Empire, had borrowed with a maturity in excess of fifty years. In need of money to buy materiel to suppress revolts against the regime, in 1893 the government took a highly unconventional approach. Having no legislative sanction to borrow directly, the finance ministry arranged a loan for the Oeste de Minas railroad company through N. M. Rothschild & Sons. It then entered into a side agreement with the company, giving the government control of the loan's sterling proceeds in London, while promising to pay the company an equivalent amount of money in Brazil (in local currency). The government further promised to take over repayment of the principal and the payment of interest. The Republic was able to directly take its own long-term foreign loan in 1895 but only after agreeing to implement policies to curb inflation and stabilize the value of the currency. A large portion of the loan converted the existing short-term debt, retiring bills Rothschild & Sons had taken; the Treasury did not have funds to redeem them outright.[27] The loan carried the largest discount at issue since Brazil borrowed at the start of the war against Paraguay in 1865.

By 1898, faced with ongoing deficits, a milréis in free fall, and rapidly rising costs of external debt service, Brazil defaulted and entered into an orderly workout with its foreign bondholders. The deal was negotiated directly by President-elect Manuel Ferraz de Campos Salles during a visit to London.[28] The accord suspended the requirement for Brazil to amortize the external debt until 1911. Interest payments to existing bondholders (along with railroad dividend guarantees) took the form of the new bonds rather than cash. Bondholders had to accept the new bonds at their face value. An increment of the new bonds was used to remove from circulation part of the paper currency. For the second time in a decade the need to adopt deflationary policies threw the economy into recession, culminating in a new banking crisis in 1900.

Recovery from the recession and strong demand for exports made it possible for Brazil to go on the gold standard in 1906. Foreign investors favorably interpreted the measure as a signal that the government would not pursue unsound fiscal and monetary policies. But Brazil's move was prompted as much by desperation as by anything else. It was the best it could do to try to recover some of the creditworthiness it had lost in the 1890s. It worked for a few years, helping Brazil get new loans abroad. When the government defaulted again in 1914, requiring yet another funding loan, its financial fall from grace was nearly complete. The default of 1931 severely limited the government's access to capital markets for decades. The postwar return to borrowing, using bank loans rather than bonds, ended badly in 1982. Call it what you will, but within a decade of the overthrow of political-fiscal institutions of the constitutional monarchy, Brazil had become decidedly debt intolerant, increasingly suffered from original financial sin, and was on the path to becoming a serial defaulter. The consequences of the fall from grace linger in the present. Twenty-plus years after taming high inflation and emerging from the last round of default, Brazil consistently has one of the highest real interest rates in the world. The succession of defaults in the century after the overthrow of the Empire left Brazil with a fiscal legacy that has proven remarkably difficult to overcome.

Theory

Two main arguments are advanced in the chapters of the text. The first is that if a ruler assigns a fiscal control right to creditors (or to a parliament in which creditor interests are protected) the government is unlikely to default, even in a fiscal downturn. If this control right is strong enough, it makes the commitment to repay credible. The second argument is that political control of incorporation hindered private financial development. This appendix presents two theoretical models that inform the analyses provided in the text. The first is the model of sovereign borrowing introduced in chapter 2 and applied in the three subsequent chapters. The second model is that of the entrepreneur's choice of organizational form under expropriation risk that is used in chapters 6 and 7.

SOVEREIGN DEBT

The basic model of sovereign borrowing involves a strategic interaction between the ruler and potential lenders as well as the consequences of particular institutional arrangements governing this interaction. Three assumptions underpin the model. The first is that borrowing is desirable; by covering deficits, borrowing smoothes taxes and public spending over time.[1] This sustains the supply of public goods while limiting efficiency-degrading distortions that tax-only finance would create. The second is that a ruler has strong incentives to default.[2] If lenders believe they will not be repaid, they do not lend. Sovereign promises to repay do not confer credibility on policy actions. The third assumption is that the ability to borrow depends on the strength of the commitment to repay. Committing to repay is valuable to lenders but indispensable for the ruler who needs money that is otherwise not available. All three assumptions are rooted in well-established theoretical propositions as well as empirical work.

Default penalties figure prominently in the literature on credible commitment. Eaton and Gersovitz emphasized how the costs of credit market exclusion could deter default.[3] Bulow and Rogoff demonstrated that a ruler could mitigate this exclusion penalty, rendering it ineffective, so long as they could purchase assets.[4] They further showed that only a stronger form of penalty could sustain lending to a sovereign state.[5]

To appreciate the importance of the default penalty, consider a ruler that seeks to borrow. Derived first are conditions under which lenders extend credit. The interaction between a ruler and lenders is modeled in the following terms.[6] The ruler values a loan (of size L) in accordance with a benefit function $B(L)$ that has diminishing returns to loan size, so that $\frac{\partial B}{\partial L} > 0$ and $\frac{\partial^2 B}{\partial L^2} \leq 0$. Financiers ($F$) can always secure a certain return by investing their capital in a safe alternative instead of lending it to the ruler. If they lend to the ruler, they do so at an interest rate i, which must be greater than or equal to the risk-free rate r. Assuming that the ruler repays the loan, the net gain to the ruler from borrowing is $B(L) - L(1+i)$, while the net gain to lenders is $L*i$.

There are five stages in the basic model. In the first stage the ruler decides whether to seek a loan. In the second stage financiers decide whether to lend to the ruler and, if so, how much and at what rate of interest. Any lending occurs under a contract that specifies an inflexible fixed repayment obligation for the borrower.

If lending takes place there is a third stage. The ruler realizes the benefits of the loan, and a player called Nature determines the fiscal circumstances (this device serves to introduce exogenous conditions that bear on the ruler's decision to repay). Lenders do not know Nature's choice beforehand and make their lending decision under uncertainty.[7] In the fourth stage if fiscal circumstances are favorable, the ruler repays. If the fiscal situation is poor, the ruler may default.

If the ruler defaults there is a fifth stage in which lenders either punish the ruler or not. Lenders can impose the penalty for default $P(x)$, which is scaled by x. The effectiveness of the penalty depends on its magnitude and the likelihood it can be applied. The parameter x captures these elements. The precise nature of the penalty is undefined in order to first focus on the impact of variation in the penalty's strength (irrespective of its form).

Let the political cost to the ruler of debt repayment be a function $C = C(T, s)$, where the taxes spent on repayment are $T = L(1 + i)$, and in which s is the fiscal outcome selected by Nature, which is either high (h) or low (l). The probability that Nature chooses a favorable fiscal outcome is p, while the probability of poor fiscal circumstances is $(1 - p)$. The repayment cost function C is continuous in the taxes required to repay and is assumed to rise at a constant or increasing rate, so that $\dfrac{\partial C}{\partial T} > 0$ and $\dfrac{\partial^2 C}{\partial T^2} \geq 0$. The total political cost to the ruler of repaying the loan in bad times is always higher than in good times: $C(T, l) > C(T, h)$.[8]

The structure of this borrowing game is portrayed in figure A.1. Potential lenders are financiers (F) who know the penalty ($P(x)$) that is available in case the ruler defaults. They decide whether to lend, how much to lend (L), and the interest rate (i) to charge. The interest rate the ruler must pay exceeds that on the risk-free alternative to the extent that repayment is uncertain. Nature (N) determines whether

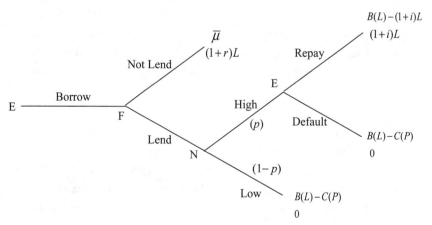

FIGURE A.1 Sovereign borrowing game with default penalties and risk premia

the fiscal situation is one in which tax revenues are sufficient to repay debt.

For the ruler to repay requires that the penalty for default must exceed the ruler's political cost of repayment:

$$C(P(x)) > C(L[1+i], s).$$

Equilibria of the game are identified by backward induction. In the last stage the ruler (labeled E for either the emperor or the executive branch of government) decides to either repay the loan L or default, incurring the penalty $P(x)$. If E repays the loan, he receives the benefits of borrowing and pays back the capital with interest, while the payoff for the financier is the return $(L(1+i))$. If E defaults, he receives the benefits of borrowing and pays the default penalty, while the lenders' rate of return on L is zero.

Consider the ruler's preferences for repayment under three different levels of the default penalty ($x \in \{a, b, c\}$, with $a < b < c$). For $x = a$ let $C(\overline{T}, h) > C(P(a))$. The cost of repaying debt exceeds the size of the penalty for default, even with high fiscal revenues. In this situation the ruler defaults with certainty. For $x = c$ let the cost of repayment always be less than the cost of default: $C(\overline{T}, l) < C(P(c))$. With such a penalty the ruler always repays, even when the fiscal outcome is poor.

At $x = b$ let the penalty equal or exceed the cost of debt service in favorable fiscal circumstances but fall short in unfavorable ones. In favorable circumstances the ruler repays, while in the low realization of income he does not, since the penalty is too small to support repayment: $C(\overline{T}, l) > C(P(b)) > C(\overline{T}, h)$. This condition defines a rationing constraint, L^C, that gives the maximum loan size at which repayment is incentive-compatible given the default penalty and the interest rate on the loan:[9]

$$L^C = \frac{P(x)}{1+i}.$$

The rationing constraint determines the supply schedule of loans to the ruler. With two possible fiscal scenarios, the supply schedule is a step function. Over the range of lending where repayment is certain, supply is perfectly elastic at the interest rate r. If the ruler's demand for loans increases to the point where the penalty does not deter default in the weak fiscal scenario, the supply schedule discontinuously shifts to i. At levels of loan demand where default is certain, the interest rate is undefined and there is no voluntary lending beyond the constraint.

Moving back to the lending stage, F knows the penalty for default that is available but does not know N's choice of fiscal circumstances. F's action depends mainly on the expected strength of the default penalty. If $x=a$ the penalty is too weak and F denies credit to the ruler even if favorable fiscal conditions are certain. If $x=c$ then F will lend, charging the risk-free rate of interest. If $x=b$, then F will lend up to the rationing constraint and charge a risk premium.

Figure A.2 portrays the rationing constraint with the penalty fixed. Consider a rationing constraint at L_L and let the ruler's demand for loans be L_i. Because the constraint is to the left of the amount demanded, the ruler would always default on the loan. Financiers anticipate default and refrain from lending. At the other extreme the ruler never defaults when the penalty is greater than the cost of repayment in poor fiscal circumstances; in terms of the figure, if the penalty exceeds L_H the rationing

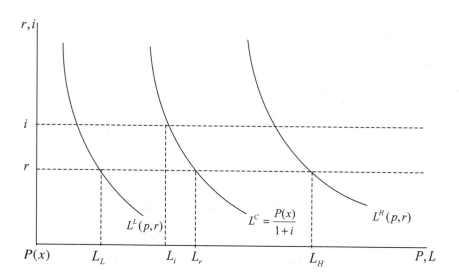

$$i = \left(\frac{1+r}{p} \right) - 1$$

FIGURE A.2 Sovereign borrowing equilibria with default penalties and risk premia constraint L^C does not bind. Loan size is determined by the first-order condition, $\dfrac{dU}{dL} = \dfrac{\partial B}{\partial L} - (1+r) = 0$, where the marginal benefit from borrowing equals the ruler's marginal cost. The ruler is able to borrow an amount L_H at the risk-free rate (r) because financiers face no uncertainty regarding repayment.

Further analysis is restricted to the range of default penalties over which loans are rationed and the ruler pays a risk premium to borrow. The rationing constraint is at L^C. Financiers are risk-neutral, so their expected payoff from lending must be at least as large as what they would receive from investing in the risk-free alternative. This certainty-equivalent payoff to lenders is given by

$$(1-p)L(0) + pL\,(1+i) \geq L(1+r)$$

where L is loan size, zero is the rate of return to lenders who suffer default, $(1+i)$ is the lenders' rate of return if the ruler repays, and $(1+r)$ is the rate of return on the risk-free alternative. The equilibrium interest rate i in terms of r and p is

$$i = \left(\frac{1+r}{p}\right) - 1$$

which includes a premium for the risk of default, based on the probability of a poor fiscal outcome. The interest rate the ruler is willing to pay must exceed r by at least this risk premium in order to elicit credit. The premium equals the spread between i and r, and decomposes as

$$s = (i-r) = (1+r)\frac{(1-p)}{p}$$

where the first term is the risk-free return on capital and the second term is the odds ratio on default.

Both the interest rate and the risk premium decline with an increase in the probability of good fiscal circumstances: $\dfrac{di}{dp} = -\dfrac{1}{p^2}(1+r)$.[10] If the probability of repayment rises, the equilibrium amount of credit increases, due to movement along the incentive compatibility constraint.[11] Note that the ruler cannot borrow more by simply paying a higher risk premium. If lenders accept a higher interest rate to supply more capital than the ceiling permits, they increase the likelihood of default.[12] The limit on the amount of credit that could be supplied to the ruler in figure A.2 approaches L_r as the probability of repayment approaches unity.

Several hypotheses tested in chapters 3, 4, and 5 emerge from the predictions of this basic model. First, submitting to a default penalty allows the ruler to obtain loans, while increases in the penalty raise the ruler's credit ceiling. Second, changes in the penalty are not necessarily the sole source of changes in the ruler's ability to borrow. If a reduction in the political cost of taxation makes the cost of loan repayment less than the default penalty, borrowing becomes possible. Any further decline in the political cost of taxation will raise the credit ceiling and reduce the risk premium. Hence, a ruler with the power to extract a greater share of output as taxes, or who simply collects taxes more efficiently, can borrow more at a given default penalty. The implication of a productivity increase in tax collection is observationally equivalent to that of an increase in the default penalty.

MONITORING AND FISCAL CONTROL

Two key institutional features give specificity to the penalty mechanism in the basic model. The first is monitoring. Imposing a penalty for default requires that creditors monitor the ruler, in the sense that they can observe the ruler's actions. The second feature is fiscal control. When creditors control the ruler's spending, they can guarantee that resources required to repay debt are available. The importance of a control right to support sovereign borrowing is an implication of Hellwig's insight that creditors seeking to penalize default must overcome their own dynamic inconsistency. The assignment to creditors of a control right over the borrower's revenue flows makes it easier for creditors to impose a penalty.[13]

These two features capture several attributes commonly held by legislative bodies related to public finance. Parliaments often demand the authority to monitor executive actions and intervene to adjust spending as a condition of supplying taxes and authorizing loans. With a default penalty of $P(b)$, a fiscal downturn can be partly or completely offset by parliamentary intervention that adjusts revenues and expenditures. This is the key difference from the basic model: repayment *may* occur in poor fiscal circumstances as well as in good ones.

These features of the model have direct counterparts in Imperial Brazil. The chamber of deputies held monitoring authority by virtue of its power to audit expenditures and review the spending made by the cabinet. It also delegated some of its monitoring authority directly to creditors, through the Junta Administrativa da Caixa de Amortização. The chamber held fiscal authority by virtue of its initiative in setting new taxes, budgeting expenditures, and passing bills to provide for debt service even in the absence of a new budget.

Several modifications incorporate these elements to the basic model; the sequence of moves is portrayed in figure A.3. The ruler who seeks to borrow submits to some degree of monitoring by creditors and gives up some fiscal control; otherwise no loans are extended. Financiers then decide to lend or not; to lend, the expected return must exceed the risk-free rate of return. If loans are extended, F then decides whether or not to monitor. F incurs a cost by monitoring, but if it does not monitor the ruler will default. If F lends, in the next stage the ruler realizes the benefits of the loan and Nature chooses the fiscal circumstances. In good fiscal circumstances the penalty for default elicits repayment. In poor fiscal circumstances F must decide to intervene or not in fiscal matters. If F declines to intervene, the ruler defaults. If F intervenes, N moves once more to determine whether the intervention is sufficient to repay debt. If insufficient, default is automatic. If sufficient, the ruler decides to either repay or to default opportunistically.

Any fiscal intervention by creditors succeeds with a probability q. This probability can be thought of in either of two ways. First, the creditors intervene in fiscal matters in a way that still leaves them uncertain over the result, but in which they expect to prevent default with probability q. Alternatively, q can be viewed as the degree of fiscal authority ceded to creditors. If creditors enjoy unlimited fiscal authority, $q=1$.

While the gross benefits of borrowing and lending are the same as in the basic model, three additional costs arising from possible courses of action figure into the strategic calculus. Financiers pay a cost M to monitor, assumed here to be a constant portion of the debt, $\frac{M(L)}{L} = m$. If lenders do not pay this cost they cannot observe the nature of default and therefore can neither intervene fiscally nor punish the ruler.[14] There is a cost to the ruler from submitting to monitoring: $\delta_1 (P)$ is increasing

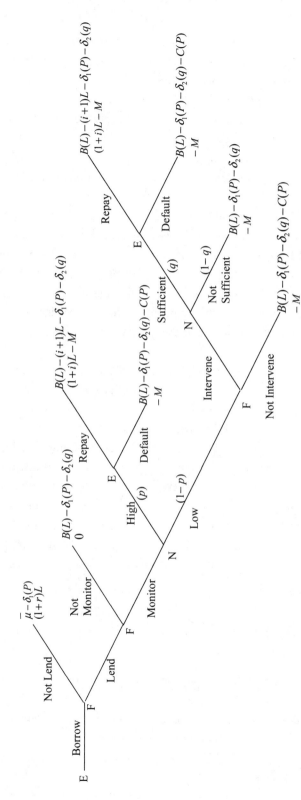

FIGURE A.3 Sovereign borrowing game with monitoring and fiscal control

in the size of the penalty. If the ruler assigns a control right to financiers, it comes at an additional cost to the ruler, δ_2 (q), that is increasing in the amount of control the ruler gives up.

Equilibria are identified by backward induction. Consider the subgame starting at the node where Nature determines the outcome of fiscal intervention by financiers ("Sufficient" or "Not Sufficient"). Insufficient intervention results in default. If intervention is sufficient, the ruler will repay the loan so long as the default penalty is large enough.

F's choice of action depends on the fiscal circumstances selected by N. In poor fiscal circumstances F will intervene to redirect revenue to debt repayment, so long as qL $(1+i) > 0$, which holds if $q > 0$. F will always intervene in the low-income state if it holds even just a small amount of fiscal authority. If N instead selects a favorable fiscal outcome, no intervention by F is required; at a default penalty $P(b)$ the financier can select a loan size and interest rate at which the ruler always repays in good fiscal circumstances.

Before Nature selects the fiscal situation, F chooses whether to monitor the ruler, which depends on m and the expected values of p and q. In poor fiscal conditions F's expected payoff from monitoring is $(1-p)$ $[qL$ $(1+i) - M]$. In the high-income scenario F's expected payoff from monitoring is $p[L$ $(1+i) - M]$. F will thus choose to monitor so long as $m < [p+q$ $(1-p)]$ $(1+i)$, that is, whenever the expected rate of return with monitoring and fiscal intervention exceeds the unit monitoring cost.

In the lending stage, whether F lends depends on whether the ruler has assigned the authorities to monitor and to exert fiscal control to creditors (which determine values of m and q for F). The interest rate required to make F at least as well off as it would be investing capital in a risk-free asset is

$$i = \left[\frac{1}{p+q\,(1-p)} \right] (1+r+m) - 1.$$

Intuitively the interest rate is a function of the cost of monitoring and degree of fiscal control the ruler concedes to creditors.[15] Increases in q reduce the equilibrium rate of interest by reducing the risk premium. So long as the ruler's costs of submitting to monitoring and delegating fiscal control are less than the benefits of borrowing, the ruler gains a surplus and thus has an incentive to establish institutional arrangements that increase the degree of fiscal control by creditors.

Figure A.4 portrays lending with both monitoring and fiscal authorities assigned to creditors. The ruler's demand for capital is L^H, with a rationing constraint of L^C. With fiscal intervention (so long as $q > 0$) the ruler can borrow a larger amount at a lower unit cost. The interest rate the ruler must pay decreases in the probabilities of favorable fiscal circumstances (p) and successful fiscal intervention (q):[16]

$$\frac{\partial i}{\partial p} = -\frac{(1-q)}{[p+(1-p)q]^2}[1+r+m] < 0, \quad \text{and}$$

$$\frac{\partial i}{\partial q} = -\frac{(1-p)}{[p+(1-p)q]^2}[1+r+m] < 0.$$

Note that if fiscal circumstances are always favorable $(p = 1)$, fiscal intervention is irrelevant to repayment. The interest rate includes the cost of monitoring but requires no premium for default risk. Likewise, if there is no chance that fiscal intervention would stave off default $(q = 0)$, then

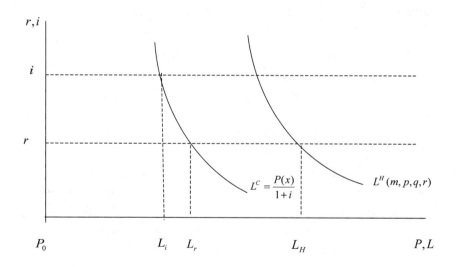

$$i = \frac{1}{[p+(1-p)q]}[1+r+m]-1$$

FIGURE A.4 Sovereign borrowing equilibria with monitoring and fiscal control there is no distinction between the outcome with fiscal intervention and without it. The risk premium is determined in that case by p.

If fiscal intervention is completely effective ($q=1$), then $i=(r+m)$, which is the risk-free rate with monitoring. Fully effective fiscal intervention in this model is analogous to the strong penalty ($P(c)$) for default in the basic model above. This is the main argument deployed in the text: if the ruler assigns a strong fiscal control right to a parliament whose majority represents creditor interests, the government is unlikely to default opportunistically, even in a fiscal downturn. Parliament's authority over fiscal affairs reduces the state's borrowing cost relative to what it would be if there was no delegation of fiscal control to creditors (since $p+(1-p)$ $q>p$ when $q>0$).

Finally, increases in both p and q attenuate each other to a certain degree. The cross partial derivative $\dfrac{\partial^2 i}{\partial p\, \partial q}>0$; the decline in the interest rate that results from an increase in the probability of favorable fiscal conditions $\left(\dfrac{\partial i}{\partial p}\right)$ is less sharp when the efficacy of a fiscal intervention is increasing. By Young's theorem the decline in the interest rate accompanying an increase in the efficacy of fiscal intervention (q) is similarly less steep when the probability of a good fiscal outcome is higher.

CREDIBLE COMMITMENT AND FINANCIAL DEVELOPMENT

If political-institutional changes that commit the ruler to repay debt also increase the credibility of sovereign promises across the board, it may improve property rights in all assets. Robinson presents a general result along these lines in which the ruler's actions matter not only vis-à-vis sovereign borrowing but also with respect to the broader capital market.[17] If the ruler can expropriate the wealth of either lenders or borrowers in the broader market (and not just those who loaned money directly to the ruler), then the private capital market exhibits credit rationing. In this scenario the ruler repays its loans only if the penalty for default exceeds the cost of the repaying sovereign debt *plus* the sum of private sector lending. Given a penalty low enough, lenders must ration credit not only to the ruler but also to private borrowers. Lending too much money will lead the ruler to default its own debt and expropriate money loaned between other parties. The effect is to reduce investment and lower the incomes of both lenders and borrowers. Securing private property depends on limiting the same sort of discretionary authority that the ruler holds over sovereign debt. The political-institutional changes required to credibly commit to repay debt should also increase lending and investment in the market.

This framework provides a useful baseline scenario for considering situations between full commitment and complete capital market failure. If sovereign commitment can be more narrowly targeted to the state's lenders, then there is no reason to expect broader financial development to result from the commitment to repay. If sovereign promises can be rendered credible in a piecemeal fashion, without committing to complete rights in financial property, then improvements in the state's creditworthiness may have no impact at all on other markets or could even come at the expense of private saving and investment. The ruler might strike bargains with entrepreneurs and asset holders to supply property rights on a purely ad hoc basis, engage in financial repression to steer private savings to the Treasury, or impose limits on business finance for narrowly particular reasons. These considerations comprise the framework underpinning the arguments in chapters 6 and 7.

Consider first the entrepreneur's choice of organizational form in the absence of political or regulatory costs. The activity the entrepreneur seeks to undertake requires more capital than can be invested as a sole proprietorship. The nature of the activity implies an efficient scale of investment that influences whether the entrepreneur prefers to use the corporate form to raise capital or instead create a partnership. The entrepreneur's return from the partnership investment is $R_p(k)$, while the return from investing in the same activity under the corporate form is $R_c(k)$. The function $R_t(k) = A_i k^\alpha$ relates the total return to the capital (k) invested in the enterprise, the elasticity of the total return with respect to capital invested (α), and the productivity of the investment (A). The entrepreneur's criterion for incorporation is $R_c(k) > R_p(k)$.

Consider three factors external to the firm that bear on the entrepreneur's choice: the cost of petitioning the government for a corporate charter (c), the probability that the petition will be approved (p), and the probability that the government will expropriate after investment has taken place $(1-s)$. The entrepreneur's choice of organizational form is modeled as a four-stage process.[18] Assume that the entrepreneur specializes in an activity for which productivity is higher in a corporation than in a partnership ($A_c > A_p$). In the first stage the entrepreneur chooses between two alternatives: organize a partnership or petition the government to incorporate. The petition cost, c, is not simply a fee but may also require the entrepreneur to persuade politicians that incorporation is warranted. The term represents the various possible lobbying expenses, bribes, and implicit losses from delay in establishing the business while the politicians consider the petition.

In the second stage the government either grants a charter to incorporate by approving the firm's statutes or it denies the petition. In the third stage, if the petition is denied the entrepreneur creates a partnership and allocates capital in the amount k to the business and the rest of their wealth ($w - c - k$) to a risk-free asset. If the government grants the charter, the entrepreneur either proceeds with incorporation or declines to incorporate. The latter choice could result from a changing assessment of expropriation risk or if government approval was conditioned on changes to the amended statutes that differed materially from what the entrepreneur had petitioned. If the entrepreneur proceeds with incorporation and raises investment capital, there is a fourth stage in which the government either honors the entrepreneur's property right or expropriates.

The conditions shaping the entrepreneur's decision are derived by backward induction. In the last stage, if the government supports the entrepreneur's property right in the corporation, the entrepreneur receives the entrepreneurial return on the portion of wealth invested in the business, and the risk-free return on the rest of their wealth:

$$V_c(k) = R_c(k) + (w - c - k)(1 + r).$$

If the government instead expropriates, there is a zero return on the business investment, but the entrepreneur gets the risk-free return on the remaining wealth. Let the probability that the government supports the entrepreneur's property right be s and the probability of expropriation be ($1 - s$). The expected return from investing in the corporation is

$$V_c(k, s) = sR_c(k) + (w - c - k)(1 + r).$$

The expected return from selecting the partnership form after having a corporate charter approved is

$$V_p(k) = R_p(k) + (w - c - k)(1 + r).$$

The entrepreneur will invest capital in the business up to the level that maximizes the total return.[19] For given levels of expropriation risk $(1-s)$, the rate of return $(1+r)$ on low-risk assets, α, and A, the optimal level of investment in the business is:

$$k_i^* = \left[\frac{\alpha s A_i}{(1+r)} \right]^{\frac{1}{(1-\alpha)}}.$$

This also determines the allocation of the entrepreneur's wealth between the business and the risk-free investment. The capital invested in the business increases in α, s, and A.

The threshold for the entrepreneur to choose to organize a corporation, conditional on the government having approved the charter, is[20]

$$s > \frac{R_p(k)}{R_c(k)}.$$

The greater the expected return under the corporate form, the higher the risk of expropriation the entrepreneur will accept when deciding how much to invest in the business.

In the second stage the entrepreneur takes into account the probability that a request to incorporate will be approved as well as the cost of seeking the charter. The government approves the entrepreneur's petition for a charter with probability p. When the condition above holds, the expected payoff to the entrepreneur from petitioning to incorporate is

$$\Pi_c = p[V_c(k, s)] + (1 - p)[V_p(k)].$$

The expected payoff from choosing the partnership form of the firm is

$$\Pi_p = R_p(k) + (w - k)(1 + r).$$

This implies that the entrepreneur will petition for a corporate charter if

$$p > \frac{c(1 + r)}{sR_c(k) - R_p(k)}.$$

This is the ratio of the opportunity cost of having sought the corporate charter in terms of the return on the risk-free investment and the expected benefit of choosing the corporate form of the firm over the partnership. If the probability of charter approval is less than the right-hand side, the entrepreneur will form a partnership, even if there is an underpinning productivity advantage for the corporation.

To define an efficiency benchmark for activities in which the return on capital of the corporate form exceeds that of the partnership, the regulatory variables are $c = \varepsilon$ (epsilon being a small administrative fee) and $p = s = 1$, petitions to incorporate are all approved with certainty at only trivial expense, and there is no risk of ex post expropriation. The entrepreneur will choose to incorporate. At the other extreme is the case in which there is no chance the government will approve the corporation $(p = 0)$. The entrepreneur will not waste money on a petition and will create the partnership. This scenario is costly to the economy; it incentivizes the entrepreneur to create the business using the organizational form that is less efficient and generates a lesser total return to capital.[21]

Two intermediate cases are relevant as well. In the first, the cost to petitioning is low $(c = \varepsilon)$, a charter will be automatically granted $(p = 1)$, but there is expropriation risk. For the entrepreneur to incorporate, the risk must be sufficiently low and the return differential in the denominator sufficiently large. Otherwise, the entrepreneur prefers the partnership form because the expropriation risk outweighs any benefits from choosing the organizational form that is better suited to the activity. Finally, the most general case is one in which there is some probability of a petition being approved, a potentially large cost to petitioning, and some risk of expropriation. If the combined costs are too high, the entrepreneur will opt for the partnership. So long as there are activities that can be more profitably undertaken using the corporate form, any institutional changes that reduce the cost of seeking a charter (c), raise the probability of approval (p), or reduce the probability of expropriation $(1-s)$ support higher levels of capital formation and increase the social surplus.

Data

The empirical analyses of the chapters on public borrowing make use of time-series data at frequencies of observation ranging from weekly to annual. Other chapters use data on banks and other private firms at intervals ranging from annual to quinquennial. This appendix details the sources of these data and the basic manipulations involved in their use.

PUBLIC DEBT

Annual fiscal-year estimates of the public debt were built up on a loan-by-loan basis from the early 1820s through 1889. Information on the stock of debt came from two sources. The first was the annual report delivered by the finance minister to the chamber of deputies at the beginning of each parliamentary session. For the few years preceding the first session in 1826, there was usually a report from the finance ministry or the Treasury that served this purpose. The second source was the published annual budget, which up to the early 1850s usually provided more detail on the debt than the finance minister's report.

External Debt: Up to 1853 the budget was used as the principal source of information on the stock of the external debt; thereafter the finance minister's report provides the numbers. Included in those used in the text are balances outstanding on the loans detailed in chapter 3, along with the Portuguese loan of 1823 for which Brazil assumed responsibility in

1825. Adjustments to the reported amounts were required in a number of instances. Occasional typographical errors in the published totals required careful reconciliation of the component figures in many years. From year to year the month for which the data were reported varied considerably. The reporting dates on the external debt were more often than not the end of June or December but were frequently reported in other months as well. The discussion of the size and structure of the debt contained in the text of the finance minister's report, all debt tables appended to the report, and the values for the debt appended to the budget were cross-checked for consistency and to help identify any sources of error. The annual figures were placed on a common footing by expressing them all as of 30 June, which was the end of the fiscal year for much of the Imperial era. This put the debt series on the same annual basis as that defined for comparable data series (exports, revenues, expenditures, and the like). In the final external debt series the data for 1829 through 1850 were those actually reported for the end of June of each year. Data from 1825 through 1828, 1851 through 1876, and 1881 through 1888 were converted from an end-of-calendar-year basis to the end of June by linear interpolation. For 1878 through 1880 the data were reported in odd months and were converted to June estimates using a weighted (by month) interpolation of the closest available observations. No figures on the stock of foreign debt were located in either the reports of the finance minister or the published budget for the calendar years 1830, 1849, 1851, 1877, and 1889. Estimates for these missing observations were obtained by interpolating the annual totals for adjoining years.

Domestic Funded Debt: In only two calendar years were no data reported on the stock of the domestic funded debt: 1830 and 1860. In every other year there was at least one report of the stock of the domestic debt in circulation; in many years there were two reports. In some instances, such as in 1872, a span of only six months separated reported values (March and September). In other cases there were intervals longer than eighteen months without an update on the stock of the domestic debt (no figure was published, for example, between March 1875 and December 1876). As in the case of the foreign debt, the month for which the domestic debt was recorded varied. Estimates for each year's end-of-June domestic debt stock were obtained by interpolating the nearest observations. Debt figures for most of the 1820s are less reliable than those for other years, since even Brazilian authorities experienced difficulty in sorting out what amounts were owed. Before the establishment of the funded debt in 1827 there were several early loans that were securitized or that otherwise paid fixed rates of interest. These included loans in 1796, 1811, 1818, and 1822. All of these instances of crown borrowing involved loans that were forced to some degree. Over time much of this earlier debt was converted to apólices of various coupon rates. The largest single category of pre-1828 domestic debt was unfunded loans made to the Treasury by the first Banco do Brasil. As those loans were converted to apólices, which was a main goal of the debt law of 1827, the stock of funded domestic debt mechanically increased.

Unfunded Debt: Most domestic debt before the law of 1827 was unfunded, a result of the heavy borrowing through the first Banco do Brasil. By the 1830s, however, the predominant form of unfunded, or floating debt, was the Treasury bill (*letra de tesouro*). Various bills had been issued as a means of payment beginning in the colonial period. No reliable indicator of their volume is available for the early postindependence era. New provisions governing their use were established in the early 1830s. The monthly amount of bills in circulation was reported regularly beginning in 1836. For the first decade of the series there were two types of bills. One type, *bilhetes de tesouro*, carried a fixed rate of interest of 6 percent. The issue of bilhetes tapered off sharply after 1844, and none remained in circulation after September 1845. Letras did not carry fixed rates like bilhetes but instead paid rates that varied with conditions in the money market and the letra's maturity. At maturity investors would receive the face value of the bill, the effective interest being the difference between the issue price and redemption price. Both types of bills were issued in anticipation of revenues within the same fiscal year.

Debt Totals: The totals of each category are summed in two steps. All types of debt were first expressed in British pounds sterling. The stock of apólices denominated in Brazilian currency was converted by using the annual average market rate of exchange, while the National Loans of 1868 and 1879 were converted to sterling at the fixed rate of 27 pence per milréis, as specified under their foreign exchange clauses. The sterling figures for the domestic debt were combined with the external debt totals for each year to give the total stock of funded public debt. To arrive at the total debt (funded and floating) the stock of Treasury bills in circulation on 30 June of each year was converted to sterling and added to the total stock of funded debt.

SEIGNIORAGE REVENUES

Funds obtained by issuing paper money were an important component of the government's fiscal resources at key moments. From 1830 through 1852 and from 1866 through 1889, nominal seigniorage is derived by taking the first difference of the annual series of the stock of paper money that had been issued by the Treasury. For the period before 1830 the banknotes issued by the first Banco do Brasil are treated as Treasury issues. The annual data draw from Brazil, *Relatório da Commissão de Inquérito* . . . , "Quadro da Emissão . . . do Extincto Banco do Brasil . . ." and "Mappa Demonstrativo da Existência . . . das Notas do Governo . . ."; and Carreira, *História Financeira*, 742–43. From 1830 and after the data are for fiscal years. Before 1830 the figures are for the calendar year and are converted to a fiscal-year basis using a two-year moving average. The series is interpolated between 1830 and 1835, 1835 and 1838, and 1838 and 1841. Occasional reductions in the currency stock between 1830 and 1852 and between 1866 and 1889 are counted as negative seigniorage. The retirements of notes between 1852 and 1866 was performed by the Banco do Brasil under the terms of its charter. While this represented a reduction in the paper currency stock, it was not a Treasury operation, and the retirements are not included in the net seigniorage series.

FISCAL DATA

Ordinary revenues, primary expenditures, and debt service outlays were reconstructed from the original source for most years. The main source for public accounts is the Treasury's *Balanço da Receita e Despeza*. The first Balanço published was for fiscal year 1831, and was the means by which the finance ministry presented its record of spending and revenues to the chamber of deputies. For the 1820s accounts had to be reconstructed from tables in the reports of the finance minister, which were considerably less detailed than the *Balanço*. In a few years for which no data were located the source used is Carreira's study. While it is the most comprehensive of the early works on government finance, it suffers from some errors and must be used with caution. In numerous instances the figures reported by Carreira diverge from those in *Balanço*. It was nonetheless the best available source for filling gaps, which fortunately was required only by exception. For 1830 no data were available in any source, and all three fiscal series are interpolated.

Fiscal years coincided with calendar years up to the end of the 1820s. The basis of the fiscal year then switched, running from the start of July until the end of June. The 1820s revenue and cost data are adjusted accordingly. The fiscal year changed again in 1887. The available figures for the year 1886 encompass three semesters, from 1 July 1886 to 31 December 1887. To obtain estimates for fiscal year 1887, the approach was to take one-half of the value for calendar year 1888 and add it to one-third of the value of the "long" 1886. Similarly, calendar year 1888 and calendar year 1889 are averaged to produce an estimate for fiscal year 1889.

The concept employed by the Brazilian Treasury from the 1830s onward in classifying ordinary revenues and outlays corresponds in most respects to modern practice. In a few areas adjustments were warranted.

Revenues: The original figures overstate ordinary revenues. The main adjustment required involved stripping out expedient sources of income. Scrutiny of revenues by category made it possible to correct the exaggerated inflows. Each year the Treasury reported a category of so-called extraordinary income. After the 1830s these extraordinary receipts came mainly from judicial fees and fines and the occasional sale of state-owned assets. Through the 1830s, however (and occasionally thereafter), extraordinary revenues included funds received from credit operations and seigniorage. At times these accounted for a large share of the government's total annual inflows. In 1824 extraordinary income was 40 percent of total revenues and included seizures of Portuguese properties and partial proceeds from the London loan. In 1827 extraordinary income rose to nearly 45 percent of total revenues and came mainly from money advanced by the Banco do Brasil and other sources of credit. In fiscal year 1828–29 more than 80 percent of the extraordinary receipts were proceeds from the sale of long-term domestic bonds. In fiscal year 1829–30 the issue of copper coins and credit operations were booked as extraordinary revenues. In 1830–31 inflows came from the issue of yet more copper coinage, proceeds from loans, and public deposits. In 1831–32 the reported total revenues included the existing balances in the Treasury as new income, along with the proceeds of credit operations and the issue of copper coins. In 1834–35 extraordinary revenues accounted for 11 percent of total receipts, deriving from a modest issue of currency and "restitution" purportedly paid from the assets of the defunct Banco do Brasil. In 1836–37, 10 percent of total revenues were extraordinary, again mainly the proceeds from new borrowing. In all of these instances extraordinary revenues were subtracted from total revenues, thereby giving a consistent measure of ordinary revenue. After the 1830s any bias that extraordinary sources of income might have created diminished greatly. What little remained consisted largely of items that derived not from pure expedients but from indemnizations, lottery revenues, and proceeds from the sales of properties, such as buildings.

Primary Expenditures: The chief adjustment to convert the reported total expenditures to a consistent measure of primary expenditure was to net out debt service payments (interest and principal). As in the case of revenues, detailed information for the 1820s is more difficult to come by, though the finance minister's report fills most gaps. For 1827 the government's outlays in London were reported in sterling, and these were converted to milréis by means of the annual rate of exchange (see below).

Debt Service: Payments on the funded debt included three components: interest payments to bondholders, amortization to retire loans, and fees to loan contractors or other financial agents who handled interest and amortization. For most years the *Balanços* provide detail sufficient enough to allow calculation of comprehensive debt service flows. For years before 1834 these had to be estimated whenever detailed data were not available in the reports of the finance minister. For example, debt service for fiscal year 1824 is partly an estimate, based on budgeted expenditures for the second half of calendar year 1823.[1] On the pre-1828 funded domestic loans (including shares of the old 1796 loan), annual coupon rates ranged from 1 percent to 6 percent. A 5 percent average coupon rate was applied to the stock of these domestic debts through 1832 to estimate the flow of interest payments. The contribution of the domestic component to overall debt service payments in this period was quite small. Interest on the London loans was estimated for 1825 and 1826 from the implicit coupon payments on the face value of the debt that had been issued to that point. From 1830 through 1833 both the domestic and foreign components of debt service were estimated from the implicit interest on the outstanding stock of both components along with any reported amortization in Rio (amortization in London had been suspended).

All payments in London were booked by the Treasury at the fictive exchange rate of 27 pence per milréis. When the market value of the milréis was less than this exchange rate, the true pecuniary cost of servicing loans denominated in sterling was greater. To account for this difference the *Balanço* statements included what the Treasury called "difference in exchange," which were the additional foreign exchange costs on transfers to London beyond those recorded at the notional parity. These are included as part of the overseas debt service payments. Summing the component series of payments across the categories of debt gives the total debt service each year.

LOAN PROCEEDS

Brazil's London loans nearly always entered the market at a discount to the loan's contracted value. Rio loans rarely raised an amount equal to or in excess of the loan's face value, so that in most instances these too were issued at a discount.

With regard to the London loans and the National Loans, calculating the actual proceeds of borrowing was straightforward. When loans were raised in installments the inflows were assigned to a fiscal year according to the date of each installment. For apólices the total volume of debt issued each year is available. Information on the loans' proceeds was not always available. When the primary market apólice price was reported, the proceeds of that year's debt issue are readily computed. In the absence of the primary market price, a three-step procedure was employed to estimate the year's proceeds. First, an adjustment factor Z_t was calculated as the ratio of the apólice's primary market price (Pp_t) to the annual average secondary market price (Ps_t) for years in which the primary market price was reported. This ratio was then interpolated to produce an estimated ratio $\hat{Z}_t$ for years in which debt was issued but no primary market price was available. For each of these years, $\hat{P}_t$ was then calculated as the product of Ps_t and $\hat{Z}_t$. The proceeds on apólice borrowing were then calculated as the product of $\hat{P}_t$ and the quantity of apólices issued. The money raised on borrowing in domestic currency was converted to pounds by using the annual average market exchange rate in order to sum it with the London issues.

Estimates of the amounts raised on London loans come from the contracts cited in appendix III. Since early pay-ins by investors were rewarded with an extra discount on the purchase of the bond, actual amounts raised on the loan could be less than the contracted amount. But as the example from the 1883 loan in chapter 3 revealed, the difference between the contracted amount and the amount raised net of early installment discounts was very slight.

PRIMARY BORROWING COSTS

Borrowing costs in the primary markets are calculated as ex ante internal rates of return at the time of borrowing. Chapters 3 and 4 present details on the computation. The data for fixed-maturity loans (all of the London loans and the National Loans in Brazil) come from loan contracts cited appendix III. For apólices the sources of the prices of new issues were the annual reports to the parliament from the finance ministers, the commercial press, and correspondence of merchants, as detailed in chapter 4.

MARKET YIELDS ON THE DOMESTIC DEBT

The bulk of Brazil's domestic funded debt consisted of 6 percent apólices. In 1886 the government executed a conversion of apólices from a 6 percent coupon to a 5 percent coupon. The new 5 percents were first quoted in the official market on 3 April 1886, and serve as the basis for the apólice price series thereafter. For convenience they are all referred to here simply as apólices (though it is important to make clear that pre-1886 5 percent apólices and the old 4 percents are not used to calculate yields or capital costs, as they were small in volume and not quoted frequently). Price quotations for apólices before 1850 come from Rio newspapers. The most important was the *Jornal do Commércio*, which carried the first reported secondary market quotations starting in 1829. Occasional gaps in its coverage were filled by the *Correio Mercantil* (intermittently during 1830–32) and *O Constitucional* (in 1831). For the pre-1850 period in general a check on the apólice prices quoted in *Jornal do Commércio* is possible at occasional intervals via the city's other commercial papers. After 1850 the main sources of apólice price quotes are the manuscript quotation books of the Rio stock exchange. Regulation originating in the commercial code of 1850 formalized the ways of quoting prices and recording the transactions of the Rio exchange beginning in March 1850. Data drawn from these registers come from ANRJ, Fundo Bolsa de Valores do Rio de Janeiro (BVRJ), Livros das Cotações Oficiais da Junta dos Corretores, Livros 13187 through 13241, Codices 5692 through 5746. The prices reported by the *Jornal do Commércio* by and large reflected the official quotes in the exchange (occasional differences were so slight as to be negligible). In 1858 the trading of apólices was unusually thin on the official market, perhaps as a result of the financial crisis that began in 1857. Price quotes were largely absent from both the stock exchange and the *Jornal do Commércio*. Curb market quotes for apólices did, however, appear in Rio's *Correio da Tarde* newspaper. There were some weeks in which no price quotation could be located in any of the available sources. Of the more than three thousand weeks covered between 1829 and 1891 to create the series, in approximately 12 percent there was no reported apólice price. These gaps were filled by cubic-spline interpolation to minimize any bias that might be imparted in the statistical manipulations of the series in chapter 5.

Yields to maturity were derived from the apólice prices in two steps. Apólices became perpetual annuities after 1838 and—since amortization had always been irregular—were likely viewed as such for most of the previous decade. Over an infinite number of payment periods, the yield to maturity is indistinguishable from the current yield. The first step, then, was to simply divide the coupon rate by the market price of the bond. The current yield is then adjusted for the semiannual coupon frequency by

$$YTM = \left(\left(1 + \frac{1}{2} \, current \, yield \right)^2 - 1 \right)$$

to give the effective annual yield, on a week-by-week basis.

YIELDS ON BRAZILIAN BONDS IN LONDON

Weekly London bond prices come from three sources. The first and most important was the *Course of the Exchange*. In a few instances missing observations were filled in by using price quotes published in the *Times* of London and the *Economist*. The main difficulty encountered with the London bonds is that no single loan circulated for the entire period under study. The series thus links runs of yields from different loans, bearing different coupons, and issued with different maturities. The different coupon rates are of some concern. Two bonds with identical risk of default and the same maturity, but differing coupon rates, will not only have different market prices but also can have different yields owing to seniority and different reinvestment risks.[2] When maturities differ for two otherwise identical bonds, their current yields may differ—one is priced higher and yields less because it is slated to mature earlier. This means that a change in the reference bond within the series, for example, from a 5 percent bond with a thirty-year maturity to a 5 percent that matures earlier than thirty years, may appear as a shift in the level of the current yield series. A partial solution is to compute the yield to maturity, rather than using the current yield, to control for differing coupon rates and maturities across the loans that comprise the subseries. The resulting yields on bonds of differing maturity then become legitimately comparable.

From 7 January 1825 through 2 December 1852, yields to maturity are calculated on bonds from the loans of 1824 and 1825. Despite being issued through separate contractors some six months apart, they were listed as a single loan on the London exchange. These had a 5 percent coupon and a maturity of 1 April 1854. When the shares of the loan of 1852 first hit the market, the bonds from the 1824 and 1825 loans quickly went above their par value, driving the yield to maturity below even that of the risk-free yield on British consols for a few weeks. The series here switches over to the 1852 bonds as soon as they appeared in order to minimize any bias from this effect.

In the rest of the 1850s and the 1860s, no single loan was quoted with the desired regularity in the London market. This left two alternatives. One was to use 4.5 percents from the loan of 1852, supplemented by price quotes for 4.5 percents from loans in 1858 and 1860. The second alternative was to use scattered observations of the 5 percents still in circulation. The 1824/1825 loans, originally set to mature in 1854, were extended by agreement with the loan contractors for ten years, meaning that those bonds were occasionally quoted as well in the 1850s. The market for the latter, however, was not very active and would require mingling price quotes of the limited number of bonds in circulation from the small loans of 1829 and 1839 with those of the 1824/1825 loans. In many instances the issue year of the 5 percent bond being quoted could not be ascertained. Because of these concerns the following approach was taken. From 10 December 1852 through 5 March 1862, the yield to maturity was calculated on bonds from the loan of 1852, bearing a 4.5 percent coupon and with a maturity of 1 December 1882. In 1862 price quotes for the 1852 loan turned scarce, necessitating a shift to bonds of another loan. To avoid interpolating over gaps as large as one month, yields beginning with the observation on 13 March 1862 and running through 28 December 1863 are based on a "composite" bond from the loans taken in 1852, 1858, and 1860. These were separate loans, in different amounts and with distinct maturities, all with a 4.5 percent coupon. They were nonetheless consistently quoted in the 1860s as if they were a single issue. Their maturities all fell within an eight-year window, and differences in their prices must have been so slight as to have been inconsequential in the eyes of most investors. The redemption date used for calculating the yield to maturity on the composite bond is a weighted average of the maturities of the individual loans, with weights derived from their relative amounts of each loan at issue.[3] The resulting blended maturity for the 1852/1858/1860 bond was 1 September 1887.

By 1864 prices for the new bonds of 1863 had appeared in the press. Given that the loan was regularly quoted in this period and does not suffer from any of the potential biases of the composite loan of 1852/1858/1860, its 4.5 percent bonds serve as the basis for calculating the yield to maturity from 1 January 1864 through 10 October 1865 (with a maturity of 1 October 1893). When Brazil took the large war loan in 1865, its bonds quickly became the most actively traded and most frequently quoted of the Brazilian issues in London. These are used in the series from 17 October 1865 until 17 March 1871. The bond had a coupon of 5 percent and matured on 1 March 1903. The remainder of the bond yield series was built up in the same way by using, in succession, bonds from the loans of 1871, 1875, 1886, and 1888, in accordance with the dates given in table A.II.1.

Potential pitfalls exist in linking the subseries of bond yields, beyond the concerns about differing maturities and coupon rates detailed above. For a bond issued at discount, as almost all Brazilian loans were, the price

Table A.II.1

Components of Brazil Sovereign Bond Yield Series, 1825–91

START OF SUBSERIES	END OF SUBSERIES	LOAN	COUPON	CONTRACTED MATURITY
7 January 1825	2 December 1852	1824/1825	5	1 April 1854*
10 December 1852	5 March 1862	1852	4.5	1 December 1882
13 March 1862	28 December 1863	1852/1858/1860	4.5	1 September 1887
1 January 1864	10 October 1865	1863	4.5	1 October 1893
17 October 1865	17 March 1871	1865	5	1 March 1903
24 March 1871	12 February 1875	1871	5	1 February 1910
19 February 1875	1 October 1886	1875	5	30 June 1915
8 October 1886	12 December 1889	1886	5	1 January 1924
20 December 1889	28 December 1894	1888	4.5	1 April 1928

* Maturity extended to 1864 by agreement with the loan contractors.

of the bond will tend to par as its maturity draws near. Similarly, bonds that trade in the market above par will tend to move back to par as the redemption date approaches. Avoiding yields that are too close in time to the maturity date is prudent.

While calculating the yield to maturity improves the comparability of bonds with differing durations or differing coupon rates, the linking of the subseries remains necessarily imperfect. Different maturities are also associated with different degrees of seniority. In a scenario of partial default, the bond due to be redeemed sooner might well be worth more, since it is more senior and more likely to be repaid first. This further complicates linking the subseries to create a single uniform yield series. In practice, these types of problems are unavoidable but can be mitigated by attention to detail. If econometric analysis returns a structural break at the point of linkage between two subseries of bonds from different loans, additional scrutiny is warranted to make sure that the shift is not an artifact of the way in which the series was constructed.

An additional risk of bias in calculating yields arises when the market price of the bond exceeds par. Under Brazil's loan contracts a portion of bonds were to be retired each year. When they were above par, that year's portion was callable by lottery drawing and would be paid at par value. Calculations of the yield to maturity in these instances should take into account the probability that the bond might be called. The "yield to call" rather than the yield to maturity would have to be computed for each future period. Multiple call scenarios with their respective probabilities (a function of how many years remained to maturity) would have to be incorporated into the estimate of yield. Outside of its computational complexity, this approach is not pursued mainly because the Empire's London bonds were infrequently priced in the market above their par values. With the exception of the run-up to the conversion loans in the late 1880s, bonds did not remain at high prices for extended periods. Bonds traded slightly above par fairly consistently from February through May in 1853; again in late June through September in 1874; from May 1881 through December 1882; April through June 1883; November and December 1883; and April 1887 through May 1889. In the latter period the Empire's bond prices were unusually high, reflecting the upcoming debt conversion to bonds with a lesser coupon and perhaps influenced by very low interest rates in the London market. But overall Brazil's bonds traded at some point above par in roughly fifty-seven months out of sixty-five years.

YIELDS ON CONSOLS IN LONDON

Converting yields to risk premia required stripping out the risk-free return on the basis of the London consol yield. Consol prices came from the same sources as the prices for Brazil's London bonds. Until 1862 the books were closed on consol trades in the weeks between the announcement of the ex-dividend date and the payment of the dividend. The *Course of the Exchange* did not normally report consol prices during the weeks when the books were closed, as trades were not officially taking place. Other sources sometimes did report prices on consols, to be settled once the closure period had ended. Whenever possible, gaps in the series during closures were filled by means of using the forward prices reported in the *Economist* and the *Times*. Where gaps persisted, the last consol price available was used.

Until April 1881 the data are for 3 percent consols, which paid interest twice yearly. In April 1881 the market value of the 3 percents exceeded par for the first time, increasing the likelihood that they would be called. This makes them unsuitable from that point forward as a measure of the long-run rate of interest. From April 1881 the data are instead based on New Gladstones, the 2.5 percent consols first issued in 1853, which also paid interest on a semester basis. For semester interest payments the yield to maturity is calculated in the same way for consols as apólices.

$$r = \left(\left(1 + \frac{1}{2} \, current \; yield \right)^2 - 1 \right).$$

The reference consol shifted again in 1884. The Conversion Act of 1884 passed under Chancellor of the Exchequer Hugh Childers authorized the conversion of outstanding 3 percents using new 2.5 percent and 2.75 percent consols; on August 8, 1884, the conversion plan began.[4] Starting in 1884 the reference consols are the New Childers, as suggested by Klovland.[5] Other than the different coupon rates, the key change in this period was the frequency of the dividend payment. The introduction of the New Childers consols shifted interest payments from a semester basis to a quarterly basis. This required a slightly different method of calculating the annual equivalent yield. For quarterly coupon payments the yield is

$$r = \left(\left(1 + \frac{1}{4} \, current \; yield \right)^4 - 1 \right).$$

EXCHANGE RATE

Weekly observations of the exchange rate in Rio de Janeiro came from newspapers and archival sources. Before 1850 the main sources for the exchange rate were the city's newspapers. The rates most often reported were those on bills of exchange rather than gold sovereigns. The bills were currency contracts to be settled in the future, usually in sixty or ninety days. Gaps in sources made it impossible to establish a Rio exchange rate for part of the 1820s. During fiscal years 1825 and 1826 there were data for only a few months of each year. If these had been scattered more or less randomly across the full twelve-month span, there would be little concern, but in both of these years the available observations were tightly clustered in time. As a result, the exchange rates used for 1825 and 1826 are those quoted in London. This creates a potential bias. Gaps between the exchange rates reported on each side of the Atlantic were as much as 10 percent (and occasionally greater) in the 1830s. But comparison of the annual rates in Rio and London for 1824 and years after 1825–26 suggests there is little reason for concern in the mid-1820s. For 1824 the average rate in Rio was 49.2 pence per milréis, while in London it was 49. For 1827 the average Rio rate was 41, while for London it was 39.5. In 1828 the average rate was 32.6 in London versus 32.9 in Rio. Weekly observations of the exchange rate in London for 1825 and 1836 came from the *Course of the Exchange*. For the rest of the 1820s the rates come from *Seminário Mercantil* from June 1823 to May 1824; *Folha Mercantil* from June to October 1824; *Diário Mercantil* from November 1824 to September 1825; *Folha Mercantil* in September of 1825; and the *Diário Mercantil* from the second half of calendar year 1826 into 1829. From 1829 to 1850 the main source was the *Jornal do Commércio*. From 1850 on, the principal sources were the same stock exchange records that provided the apólice price quotations. In the aftermath of the financial crisis of 1857 official quotes for exchange rates became sparse, but the *Correio da Tarde* published regular quotations drawn from the curb market for most of 1858.

For thirteen months, from July 1876 until August 1877, quotations for pound-milréis exchange contracts vanished from both the financial press and the official transactions of the exchange. The gap in the data was filled by using the rate at which the Treasury remitted its funds to London. In most instances these were remittances from the main Treasury office in Rio. The remittances were made at irregular intervals, giving observations that were less frequent than desired. One concern is whether the rate at which the Treasury actually remitted was representative of market rates. Comparisons of market-based rates from the period before and after the thirteen-month interval reveal that the differences between the Treasury's rate of exchange and the rate quoted in the market were minuscule. The annual series of exchange rates was placed on a fiscal-year basis by taking an unweighted average of weekly quotes over each twelve-month interval from 1 July to 30 June.

DATA ON BANKS AND COMPANIES

Chapters 6 and 7 rely mainly on published primary sources and newspapers. For companies the *Jornal do Commércio* intermittently reported tables with the capital stock of the joint-stock firms listed on the Rio de Janeiro stock exchange. Occasional summary data, cited in the chapters, appeared in annual reports of cabinet ministers.

The semester or annual reports of banks to their shareholders were, in a number of instances, published as separate volumes. Many of those that have survived are available in the periodicals section of the Biblioteca Nacional. The London and Brazilian Bank annual reports to shareholders are available in the archive of the Bank of London and South America at University College, London. Summary financial statements of banks for years in which no separate reports were available came from the *Jornal do Commércio* and the *Diário Oficial do Império*.

Primary Market Borrowing Costs

SOURCES AND METHOD

The interest rate the Brazilian government agreed to pay on a new loan was the ex ante cost of capital implied by the loan contract. This is not the same as the interest rate that Brazil paid ex post. The ex post rate depended on the timeliness of interest payments, the frequency of amortization, and the amounts actually paid in fees to the contractor handling the service on the loan. The ex ante cost of capital differs as well from the rate of return to the bondholder who acquired bonds at issue and held them until maturity. Like the ex post cost of capital, bondholder returns depended on the timeliness of interest payments. They did not include fees that the government paid to intermediaries, which meant they were always less than the government's ex ante borrowing rate even when the government strictly complied with the terms of the loan contract.

The distinction is important because only the ex ante interest rate reveals the market's appraisal of creditworthiness at the time of lending (the ex post measure reveals whether lenders were justified in their ex ante appraisal of the borrower's reliability). What the borrower commits to pay is detailed in the contract between the borrower and the intermediary handling the loan: interest, regular amortization, onetime fees at issue, recurring fees for handling interest payments and amortization drawings, the additional discount at issue resulting from the use of installments to raise the loan, and the settlement of any balance of principal at the loan's maturity. For fixed maturity loans, like those in London and the National Loans in Brazil, the interest rate is derived from the internal rate of return, $(1+i)$, in the expression

$$M = \sum_{t=0}^{T} \left[\frac{D_t + A_t + Fd_t + Fa_t}{(1+i)^t} \right] + \frac{B}{(1+i)^T}$$

where M is the money raised, D is the semester interest payment on bonds in circulation, A is the prescribed amortization along with interest payments to the sinking fund on bonds already retired, Fd and Fa are fees on interest payments and amortization drawings, T is the loan's term, and B is the balance (if any) to be paid off at maturity. There is no closed-form solution for the internal rate of return, and it is calculated using numeric techniques. Because interest was paid on a semester basis, the calculation gives a semester interest rate, which is converted to an annual equivalent rate: $i_a = (1+i_s)^2 - 1$.

Interest rates for the loans issued in London and for the fixed-maturity National Loans taken in Brazil depended on specific details set out in each loan contract. Several considerations are warranted in using the contractual provisions to compute the ex ante cost of borrowing. The present value of the cash raised was less when the money came to the Treasury in installments. Disbursement by installment was commonly used when the intermediary raised the loan through a public subscription of bonds. The delay in receiving the borrowed money reduced its value and raised the loan's cost. The borrower had to pay interest from the start date of the contract on money it received only later. In such cases the present value of the loan on the date that interest began to accrue is calculated by discounting each installment by a daily interest rate implied by the coupon rate on the loan, taking into account the number of days that elapsed between the signing of the contract and each installment.

The amount of the cash raised was further reduced when subscribers received rebates for early completion of their installments. Such information survives for only a few loans, such as that of 1883. On the basis of the reported cash flows, the difference this made to the estimates here is slight. Of 4 million pounds sterling, the discounts for early installments came to only around 1.4 percent (see *RMF* 1884, table 7). The total amount rebated could not be anticipated at the time the loan was first contracted and is disregarded in the calculations of chapter 3.

Loans that Brazil received in a single payment were those in 1839, 1843, 1852, the maturity extension of 1854, and the loan of 1859. All of these either securitized existing unfunded debts or refinanced outstanding issues of bonds. Loans taken under installments were those of 1824, 1825, 1829, 1858, 1860, 1863, 1865, 1871, 1875, 1883, 1886, 1888, and 1889. It is not useful to detail in every case the precise adjustments made to the amounts of money raised. An illustration is provided in the discussion in chapter 3, using the case of the loan of 1871. The main implication is that installment loans had higher effective rates of interest than loans made under identical terms and conditions but which were provided in whole from the time of contracting.

A second adjustment involves the terms of amortization and the fees involved. Loan contracts required amortization either by purchasing bonds in the open market or by lottery drawing. Purchase was used whenever bonds traded at less than their par value. Loan contractors used drawings to retire bonds whenever the bond's market price exceeded the par value. The National Loan of 1865 mandated amortization at par, irrespective of the bonds' market price. Amortization fees to the loan contractor differed depending on the way amortization took place. To make the results of the internal rate of return calculations comparable over loans, the calculation of fees assumes that bonds were called and retired at face value. Some loan contracts required amortization on a semester basis, while others indicated the annual amount. The computation of the return was tailored, by loan, to account for this feature.

The interest payments on domestic loans raised through the issue of apólices did not involve intermediaries and were handled directly by the Treasury. Amortization was suspended indefinitely in 1838, making the apólices perpetual interest-bearing securities. The ex ante return on apólice issues through 1838 was calculated like that for the London loans. The adjustment for computing the interest rate on apólice loans after 1838 in chapter 4 is to calculate the internal rate of return on an infinite stream of coupon payments, using the bond's initial issue price (P):

$$P = \sum_{t}^{\infty} \frac{coupon_t}{(1 + i_A)^t},$$

which in the limit approaches

$$i_A \cong \frac{coupon}{P}.$$

Because interest was paid by semester it is adjusted to an annual rate. The government's cost of borrowing using apólices of identical coupon rates varied solely with the initial issue price of the loan.

The following sources were used to estimate the cost of domestic borrowing presented in Figure 4.7: for 1828, Samuel, Phillips (SP) to Nathan Mayer Rothschild (NMR), RAL XI/38/215B, 17 January 1828, and 16 February 1828; for 1829: SP to NMR, 12 July 1828, and 13 December 1828; Macedo, *Tratado do Cavalleiro Hennet*, pp. 142–44; Anexo B, "Quadro das Apólices . . . ," *Relatório da Commissão . . . 1859*; 1830: SP to NMR, 28 January 1830, 8 February 1830; 1832: SP to NMR, 16 October 1831; 1833–36: Anexo B, "Quadro das Apólices . . . ," *Relatório da Commissão . . . 1859*; 1837–38: *RMF*, 1839; Anexo B, "Quadro Demonstrativo das Apólices de Fundos Públicos"; 1839: Anexo B, "Quadro das Apólices . . . ," *Relatório da Commissão . . . 1859*; 1841: *RMF* 1841, table 7-A; *RMF* 1843A, table 21; 1842: *RMF* 1843A, table 21; 1843: SP to NMR, 15 September 1842, *RMF* 1843B, table 3; 1844: *RMF* 1844, table 6; *RMF* 1845A, table 5; 1845: *RMF* 1845B, table 6; 1846: *RMF* 1846, table 11; 1847: *RMF* 1847, table 6; 1849: *RMF* 1850A, table 11; 1850: *RMF* 1850B, table 7; 1851: *RMF* 1851, p. 12, table 8; 1852: *RMF* 1852, table 8; 1853: *RMF* 1854, p. 3, table 11; 1861: *RMF* 1862, p. 15; 1863: *RMF* 1864A, p. 8; "Retrospecto Anual" (RA), *Jornal do Commércio* (*JdoC*), 7 January 1863; 1869: RA, *JdoC* for 1869, 7 January 1870; 1870: RA, *JdoC* for 1870, 7 January 1871; 1871: *RMF* 1871, p. 10; 1876: *RMF* 1877A, p. 33; 1877: *RMF* 1877B, pp. 18–19; 1879: *RMF* 1879, table 10; *RCJC* for 1879, p. 43; 1887: *RMF* 1886, "Contrato feito com o Banco do Brasil"; *RMF* 1887, p. 58. For most annual observations the interest rate is based on a weighted average of apólice issue prices during a single fiscal year. In cases where new borrowing ran over fiscal year cutoffs, loan prices were assigned to the fiscal year in which the bulk of the bond issue took place. In the mid-1840s the specific months of issue were not reported, so that the fiscal year matching is approximate.

For borrowing in London, and borrowing with fixed-maturity loans in Brazil, the contracts located and consulted are listed below.

LOAN AGREEMENTS OF THE EMPIRE OF BRAZIL

1824: AMFF 71.11.54, "[Agreement for General Bond] Between Felisberto Caldeira Brant and Manoel Rodrigues Gameiro Pessoa, Plenipotentiaries, and Messrs. Bazett, Colvin, Crawford & Co., Messrs. Fletcher, Alexander, & Co., and Messrs. Thomas Wilson & Co.," 7 June 1824; ANRJ, Série Diplomacia, Manuscritos, [BR AN Rio] Q1 O DIL 89, "[Bond Certificate] Loan of £3,000,000 Sterling Money for the Service of the Brazilian Empire," 7 June 1824.

1825: RAL 000/336/4, "An Agreement . . . Between Felisberto Caldeira Brant . . . and Chevalier Manoel Rodrigues Gameiro Pessoa . . . and Nathan Mayer Rothschild of the City of London . . . ," 12 January 1825; RAL 000/401/A, "Abstract of the Brazil Loan Contract 1825 Between the Brazilian Gov't FC Brant MRG Pessoa and NM Rothschild, 12 January 1825"; AMFF 77.11.201B, "[Contract] N. M. Rothschild to the General Felisberto Caldeira Brant and Chevalier Manoel Rodrigues Gameiro Pessoa, Plenipotentiaries of His Majesty the Emperor of the Brazils," n.d.

1829: AMFF 77.11.57, and RAL 000/336/4, "An Agreement Between . . . Viscount de Itabayana . . . and Nathan Mayer Rothschild . . . ," 3 July 1829; AMFF 77.11.57A, "Private Agreement Between . . . Viscount de Itabayana . . . and Nathan Mayer Rothschild," 3 July 1829; AMFF 77.11.57B, "An Agreement Between . . . Viscount of Itabayana and Messrs. Thomas Wilson & Co. merchants of the City of London," 3 July 1829; AMFF 77.11.57C, "Private Agreement Between . . . Viscount of Itabayana . . . and Messrs. Thomas Wilson & Co.," 3 July 1829.

1839: *RMF* 1838, p. 19; *RMF* 1875, Annexo B, "Tabella das diversas condições dos empréstimos levantados pelo Brazil em Londres desde o anno de 1824."

1843: AMFF 77.11.58, "Notarial Certificate of the Deposit at the Bank of [the] General Bond and Full Powers for [the] Brazilian Fund [of] 1843," 20 May 1843.

1852: RAL 000/336/2, "Loan of £954,250 Sterling for the Service of the Brazilian Empire," 6 September 1852 (Notarized Copy, 12 November

1852); *RMF* 1853, [Table] 43, "Traducção do Contracto do Empréstimo de £1.040.600."

1858: RAL 000/336/2, "1858. Empire of Brazil. Loan of £1,425,000 Sterling," 19 May 1858; *RMF* 1859, Anexo 1, "Contracto para Levantamento do Empréstimo de 1858."

1859: AMFF 71.11.63, "1859. Empire of Brazil. Loan of £508,000 sterling for the Financial Service of the Empire of Brazil," n.d.; AMFF 71.11.63A, "Memorandum of Loan, 23 February 1859"; *RMF* 1859, Anexo 2, "Condições do Contracto para pagamento do Resto do Empréstimo de 1829."

1860: RAL 000/336/2, "1860. Empire of Brazil. Loan of £1,210,000 Sterling for Advances to be Made to Promote Industrial Undertakings," 16 March 1860; [Prospectus] "Imperial Brazilian Loan at 4½ Per Cent"; *RMF* 1861, p. 6; *RMF* 1860, pp. 16–17.

1863: RAL 000/336/2, "1863. Empire of Brazil Loan of £3,300,000 Sterling;" [Prospectus] "Imperial Brazilian 4½ per Cent Loan 1863, for £3,300,000"; *RMF* 1864, Anexo B, "Empréstimo de 1863."

1865: AMFF 77.11.69, [Agreement between Baron of Penedo and N. M. Rothschild and Sons], "1865. Empire of Brazil. Loan of £5,000,000 Sterling," 23 September 1865; AMFF 77.11.69A, "Memorandum of an Agreement . . . Between the Imperial Brazilian Government by His Excellency the Baron do Penedo . . . and Baron Lionel Nathan de Rothschild, Sir Anthony Rothschild, Baron Nathaniel de Rothschild, and Baron Mayer Amschel de Rothschild . . . ," 12 September 1865; [Prospectus] "Imperial Brazilian 5 per Cent Loan of 1865, for £5,000,000 Sterling"; *RMF* 1866, Annexo A, "Empréstimo de 1865. Contracto."

1868 (National Loan): AMFF 77.11.37, [Bond certificate] Empréstimo Nacional do 1868, issued under Decreto 4.244, 15 September 1868.

1871: RAL 000/401C, "Memorandum of Contract for the Loan of £3,000,000 Sterling," 23 February 1871; RAL 000/336/2, [General bond], 26 April 1871; [Prospectus] "Imperial Brazilian 5 per Cent Loan of 1871, for £3,000,000 Sterling"; *RMF* 1871, pp. 13–14, "Memorandum de Contracto para o Empréstimo de £3.000.000 sterlinas . . ."

1875: RAL 000/401C, "Memorandum of Agreement . . . Between the Imperial Brazilian Government by his Excellency the Baron do Penedo . . . and Baron Lionel Nathan de Rothschild, and Sir Anthony Rothschild Baronet . . . ," 18 January 1875; [Prospectus] "Imperial Brazilian 5 per Cent Loan of 1875 for £5,000,000 Sterling"; *RMF* 1875, Anexo B, "Contracto do Empréstimo de 1875 e Condições dos Empréstimos Externos."

1879 (National Loan): RAL 000/337/2 [Bond Certificate], "Império do Brazil, Empréstimo de 1879"; *CLB*, Decreto 7381, 19 July 1879.

1883: [Prospectus] "Imperial Brazilian 4½ per Cent Loan of 1883, for £4,000,000 Sterling"; *RMF* 1883, Annexo A, "Memorandum do Contrato do Empréstimo Externo de 1883 e breve notícia sobre os empréstimos contrahidos pelo Brazil na praça de Londres desde 1824"; RAL 000/336/3 [General Bond], 11 May 1883.

1886: RAL 000/401D, "Memorandum of Contract for the Loan of £6,000,000 Sterling in 5 per Cent Stock"; RAL 000/336/3, [General Bond] 26 May 1886; [Prospectus] "Imperial Brazilian 5 per Cent Loan of 1886, for £6,000,000 Sterling"; *RMF* 1886, Anexo B, Operações de Crédito, "Empréstimo de 1886. £6.000.000 reaes ou £6.431.000 nominaes. Contrato Preliminar."

1888: RAL 000/336/3, "[General Bond] Empire of Brazil. 4½ % Loan of 1888"; [Prospectus] "Imperial Brazilian 4½ per Cent Loan of 1888, for £6,000,000 Sterling."

1889: RAL 000/336/3, "1889 Brazilian Loan Contract Between . . . Conselheiro Bacharel José Antonio de Azeredo Castro . . . and N. M. Rothschild & Sons," 30 September 1889; RAL 000/336/3, "Brazil 4% Loan of 1889, General Agreement," 29 April 1890; [Prospectus] "Conversion and Redemption of the Imperial Brazilian Five Per Cent Loans of 1865, 1871, 1875, and 1886."

1889 (National Loan): Decreto no. 10.322, 27 August 1889. For the issue fee, see Rui Barbosa, *Obras Completas*, vol. 16, no. 6, p. 301.

NOTES

CHAPTER 1. INTRODUCTION

1. Borrowing in London was cheaper for Brazil in 1824 and 1825 than in 1829, a result partly of the lending boom still under way in London and partly of the fact that Brazil had not yet had trouble making interest payments. For the costs of the government's London borrowing, see chapter 3.

2. Loans taken by the government in the domestic market before 1831 were cheaper, but not by much, costing some 11.5 percent per year in 1828. The cost of the last loan in 1889 was identical to the cost of borrowing in sterling in London, as Brazil had gone on gold. Chapter 4 provides estimates of primary market borrowing costs in Rio de Janeiro.

3. Historians had long emphasized the financial importance of the institutional changes wrought by the Glorious Revolution; see Dickson, *The Finan-*

cial Revolution in England. For the political background to the institutional and economic changes of the Glorious Revolution, see Pincus, *1688: The First Modern Revolution,* 366–99. The now-classic argument for the connection between institutional change, the credible commitment to repay sovereign debt, and financial development in the British case is North and Weingast, "Constitutions and Commitment." North and Weingast's paper inspired a body of work that alternately disputed, confirmed, or added to their argument. Those studies are cited below at the appropriate points.

4. Stasavage, *States of Credit,* 70–131.
5. North and Weingast, "Constitutions and Commitment."
6. Salvucci, *Politics, Markets, and Mexico's "London Debt,"* 14–16.
7. For these early arguments, and energetic rebuttals by a staunch defender and participant, see Figueiredo [visconde de Ouro Preto], *A Década Republicana.*
8. Prado Junior, *História Econômica do Brasil,* 201.
9. Furtado, *A Formação Econômica do Brasil,* 139.
10. Rodrigues, *Atas do Conselho do Estado,* 10:xxviii.
11. Spain holds the unenviable record for the most defaults, and Philip II alone defaulted four times in the late sixteenth century; see Drelichman and Voth, *Lending to the Borrower from Hell.*
12. In light of Rodrigues's characterization, the relative dearth of research on the Imperial debt is a peculiar elision. The emphasis to date in analyses of Brazilian state building at the national level—where one might think that the relevance of sovereign borrowing in particular would be most direct—is on other issues: the backgrounds of high-office holders, the workings of patronage, the nature of partisan organization, and ideology. For leading examples, see Mattos, *O Tempo Saquarema;* Barman, *Brazil: The Forging of a Nation;* Graham, *Patronage and Politics;* Salles, *Nostálgia Imperial;* Needell, *Party of Order,* along with the essays in Jancsó, ed., *Brasil: Formação do Estado e da Nação.* Some of the more recent works related to state building are tightly regional in focus, such that government borrowing might seem to be naturally outside its scope. See, for example, Bieber, *Power, Patronage, and Political Violence;* Mosher, "Political Mobilization, Party Ideology, and Lusophobia." Although long-term funded borrowing by provincial governments added fully 10 percent on top of the central government's debt by the end of the Empire, province-level studies of state building have yet to illuminate the politics and economics of the provincial public debt or the contours of markets for provincially issued securities.
13. It also does not give short shrift to other elements that matter for economic growth. Obviously, sustained economic growth occurs across a broad front, with factors beyond finance playing important roles, including factor endowments, education and human capital formation, transport costs, and transaction costs more generally, among others.
14. Suzigan, *Indústria Brasileira: Origem e Desenvolvimento,* 78.
15. Haber, "The Efficiency Consequences of Institutional Change."

16. For a useful exposition of this problem and its implications for competition in the financial sector, see Perotti and Volpin, "Lobbying on Entry" (2004).

17. Bates and Lien, "A Note on Taxation, Development, and Representative Government."

18. Weingast, "The Political Foundations of Democracy and the Rule of Law."

19. Cox, "War, Moral Hazard, and Ministerial Responsibility."

20. See Salvucci, Politics, Markets, and Mexico's "London Debt," 100–105; Dawson, The First Latin American Debt Crisis, 92–173; Marichal, A Century of Debt Crises in Latin America, 43–67; Tenenbaum, The Politics of Penury, 28–29; Gootenberg, Between Silver and Guano, 22; Liehr, La Deuda Pública en América Latina, passim.

21. Salvucci, Politics, Markets, and Mexico's "London Debt," 102–3.

22. Dawson, The First Latin American Debt Crisis, 179–83. Most of the newly independent Latin American nations had borrowed in London using bonds in the 1820s, including one country that did not even exist (Poyais). Those that did not borrow were Bolivia, Paraguay, and the newly created Uruguay.

23. Marichal, A Century of Debt Crises in Latin America, 43–125.

24. Stone, "The Composition and Distribution of British Investment in Latin America," table 14, table 17.

25. The more successful cases of reentry into the international capital market before 1880 in Spanish America included Chile in the 1840s, some of the provincial governments of Argentina, and the national government of Peru at the start of the country's guano boom.

26. English, "Understanding the Costs of Sovereign Default"; Wallis, Grinath, and Sylla, "Sovereign Default and Repudiation."

27. On the concept and its evolution, see Eichengreen and Hausmann, "Exchange Rates and Financial Fragility," 330; Eichengreen, Hausmann, and Panizza, "The Pain of Original Sin," 13; Eichengreen, Hausmann, and Panizza, "Currency Mismatches, Debt Intolerance, and Original Sin," 147–50.

28. Reinhart, Rogoff, and Savastano, "Debt Intolerance," 1.

29. The first foreign default was negotiated by Brazil's president-elect, resulting in the Funding Loan of 1898. The loan covered interest on the outstanding foreign debt, on the National Loans fixed in sterling and gold, and on railroad dividend guarantees. These obligations were initially paid with new bonds, not cash, and at their face value, not at the market price. Debt holders thus saw the value of their interest "payments" shaved considerably. On the Funding Loan, see Abreu, "Os Funding Loans," 519–24.

30. 't Hart, Jonker, and Zanden, A Financial History; North and Weingast, "Constitutions and Commitment"; Rousseau and Sylla, "Financial Systems, Economic Growth, and Globalization."

31. On the merits and role of case studies for more general propositions, see George and Bennett, Case Studies and Theory Development.

32. The emphasis on institutions occupies a vast literature, beginning with pioneering works in economic history by North and Thomas (The Rise of the

Western World), and is now common in economics and political science; see Shepsle, "Studying Institutions"; Acemoglu and Johnson, "Unbundling Institutions."

33. At several moments the size of Brazil's debt was overshadowed by that of other Latin American borrowers. In the years immediately preceding its 1876 default, Peru's external funded debt was larger than Brazil's. By 1885 the net foreign debt of Brazil's central government was 23 million pounds, while that of the Argentine central government was only 14 million pounds. However, the Argentine provinces (mainly Buenos Aires) collectively had their own foreign debts of nearly 12 million pounds, while Brazil's provinces would have added much less to Brazil's overall government indebtedness; Stone, "The Composition and Distribution of British Investment in Latin America,"appendix D. Irrespective of differences in the amount of borrowing, no state consistently serviced its debt as reliably as Brazil.

34. Abreu, "A Dívida Pública Externa"; Bouças, *História da Dívida Externa;* Carreira, *História Financeira e Orçamentária.*

35. The view that London merchant bankers or external borrowing in general worked against Brazil dates from the criticisms of Bernardo de Vasconcelos and other nativists in the late 1820s and early 1830s, repeated with a vengeance a century later in Barroso, *Brasil, Colônia de Banqueiros.* For a more recent reformulation of the claim that Brazil relied excessively on foreign borrowing to its long-term detriment, see Centeno, "Blood and Debt." Evidence in chapters 3 and 4 below falsifies the claim.

36. Rousseau and Sylla, "Financial Systems, Economic Growth, and Globalization," 393–98.

37. Most of Brazil's major commercial banks were based in Rio de Janeiro. Restricting the examination to those companies listed on the Rio de Janeiro stock exchange makes it unavoidably incomplete. A number of companies were scattered across the provinces and issued stock but did not list or trade on the Rio exchange. If a firm did not list shares in Rio, then it did not really list at all. In São Paulo there was no formal stock exchange until the 1890s, after the period of consideration here; see Hanley, *Native Capital.*

38. The principal exception was railroads, but even these were shaped by an array of subsidies and regulations that channeled numerous projects to areas where they were less needed, while undersupplying them where they would have had more value; see Summerhill, "Institutional Determinants of Railway Subsidy and Regulation."

CHAPTER 2. SOVEREIGN BORROWING AND IMPERIAL DEBT POLICY

1. On the crises, see Marichal, *A Century of Debt Crises in Latin America,* 229–39.

2. Eaton, Gersovitz, and Stiglitz, "A Pure Theory of Country Risk"; Bulow and Rogoff, "Sovereign Debt: Is to Forgive to Forget?"

3. Kydland and Prescott, "Rules Rather Than Discretion"; Fischer, "Dynamic Inconsistency, Cooperation and Benevolent Dissembling Government"; Lucas and Stokey, "Optimal Fiscal and Monetary Policy." Time inconsistency proves to be a problem for lenders as well as borrowers; creditors confronted with default may find it difficult to apply the penalty; Hellwig, "A Model of Borrowing and Lending with Bankruptcy."

4. Eaton, Gersovitz, and Stiglitz, "A Pure Theory of Country Risk," 488.

5. Sachs and Cohen, "LDC Borrowing with Default Risk," 22; Bulow and Rogoff, "A Constant Recontracting Model of Sovereign Debt," 156; Eaton, Gersovitz, and Stiglitz, "A Pure Theory of Country Risk," 499–502.

6. Tomz and Wright, "Do Countries Default in 'Bad Times'?"

7. Edwards, "LDC Foreign Borrowing and Default Risk"; Catão, Fostel, and Kapur, "Persistent Gaps and Default Traps"; Hilscher and Nosbusch, "Determinants of Sovereign Risk."

8. Eaton and Gersovitz, "Debt with Potential Repudiation"; Cole and Kehoe, "Models of Sovereign Debt: Partial Versus General Reputations"; Tomz, *Reputation and International Cooperation.*

9. Bulow and Rogoff, "Sovereign Debt: Is to Forgive to Forget?"

10. Wright, "Reputations and Sovereign Debt."

11. Greif, Milgrom, and Weingast, "Coordination, Commitment, and Enforcement"; Weingast, "The Political Foundations of Limited Government," 238–44.

12. If the ruler has borrowed within the rationing constraint, the marginal loan has a net value of zero to the ruler; if the ruler is rationed credit, then the marginal loan has the lowest net value to the ruler of all loans.

13. Bulow and Rogoff, "A Constant Recontracting Model of Sovereign Debt," 158–59.

14. For the dependence of borrowing on sufficiently strong penalties for default, see Eaton, Gersovitz, and Stiglitz, "A Pure Theory of Country Risk," 486–92; and Bulow and Rogoff, "A Constant Recontracting Model of Sovereign Debt," 156.

15. Examples of political (rather than economic) models of debt include Weingast, "The Political Foundations of Limited Government"; Dixit and Londregan, "Political Power and the Credibility of Government Debt"; Schultz and Weingast, "The Democratic Advantage"; Kohlscheen, "Sovereign Risk: Constitutions Rule"; Stasavage, *Public Debt and the Birth of the Democratic State;* Cox, "Sovereign Debt, Policy Stability, and Bargaining Efficiency."

16. These included the earmarking of tax revenues for debt service in Venice and Florence and the delegation of revenue collection to a creditors' association in Genoa; Fratianni and Spinelli, "Italian City-States and Financial Evolution."

17. 't Hart, *The Making of a Bourgeois State,* 173–80. Ironically, its roots were in Hapsburg debt policy; Tracy, *A Financial Revolution in the Habsburg Netherlands.*

18. North and Weingast, "Constitutions and Commitment," 816–17. On the potential for political penalties to support international lending, see Bulow and Rogoff, "A Constant Recontracting Model of Sovereign Debt," 158–59.

19. Epstein, *Freedom and Growth*, 24–25; O'Brien, "Fiscal Exceptionalism," 245–64.

20. Sussman and Yafeh, "Institutional Reforms, Financial Development, and Sovereign Debt." Stasavage finds that the British government's borrowing costs fell principally with Whig control of the government; Stasavage, "Credible Commitment in Early Modern Europe."

21. Clark, "Political Foundations of Modern Economic Growth"; Quinn, "The Glorious Revolution's Effect on British Private Finance."

22. Robinson, "Debt Repudiation and Risk Premia."

23. North and Weingast, "Constitutions and Commitment," 808; Cox, "Was the Glorious Revolution a Constitutional Watershed?" 584.

24. Dincecco, *Political Transformations and Public Finances*, 96–97.

25. Hellwig, "A Model of Borrowing and Lending with Bankruptcy," 1895–1900.

26. Bulow and Rogoff, "A Constant Recontracting Model of Sovereign Debt," 156–57.

27. North and Weingast, "Constitutions and Commitment," 821–28.

28. Stasavage, "Private Investment and Political Institutions."

29. Rousseau and Sylla, "Financial Systems, Economic Growth, and Globalization," 374–77.

30. King and Levine, "Finance and Growth"; Levine, "Financial Development and Economic Growth"; Levine and Zervos, "Stock Markets, Banks, and Economic Growth"; Rajan and Zingales, "Financial Dependence and Growth."

31. See, for example, Eaton and Gersovitz, "Some Curious Properties of a Familiar Model of Debt and Default"; Weingast, "The Political Foundations of Limited Government,"

32. Robinson, "Debt Repudiation and Risk Premia."

33. Cox, "Was the Glorious Revolution a Constitutional Watershed?" 586–90.

34. Article 179, section 23; see Rodrigues, *Constituição Política do Império do Brasil*, 141–55.

35. Bueno, *Direito Público Brasileiro*, 431.

36. Article 15, sections 13 and 14; Rodrigues, *Constituição Política do Império do Brasil*, 19.

37. Bueno, *Direito Público Brasileiro*, 537–46.

38. Silva Torres [de Alvim] [visconde de Jerumerin], *Memória Sobre o Crédito em Geral*, 52–53.

39. *Constituição*, article 15, paragraph 10.

40. Article 172 obligated the cabinet to propose the annual budget to the chamber of deputies for deliberation and amendment. After 1830 the cabinet had a deadline of 8 May each year (roughly the opening of the legislative session) to present its proposed budget to the Finance Ministry as well as its proposed

size for the army and navy. It had until 15 May to present the budget proposals of all of the ministries; *CLB*, Lei of 15 December 1830, articles 41 and 42.

41. Bueno, *Direito Público Brasileiro*, 109–10; Sousa, *Analyse e Commentario da Constituição Política do Império do Brazil*, 208–11.

42. For brief mentions, see Dodsworth, *Organizações e Programas Ministeriais*, 35; Bouças, *História da Dívida Externa*, 48–49; Reis, *Dívida do Brasil*, 60–61.

43. *RMF* 1831, 15.

44. For both the full proposal and the commission's *parecer*, see Brazil, Câmara dos Deputados, *Proposta do Governo Sobre a Suspensão do Pagamento*.

45. *ACD*, 7 June 1831, 129–30.

46. *ACD*, 9 June 1831, 147. Vasconcelos blamed the sudden weakness in the market for public debt cited by Cunha Mattos on the "English merchants" who, Vasconcelos claimed, were selling their bonds to take profits.

47. *ACD*, 11 June 1831, 155.

48. Bueno, *Direito Público Brasileiro*, 99–100. Similarly, "if the government has [borrowing] authority, the guarantee that only the legislative branch can tax the nation would be meaningless, and each ministry would saddle the country with new debt, so long as the public credit lasts"; Sousa, *Analyse e Commentario da Constituição Política do Império do Brazil*, 139.

49. See Calmon's comments in *ACD*, 3 September 1836, 256–57; and those of Vasconcelos on 10 September 1836, 286–87.

50. *CLB*, Decreto 50, 17 October 1836, provided the credit by recourse to either a fiscal surplus (if there was one) or a domestic loan using apólices.

51. Silva, *Memórias do Meu Tempo*, 190–99.

52. *ACD*, 13 January 1879, 405.

53. The main exception is the fiscal year 1830–31 (along with the first semester of calendar year 1830), for which it has not been possible to locate parliamentary sanction of either debt service or the budget more generally.

54. Roure, "Formação do Direito Orçamentário Brasileiro," 574–75.

55. *Constituição do Império do Brazil*, article 172.

56. *CLB*, Lei of 15 December 1830, article 38.

57. The time in session each year is counted from the day deputies began their presession deliberations until the emperor formally closed the session (inclusive of special sessions). The dates come from the *Anais* of the chamber; Carvalho, *A História das Dissoluções da Camara dos Deputados;* and Gama, *Regimento Interno do Senado*.

58. *CLB*, Lei 58, 8 October 1833, article 43.

59. *CLB*, Lei 514, 28 October 1848, articles 52 and 53; Lei 589, 9 September 1850, article 4, paragraphs 1 through 3.

60. *CLB*, Lei 1177 of 9 September 1862, articles 12 and 13; *RMF* 1863, 6.

61. *RMF* 1875, "Proposta," 14.

62. It did so by passing a *prorrogativa* to cover the first semester of the new fiscal year; *CLB*, Lei 2585, 3 July 1875.

63. Chamber authorization for new borrowing was in the budget for 1876; *CLB*, Lei 2640, 22 September 1875.

64. This was the Caixa de Amortização; Oliveira, *Systema Financial do Brazil*, 159; *CLB*, Lei of 15 November 1827, articles 41, 42, 44.

65. *CLB*, Decreto of 8 October 1828, "Plano do Regimento interno da Caixa de Amortização da Dívida Nacional," chapter 1.

66. ANRJ, Fundo Caixa de Amortização-Balanços, Caixa 460, "Balanço Geral da Caixa d'Amortisação da Dívida Nacional no anno financeiro de 1840–1841"; "Quadro Demonstrativo das Transacções da Caixa d'Amortisação da Dívida Nacional deste Corte [1849–50]." Information on Treasury compliance moved quickly across the Atlantic. See, for example, RAL XI/38/215 B99, Samuel, Phillips & Co. to Nathan M. Rothschild, 20 September 1831.

67. Vasconcellos and Smith de Vasconcellos, *Archivo Nobiliarchico Brasileiro*, 387–88; Pang, *In Pursuit of Honor and Power*, 122–23; Plancher-Seignot, *Almanak Imperial . . .* , 160.

68. Blake, *Diccionário Bibliográphico*, 3:278; Plancher-Seignot, *Almanak Imperial . . .* , 160; Filho, *Folhinha Commercial . . . (1842)*, 95–123; Franco, *História do Banco do Brasil*, 201, 274, 304, 317; Mathias, *Comércio, 173 Anos de Desenvolvimento*, 361.

69. Matrícula (registration) as *negociante de atacado*, Joaquim Antonio Ferreira, ANRJ, Real Junta do Commercio, caixa 444, 1814; Vasconcellos and Smith de Vasconcellos, *Archivo Nobiliarchico Brasileiro*, 170–71; Florentino, *Em Costas Negras*, 254, 266–67.

70. Vasconcellos and Smith de Vasconcellos, *Archivo Nobiliarchico Brasileiro*, 207–8; Matrícula as *negociante de grosso trato*, Francisco José da Rocha Filho, ANRJ, Real Junta do Commércio, caixa 394, 1822; Florentino, *Em Costas Negras*, 256, 266–67.

71. Matrícula, *mercador de retalho*, ANRJ, Real Junta do Commercio, caixa 397, 1809; Vasconcellos and Smith de Vasconcellos, *Archivo Nobiliarchico Brasileiro*, 26; Dodsworth, *Organizações e Programas Ministeriais*, 183.

72. Vasconcellos and Smith de Vasconcellos, *Archivo Nobiliarchico Brasileiro*, 26, 122.

73. Nogueira and Firmo, *Parlamentares do Império*, 422–23; Vasconcellos and Smith de Vasconcellos, *Archivo Nobiliarchico Brasileiro*, 210.

74. Vasconcellos and Smith de Vasconcellos, *Archivo Nobiliarchico Brasileiro*, 436–37; Sweigart, "Financing and Marketing Brazilian Export Agriculture," 291.

75. Vasconcellos and Smith de Vasconcellos, *Archivo Nobiliarchico Brasileiro*, 309–10; Mathias, *Comércio, 173 Anos de Desenvolvimento*, 361; Nogueira and Firmo, *Parlamentares do Império*, 393.

76. Dome, *The Political Economy of Public Finance in Britain*, 5–7.

77. *RMF* 1884, 10.

78. The same was true in much of republican Spanish America as well; Gootenberg, *Between Silver and Guano*, 101; Marichal, "Una Difícil Transición Fiscal," 43–52.

79. Dewey, *Financial History of the United States*, 110–474, passim.
80. Care has been taken to isolate that portion of revenues that were legitimately "ordinary." Appendix II provides detail on the adjustments to the total revenues.
81. Summary figures on total revenues and expenditures are available in Cavalcanti, *Resenha Financeira do Ex-Império do Brazil*, 328; Carreira, *História Financeira e Orçamentária*, 660–61.
82. The source for recalculating revenues and expenditures in most years is the original statements of accounts presented to the chamber; Brazil, *Balanço da Receita e Despesa*. Figures for actual outlays on debt service (internal and external, funded and unfunded) become available only in 1833. Detail on the derivation pre-1833 revenues and expenditures, including outlays on debt service, is presented in appendix II.
83. Brazil, Câmara dos Deputados, *Parecer da Commissão de Fazenda*, Letra I, [Quadro] no. 8, "Estado de Dívida Passiva do Thesouro Público no fim do Anno de 1824," 145–48.
84. Sturz, *A Review, Financial, Statistical, and Commercial*, 4–7.
85. Reis, *Dívida do Brasil*, 27; Neves, *Corcundas e Constitucionais*, 364; Sturz, *A Review, Financial, Statistical, and Commercial*, 9.
86. The first systematic tally of Brazil's recognized debts after independence is for 30 June 1823 and came to almost 12 million milréis; Brazil, Ministério da Fazenda, *Exposição do Estado da Fazenda Pública*, 32–34. Market exchange rates in the second half of 1823 were between 49.5d and 52d per milréis (see the *Seminário Mercantil*, weekly issues between June and December 1823). To arrive at the figure in the text, 12 million milréis are converted to dollars at 0.2125 pounds per milréis, and 4.81 dollars per pound; for the dollar-pound rate, see Officer, "Dollar-Sterling Mint Parity," 592.
87. Sturz, *A Review, Financial, Statistical, and Commercial*, 20.
88. Early mention of apólices issued by provincial governments can be found in RA 1848, *Jornal do Commércio*, 14 January 1849.
89. The funded share of this debt was less, some 60.3 million milréis; Cavalcanti, *Resenha Financeira do Ex-Império do Brazil*, 284.
90. For debt figures, see the essays in Liehr, *La Deuda Pública en América Latina*. Exchange rates taken from the *Statesmen's Year Book*.
91. In a number of these there was no domestic debt to speak of, so that the external ratio indicated the overall debt ratio; Reinhart, Rogoff, and Savastano, "Debt Intolerance," 13.
92. Brazil's pre-1900 GDP data series suffer from several known weaknesses and are useful mainly for indicating income fluctuations. The chief exception is the carefully constructed estimate for the early 1870s; Reis, "A Renda por Cápita dos Municípios Brasileiros."
93. Reinhart, Reinhart, and Rogoff, "Public Debt Overhangs," 79–82.
94. Sargent and Velde, "Macroeconomic Features of the French Revolution," 477–79.

95. See Bohn, "The Behavior of U.S. Public Debt and Deficits," 949–53.
96. For estimates of the low rate of per capita economic growth in the nine-teenth century, see Leff, *Underdevelopment and Development in Brazil*, 1:32–34.
97. The unit root tests include the augmented Dickey-Fuller (ADF) test, the generalized least-squares variant of the ADF test, the Phillips-Perron test, and the Ng-Perron (NP) test with the modified Akaike criterion. In all but the Ng-Perron test the hypothesis of a unit root was rejected at the 1 percent level of significance. While the NP test could not reject a unit root at conventional levels of significance, the Kwiatkowski-Phillips-Schmidt-Shin test did not reject the hypothesis that the series was stationary. For proof that the absence of a unit root in the deficit is sufficient for fiscal sustainability, see Bohn, "Are Stationarity and Cointegration Restrictions Really Necessary for the Intertemporal Budget Constraint?" 1840–41.
98. This normalization reduces heteroskedasticity. GDP is customarily used as the denominator, but as no reliable annual series exists for most of the nineteenth century, exports are used instead. It is quite likely that export fluctuations were correlated with changes in GDP.
99. For the condition, see Bohn, "The Behavior of U.S. Public Debts and Deficits," 950–51.
100. Trehan and Walsh, "Testing Intertemporal Budget Constraints," 208–13.
101. The primary market interest rates are derived in chapters 3 and 4.
102. Barro, "U.S. Deficits since World War I," 204–7; Bohn, "The Behavior of U.S. Public Debts and Deficits," 951–53.
103. For the personal tax, *CLB*, Lei 1507, article 10, 26 September 1867; on the tax on the salaries of public employees, Regulamento 3977, 12 October 1867, and Decreto 1750, 20 October 1869; on the stamp tax, Decreto 4354, 17 April 1869; for the tax on industries and professions, Decreto 4346, 23 March 1869; and on the property transmission tax, Decreto 4355, 17 April 1869.

CHAPTER 3. TROPICAL CREDIBILITY ON LOMBARD STREET

1. Montezuma's barb was part of an attack on the cabinet over the terms of the 1865 loan raised to support the war effort against Paraguay; Jequitinhonha, *Reflexões Sobre as Finanças do Brasil*, 53.
2. Baxter, "The Recent Progress of National Debts," 5–6.
3. In some cases the amount of money received was less than what was contracted because of a provision that provided a rebate to lenders who fully paid the issue price of their bonds in advance of the installment deadlines. This amount could not be anticipated at the time the loan was taken, but in any case was small. See appendix III for an example.
4. On the capital spillovers from Britain in the nineteenth century, see Jenks, *The Migration of British Capital*; Feis, *Europe, the World's Banker*; Stone, "The Composition and Distribution of British Investment in Latin America."
5. Dawson, *The First Latin American Debt Crisis*, 249.

6. Michie, *The London Stock Exchange*, 53.

7. Morgan and Thomas, *The Stock Exchange*, 81.

8. Michie, *The London Stock Exchange*, 54–57.

9. Neal, "The Financial Crisis of 1825."

10. Dawson, *The First Latin American Debt Crisis*, 110–73; Marichal, *A Century of Debt Crises in Latin America*, 43–55. Greece, Portugal, and Spain also defaulted; Michie, *The London Stock Exchange*, 57.

11. Jenks, *The Migration of British Capital*, 48.

12. For most of the nineteenth century the term *underwriting* was not used by the financial community in London and was not explicitly a form of insurance in the loan contracts; Finnie, *Capital Underwriting*, 2–4.

13. Jenks, *The Migration of British Capital*, 276–77.

14. Flandreau and Flores, "Bonds and Brands."

15. The sons of Mayer Amschel Rothschild in Frankfurt went on to establish banking concerns in Paris, Vienna, and Naples, in addition to Nathan M. Rothschild's banking house in London; Ferguson, *The House of Rothschild*, xiv–xxv.

16. Ibid., xxiv, 292.

17. Barman, "Rothschild and Brazil"; Shaw, "Rothschilds and Brazil."

18. *Times*, 12 January 1825; *Times*, 26 January 1825.

19. The Brazilian minister in London, in defending against accusations that the 1863 loan was too expensive because he did not use a competitive bidding process, pointed out that dealing directly with a high-quality intermediary linked the government's credit to that of the intermediary; Moreira [Barão de Penedo], *O Empréstimo Brasileiro*, 43.

20. *Bullionist*, 27 January 1883.

21. Morgan and Thomas, *The Stock Exchange*, 81–82.

22. The provisions of the loans are taken from the original contracts, along with published prospectuses and manuscript memoranda. The sources for information on each loan are detailed at appendix III.

23. This was the case, for example, with Brazil's 1829 loans, when the bankers took the entire loan without public subscription. N. M. Rothschild & Sons took the 1852 loan in its entirety as well.

24. The claim that Brazil did not have access to the London capital market in this period is inaccurate; Ferguson, *The House of Rothschild*, 68. The government simply contracted with other financial agents to arrange loans in 1839 and 1843, having dismissed Rothschild from the agency when Bernardo de Vasconcelos was finance minister.

25. Barman, "Rothschild and Brazil," 40.

26. *RMF* 1880, 4.

27. Ferguson, *The House of Rothschild*, 345.

28. *RMF* 1883, Annexo A, 10–11; Fenn and Nash, *Fenn's Compendium (1889)*, 393; [Prospectus] "Imperial Brazilian 4 1/2 per Cent. Loan 1863"; RAL, 000/336/2, "1863. Empire of Brazil. Loan of £3,300,000 Sterling."

29. Summerhill, *Order Against Progress*, 58–105.
30. The first parliament was not seated until 1826, and the first budget was not passed until 1828; Sturz, *A Review, Financial, Statistical, and Commercial*, 14–17.
31. Ibid., 9–10.
32. AMFF 77.11.54, "[Agreement for General Bond] Between Felisberto Caldeira Brant and Manoel Rodrigues Gameiro Pessoa, Plenipotentiaries, and Messrs. Bazett, Colvin, Crawford & Co., Messrs. Fletcher Alexander & Co., and Messers Thomas Wilson & Co.," 7 June 1824; Brazil, Câmara dos Deputados, *Parecer da Commissão de Fazenda*, 118–24; Fortune, *Fortune's Epitome*, 70; Field and Fortune, *Fortune's Epitome*, 175–76.
33. Brazil, Câmara dos Deputados, *Parecer da Commissão de Fazenda*, 116–17.
34. AMFF 77.11.201B, Rothschild to the General Felisberto Caldeira Brant and the Chevalier Manoel Rodrigues Gameiro Pessoa, Plenipotentiaries of His Majesty the Emperor of the Brazils, n.d.
35. RAL 000/336/4, "Abstract of Brazilian Loan Contract 1825"; Brazil, Câmara dos Deputados, *Parecer da Commissão de Fazenda*, 127–33. The Imperial government maintained old colonial monopolies on diamond mining and Brazil wood for a time after independence, and these were used along with cash to remit interest to loan contractors in London. See, for example, AMFF 77.11.201.A, Rothschild to Mattos, 19 February 1831, regarding losses of Brazil wood shipments in 1827 and 1830.
36. Sturz, *A Review, Financial, Statistical, and Commercial*, 11–12.
37. "Convenção adicional ao Tratado de Amizade, e Aliança de 29 de Agosto de 1825 . . . ," in Lima, *História Diplomática do Brazil*.
38. Dawson, *The First Latin American Debt Crisis*, 170–71.
39. Rodrigues, *Atas do Conselho do Estado*, Sessão 19, 15 November 1828, 2:51–52.
40. *RMF* 1834, 9; *RMF* 1835, 1–2; *RMF* 1836, 24.
41. Rodrigues, *Atas do Conselho do Estado*, 2:49, 51–52, 55–56.
42. That the loan was raised not by a specific legislative act but "with the advice of his [Dom Pedro I's] Council of State" was noted by the contractors. This feature may have given the contractors more pause than it did the cabinet in Rio; AMFF 77.11.57, "An Agreement Between . . . Viscount Itabayana . . . and Nathan Mayer Rothschild . . . ," 3 July 1829.
43. Fenn, *Fenn's Compendium* (1840), 54; RAL 000/336/4, "An Agreement . . . Between . . . Viscount Itabayana . . . and Nathan Mayer Rothschild . . . ," 3 July 1829; AMFF 77.11.57B, "An Agreement Between . . . Viscount of Itabayana . . . and Messrs. Thomas Wilson and Co.," 3 July 1829.
44. AMFF 77.11.57C, "Private Agreement Between . . . Viscount of Itabayana . . . and Messrs. Thomas Wilson & Co.," 3 July 1829; AMFF 77.11.57A, "Private Agreement Between . . . Viscount of Itabayana . . . and Nathan Mayer Rothschild," 3 July 1829.
45. Sturz, *A Review, Financial, Statistical, and Commercial*, 13–14.

46. *RMF* 1833, 8. A curb market clearly existed for the bonds, and their price was first quoted in the *Course of the Exchange* in July 1829; transactions and price quotes were very patchy until the intermediaries began to place more of the bonds in the secondary market in 1832.

47. *RMF* 1834, 9.

48. The prices of apólices hovered in the high 80s in the first half of 1838 but fell in early 1839, pushing yields above 8.6 percent; *Jornal do Commércio,* various issues, 1838 and 1839.

49. *RMF* 1839, 19.

50. *Times,* 14 February 1839; Carreira, *História Financeira e Orçamentária,* 264–65.

51. *RMF* 1843, 16, table 23.

52. Only a handful of new loans were made to foreign governments in the 1840s; Clarke, "On the Debts of Sovereign and Quasi-Sovereign States," 314.

53. Carreira, *História Financeira e Orçamentária,* 287–89; AMFF 77.11.58, "Notarial Certificate of the Deposit at the Bank of General Bond and Full Powers for Brazilian Fund 1843, original bond between Sir Isaac Lyon Goldsmid and Jozé Marques Lisboa, Minister Plenipotentiary at the Court of St. James, on behalf of Emperor Pedro II," 20 May 1843.

54. Saquarema refers to the original Conservative party leaders; Itaboraí was a major figure in Imperial politics, and his brother would later sit on the junta overseeing the management of the public debt; see the discussion in chapter 2.

55. *RMF* 1853, 9–10, Tabela 10; AMFF 77.11.229, Joaquim José Rodrigues Torres to Messrs. Goldsmid, King, & Thompson [copy], 14 May 1852. Accompanying Rodrigues Torres's instructions were gold bars, 24,000 gold sovereigns, and £6,000 in drafts; *Times,* 7 May 1852 and 8 May 1852.

56. *RMF* 1866, 8.

57. Fenn and Nash, *Fenn's Compendium* (1874), 263; *RMF* 1883, annex A, 7.

58. Clarke, "On the Debts of Sovereign and Quasi-Sovereign States," 314.

59. RAL 000/336/2, 1852, "Loan . . . for the Service of the Brazilian Empire," 12 November 1852; *RMF* 1853, [annex] N. 43.

60. The essence of funded debt involved assigning a specific source of revenues for the service of a specific loan. Later, reducing the specificity of the funding avoided problems arising from the potential inadequacy of any particular revenue source. Debt service came to be an annual commitment of the government, to be drawn from all revenues irrespective of source; Oliveira, *Systema Financial do Brazil,* 140–41.

61. *Times,* 22 July 1854, 8.

62. AMFF 77.11.313, "[Agreement between] Sérgio Teixeira de Macedo, Enviado Extraordinário e Ministro Plenipotenciário e N. M. Rothschild & Filhos," 20 June 1855. The contract was effective for three years and automatically renewed each year thereafter unless one party gave at least six months' notice of its cancellation.

63. In 1852 the first guarantee of shareholder dividends was granted by the government to try to attract railroad investment, while in 1853 the cabinet engineered the creation of a super bank in the form of the new Banco do Brasil.

64. RAL 000/336/2, "1858. Empire of Brazil. Loan of £1,425,000 Sterling for the Railway 'Dom Pedro II'"; *Times*, 26 May 1858. The railroad in 1858 was still a private concern, the construction of which had stalled. Eventually the government would buy it outright; see El-Kareh, *Filha Branca de Mãe Preta*.

65. Clarke, "On the Debts of Sovereign and Quasi-Sovereign States," 315.

66. *RMF* 1859, 9–16.

67. On the Recife and San Francisco Railway, see Summerhill, *Order Against Progress*, 44, 47, 64. On the Mucury company, see Barton, "Making the Mucurí." On the União e Indústria road, see Giroletti, *Industrialização de Juiz de Fora*.

68. *RMF* 1861, 6.

69. Moreira [Barão de Penedo], *O Empréstimo Brasileiro*, 47.

70. [Prospectus] "Imperial Brazilian Loan at 4½ Per Cent"; RAL 000/336/2, "1860 Empire of Brazil Loan of £1,210,000 Sterling for advances to be made to promote Industrial Undertakings"; *Times*, 19 March 1860.

71. See Graham, "A Questão Christie."

72. *RMF* 1864A, 8.

73. RAL 000/336/2, "1863. Empire of Brazil. Loan of £3,300,000 Sterling"; [Prospectus] Imperial Brazilian 4½ per Cent. Loan 1863, for £3,300,000.

74. *RMF* 1866, 9. On the terms of the loan and the detailed instructions and communications, see Brazil, Ministério da Fazenda, *Correspondência entre o Ministério da Fazenda e a Legação em Londres*.

75. *RMF* 1866, 7, 8–10; [Prospectus], "Imperial Brazilian 5 per Cent. Loan of 1865, for £5,000,000 Sterling."

76. *RMF* 1866, 11.

77. *Times*, 19 September 1865. By 1866 the government had exhausted the receipts from the loan. In the face of expectations of further heavy outlays on the war, the milréis began what would become its largest decline against the pound since the 1830s; *RMF* 1868, 8–9.

78. Contemporary critics glossed over the fact that the 1860 loan was less successful than its initial issue price suggested. The government placed the bonds with investors by paying a simple commission rather than by having the loan taken "firm" by the Rothschilds, and the subscribers were slow to take up the issue.

79. Clarke, "On the Debts of Sovereign and Quasi-Sovereign States," 315; Moreira [Barão de Penedo], *O Empréstimo Brasileiro*, 28–29.

80. For a thorough contemporary critique that addressed not only the loan's terms but also the foreign policy that led to borrowing, see Jequitinhonha, *Reflexões Sobre as Finanças do Brasil*, 58–59, 63–66.

81. The minister pointed out that prices for U.S., Egyptian, and Italian bonds were also low at the time of issue; *RMF* 1866, 9.

82. [Prospectus] "Imperial Brazilian 5 per Cent. Loan of 1871, for £3,000,000 Sterling"; RAL 000/401C, "Memorandum of Contract for the Loan of £3,000,000 Sterling in 5 per Cent Stock for the service of the Brazilian Empire," London, 23 February 1871.

83. *RMF 1871*, 11.

84. Among low-income nations only Russia borrowed on terms as favorable as those commanded by the Empire in these years; Clarke, "On the Debts of Sovereign and Quasi-Sovereign States," 317.

85. *New York Herald*, 20 June 1874.

86. *Times*, 7 October 1874; *Financier*, 14 October 1874; *Pacific Mail*, 16 November 1874; *Financier*, 24 December 1874.

87. *Financier*, 14 and 19 January 1875; *Times*, 15 January 1875; *Money Market Review*, 23 January 1875.

88. RAL 000/401C, "Memorandum of an Agreement . . . ," 18 January 1875.

89. RAL 000/336/3, [General Bond], 11 May 1883.

90. *Financier*, 25 January 1883; *Bullionist*, 27 January 1883; *Statist*, 27 January 1883.

91. RAL 000/336/3, [General Bond], 26 May 1886; RAL 000/401D, "Memorandum of Contract for the Loan of £6,000,000 Sterling in 5 per Cent Stock"; [Prospectus] Imperial Brazilian 5 per Cent. Loan of 1886 for £6,000,000 Sterling.

92. *RMF 1886*, 20–21; *Financial News*, 3 March 1886.

93. *RMF 1888*, 32; RAL 000/336/3, "Empire of Brazil 4¹/₂% Loan of 1888 for £6,000,000 Sterling"; [Prospectus] Imperial Brazilian 4¹/₂ per Cent. Loan of 1888 for £6,000,000 Sterling.

94. [Prospectus] "Conversion and Redemption of the Imperial Brazilian Five Per Cent. Loans of 1865, 1871, 1875, 1886"; RAL 000/336/3, "Brazilian 4% Loan of 1889 for £19,875,000."

95. *Revista Illustrada*, 12 October 1889, 4.

96. *RMF 1859*, table 7.

97. *RMF 1859*, 9–16.

98. RAL 000/401C, "Memorandum of Contract for the Loan of £3,000,000 Sterling in 5 per Cent Stock for the service of the Brazilian Empire," 23 February 1871.

99. *RMF 1883*, 30.

100. The internal rate of return in the expression is computed by using numeric techniques since there is no closed-form solution for i. Given that there can be multiple rates of return that solve the expression, in practice the approach was to begin with an arbitrarily low i, at the lowest pre-1889 coupon rate of 4.5 percent, and increase the value of i in increments of 0.05 until the right-hand side of the expression attained the value of the money actually raised on the loan.

101. The values for these variables for each loan come from the contracts and are detailed in appendix III.

102. Contemporaries, like modern historians of sovereign debt, understood that the consol yield indicated the risk-free return; Moreira [Barão de Penedo], *O Empréstimo Brasileiro*, 22–24.

103. The movements in Brazil's primary market borrowing costs mirror the changes in yields reported in chapter 5.

104. Abreu estimates the ex post internal rate of return on these loans and the returns to bondholders. Both measures differ from the ex ante borrowing costs derived here. Only the ex ante return can indicate the state's creditworthiness at the time the loan was extended. For the estimates of realized returns, see Abreu, "Brazil as a Debtor," 777.

105. Because loan costs included fees paid at issue, along with debt-service fees that would run for decades into the future, the ex ante capital cost to the government on a loan exceeded the ex post return to the bondholders. This difference was the transaction cost of borrowing.

106. The default probability would clearly vary with the scenario. So long as the same default scenario is used for each loan, the direction and proportions of the changes in the default probability over time are preserved.

107. This is the approach taken by Fogel in estimating the probability of default on Union Pacific bonds; Fogel, *The Union Pacific Railroad*.

108. The calculation assumes a bondholder who would have kept the bond until maturity.

109. This is computed as the internal rate of return that sets the issue price equal to the sum of the discounted stream of coupon payments and the redemption value at maturity.

110. The expected likelihood of default for bondholders is inversely related to the severity of the default. Repudiation is less likely than delayed interest or a unilateral write-down.

111. Baxter, "The Recent Progress of National Debts," 7–8.

112. See, for example, the discussion in Reinhart and Rogoff, *This Time Is Different*, 119–27.

113. On the trade-off between the discretion that nominal debt allows and the creditworthiness that indexed debt can provide, see Bohn, "Why Do We Have Nominal Government Debt?"; Calvo and Guidotti, "Indexation and Maturity."

114. That debt structure can incentivize government performance on its loans is analogous to the finding in corporate finance that the firm's capital structure matters in the likelihood that the firm repays debt; Diamond, "Debt Maturity Structure and Liquidity Risk."

115. Chang and Velasco, "Banks, Debt Maturity, and Financial Crises."

116. Reinhart and Rogoff, *This Time Is Different*, 21–47.

117. In 1846 the parliament fixed the rate at which the Treasury would accept gold at customs stations to pay duties in milréis, implicitly defining the legal exchange rate between the pound and the milréis.

CHAPTER 4. BORROWING ON RUA DIREITA

1. *Almanach do Rio de Janeiro,* 164.
2. *Jornal do Commércio,* 17 March 1828; *Jornal do Commércio,* 24 March 1828.
3. *Jornal do Commércio,* 17 April 1828. While the Mesquita, Rego, and Rocha bid was part of the first issue of the new debt, it was not the first tranche of the loan. In January the Treasury had approached Samuel, Phillips & Co. to buy bonds at 65 but the firm would go no higher than 60. Other parties took them at 65; RAL XI/38/21, Samuel, Phillips & Co. to Nathan M. Rothschild, 17 January 1828.
4. On Rothschild's orders for apólices, see RAL, XI/38/215 Box B, Samuel, Phillips & Co. to Nathan M. Rothschild, 8 February 1830; and on the demand for apólices from the City, see Samuel, Phillips & Co. to Nathan M. Rothschild, 6 April 1830.
5. Historians working with probate inventories from the nineteenth century have found holdings of apólices by upper- and middle-income Brazilians outside of Rio de Janeiro; see, for example, Mattoso, *Bahia, Século XIX,* 628–42; Mello, *Metamórfoses da Riqueza,* 79–80.
6. Alencar, *Lucíola,* 231.
7. Alencar, *Senhora,* 29.
8. Assis, *Dom Casmurro,* 33.
9. Though foreign and domestic creditors may be distinguished in both practice and under the law, the economically relevant distinction involved location; securities that were held within Brazil were domestic by this criterion.
10. The inconvertibility of the currency meant that the government did not commit to exchange the milréis for gold or silver at a fixed rate. Because Brazil was not on a specie standard, holders of domestic apólices took on risk that their bonds' value could fall in inflation-adjusted terms and in terms of the pound sterling.
11. Since private saving depends partly on reducing the uncertainty about the security of wealth, an improvement in the sovereign's commitment to property rights can elicit an increase in the supply of savings. Higher savings can help increase funds to lend to the state and boost investment in business. That an increase in savings might boost lending to government figures as an assumption in Drazen, "Towards a Political-Economic Theory of Domestic Debt," 164–67. That higher saving might spill over to private sector activities, increasing the capital stock, is derived in Robinson, "Debt Repudiation and Risk Premia," 8–12. In Brazil the increased security of financial property rights after 1824 may well have had both effects, though the main focus here is on the public sector.
12. The course of the war during 1868 is detailed in Doratioto, *Maldita Guerra,* 309–82.
13. Such claims have a long tradition, rooted in a circumscribed focus on foreign borrowing; Doin, *O Café, a Dívida Externa e a Modernização do Brasil,* 103–27; Centeno, "Blood and Debt," 1565–1605.

14. *RMF* 1879, table 19.
15. The data in the figure exclude short-term borrowing and expedients. They are gross inflows of resources and are not adjusted for the increase in debt service outlays that they imply at the time they were obtained. Their derivation is detailed in appendix II.
16. In addition to new London loans in 1852 and 1858, in 1854 the government extended by ten years its loans from 1824–25, with the bondholders' approval.
17. The Treasury issued gold and silver coins at various intervals, but these traded at a premium relative to its own notes. Because the coins circulated outside of the country and foreign coins circulated within Brazil, estimates of the metallic component of the currency stock are fragile; Lago, "Balança Comercial, Balanço de Pagamentos e Meio Circulante," 502–3.
18. The sources for seigniorage revenues are presented in appendix II.
19. The correlation between the amount (as percentages over tax revenues) raised by seigniorage and that raised through domestically funded borrowing was reasonably high at 0.48. The correlation between either of those and the funds raised on foreign borrowing was effectively zero.
20. On the evolution of the components of the currency stock and monetary policy under the Empire more generally, see Peláez and Suzigan, *História Monetária do Brasil*, 53–135.
21. Cavalcanti, *Elementos de Finanças*, 401–2.
22. *Financier*, 12 November 1875.
23. *RMF* 1865, 10.
24. *RMF* 1877A, 39.
25. Cavalcanti, *Elementos de Finanças*, 406–14; Adams, "Caixa Econômica."
26. *RMF* 1878, 32. Other accounts included very old debts in Mato Grosso for which creditors could not be located, and, later the money accumulated in the emancipation fund.
27. Brazil, Câmara dos Deputados, *Parecer da Commissão de Fazenda*, Letra I, [Quadro] no. 8, "Estado de Dívida Passiva do Thesouro Público no fim do Anno de 1824," 145–48.
28. The only modern treatment is found in Levy, "The Brazilian Public Debt." Otherwise there is little discussion of the domestic debt in the historiography of the Empire.
29. *CLB*, Lei of 15 November 1827, Título IV; Oliveira, *Systema Financial do Brazil*, 157; RAL XI/38/215 B1, Samuel, Phillips & Co. to Nathan M. Rothschild, 7 January 1828.
30. Of the Rio brokerage firm Bueschantal [*sic*] & Duval; *Almanach do Rio de Janeiro*, 170. Buschental later made loans alongside the barão de Mauá to the Argentine government after the defeat of Rosas; Marichal, "Liberalism and Fiscal Policy," 99; Montero Bustamante, *Estampas del Montevideo Romántico*, 23–29.
31. March Brothers was a Rio-based merchant firm; *Almanach do Rio de Janeiro*, 169. Naylor Brothers was headed in Rio by Jorge [George] Naylor and was ac-

tive in local commerce and finance from the 1820s through at least the early 1840s; *Almanak dos Negociantes do Império do Brasil*, 193; Seignot-Plancher, *Almanak Nacional . . .* , 49; Filho, *Folhinha Commercial . . .* (1842), 97.

32. *RMF* 1866, 12.

33. The London risk premium did exceed the Rio risk premium on occasion in the 1840s.

34. Oliveira, *Systema Financial do Brazil*, 161–63.

35. *RMF* 1838, 16; *RMF* 1841, 14–15; "Regulamento para execução da lei no. 241 de 29 de novembro de 1841," visconde de Abrantes, 15 January 1842, ANRJ, BRAN Rio 22.0.3709.

36. *CLB*, decree 91, 23 October 1839, table A.

37. See, for example, *CLB*, decree 158, 18 September 1840, table B. In 1845, Finance Minister Manoel Alves Branco, the architect of the new tariff schedule applied in 1844, stressed that the government "should not amortize the internal and external debt while there are not sufficient balances for other expenditures"; *RMF* 1845A, 13; *RMF* 1845B, 12.

38. *RMF* 1832, 11.

39. See the discussion in the council of state on how to borrow under the law of 23 September 1829; Sessão 38, 30 January 1830, Rodrigues, *Atas do Conselho de Estado*, 2:99–100.

40. *Times*, 20 October 1824. These indemnities to the Portuguese crown and individuals came in addition to Brazil's assumption in 1825 of Portugal's London loan of 1823.

41. RAL XI/38/215 B30, communicating that the Rio government had settled with the British minister (Lord Ponsonby) for "prizes illegally made of British Vessels & Cargoes in the Rio da Prata," to the tune of 450,000 pounds sterling to be paid in apólices; RAL XI/38/215 B102, 5 November 1831; RAL XI/38/215 B118, 3 July 1832; RAL XI/38/215 B125, 17 September 1832; RAL XI/38/215 B128, 22 October 1832.

42. The problem became particularly acute by the end of the war against Paraguay. The Treasury had to collect and hold large sums of cash to accommodate the Treasury bills maturing each month; *RMF* 1871, 10; *RMF* 1883, 34.

43. *RMF* 1851, 13.

44. *RMF* 1861, 7, 13–15, and table 38; *CLB*, Lei 1083, 22 August 1860. The response from shareholders in the Recife and Bahia railroad lines was tepid but stronger in the case of the Dom Pedro II line.

45. *RMF* 1868, 13.

46. By way of example, in 1888 more than 16 percent of the total stock of apólices changed hands, according to the registries of the Caixa; *RMF* 1889, Anexo D, "Relatório do Inspector da Caixa de Amortização," 3.

47. *Times*, 14 October 1879.

48. *RMF* 1883, 34.

49. *CLB*, Lei 3229, 3 September 1884, implemented by decreto 9581, 17 April 1886.

50. Blake, *Diccionário Bibliográphico*, 2:408–9; *AL* 1876, 595; *AL* 1880, 603.
51. Belisário had skin in the game, so to speak; fully 50 percent of his wealth consisted of Imperial bonds at the time of his death in 1889; Colson, "Destruction of a Revolution," 769–70.
52. *Buenos Ayres Standard,* 31 April 1886.
53. *RCJC* 1886, 31.
54. *RMF* 1887, 56–57.
55. On the postabolition subsidies for agricultural lending that ultimately led to the National Loan of 1889, see Schulz, *The Financial Crisis of Abolition,* 65–75.
56. *Times,* 15 September 1868; *Times,* 23 September 1868.
57. *Times,* 28 October 1868.
58. *CLB,* decree 4244, 15 September 1868; *Jornal do Commércio,* 18 September 1868.
59. RA for 1868, *Jornal do Commércio,* 6 January 1869.
60. See, for example, letters printed in the *Jornal do Commércio* on 8, 9, 10, 13, 14, 16, 20, and 23 September and 2 October 1868.
61. *RCJC* 1874.
62. RA 1868, *Jornal do Commércio,* 6 January 1869, Table 24.
63. Based on fiscal year averages, the milréis in 1871 had not recovered to its prewar level but had increased in value by 20 percent over what it had been worth in 1868 when the bonds were first issued.
64. *Times,* 28 June 1879; *Morning Post,* 23 July 1879; *Times,* 24 June 1879.
65. *RMF* 1880, Tabela 8; *Money Market Review,* 23 August 1879; *Times,* 1 September 1879.
66. *RMF* 1880, table 7.
67. *RMF* 1880, 26.
68. For the first dividend on the 1879 loan the government paid bondholders in paper money. However, it made the conversion from sterling based on the ninety-day exchange rate. Bondholders' complaints caused the government to adjust the payment using the more favorable spot rate of exchange instead. *RCJC* 1880, 35.
69. *Times* 21 May 1880. In early 1879 the share of the 1868 bonds held by British subjects was less than 10 percent, and the share held by foreigners in general was less than one-fourth. The Finance Ministry ceased reporting the nationality of the bondholders after 1880. Within a few years the commercial press indicated that most of the 1879 loan and a good portion of the 1868 loan had indeed shifted abroad; *RCJC* 1883, 34; *RCJC* 1884, 35.
70. *Times,* 25 May 1880.
71. *RCJC* 1881, 39.
72. *Money Market Review,* 17 July 1880. Whether Brazil could "descend" into a "breach of faith" was clearly a function of the institutions governing debt policy; in the decade after the overthrow of the monarchy the republican government would default and indeed pay "in depreciated paper."

73. *CLB*, decree 10322, 27 August 1889.
74. *CLB*, decree 823-B, 6 October 1890.
75. Brazil, Tesouro Publico Nacional, *Situação Financeira do Tesouro*, table 5.
76. On Johnston, *AL* 1844, 223; and Bacha and Greenhill, *150 Anos de Café*, 145–47. By the late 1870s the business, passed to his sons, had become one of Rio's largest coffee exporting firms; *RCJC* 1879, 39–40.
77. *RMF* 1844, table 6; Moreira was a prominent merchant who in the late 1830s had served on the commission to convert the old customshouse into the new commercial exchange; see *AL* 1844, 216, 218.
78. *RMF* 1846, table 11.
79. *RMF* 1851, 12–14; *RMF* 1852, table 8. As broker-dealers Gomes & Paiva loaned money and traded in precious metals, foreign currencies, Imperial and provincial apólices, Treasury bills, and commercial paper; *AL* 1850, 320; *AL* 1851, 371.
80. Here and elsewhere in the text references to market prices are based on end-of-week observations in Rio de Janeiro using the sources detailed in appendix II.
81. *RMF* 1852, 12, table 8.
82. RA 1852, *Jornal do Commércio*, 15 January 1853; *RMF* 1852, table 8.
83. *RMF* 1854, table 11.
84. The bank sold these bonds, redeeming paper currency under its contract with the government as a bank of issue; RA 1861, *Jornal do Commércio*, 2 January 1862. Gomes & Filhos was a private bank that traded in foreign currencies, public securities, stocks, and discounters of commercial paper; *AL* 1861, 582.
85. RA 1863, *Jornal do Commércio*, 7 January 1864; *RMF* 1864A, 8.
86. Despite holding assets of more than 17 million milréis, including nearly 7 million milréis in apólices, Gomes & Filhos was one of the main banking houses to fail in the financial crisis of 1864; RA 1864, *Jornal do Commércio* (supplemento), 9 January 1865. Montenegro, Lima & Cia. also failed; Brazil, *Relatório da Commissão . . . Inquérito Sobre as Causas Principaes . . .*, Documentos Anexos, Serie B, Documentos relativos à Casa Bancária de Gomes & Filhos, 7–35; and Documentos relativos a Casa Bancária de Montenegro, Lima & Cia., 37–47.
87. Brazil, Tesouro Nacional, *Relatório e Projecto de Lei*.
88. *Almanak dos Negociantes do Império do Brasil*, 191; Surigue, *Almanak Geral. . . . (1838)*, 174; *AL* 1844, 220; *AL* 1868, 501.
89. On the Teixeira Leites in Vassouras, see Stein, *Vassouras: A Brazilian Coffee County*, 17–20; Melo and Falci, "Eufrásia Teixeira Leite." On the directors of the Banco Commercial e Agrícola in Rio, see *AL* 1858, 441. For the investors in the Banco Industrial e Mercantil, see ANRJ, Junta do Comércio, Livro 424, Registro 7, Galeria 3.
90. On Carvalho, see Vasconcellos and Smith de Vasconcellos, *Archivo Nobiliarchico Brasileiro*, 43–44, 74–75, 398–99; *AL* 1868, 488, 597. The second barão

do Amparo would become an initial investor in the Banco Industrial e Mercantil, together with the aforementioned barão de Vassouras.

91. The connections between the Teixeira Leites and other members of the *provincial* elite were more extensive than sketched here. See the genealogies in Needell, *Party of Order*, 328–31.

92. *RCJC* 1869; *RMF* 1871, 10.

93. *RCJC* 1876, 33.

94. Total issues in 1875–76 were nearly 8.7 million milréis; *Times*, 2 February 1877; *RMF* 1877A, 33; *RMF* 1877B, Tabela 19, 18–19.

95. *RCJC* 1877, 34.

96. *RMF* 1879, 16; *RCJC* 1879, 43. Wagner was a resident foreign merchant whose principal activity was trade; *AL* 1861, 42. Irapuá was from Minas Gerais and had built a ranching fortune in Rio Grande do Sul; Vasconcellos and Smith de Vasconcellos, *Archivo Nobiliarchico Brasileiro*, 197. A parliamentary dispute over the loan, among other financial issues, became a question of confidence in the cabinet within the chamber of deputies; see the discussion in chapter 2 above, and *Times*, 4 February 1879.

97. *RMF* 1880, table 8; *RCJC* 1879, 44–45.

98. Cavalcanti, *Elementos de Finanças*, 392.

99. *RMF* 1886, annex B, 6–10.

100. *Financial News*, 27 July 1886; *South American Journal*, 1 May 1886.

101. Francisco de Figueiredo (visconde, and later conde) was one of the most important banking investors of the late Imperial era. He had initial investments of nearly three thousand shares of the Banco Internacional in 1888, two hundred shares of the Banco del Credere in 1886, and one hundred shares of the Banco União do Crédito in 1885, among other businesses. Such holdings easily placed him among the top financiers in Brazil; Vasconcellos and Smith de Vasconcellos, *Archivo Nobiliarchico Brasileiro*, 152; ANRJ, Junta Comércial, Livro 26, registro 267; Livro 24, registro 523; Livro 23, registro 496.

102. Investors who lived in the larger provinces could subscribe through the provincial branch of the Treasury; Cavalcanti, *Elementos de Finanças*, 386.

103. Cavalcanti, *Resenha Financeira do Ex-Império do Brazil*, 28.

104. *RMF* 1838, "Estabelecimentos Possuidores de Fundos Públicos." This caixa of 1838 pooled the savings of its members and functioned like an investment club. It had no relation to the government-created caixa that appeared in the 1860s; see Adams, "Caixa Econômica," 2–3.

105. RA 1872, *Jornal do Commércio*, 4 January 1873.

106. *RBB*, 1877, "Balanço." The bank's stake in apólices at the end of the fiscal year was some 27 million milréis, which was not a trivial position for the bank and certainly not typical of its portfolio. The bonds accounted for more than 20 percent of the bank's total assets and equaled more than 80 percent of the bank's paid-in equity.

107. This does not count the large National Loan of 1889, which was taken in fiscal year 1890.

108. This figure includes around 27 percent of the total proceeds from the 1889 National Loan, which was the amount that had been paid in to the Treasury under the contract by the time the army overthrew the constitutional monarchy.

109. Even without a shift in the demand for credit, an increase in the penalty for default increases the volume of lending (to meet existing demand) and reduces the interest rate.

110. Wright, "Reputations and Sovereign Debt."

111. For the discounted bills, see *RBB*, 1887, 13. For the amounts in circulation, see figure 4.3.

112. RAL XI/38/215 B3, Samuel, Phillips & Co., to Nathan M. Rothschild, Rio de Janeiro, 16 February 1828; RAL XI/38/215 B18, 13 October 1828.

113. RAL XI/38/215 B24, 13 December 1828.

114. *RMF* 1835, 10–11, 15.

115. *RMF* 1838, "Quadro demonstrativo da Apólices de Fundos Públicos de juro de 6 per cento."

116. *RMF* 1844, table 6.

117. RA 1851, *Jornal do Commércio*, 14 January 1852.

118. *Times*, 2 August 1876.

119. *RCJC* 1877, 34; *Telegraph*, 27 January 1879.

120. *RMF* 1851, 12–14, table 8.

121. *RMF* 1852, 12, Tabela 8; RA 1852, *Jornal do Commércio*, 15 January 1853.

122. RA 1860, *Jornal do Commércio*, 7 January 1861.

123. RA 1861, *Jornal do Commércio*, 2 January 1862.

124. *RMF* 1864A, 8.

125. *RMF* 1871, 10.

126. *RMF* 1877A, 33; *RCJC* 1879, 43; *RMF* 1879, table 10.

127. Barbosa, *Obras Completas*, 151–52, 159–62, 301–2.

128. *RMF* 1854, table 11.

129. *RCJC* 1876, 33; *Times*, 2 February 1877; *RMF* 1877B, table 19; 18–19.

130. *RMF* 1879, table 19. Taking further into account the minuscule 4 percent and 5 percent issues up to 1879, along with the National Loans of 1868 and 1879, the government received 308.9 million milréis on obligations of 352.6 million milréis, or an average overall issue price of 87.6 percent of par.

131. The amortization schedule implied under the law was typical of the era, being based on the system advocated by Richard Price (and implemented by Pitt) in late-eighteenth-century Britain; Oliveira, *Systema Financial do Brazil*, 115–30.

132. The calculation takes into account the payment frequency of interest and amortization. Because interest was paid twice yearly, the calculation produces a semester interest rate, which is then annualized as $i_A = (1 + i_S)^2 - 1$.

133. The price of a new bond in this case is the present value of future coupon payments to infinity, $P = \sum_{t}^{\infty} \dfrac{coupon_t}{(1 + i_B)^t}$. In the limit this expression equals the

current yield at issue, $i_B \cong \dfrac{coupon_t}{P}$. Like estimate A, estimate B is adjusted to account for the semester frequency of interest payments.

134. Appendix III gives the sources of the loan's price in each instance of borrowing for which the information could be located.

135. Primary market prices for issues of apólices in the years 1866–68 were not located. Prices were, however, available for even larger issues in 1869 and 1870, which presents reasonable, if incomplete, coverage of borrowing costs during the war against Paraguay.

136. Note that the National Loan of 1868 did not involve fees on issue or service since the Caixa de Amortização in Rio administered the loan. The Rothschilds handled service in Europe on the 1879 loan. As such there were in practice fees of an unknown amount. These fees were not contracted under the loan per se and do not figure in the estimated cost of capital at issue.

137. Although wartime issue prices are available for some tranches of apólices, they are not available for every year in which borrowing took place, including 1867 and 1868.

138. In Rio, unlike London, there was little difference between the bond investor's expected return and the state's borrowing costs on most of the apólice-based borrowing, since there were no fees to bankers and the bonds were perpetual after 1838. The chief exception was the large issue of 1886, on which the Banco do Brasil charged an issue fee; *RMF* 1886, annex, 6–10.

139. For the broad concept of original sin, see Eichengreen and Hausmann, "Exchange Rates and Financial Fragility." For a revised statement, see Eichengreen, Hausmann, and Panizza, "Currency Mismatches, Debt Intolerance, and Original Sin," 147–50.

140. Domestic long-maturity borrowing became more widespread in the first part of the twentieth century; Reinhart and Rogoff, *This Time Is Different*, 105–6.

141. The Republic that followed the Empire also relied on the domestic capital market, but under the new institutions borrowing became more difficult in the 1890s (see chapter 8 for discussions of some of the reasons for this shift and its implications).

CHAPTER 5. TURNING POINTS

1. Baxter, "The Recent Progress of National Debts," 4, 7.

2. Bonds exhibit a variety of risks: interest rate risk, inflation risk, reinvestment risk, liquidity risk, and default risk. Credit risk that is unique to the borrowing state is alternately referred to as the default premium, the risk premium, or country risk.

3. Bond prices and yields move inversely; higher default risk will reduce a bond's price and increase its yield, while less risk will raise the bond's price and reduce its yield.

4. Sussman and Yafeh, "Institutional Reforms, Financial Development, and Sovereign Debt," 15; Stasavage, "Credible Commitment in Early Modern Europe," 164–74; Stasavage, "Partisan Politics and Public Debt."

5. Cox, "Was the Glorious Revolution a Constitutional Watershed?" 54.

6. Sussman and Yafeh, "Institutional Reforms, Financial Development, and Sovereign Debt," 6.

7. Since government may borrow only occasionally, in periods in which it exhibits extremely high risk of default it may not be able to borrow at all. It is conceivable, then, that some intervals between new loans could conceal immeasurably high credit risk.

8. Willard, Guinnane, and Rosen, "Turning Points in the Civil War."

9. Another approach to identifying changes in sovereign risk is to focus on the largest "yield fluctuations," as Ferguson did for European states in the nineteenth century. The approach focuses exclusively on the largest *increases* in the bond yield. Some events that abruptly raised yields, such as the Revolutions of 1848, quite likely were turning points. But visual inspection of the yield series for the major European states is sufficient to suggest that many of these large increases in sovereign risk for European states were short-term changes, not structural shifts; Ferguson, "Political Risk and the International Bond Market," 78, 105–7.

10. The bonds that the Empire issued in London were never listed or quoted in Brazil. While some individuals and banking organizations in Brazil owned them, they found no active formal market there and give no indication of having been traded on anything other than an exceptional basis.

11. *RMF 1877A*, 32.

12. $\frac{\partial s}{\partial p} = -\frac{(1+r)}{p^2} < 0$,   and $\frac{\partial s}{\partial (1-p)} = \frac{(1+r)}{p} > 0$.

13. For more than half a century after the Glorious Revolution the bonds of Holland remained less risky than those of Britain. By 1824, however, no state's bonds consistently exhibited lower levels of risk than those of the British.

14. The yield-to-maturity is the expected internal rate of return, i, on the bond when purchased at time t, given by

$$P_t = \sum_{t}^{T} \frac{coupon_t}{(1+i)^t} + \frac{P_R}{(1+i)^T}.$$

Where P_t is the market price of the bond, which is equal to the discounted stream of remaining future coupon payments and the discounted value of the redemption price (P_R) of the bond at maturity in year T. *Coupon* is the coupon rate on the bond. The yield to maturity, i, cannot be isolated in the expression and is determined in practice by the use of numeric techniques.

15. The series is extended slightly past the fall of the Empire in 1889 for statistical reasons related to the trimming parameter in the structural breaks estimation below.

16. If bonds were trading at or above par, a lottery would select the bonds to be redeemed at par. This prospect made precise yield-to-maturity calculations even more difficult for investors. A comparison of the yield-to-maturity that

takes into account the lottery redemption feature and one that ignores it shows that they are remarkably similar; see Mauro, Sussman, and Yafeh, *Emerging Markets and Financial Globalization*, 41–45. For Brazil the differences would have been especially small; its London bonds rarely traded above par, so a lottery drawing was not relevant in most years.

17. $P_t = \sum_{t}^{\infty} \dfrac{coupon_t}{(1+r_c)}$

where P_t is the net present value of the bond given by its market price, *coupon* is the interest payment implied by the annual coupon rate, t is the time index, and r_c is the internal rate of return. In the limit this is the same as the current yield but is adjusted for the frequency of coupon payments:

$$r_{YTM} = \left(\left(1 + \frac{r_{Ct}}{2} \right)^2 - 1 \right).$$

18. Klovland, "Pitfalls in the Estimation of the Yield on British Consols."
19. This required a slightly different calculation of the annual equivalent yield to maturity:

$$r_{YTM} = \left(\left(1 + \frac{r_{Ct}}{4} \right)^4 - 1 \right).$$

20. The shifts in the volatility of the series themselves serve as a proximate cause of changes in the level of the risk premium, since a more volatile stream of returns is viewed by investors as intrinsically more risky.
21. Willard, Guinnane, and Rosen, "Turning Points in the Civil War"; Bai and Perron, "Estimating and Testing"; Bai and Perron, "Computation and Analysis."
22. The procedure developed by Bai and Perron makes it possible to identify breaks by using a linear model and least-squares regression; Bai and Perron, "Estimating and Testing"; Bai and Perron, "Computation and Analysis."
23. The series suffers from heteroskedasticity in levels, but kurtosis is even more pronounced in logarithms. Since the Bai-Perron procedure uses standard errors corrected for heteroskedasticity and autocorrelation, the estimation proceeds with the data in levels.
24. While Bai and Perron restrict the applicability of their approach to stationary data series, the technique still performs reasonably well when there is high persistence in the series (nearing nonstationarity); see Paye and Timmermann, "Instability of Return Prediction Models."
25. The Zivot-Andrews test allows for one endogenously selected structural break. The results were robust to different maximum lag lengths (with the lag length selected through the Akaike Information Criterion) ranging from four weeks to fifty-two weeks.
26. To further allow the largest possible number of breaks, the required trimming parameter is set at 5 percent of each end of the data series.

27. Based on the UD max and WD max statistics in the Bai-Perron procedure, which derive from the global minimization of the sum of squared residuals from the regression equations.

28. Breaks are estimated by using the sequential procedure, which involves a series of Wald tests of the null hypothesis of no breaks, against alternative hypotheses of various numbers of breaks.

29. The estimates are conservative in that they reduce the chance of rejecting the hypothesis of a constant mean in favor of a break, when in fact there is no break in the series. The confidence intervals are also asymmetric, which provides better coverage if the data series verges on nonstationarity; Bai and Perron, "Computation and Analysis," 15.

30. The break dates, along with their confidence intervals, must be evaluated in light of the time required both for news to travel from Brazil to London and for the news to settle—that is, to be verified as true or likely to be true rather than just rumor or conjecture. Before the transatlantic telegraph, news took several weeks at best to travel from Rio to London. Once the telegraph was connected in the 1870s between the northeast and Europe and then from Rio to the northeast, news could travel nearly instantaneously but still required verification.

31. Note that the base of the series changes in December 1852 from the bonds of the loans of 1824/1825 to the bonds of the new loan of 1852. This switch comes after the break but inside the 90 percent confidence interval. The change is unavoidable, even desirable, for the estimation. As a practical matter the 1852 loan quickly became the most frequently traded Brazilian issue in the market, while quotations of the earlier loans became more difficult to locate. Since the new loan had a lower coupon rate, it created reinvestment risk, which would have *increased* the risk premium if the switch in the subseries was the source of the break. One would also expect the risk premium to increase as an artifact switching to bonds of a more junior loan. That the break instead generated a dramatic decline in risk points to the shift as a fundamental one, not an artifact.

32. *RMF* 1853, 9–10; *Times,* 7 May 1852; *Times,* 8 May 1852; AMFF 77.11.229, Joaquim José Rodrigues Torres to Messrs. Goldsmid, King, & Thompson [copy], 14 May 1852.

33. "Tradução do Contracto do Empréstimo de £1,040,600," *RMF* 1853, [annex] no. 43; RAL 000/336/2, "Loan . . . for the Service of the Brazilian Empire," 6 September 1852.

34. *Economist,* 17 January 1852.

35. *Times,* 21 February 1852. The battle in which Rosas was defeated was also fought in early February; news of earlier progress in the campaign against Rosas was reported that week as well; *Times,* 23 February 1852. News of Rosas's final defeat arrived in Southampton on 13 March and falls easily within the confidence window around the break; *Times,* 15 March 1852.

36. *Economist,* 14 August 1852.

37. The Alves Branco tariff did not elevate customs revenues over what the previous "pro-British" tariff had done, a point first made by Adalton Diniz, "O Tratado de Comércio com a Inglaterra e a Receita Fiscal do Império Brasileiro no Período de 1821 a 1850" (ms. 2005). Its end did not adversely impact government revenue, according to reworked tariff figures; Villela, "Política Tarifária no II Reinado," 35–68.

38. Dodsworth, *Organizações e Programas Ministeriais*, 119–22; Needell, *Party of Order*, 202–11.

39. *Times*, "Brazil and River Plate Mails," 2 September 1859.

40. *Times*, 11 January 1859.

41. *Times*, 7 September 1859.

42. Note that the confidence interval includes the shift in the base of the series from one loan (1852/1858/1860 composite) to another (1863) in table A.II.1. However, the change did not involve a different coupon rate, and the only alteration was a relatively slight change in the seniority of the loan used for the subseries. This seems unlikely to have caused the mean of the yield series to durably shift.

43. On the speech to the parliament, see *Times*, "Brazil and River Plate Mails," 4 June 1864. The near expiry of the deadline ultimately established by the Brazilians was reported in London as well, accompanied by reports that Brazil had twenty warships standing by at Montevideo and a large ground force on the border; *Times*, 20 September 1864.

44. *Times*, "Brazil and River Plate Mails," 3 September 1864.

45. "Great military preparations are going on in Asunción," *Times*, 7 November 1864.

46. Dodsworth, *Organizações e Programas Ministeriais*, 137–38.

47. The confidence interval includes the change in the base of the series in March 1871; there was no change in the coupon rate, just a change in the seniority of the loan—which should raise the risk premium, not lower it.

48. *Times*, 25 December 1869. The paper also offered a lengthy editorial indictment of the cruelty of the Solano López regime during the conflict on 24 December 1869.

49. Doratioto, *Maldita Guerra*, 419–55.

50. On the contrary, emancipation measures were accompanied by calls for indemnities to slave owners, which would have increased the debt burden and been more likely to raise the risk premium. Because of the question of indemnities and the implied need to finance them, proposals to end slavery would be more likely to raise the risk premium than to lower it.

51. Seckinger, *The Brazilian Monarchy and the South American Republics*, 145–46.

52. In this same period the chief determinant of large movements on the risk premia for European states—whether breaks or "blips"—was war; Ferguson, "Political Risk and the International Bond Market," 77–83.

53. Brazil's 4 percent apólices and the early 5 percents made up only a small share of the domestic debt. These were relatively illiquid, thinly traded, and

so infrequently quoted in newspapers and stock exchange ledgers as to rule out their use in statistical assessments. The National Loans of 1868 and 1879 cover only a portion of the period of interest, and their fixed exchange clauses made them far more similar to the London bonds than apólices.

54. ANRJ, Série Bolsa de Valores do Rio de Janeiro, Junta de Corretores de Fundos Públicos da Cidade do Rio de Janeiro, "Livros de Registro Oficial de Cotações de Títulos e Valores," years 1850–95. See appendix II.

55. Like consols, the apólice's yield to maturity was the internal rate of return that satisfies:

$$P_{At} = \sum_{t}^{\infty} \frac{coupon_t}{(1+r_{At})^t} \cong \frac{coupon_t}{r_{At}},$$

where P_{At} is market price at time t, *coupon* is the interest payment implied by the annual coupon rate, t is the year, and r_{At} is the internal rate of return. Taking the limit as the number of dividend payment periods goes to infinity, the yield to maturity at time t simplifies to the current yield.

56. Given semester payouts, the annual yield at any point in time is given by

$$r_{at} = \left(\left(1 + \frac{r_{At}}{2} \right)^2 - 1 \right).$$

57. On this episode, see Macaulay, *Dom Pedro*, 240–53.

58. Results from the standard unit root tests (Augmented Dickey Fuller and Phillips-Perron) do not rule out a unit root in the Rio risk premium series at all levels of statistical significance. Allowing for one endogenously selected structural break, the Zivot-Andrews test rejected the null of a unit root in the Rio risk series at the 1 percent level. The robustness of the result was checked by using lag lengths ranging from four to fifty-two lags.

59. The tests using the largest F statistic (supF(L+1/L) test), the sequential procedure, and repartition procedure all indicate four breaks in the series at the 1 percent level of significance. The locations of three of the breaks under the repartition procedure are nearly identical to those under the sequential procedure, while the fourth differs by forty-one weeks.

60. While the data here are in levels, transforming them to logarithms still gives four breaks, and at identical or nearly identical points in time.

61. *Jornal do Commércio*, 24 November 1834; 29 November 1834; 6 December 1834; Barman, *Brazil: The Forging of a Nation*, 178.

62. *Jornal do Commércio*, 20 December 1834. See also Andrade, *A Guerra dos Cabanos*.

63. There is nothing sacrosanct about the interval of time defined by the 90 percent confidence interval. In most instances its use limits the search for the "cause" of a break point to events that are relatively close by in time. The 95 percent confidence interval expands the window around the break in which events can be considered at a conventionally acceptable level of statistical significance.

64. The revolt began in January 1835, the first news of its imminence appearing late in the month; *Jornal do Commércio,* 25 January 1835; Cleary, "Lost Altogether to the Civilised World," 121–30.

65. See especially *Jornal do Commércio,* 6 May 1836, 7 May 1836, and 4 June 1836.

66. *Jornal do Commércio,* 26 May 1836. On the revolt's origins, see Harris, *Rebellion on the Amazon,* 176–220. Other events that historians identify as important occurred inside the window around the 1834 break but collectively were ambiguous in their implications for the market. There was the brief, abortive uprising by slaves in Salvador—soon reported in Rio—which was put down by local forces in short order; *Jornal do Commércio,* 10 February 1835; Reis, "Slave Resistance in Brazil." The revolt's impact on the bond market was trivial.

67. Barman, *Brazil: The Forging of a Nation,* 182.

68. The Bahian uprising began in November 1837 and was definitively put down by April 1838; Kraay, "As Terrifying as Unexpected."

69. On the start of the Balaiada and the waning prospects of the Empire more generally, see Barman, *Brazil: The Forging of a Nation,* 200, 210.

70. There is an extensive literature on the revolt by both contemporaries and historians. For modern studies, see Naro, "Safeguarding Portugal's Colonial Legacies"; Mosher, "The Struggle for the State"; Barman, *Brazil: The Forging of a Nation,* 232.

71. See, for example, *Jornal do Commércio,* 7 July 1848 and 23 July 1848.

72. The first reports that Rosas had fallen did not appear in print in Rio until February; see *Jornal do Commércio,* 4 February 1852 and 11 February 1852.

73. This is true even if one were to restrict attention solely to events after 1848. A variety of other events fall within this very broad window, including the entire confidence interval for the third break and the resumption in 1851–52 of the regular amortization of the London bonds, described above—though there was no resumption of sinking fund payments on the Rio bonds.

74. Eaton and Gersovitz, "Debt with Potential Repudiation"; Diamond, "Reputation Acquisition in Debt Markets"; Cole, Dow, and English, "Default, Settlement, and Signalling"; English, "Understanding the Costs of Sovereign Default"; Wright, "Reputations and Sovereign Debt."

75. Reinhart, Rogoff, and Savastano, "Debt Intolerance."

76. In a reputational model lenders focus on the borrower's record of repayment—creditworthiness at any given moment is necessarily retrospective, since it is the only information available. In the institutional model lenders focus on whether the political penalty for default is still in effect and is likely to persist.

77. Tomz, *Reputation and International Cooperation,* 19–20.

78. All of the regressions in the table use ordinary least squares and compute HAC standard errors with Andrews bandwidth selection.

79. Here I use the Davidson-McKinnon "J" test for non-nested models; see Caporale and Grier, "Time Series Tests for the Influence of Politics," 85.

80. The dummy variable for the first interval is suppressed in favor of a regression constant. The regression returns the results of the structural breaks analysis of table 5.2, differing by the constant term in the equation and by the slightly longer span of the series (the structural breaks procedure has to trim the series to reliably locate possible break points closer to the beginning and end of the series).

81. One might be inclined to simply combine the structural breaks and the payment history variable into a single regression and perform the associated nested hypothesis tests. The rationale for doing so is not clear. The existence of breaks is inconsistent with the reputational model put forth by Tomz. In any case, an ad hoc specification that adds the interest payment index as a variable in the structural breaks regression leaves the signs of the coefficients and the statistical significance of the break point dummies intact. The estimated coefficient on the reputational index is not significant (results available on request).

CHAPTER 6. CONTROLLING CAPITAL

1. It was the third bank to use that name to be authorized under the law and the second to establish operation.

2. By the commercial code of 1850 corporations were always joint-stock concerns with limited liability. In general these attributes are separable; corporations need not have tradable shares, and joint-stock companies need not enjoy limited liability. Under Brazilian law the *sociedade anônima* was the only form of incorporation available; it existed only through the issue of shares and conferred on its investors limited liability.

3. Guimarães, "Bancos, Economia e Poder no Segundo Reinado," 74–83.

4. Discount rates taken from "Quadro do curso do câmbio entre a Praça do Rio de Janeiro e as de Londres . . . durante o period de 1850 a Março de 1860," in Brazil, Commissão de Inquérito, *Relatório da Commissão de Inquérito . . .*

5. Cavalcanti, *O Meio Circulante Nacional*, 73–75.

6. *RMF* 1853, 13.

7. *CLB*, Lei 683, 5 July 1853; Lei 688, 15 July 1853.

8. *CLB*, Lei 556, 25 June 1850, article 295.

9. "A necessidade da fusão é inquestionável"; *Jornal do Commércio*, 12 July 1853.

10. Barman, "Business and Government in Imperial Brazil," 248–49.

11. *CLB*, Decreto 1223, 31 August 1853.

12. *CLB*, Decreto 1487, 13 December 1854.

13. Various facets of the episode have been addressed by historians, mainly in writing about the origins of the 1854 Banco do Brasil. Important details are selectively recalled by Mauá in his autobiography; Mauá, *Autobiografia*, 211–20, 259–60. The episode is expertly reconstructed in Barman, "Business and Government in Imperial Brazil," 242–57. Biographers tend to support the view that the government was to blame for Mauá's recurrent problems in banking, which ultimately resulted in his bankruptcy in the 1870s; see, for

example, Caldeira, *Mauá*, 307–12. Government was certainly responsible for the restrictions on the organizational form that Mauá's businesses could take. As for his performance as a banker per se, Barman's assessment was that Mauá's difficulties were largely a result of his own doing. This does not change the fact that entrepreneurs confronted a limited set of options for pooling capital.

14. Garner, "In Pursuit of Order," 388–89.
15. Milet, *O Meio Circulante e a Questão Bancária*, 14.
16. Freedeman, *Joint-Stock Enterprise in France*, 47–65. The French *comandite par actions* was eliminated by new legislation in 1856, but a similar form was authorized in 1863, and legislation in 1867 lifted restrictions on incorporation, giving entrepreneurs who wished to raise large amounts of capital another option.
17. North and Weingast, "Constitutions and Commitment," 824–28, and Rousseau and Sylla, "Financial Systems, Economic Growth, and Globalization," 374–77, stress the primacy of sound public finance for financial development.
18. Robinson, "Debt Repudiation and Risk Premia," 8–10.
19. Levy, *A Indústria do Rio de Janeiro*, 39–101; Hanley, *Native Capital*, 30, 63–68; Musacchio, *Experiments in Financial Democracy*, 32–42.
20. The rapid expansion of the number of joint-stock firms in 1889 corresponds to the contemporaneous creation of a vast liquidity bubble (see below and chapter 8).
21. The obstacles to financial development through the banking channel are addressed in detail in chapter 7.
22. The size of this effect would depend on the extent of reductions of the cost of capital and the stimulus to savings induced by the improvement to financial intermediation.
23. *CLB*, Lei 556, 15 June 1850 (*Código Commercial do Império do Brazil*), articles 300–28.
24. *CLB*, Lei 3150, 4 November 1882, articles 35–42.
25. *CLB*, Lei 3150, 4 November 1882, article 34; Decreto 8821, 30 December 1882, articles 145–48.
26. The only bank to operate in Rio de Janeiro with this authorization between the demise of the first Banco do Brasil in 1829 and the creation of Mauá's bank in 1851 was the Banco Commercial; Franco, *Os Bancos do Brasil*, 27–31.
27. Internal considerations in determining the organizational form of the firm are detailed and formalized in Lamoreaux and Rosenthal, "Legal Regime and Business' Organizational Choice."
28. The figure for joint-stock companies is based on all companies registered, while the figure for partnerships is based on a 10 percent random sample of all newly registered *comandita* partnerships. Newly registered joint-stock companies and partnerships for 1851–65 from *Relatório do Ministério da Justiça*, 1866.

29. Sweigart, "Financing and Marketing Brazilian Export Agriculture," 254.
30. See La Porta et al., "Law and Finance"; La Porta et al., "Legal Determinants of External Finance."
31. Harris, *Industrializing English Law*, 282–86.
32. For an overview of those of the Pomabline era, see Carnaxide, *O Brasil na Administração Pombalina*, 67–142.
33. This is the Portuguese *lei da boa razão* of 18 August 1769.
34. Even if an entrepreneur formed a corporation in line with the law of another country, the law of good reason provided no guarantee that the firm could operate in Brazil.
35. *CLB*, decree 575, 1 October 1849.
36. *CLB*, Lei 556, 15 June 1850 (Código Commercial do Império do Brazil), articles 295–299; Lei 3150, 4 November 1882, article 2, section 2; decree 8821, 30 December 1882.
37. *CLB*, Lei 3150, 4 November 1882, article 7, section 2.
38. It was the removal of this provision from commercial legislation by the military-led government in 1890 that helped make investment fraud a prominent feature of the stock market bubble in Brazil in 1890–92.
39. *CLB*, Lei 1083, 22 August 1860, article 2, section 3.
40. *CLB*, Decreto 2711, 19 December 1860, chapter 1, article 9, section 1.
41. Garner, "In Pursuit of Order," 381–420.
42. Brazil, *Relatório do Ministério de Agricultura, Comércio, e Obras Públicas*, 1868, 129.
43. In 1865 Senator Nabuco de Araújo, in his capacity as minister of justice, proposed to the chamber a reform project on *sociedades anônimas*. The chamber considered a separate proposal of this type in 1877; *Annaes do Senado*, 24 February 1882, 214.
44. See, for example, the debate in the chamber of deputies, *ACD*, 30 June 1879, 224–32; 3 July 1879, 7–13; 7 July 1879, 58–64.
45. *Annaes do Senado*, 7 October 1880, 606–12; 24 February 1882, 213–16; 17 June 1882, 9–16. Discussions continued through July and August of 1882, and the measure first introduced in the chamber in 1879 was approved by the senate only on 14 September 1882.
46. *CLB*, Lei 3150, 4 November 1882, article 1; decree 8821, 30 December 1882, article 130, section 4, and article 133.
47. Lamoreaux and Rosenthal, "Legal Regime and Business' Organizational Choice."
48. Alternatively, it could be that the elasticity of the return with respect to capital is higher for the corporation than for the partnership. Then the corporation would have a higher return than a partnership even if both had the same level of productivity and amount of capital.
49. Institutions that restrict entrepreneurial choice of the form of the firm could thus make the economy smaller by reducing capital formation or by lowering productivity. See appendix I for the derivation of the conditions that lead

the entrepreneur to organize a partnership, when a corporation would be preferred in the absence of restrictive chartering.

50. The same result obtains in any situation in which the numerator exceeds the denominator (since p is defined to never exceed one), such as when the cost of the petition is too high or when the risk of expropriation is too large.

51. Many first-time charters to foreign firms were awarded to companies with established operations outside of Brazil and simply authorized the opening of a branch. The emphasis of the analysis in any case is the impact of restrictions on the domestic capital market.

52. The standard source for all authorizations is Brazil, Departmento Nacional de Indústria e Comércio, *Sociedades Mercantis Autorizadas a Funcionar no Brasil.* A sample of charters was cross-checked at various intervals against contemporary published decrees.

53. Augmented Dickey-Fuller tests and Phillips-Perron tests reject a unit root at most of the conventional levels of significance.

54. The number of breaks was determined by selecting the best-fit model through the Bayesian Information Criterion.

55. Because they stop just short of 1889, the figures do not reflect the impact of rapidly rising liquidity that resulted from legislation liberalizing new banks of issue. This eleventh-hour effort by the Imperial government was tailored to try to stymie growing dissatisfaction with the regime.

56. The estimates derive from figures published in the "Companhias Públicas" column that irregularly appeared in the *Jornal do Commércio.*

57. "Companhias Públicas," *Jornal do Commércio,* 15 December 1853.

58. The authorized capital for the firms registered in 1851 was much greater than this, more than 9 million milréis; "Mappa das Companhias ou Sociedades Anônymas registradas no Tribunal do Commércio da Capital do Império," *Relatório do Ministério da Justiça,* 1866.

59. RA 1851, *Jornal do Commércio,* 14 January 1852.

60. This includes every listed joint-stock company in Rio. It excludes Mauá's bank, since it was a limited partnership that operated briefly with shares, not a corporation.

61. See the discussion of Treasury bills in chapter 4.

62. On subsidy to railroads, see Summerhill, *Order Against Progress,* 38.

63. One of the few attempts to test whether restrictions on corporate entry limited the growth of capital markets dismisses any role for the 1882 reform; Musacchio, *Experiments in Financial Democracy,* 36–37. However, the test relies on a comparison of new charters in Brazil and new listings on the Rio stock exchange. Listings in Rio need not necessarily accompany increases in charters for all of Brazil because many corporations did not list in Rio. For example, in 1867 there were twenty-four Brazilian firms based in Rio that listed on the stock exchange. Twenty-eight more Brazilian corporations were scattered across the provinces, none of which listed in Rio. Comparing the number of new charters for Brazil as a whole to the number of new firms

listed on the Rio exchange cannot gauge the capital market impact of the 1882 liberalization of incorporation. For the corporations in 1867, see "Relação das Companhias nacionaes e estrangeiras que funccionam no Império," Brazil, *Relatório do Ministério de Agricultura, Comércio, e Obras Públicas,* 1867, annex T.

64. Because the confidence interval on the break is large there is some chance it came even earlier than 1887. Given that the upper limit on the interval is 1887, the result rules out any role for the 1890 regulatory changes that further loosened restrictions on company formation.

65. It is a common conjecture that rising coffee prices in the later 1880s played an important role in the increase in joint-stock investment. The average wholesale price of coffee in Rio in the 1880s was, however, less than that in the 1870s. Legal restrictions on organizational form and credit, not coffee prices, were the principal constraint on the number of companies and their capital stock.

CHAPTER 7. CONCENTRATION AND CRONYISM

1. Sweigart, "Financing and Marketing Brazilian Export Agriculture," 143–44.

2. *RMF* 1874, 121; see also Brazil, Ministério da Fazenda, *Additamento as Informações Sobre o Estado da Lavoura,* 10.

3. Brazil, Ministério da Fazenda, *Informações Sobre o Estado da Lavoura,* "Annexos," for Espírito Santo, 77; Rio Grande do Sul, 103; Rio Grande do Norte, 89; Minas Gerais, 114; São Paulo, 146; Pernambuco, 160; Paraiba, 125.

4. Sylla, "U.S. Securities Markets and the Banking System."

5. Perotti and Volpin, "Lobbying on Entry," 11–15. The same problem existed in some states in the antebellum United States where bank entry proved difficult because of regulatory restrictions and political barriers; Sylla, "U.S. Securities Markets and the Banking System," 95–96.

6. Peláez and Suzigan, *História Monetária do Brasil,* 395–401.

7. Ibid., 85–100.

8. *AL* 1886, 1211, 1215–16.

9. *RBB,* 1866.

10. *AL* 1886, 1213, 1219.

11. Work on the roles of both banks and markets in financial development suggests that much of the debate may have been misdirected, since banks and securities markets appear to be viable substitutes; Levine and Zervos, "Stock Markets, Banks, and Economic Growth."

12. Gerschenkron, *Economic Backwardness,* 5–30.

13. Guinnane, "Delegated Monitors, Large and Small," 73–75.

14. Sweigart, "Financing and Marketing Brazilian Export Agriculture," 194–201.

15. Brazil was not unique in providing creditor protections. In periods during which the United States had federal bankruptcy protections in the nineteenth century debtors were heavily favored under the law; Berglöf and Rosenthal, "Power Rejected." The difference in the Brazilian case was that

the legally mandated process for foreclosure on land potentially cost much more than the collateral was worth.

16. *RMF* 1874, 121; see also Brazil, Ministério da Fazenda, *Additamento as Informações Sobre o Estado da Lavoura*, 10.

17. In England, Prime Minister Robert Peel's legislation in 1844 imposed restrictions that limited bank entry, but the preponderance of legislation, including acts passed in 1826, 1857, and 1862, liberalized joint-stock banking and promoted entry; Newton and Cottrell, "Banking Liberalisation in England and Wales," 76–77.

18. Piñeiro, "Negociantes, Independência e o Primeiro Banco do Brasil," 89–91.

19. Franco, *Os Bancos do Brasil*, 27–31.

20. The public finance logic behind the creation of superbanks is pervasive: Broz and Grossman, "Paying for Privilege"; Calomiris, "Motives of U.S. Debt-Management Policy," 69–79; Maurer and Gomberg, "When the State Is Untrustworthy," 1087–1105; Tattara, "Paper Money But a Gold Debt," 125.

21. *CLB*, Decreto 1223, 31 August 1853, article 56.

22. This concern was apparent in the debates between "metalists" (*metalistas*) and "paperists" (*papelistas*) during the Second Reign. These debates centered on the preferred means of backing for banknotes in banks of issue. The two positions were roughly analogous to the contemporaneous debate between the currency school and the banking school in Britain; Guimarães, "Bancos, Economia e Poder no Segundo Reinado"; Villela, "The Political Economy of Money and Banking," 37–42.

23. Franco, *Os Bancos do Brasil*, 15–51.

24. *CLB*, Lei 1083, 22 August 1860, article 1; decree 2711, 19 December 1860, article 1.

25. *CLB*, Decreto 2711, 19 December 1860, article 1, section 2.

26. *CLB*, Lei 3150, 4 November 1882, article 1, section 1.

27. *CLB*, Decreto 8821, 30 December 1882.

28. Schulz, *The Financial Crisis of Abolition*, 66–68.

29. *RMF* 1889, 26–32.

30. For 1 milréis of gold held in its vault, the bank could print and issue 2 milréis in notes, which it could then lend at interest. By considering four assumptions it is possible to calculate the impact of a change in the note-to-gold issue ratio on the rate of return to the issue of notes. Assuming (1) the cost of printing and signing notes was negligible, (2) loans were repaid as contracted, (3) parity between gold and the bank's notes (convertibility) was maintained, and (4) the return the bank could earn (π) by investing its gold elsewhere was at least what the bank could charge on its own discounting activities, then at a 2:1 ratio the return to the bank from issuing was $(2^*\pi)/1 = 2$ π per year. If the discount rate was 7 percent, the profitability of issue was $(2\$000 * 0.07)/1\$000 = 14$ percent. Increasing the issue ratio raised the return to the bank from issue by the discount rate. Elevating the ratio to 3:1 raised the profits from issuing notes to 21 percent.

31. *RMF* 1877, 33–35.
32. *RMF* 1879, 23–24. The chief features of this second effort were to eliminate the amortization section at the Ministry of Finance; place government deposits with the Banco do Brasil, where they would earn interest and where the government could draw on short-term credit; and run the government's foreign exchange transactions for overseas debt service through the bank.
33. *RMF* 1880, 5, 27.
34. Sweigart, "Financing and Marketing Brazilian Export Agriculture," 140–46.
35. *Times*, 14 May 1875.
36. Mauá's financial troubles stemmed primarily from loans he had extended to the government of Uruguay; *Financier*, 20 May 1875; Caldeira, *Mauá*, 495–526.
37. The largest amount of aid went to the Banco do Brasil, which paid the lowest rate of interest on the borrowing, a little over 1 percent. The Banco Rural e Hypothecário paid around 2 percent for its loans, while the Deutsch Brasilianische Bank, which ended up liquidating, paid around 3.6 percent, still a bargain by the standards of the day; *RMF* 1877A, table 9.
38. For the information on these banks in 1873, see *RMF* 1874, 109–33, and table 14.
39. One of the most prominent financiers of the Second Reign, the visconde de Figueiredo was an investor in various Rio banks and personally loaned money to the provincial government of Rio Grande do Sul; *RCJC* 1881, 39.
40. The data used here are from joint work done with Joseph Ryan. Building the data series required scrutiny of more than five thousand credit contracts from the Second Notary Office (Segundo Ofício de Notas) ledgers held in at ANRJ, for the period from 1835 (when interest rates were first recorded in an appreciable portion of the contracts) through 1889. The loans recorded in the Segundo Ofício were compared with the loans of all notary offices at ten-year intervals and were quite representative; Ryan, "Credit Where Credit Is Due," 49–60.
41. The mean of the private interest rate series in figure 7.1 is 12.4 percent. The mean of the annual apólice yield series for the same period is 6.6 percent. The spread fell slightly in the latter decades of the period.
42. A Zivot-Andrews test returns a structural break in the mean of the interest rate series in 1868.
43. For the evolution of commercial banks, see Levy, "História dos Bancos Commerciais"; Peláez, "The Establishment of Banking Institutions in a Backward Economy"; Peláez and Suzigan, *História Monetária do Brasil*, 44–121. Consolidated accounts for the assets and operations of the entire banking sector do not exist. Decree 2679 of 3 November 1860 required joint-stock banks to submit statements of their operations regularly to the Ministry of Finance. In 1866 the ministry was still trying to get banks to comply with the reporting requirement; *RMF* 1866, 17. Statements of operations intermittently published by the ministry rarely included full balance sheets and

almost never included statements of income and expenditure. Joint-stock banks were required to also publish their balance sheets regularly in public sources (table 7.1 is crafted from these).

44. The index is normalized here such that a value approaching unity indicates an increasingly monopolized market, while a value approaching zero indicates increasingly perfect competition.

45. These are the standards employed by U.S. government agencies today in assessing, for example, the market impact of proposed mergers.

46. Though attention here is restricted to banks in Rio de Janeiro, the financial center of Brazil, the markets for bank loans in the country's other main ports, which often had only one or two joint-stock banks at most, were likely even more concentrated.

47. The initial directors of the bank are identified in terms of the officeholding and business professions. Political offices are given in Nogueira and Firmo, *Parlamentares do Império,* supplemented by information in Dodsworth, *Organizações e Programas Ministeriais.* Merchant registrations are from ANRJ, Junta Commercial, "Registro de Matrícula dos Comerciantes, Corretores, agentes de Leilões, Trapicheiros e administradores de armazéns, de depósitos, do Tribunal do Comércio da Capital do Império," supplemented by information on occupations in the *Almanak Laemmert* for 1854.

48. *AL* 1866, 401–3, 419, 424.

49. *AL* 1868, 421.

50. *AL* 1872, 418, 551; *AL* 1886, 1210.

51. *AL* 1873, 457, 509.

52. *AL* 1875, 572.

53. *AL* 1858, 504; *RBB* 1865.

54. See *RBB* for 1861–64, and Nogueira and Firmo, *Parlamentares do Império,* 307–8; Garner, "In Pursuit of Order," 814.

55. *RBB* 1866; Nogueira and Firmo, *Parlamentares do Império,* 296–97.

56. *AL* 1886, 1209–10.

57. *RBB* 1867; Nogueira and Firmo, *Parlamentares do Império,* 214–15.

58. *RBB* 1877–80, 1888–89; Nogueira and Firmo, *Parlamentares do Império,* 391.

59. *RBB* 1872–76, 1881–86; Nogueira and Firmo, *Parlamentares do Império,* 134.

60. *AL* 1872, 437; *AL* 1874, 520; Dodsworth, *Organizações e Programas Ministeriais,* 297; Garner, "In Pursuit of Order," 816.

61. *AL* 1875, 571; *AL* 1878, 556; Nogueira and Firmo, *Parlamentares do Império,* 400.

62. *AL* 1886, 1212, Nogueira and Firmo, *Parlamentares do Império,* 249, 402.

63. *AL* 1886, 1213.

64. *Times,* 24 April 1879; *Money Market Review,* 14 June 1879.

65. Urban real estate accounted for less than 6 percent. For the breakdown of the mortgages by province and municipality, see *RBB* 1880, 24–26.

66. Sweigart, "Financing and Marketing Brazilian Export Agriculture," 147–48.

67. *RBB* 1885, 21–26.

68. The only new mortgages after mid-decade were rollovers, or mortgages granted to buyers of properties sold to them by the bank. On the delinquency rate in 1887, see *RBB* 1887, 23–24.
69. *CLB*, Lei 3263, 18 July 1885.
70. *RBB* 1887, 14; *RCJC* 1887, 12; *RBB* 1888, 9.
71. *Revista Illustrada*, 4 August 1888, 5.
72. *RMF* 1886, 16–17.
73. Figueiredo's Banco Internacional had also availed itself of the Treasury's line of credit; *RMF* 1888, 10.
74. *RMF* 1889, 29–31.
75. Franco, *Reforma Monetária*, 54–55; *RMF* 1889, 27–29.
76. *CLB*, Lei 3403, 24 November 1888; Decreto, 5 January 1889.
77. *RCJC* 1889, "Lista dos Bancos pecuniariamente protegidos pelo Thesouro Nacional em 1889."
78. *CLB*, Decreto 10262, 6 July 1889, article 3.
79. Compare *RCJC* 1889, table 32, "Quadro de Títulos de Renda e Acções . . ." and *RCJC* 1888, table 32, "Preços Extremos das Acções da Companhias. . . ."
80. *RCJC* 1889, 34; Cavalcanti, *Resenha Financeira do Ex-Império do Brazil*, 54–60.
81. *Revista Illustrada*, 5 October 1889, 8.
82. This point and the larger argument are expertly elaborated in Schulz, *The Financial Crisis of Abolition*, 59–78.
83. Weingast, "The Economic Role of Political Institutions." The conditions under which a federal division of authority generates policy competition among subnational units of the federation may well be peculiar to the configuration of federalism in the United States. For a critique and qualification of the general argument, see Treisman, *The Architecture of Government*, 74–103.
84. Chartering activity was not uniform across states, however, and varied considerably by region. Bodenhorn, *State Banking in Early America*, 72–248 *passim*.
85. Lamoreaux, *Insider Lending*, 52–83; Wallis, "Constitutions, Corporations, and Corruption."

CHAPTER 8. FALL FROM GRACE

1. LMA, CLC/B/110/MS19075, Hambro to Charles Sautter, Banque de Paris et Pays Bas, n.d. [around 16–17 July 1889]. The bank was the Paris-based progeny of a Franco-Dutch banking merger in the 1870s and had partnered with Baring Brothers in lending to governments. The other three firms were London businesses that had begun as merchants and over time came to specialize mainly in banking.
2. Schulz, *O Exército na Política*, 121–40.
3. "We have shown this letter to Messrs. Baring Brothers & Co. and likewise to Messrs. Brown Shipley & Co. who quite share our own views"; [Private]

Hambro & Son to Banque de Paris & des Pays Bas, 6 December 1889, LMA, CLC/B/110/MS19075.

4. Colson, "Destruction of a Revolution," 197–285; Carvalho, *Construção da Ordem—Teatro de Sombras,* 213–16.
5. See *RCJC* 1890, 9, for the quotation and 10–13 for the new companies.
6. See Levy, "O Encilhamento"; Levy, *História da Bolsa de Valores,* 172.
7. On the banking sector in particular under the Republic, see Triner, *Banking and Economic Development.*
8. Hanley, *Native Capital,* 100–101.
9. Suzigan, *Indústria Brasileira: Origem e Desenvolvimento,* 78.
10. On manufacturing in general, see Versiani, "Industrial Investment in an 'Export' Economy"; Suzigan, *Indústria Brasileira: Origem e Desenvolvimento;* Fishlow, "Origins and Consequences of Import Substitution."
11. And their use was ephemeral. There were some large new issues between 1904 and 1913, but overall corporate bond issues were very small in most years. After 1913 debenture finance fell off to trivial levels. The presumed takeoff in debentures after 1890 is difficult to detect, save for indicators that use a sharply depressed GDP in the denominator for the decade of the 1890s. Compare figure 2.5 on page 46 with figure 2.7 on page 49 in Musacchio, *Experiments in Financial Democracy,* 45–50.
12. Levy, *História da Bolsa de Valores,* 176.
13. Haber, "The Efficiency Consequences of Institutional Change."
14. Schulz, *The Financial Crisis of Abolition,* 122.
15. RAL 000/336/3, "Brazil 4% Loan of 1889, General Agreement," 29 April 1890.
16. Peláez and Suzigan, *História Monetária do Brasil,* 129–34.
17. Franco, *Reforma Monetária,* 101–33.
18. Perhaps in part a reaction to the extreme price inflation of the early Republic, the Constitution of 1891, otherwise highly federal in nature, restricted state governments from chartering note-issuing banks.
19. For the evolution of the risk premium (based on the current yield) in the 1890s, see Triner and Wandschneider, "The Baring Crisis and the Brazilian Encilhamento"; Abreu, "Brazil as a Debtor." Measures of the risk premium that extend the series discussed in chapter 5 into the 1890s, based on the yield to maturity, tell the same story.
20. The change did little to raise the government's standing in debt markets. Floriano's tenure was wracked by armed revolts, placing the viability of new political institutions further in doubt.
21. This shift had other important implications as well. The political machines that dominated state politics, especially in the most economically successful states, became the centers of much of the political action under the Republic. Regional oligarchies determined the outcomes of presidential elections before they happened. National-level policies increasingly reflected the dynamic among the dominant states.

22. Figueiredo [visconde de Ouro Preto], *A Década Republicana*, 160.
23. Information on apólice issues and conversions in the 1890s is drawn from the annual *Relatório* of the finance minister for the years 1890–99.
24. Triner and Wandschneider, "The Baring Crisis and the Brazilian Encilhamento"; Mitchener and Weidenmier, "The Baring Crisis and the Great Latin American Meltdown."
25. Franco, *A Década Republicana*, 77–80.
26. RAL 000/401/E, "Contract . . . Between the Government of the Republic of Brazil . . . and Messrs. N.M. Rothschild & Sons," 3 June 1892 (copy at AMFF 77.11.422).
27. [Prospectus] "Brazilian Government 5 Per Cent Loan for £6,000,000 Sterling, of which £2,000,000 are for the Repayment of the Treasury Bills dated the 1st of February 1895."
28. [Prospectus] "United States of Brazil Funding Scheme," 15 June 1898.

APPENDIX I. THEORY

1. Barro, "On the Determination of the Public Debt."
2. Kydland and Prescott, "Rules Rather Than Discretion"; Lucas and Stokey, "Optimal Fiscal and Monetary Policy."
3. Eaton and Gersovitz, "Debt with Potential Repudiation."
4. Bulow and Rogoff, "Sovereign Debt: Is to Forgive to Forget?"
5. Bulow and Rogoff, "A Constant Recontracting Model of Sovereign Debt," 158–59.
6. This basic model is adapted from those in Eaton and Gersovitz, "Debt with Potential Repudiation," 290–93; Eaton, Gersovitz, and Stiglitz, "A Pure Theory of Country Risk," 486–89; Sachs and Cohen, "LDC Borrowing with Default Risk," 12–21; Eaton and Gersovitz, "Some Curious Properties of a Familiar Model of Debt and Default"; Weingast, "The Political Foundations of Limited Government," 224–26; and Schultz and Weingast, "Limited Governments, Powerful States."
7. Allowing only two states of the public sector's fiscal conditions simplifies the exposition; the general result is unchanged when allowing for more varied fiscal circumstances.
8. Note that $C(0, s) = 0$; when there is no debt to repay, there is obviously no political cost to the government, irrespective of the state of the economy.
9. The rationing constraint as defined here impacts only the quantity of borrowing. Rationing may also occur on other attributes of the loan, such as loan maturity. A borrower whose willingness to repay is unclear to lenders may, for example, receive loans that require repayment relatively soon.
10. And it does so at an increasing rate, since $\dfrac{d^2 i}{dp^2} = \dfrac{2}{p^3}(1 + r) > 0$. Note that the derivatives are the same for both the interest rate i and the risk premium S. Any decline in the probability of repayment rapidly increases the size of the risk premium.

11. Substituting $i = \left(\dfrac{1+r}{p}\right) - 1$ into $L^c \leq \dfrac{P(x)}{1+i}$ gives $L^c_r \leq \dfrac{pP(x)}{1+r}$. Then, for a given $P(x)$ and risk-free return, the single rationing constraint plotted with respect to i separates into a family of rationing constraints L^c_r, each of which corresponds to a different probability of the high realization of income. Increases in p shift L^c_r to the right, raising the maximum loan size for a given rate r. Expressing the incentive compatibility constraint in terms of i gives a single rationing schedule L^c.

12. Charging a higher interest rate to justify lending may work against the lender and increase the likelihood of default in two ways. It can elicit borrowers that wholly intend to default. It can also encourage riskier uses of the funds, which are less likely to result in repayment of the loan; Stiglitz and Weiss, "Credit Rationing in Markets with Imperfect Information."

13. Hellwig, "A Model of Borrowing and Lending with Bankruptcy." For a model of sovereign borrowing in which monitoring of the executive is critical not only for borrowing but also for the creation of a representative assembly, see Stasavage, States of Credit, 72–77.

14. In the extreme case in which the ruler defaults solely because of an inability to repay, the threatened penalty does not elicit repayment, and applying the penalty is inefficient for the creditors. Only by monitoring is it possible for lenders to assess the degree to which a default might be due strictly to an inability to repay.

15. Note that the interest rate here is not comparable to that of the basic model. This is owing to the fact that borrowing at the original rate i is not feasible (except in the case when $M = 0$) since it would require F to refrain from monitoring and as a result to decline to lend.

16. As in the case of the basic model, the second derivatives of the interest rate with respect to the probability of repayment are positive, and the spread between the risk-free rate and the government's borrowing rate opens rapidly with a decline in the probability of repayment.

17. Robinson, "Debt Repudiation and Risk Premia," 9–11.

18. This is a decision problem for the entrepreneur, not a complete game; the government's payoffs and decisions are not made explicit, and there is no strategic interaction. A complete specification of the game is not required in order to be able to identify the direction of the effect of regulatory changes on the entrepreneur's decision.

19. The return function is, by convention, assumed to increase in k but at a decreasing rate, making it concave.

20. Under the assumption that the source of differential return is productivity, this condition is equivalent to $s > \dfrac{A_s}{A_c}$.

21. The same result obtains in any situation in which the numerator exceeds the denominator (since p cannot exceed one), such as when the cost of the petition is too high or when the risk of expropriation is too large.

APPENDIX II. DATA

1. Brazil, Ministério da Fazenda, *Exposição do Estado da Fazenda Pública*, 22–24.
2. Reinvestment risk exists when the bondholder's proceeds from a bond with a higher coupon rate can be reinvested only at a lesser coupon.
3. The maturity on the 1852 loan was December 1, 1882, with a weight of 0.264; there was a maturity of June 1, 1888 on the 1858 loan, with a 0.387 weight; and the 1859 loan had a maturity of June 1, 1890, with a weight of 0.348.
4. Wormell, ed., *National Debt in Britain, 1850–1930*, 170–71.
5. Klovland, "Pitfalls in the Estimation of the Yield on British Consols."

BIBLIOGRAPHY

ARCHIVES

Acervo do Museu da Fazenda Federal, Rio de Janeiro (AMFF). Materials held by the museum are cited by call number and the document name or title. In the case of correspondence the citation also includes the initiator, recipient, and date, when available.

Arquivo Nacional, Rio de Janeiro (ANRJ). Manuscript materials in the archive are cited in the notes indicating the collection in which they are stored, along with any other document-specific cataloging information. A single document may have more than one way of being referenced because of changes in cataloguing. In such cases the most recent indication is the one used.

London Metropolitan Archive (LMA)

Rothschild Archive, London (RAL). Citations to each loan contract or memorandum provide the container number, the date of the contract, and the contract's heading. Correspondence is cited in the same manner.

NEWSPAPERS

Buenos Ayres Standard
Bullionist
O Constitucional
Correio da Tarde
Correio Mercantil
Course of the Exchange
Economist
Financial News

Financier
Investor's Monthly Manual
Jornal do Commércio
Money Market Review
Morning Post
New York Herald
Pacific Mail
Retrospecto Commercial do Jornal do Commércio
The Rio News
Statist
Telegraph
The Times (London)

BOOKS AND ARTICLES

Abrantes, Marques de. *O Empréstimo de 1865*. Rio de Janeiro: Typographia do Correio Mercantil, 1865.

Abreu, Marcelo de Paiva. "A Dívida Pública Externa do Brasil, 1824–1931." *Estudos Econômicos* 15, no. 2 (1985).

———. "Os Funding Loans Brasileiros, 1898–1931." *Pesquisa e Planejamento Econômico* 32, no. 3 (2002): 514–40.

———. "Brazil as a Debtor, 1824–1931." *Economic History Review* 59, no. 4 (2006): 765–87.

Acemoglu, Daron. "Politics and Economics in Weak and Strong States." *Journal of Monetary Economics* 52, no. 7 (2005): 1199–1226.

Acemoglu, Daron, and Simon Johnson. "Unbundling Institutions." *Journal of Political Economy* 113, no. 5 (2005): 949–95.

Acemoglu, Daron, Simon Johnson, and James A. Robinson. "The Colonial Origins of Comparative Development: An Empirical Investigation." *American Economic Review* 91, no. 5 (2001): 1369–1401.

Adams, Alison. "The Caixa Econômica: A Social and Economic History of Popular Banking in Rio de Janeiro, 1821–1929." Ph.D. diss., Harvard University, 2005.

Alencar, José Martiniano de. *Senhora*. Rio de Janeiro: Garnier, 1926.

———. *Lucíola*. Rio de Janeiro, Paris: Garnier, n.d.

Almanach Civil, Politico e Commercial da Cidade da Bahia para o Anno de 1845. [Salvador], Bahia: Typographia de M. A. da Silva Serva, 1845.

Almanach do Rio de Janeiro. Rio de Janeiro: Impressão Régia, 1827.

Almanak Administrativo, Mercantil e Industrial da Côrte e da Capital da Província do Rio de Janeiro [Almanak Laemmert]. Rio de Janeiro: Eduardo e Henrique Laemmert, 1843–89.

Almanak dos Negociantes do Império do Brasil. Rio de Janeiro: Typographia de Plancher-Seignot, 1827.

Andrade, Manuel Correia de Oliveira. *A Guerra dos Cabanos*. Rio de Janeiro: Conquista, 1965.

Assis, Machado de. *Dom Casmurro*. Edited by Maximiano de Carvalho e Silva. São Paulo: Companhia Melhoramentos de São Paulo, 1966.

Bacha, Edmar Lisboa, and Robert Greenhill. *150 Anos de Café*. Rio de Janeiro: Salamandra Consultoria, 1993.

Bai, Jushan, and Pierre Perron. "Estimating and Testing Linear Models with Multiple Structural Changes." *Econometrica* 66, no. 1 (1998): 47–78.

———. "Multiple Structural Change Models: A Simulation Analysis." In *Econometric Theory and Practice*, edited by Dean Corbae, Steven N. Durlauf, and Bruce E. Hansen, 212–38. Cambridge: Cambridge University Press, 2006.

———. "Computation and Analysis of Multiple Structural Change Models." *Journal of Applied Econometrics* 18 (2003): 1–22.

Banco do Brasil. *Relatório*: Various, 1853–89.

Barbosa, Rui. *Obras Completas de Rui Barbosa*. Vol. 16, no. 6. Rio de Janeiro: Ministério da Educação e Saúde, 1948.

Barman, Roderick J. "The Role of the Law Graduate in the Political Elite of Imperial Brazil." *Journal of Interamerican Studies and World Affairs* 18, no. 4 (1976): 423–50.

———. "Business and Government in Imperial Brazil: The Experience of Viscount Mauá." *Journal of Latin American Studies* 13, no. 2 (1981): 239–64.

———. *Brazil: The Forging of a Nation, 1798–1852*. Stanford: Stanford University Press, 1988.

———. *Citizen Emperor: Pedro II and the Making of Brazil, 1825–1891*. Stanford: Stanford University Press, 1999.

———. "Nathan Mayer Rothschild and Brazil: The Role of Samuel Phillips & Co." *The Rothschild Archive: Review of the Year April 2002–March 2003* (2003): 38–45.

Barro, Robert J. "On the Determination of the Public Debt." *Journal of Political Economy* 87, no. 5 (1979): 940–71.

———. "U.S. Deficits Since World War I." *Scandinavian Journal of Economics* 88, no. 1 (1986): 195–222.

———. "Optimal Management of Indexed and Nominal Debt." *Annals of Economics and Finance* 4 (2003): 1–15.

Barros, Eudes. *A Associação Comercial no Império e na República*. Rio de Janeiro: Associação Comercial do Rio de Janeiro, 1959.

Barroso, Gustavo. *Brasil, Colônia de Banqueiros (História dos Empréstimos de 1824 a 1934)*. Rio de Janeiro: Civilização Brasileira, 1934.

Barton, Matthew M. "Making the Mucurí: Entrepreneurialism and Private State Building Ventures in 1850s Brazil." Manuscript, University of Chicago, 2013.

Bates, Robert, and Da-Hsiang Donald Lien. "A Note on Taxation, Development, and Representative Government." *Politics and Society* 14 (1985): 53–70.

Baxter, Dudley. "The Recent Progress of National Debts." *Journal of the Statistical Society* 37 (1874): 1–14.

Bayley, Rafael. *The National Loans of the United States from July 4, 1776 to June 30, 1880.* New York: B. Franklin, 1881 [reprint 1970].

Bencivenga, Valerie R., and Bruce D. Smith. "Financial Intermediation and Endogenous Growth." *Review of Economic Studies* 58, no. 2 (1991): 195–209.

Berglöf, Erik, and Howard Rosenthal. "Power Rejected: Congress and Bankruptcy in the Early Republic." Manuscript, 2004.

Bethell, Leslie. *The Abolition of the Brazilian Slave Trade, 1807–1869.* Cambridge: Cambridge University Press, 1970.

Bieber, Judy. *Power, Patronage, and Political Violence: State Building on a Brazilian Frontier, 1822–1889.* Lincoln: University of Nebraska Press, 1999.

————. "A 'Visão do Sertão': Party Identity and Political Honor in Late-Imperial Minas Gerais, Brazil." *Hispanic American Historical Review* 81, no. 2 (2001): 309–42.

Blake, Augusto Victorino Alves Sacramento. *Diccionário Bibliográphico Brazileiro.* 7 vols. Rio de Janeiro: Imprensa Nacional, 1883–1902.

Bodenhorn, Howard. *State Banking in Early America: A New Economic History.* New York: Oxford University Press, 2003.

Bohn, Henning. "Why Do We Have Nominal Government Debt?" *Journal of Monetary Economics* 21 (1988): 127–40.

————. "The Behavior of U.S. Public Debt and Deficits." *Quarterly Journal of Economics* 113, no. 3 (1998): 949–63.

————. "Are Stationarity and Cointegration Restrictions Really Necessary for the Intertemporal Budget Constraint?" *Journal of Monetary Economics* 54 (2007): 1837–47.

Bordo, Michael D., Alan M. Taylor, and Jeffrey G. Williamson. *Globalization in Historical Perspective.* Chicago: University of Chicago Press, 2003.

Bouças, Valentim F. *História da Dívida Externa.* Rio de Janeiro: Jornal do Commércio, 1950.

Brazil. *Balanço da Receita e Despesa do Império.* Rio de Janeiro: Typographia Nacional, 1830–89.

————. *Relatório da Commissão Encarregada Pelo Governo Imperial Por Avisos de 10 de Outubro e 28 de Dezembro de 1864 de Proceder a um Inquérito Sobre as Causas Principaes e Accidentaes da Crise do Mez de Setembro de 1864.* Rio de Janeiro: Typographia Nacional, 1865.

————. *Breve Notícia do Estado Financeiro das Provincias, Organizada Por Ordem de S. Ex. o Sr. Barão de Cotegipe, Presidente do Conselho de Ministros.* Rio de Janeiro: Imprensa Nacional, 1887.

————. *Código Brasiliense, ou Collecção das Leis, Alvarás, Decretos, Cartas Régias, &C. Promulgadas no Brasil Desde a Feliz Chegada do Príncipe Regente N. S. a Estes Estados com Hum Índice Chronologico.* Vol. 3. Rio de Janeiro: Typographia Imperial e Nacional, n.d.

————. *Collecção das Leis do Brasil.* Rio de Janeiro: Typographia Nacional, various years.

Brazil. Câmara dos Deputados. *Parecer da Commissão de Fazenda da Câmara dos Deputados da Assemblea Geral Legislativa do Império do Brazil.* Rio de Janeiro: various, 1826.

———. *Proposta do Governo Sobre a Suspensão do Pagamento da Dívida Externa.* Rio de Janeiro: Typographia Nacional, 1831.

———. *Annaes da Câmara dos Deputados.* Rio de Janeiro: various years.

Brazil. Commissão de Inquérito. *Relatório da Commissão de Inquérito Nomeada Por Aviso do Ministério da Fazenda, de 10 de Outubro 1859.* Rio de Janeiro [1860].

Brazil. Departmento Nacional de Indústria e Comércio. *Sociedades Mercantis Autorizadas a Funcionar no Brasil, 1808–1946.* Rio de Janeiro: Imprensa Nacional, 1947.

Brazil. Ministério da Agricultura, Comércio, e Obras Públicas. *Relatório.* Rio de Janeiro: various, 1861–1889.

Brazil. Ministério da Fazenda. *Exposição do Estado da Fazenda Pública.* Rio de Janeiro: Typographia Nacional, 1823.

———. *Relatório.* Rio de Janeiro: Typographia Nacional, 1828–1889.

———. *Correspondência entre o Ministério da Fazenda e a Legação em Londres no Empréstimo Contrahido em 1865.* Rio de Janeiro: Typographia Nacional, 1866.

———. *Informações Sobre o Estado da Lavoura.* Rio de Janeiro: Typographia Nacional, 1874.

———. *Additamento as Informações Sobre o Estado da Lavoura.* Rio de Janeiro: Typographia Nacional, 1874.

———. *Relatório e Projecto de Lei da Commissão Encarregada de Rever e Classificar as Rendas Geraes, Provinciaes e Municipais do Império.* Rio de Janeiro: Typografia Nacional, 1883.

Brazil. [Thesouro Nacional]. *Quadros dos Impostos Provinciaes Organizados no Thesouro Nacional.* Rio de Janeiro: Typographia Nacional, 1877.

Brazil. Tesouro Nacional. *Relação dos Subscritores do Empréstimo Nacional de 1868 com o Número das Ações Pedidas e o das Distribuidas.* Rio de Janeiro: Typographia Nacional, 1868.

Brazil. Tesouro Público Nacional. *Situação Financeira do Tesouro Durante Os Anos de 1837 e 1838.* Rio de Janeiro: Typographia Nacional, n.d.

Broz, J. Lawrence, and Richard S. Grossman. "Paying for Privilege: The Political Economy of Bank of England Charters, 1694–1844." *Explorations in Economic History* 41, no. 1 (2004): 48–72.

Bueno, José Antônio Pimenta. *Direito Público Brasileiro e Análise da Constituição do Império.* Rio de Janeiro: Typographia Imperial e Constitucional de J. Villeneuve, 1857.

Bulow, Jeremy, and Kenneth Rogoff. "Sovereign Debt: Is to Forgive to Forget?" *American Economic Review* 79, no. 1 (1989): 43–50.

———. "A Constant Recontracting Model of Sovereign Debt." *Journal of Political Economy* 97, no. 1 (1989): 155–78.

Caldeira, Jorge. *Mauá: Empresário do Império*. São Paulo: Companhia das Letras, 1995.

Calomiris, Charles W. "The Motives of U.S. Debt-Management Policy, 1790–1880: Efficient Discrimination and Time Consistency." In *Research in Economic History*, edited by Roger L. Ransom and Richard Sutch, 67–105. Greenwich: JAI Press, 1991.

Calvo, Guillermo, and Pablo Guidotti. "Indexation and Maturity of Government Bonds: An Exploratory Model." In *Capital Markets and Debt Management*, edited by Rudiger Dornbusch and Mario Draghi, 52–81. Cambridge: Cambridge University Press, 1990.

Caporale, Tony, and Kevin Grier. "How Smart Is My Dummy? Time Series Tests for the Influence of Politics." *Political Analysis* 13, no. 1 (2005): 77–94.

Carnaxide, Antonio de Sousa Pedroso. *O Brasil na Administração Pombalina (Economia e Política Externa)*. São Paulo: Companhia Editora Nacional, 1940.

Carreira, Liberato de Castro. *O Orçamento do Império Desde sua Fundação*. Rio de Janeiro: Typographia Nacional, 1883.

———. *História Financeira e Orçamentária do Império do Brasil Desde a Fundação*. Brasília: Senado Federal, 1980 [reprint].

Carvalho, José Murilo de. *A Construção da Ordem—Teatro de Sombras*. 2d ed. Rio de Janeiro: Editora UFRJ, 1996.

Carvalho, Visconde de Souza. *A História das Dissoluções da Camara dos Deputados*. Rio de Janeiro: Typographia União, 1885.

Catão, Luis, Ana Fostel, and Sandeep Kapur. "Persistent Gaps and Default Traps." *Journal of Development Economics* 89 (2009): 271–84.

Cavalcanti, Amaro. *Resenha Financeira do Ex-Império do Brazil em 1889*. Rio de Janeiro: Imprensa Nacional, 1890.

———. *O Meio Circulante Nacional, Resenha e Compilação Chronológica de Legislação e de Factos*. Rio de Janeiro: Imprensa Nacional, 1893.

———. *Elementos de Finanças (Estudo Theórico-Prático)*. Rio de Janeiro: Imprensa Nacional, 1896.

Cavalcanti, Nireu Oliveira. "O Comércio de Escravos Novos no Rio Setecentista." In *Tráfico, Cativeiro e Liberdade: Rio de Janeiro, Séculos XVII–XIX*, edited by Manolo Florentino, 15–77. Rio de Janeiro: Civilização Brasileira, 2005.

Centeno, Miguel Angel. "Blood and Debt: War and Taxation in Nineteenth-Century Latin America." *American Journal of Sociology* 102, no. 6 (1997): 1565–1605.

Chang, Roberto, and Andrés Velasco. "Banks, Debt Maturity, and Financial Crises." *Journal of International Economics* 51 (2000): 169–94.

Clark, Gregory. "The Political Foundations of Modern Economic Growth: Britain, 1540–1800." *Journal of Interdisciplinary History* 26, no. 4 (1996): 563–88.

———. "Debt, Deficits, and Crowding Out: England, 1727–1840." *European Review of Economic History* 5, no. 3 (2001): 403–36.

Clarke, Hyde. "On the Debts of Sovereign and Quasi-Sovereign States, Owing by Foreign Countries." *Journal of the Statistical Society of London* 41, no. 2 (1878): 299–347.

Cleary, David. "'Lost Altogether to the Civilised World': Race and the Cabanagem in Northern Brazil, 1750 to 1850." *Comparative Studies in Society and History* 40, no. 1 (1998): 109–35.

Cole, Harold, James Dow, and William B. English. "Default, Settlement, and Signaling: Lending Resumption in a Reputational Model of Sovereign Debt." *International Economic Review* 36, no. 2 (1995): 365–85.

Cole, Harold L., and Patrick J. Kehoe. "The Role of Institutions in Reputation Models of Sovereign Debt." *Journal of Monetary Economics* 35, no. 1 (1995): 45–64.

———. "Models of Sovereign Debt: Partial Versus General Reputations." *International Economic Review* 39, no. 1 (1998): 55–70.

Colson, Roger Frank. "The Destruction of a Revolution: Polity, Economy, and Society in Brazil, 1750–1895." Ph.D. diss., Princeton University, 1979.

Cox, Gary W. "Sovereign Debt, Policy Stability, and Bargaining Efficiency." Stanford University, 2010.

———. "War, Moral Hazard, and Ministerial Responsibility: England after the Glorious Revolution." *Journal of Economic History* 71, no. 1 (2011): 133–61.

———. "Was the Glorious Revolution a Constitutional Watershed?" *Journal of Economic History* 72, no. 3 (2012): 567–600.

Dawson, Frank G. *The First Latin American Debt Crisis: The City of London and the 1822–25 Loan Bubble.* New Haven: Yale University Press, 1990.

Dewey, Davis. *Financial History of the United States.* 11th ed. New York: Longmans, Green, 1931.

Diamond, Douglas W. "Reputation Acquisition in Debt Markets." *Journal of Political Economy* 97, no. 4 (1989): 828–62.

———. "Debt Maturity Structure and Liquidity Risk." *Quarterly Journal of Economics* 106 (1991): 709–37.

Dickson, P. G. M. *The Financial Revolution in England: A Study in the Development of Public Credit, 1688–1756.* New York: Macmillan and St. Martin's, 1967.

Dincecco, Mark. *Political Transformations and Public Finances: Europe, 1650–1913.* Cambridge: Cambridge University Press, 2011.

Dixit, Avinash, and John Londregan. "Political Power and the Credibility of Government Debt." *Journal of Economic Theory* 94 (2000): 80–105.

Dodsworth, Jorge João [Barão de Javari]. *Organizações e Programas Ministeriais: Regime Parlamentar no Império.* 2d ed. Rio de Janeiro: Arquivo Nacional, 1962.

Doin, José Evaldo de Mello. *O Café, a Dívida Externa e a Modernização do Brasil.* Franca, Brazil: Faculdade de História, Direito e Serviço Social, UNESP Franca, 1986.

Dome, Takuo. *The Political Economy of Public Finance in Britain, 1767–1873.* London: Routledge, 2004.

Doratioto, Francisco. *Maldita Guerra: Nova História da Guerra do Paraguai*. São Paulo: Companhia das Letras, 2002.

Drazen, Allan. "Towards a Political-Economic Theory of Domestic Debt." In *The Debt Burden and Its Consequences for Monetary Policy*, edited by Guillermo Calvo and Mervyn King, 159–78. New York: St. Martin's Press, 1998.

Drelichman, Mauricio, and Hans-Joachim Voth. *Lending to the Borrower from Hell: Debt, Taxes, and Default in the Age of Philip II*. Princeton: Princeton University Press, 2014.

Eaton, Jonathan, and Mark Gersovitz. "Debt with Potential Repudiation: Theoretical and Empirical Analysis." *Review of Economic Studies* 48, no. 2 (1981): 289–309.

———. "Some Curious Properties of a Familiar Model of Debt and Default." *Economics Letters* 48 (1995): 367–71.

Eaton, Jonathan, Mark Gersovitz, and Joseph Stiglitz. "A Pure Theory of Country Risk." *European Economic Review* 30 (1986): 481–513.

Edwards, Sebastian. "LDC Foreign Borrowing and Default Risk: An Empirical Investigation, 1976–80." *American Economic Review* 74, no. 4 (1984): 726–34.

Eichengreen, Barry, and Ricardo Hausmann. "Exchange Rates and Financial Fragility." In *New Challenges for Monetary Policy*, 329–68. Kansas City: Federal Reserve Bank of Kansas City, 1999.

———. *Other People's Money: Debt Denomination and Financial Instability in Emerging Market Economies*. Chicago: University of Chicago Press, 2005.

Eichengreen, Barry, Ricardo Hausmann, and Ugo Panizza. "The Pain of Original Sin." In *Other People's Money: Debt Denomination and Financial Instability in Emerging Market Economies*, 13–47. Chicago: University of Chicago Press, 2005.

———. "Currency Mismatches, Debt Intolerance, and Original Sin: Why They Are Not the Same and Why It Matters." In *Capital Controls and Capital Flows in Emerging Economies: Policies, Practices and Consequences*, edited by Sebastian Edwards, 121–64. Chicago: University of Chicago Press, 2007.

El-Kareh, Almir Chaiban. *Filha Branca de Mãe Preta: A Companhia da Estrada de Ferro D. Pedro II (1855–1865)*. Petrópolis: Vozes, 1982.

English, William B. "Understanding the Costs of Sovereign Default: American State Debts in the 1840's." *American Economic Review* 86, no. 1 (1996): 259–75.

Epstein, S. R. *Freedom and Growth: The Rise of States and Markets in Europe, 1300–1750*. New York: Routledge, 2000.

Falas do Trono Desde o Ano de 1823 Até o Ano de 1889. Belo Horizonte: Editora Itatiaia, 1993 [reprint].

Feis, Herbert. *Europe, the World's Banker, 1870–1914: An Account of European Foreign Investment and the Connection of World Finance with Diplomacy Before the War*. New York: Council on Foreign Relations, 1930.

Fenn, Charles. *A Compendium of the English and Foreign Funds and the Principal Joint Stock Companies*. London: Sherwood, Gilbert, and Piper, 1837.

———. *A Compendium of the English and Foreign Funds and the Principal Joint Stock Companies.* 3d ed. London: Sherwood, Gilbert, and Piper, 1840.

Fenn, Charles, and Robert Lucas Nash. *Fenn's Compendium of the English and Foreign Funds.* 12th ed. London: Effingham Wilson, 1874.

———. *Fenn's Compendium of the English and Foreign Funds.* 14th ed. London: Effingham Wilson, 1889.

Ferguson, Niall. *The House of Rothschild: The World's Banker, 1849–1999.* New York: Viking, 1999.

———. "The First 'Eurobonds': The Rothschilds and the Financing of the Holy Alliance, 1818–1822." In *The Origins of Value,* edited by William N. Goetzmann and K. Geert Rouwenhorst, 313–26. Oxford: Oxford University Press, 2005.

———. "Political Risk and the International Bond Market Between the 1848 Revolution and the Outbreak of the First World War." *Economic History Review* 59, no. 1 (2006): 70–112.

Field, John, and T[homas] Fortune. *Fortune's Epitome of the Stocks and Public Funds.* 14th ed. London: Sherwood, Gilbert, and Piper, 1838.

Figueiredo [visconde de Ouro Preto], Afonso Celso de Assis. *A Década Republicana.* 2d ed. 2 vols. Vol. 1. Rio de Janeiro: Typographica do Brazil, 1902.

Filho, Viuva Ogier e. *Folhinha Commercial, ou Pequeno Almanak do Rio de Janeiro.* Rio de Janeiro: Typographia dos Editores Viuva Ogier e Filho, 1842.

———. *Folhinha Commercial, ou Pequeno Almanak do Rio de Janeiro.* Rio de Janeiro: Typographia dos Editores Viuva Ogier e Filho, 1843.

Finnie, David. *Capital Underwriting: An Account of the Principles and Practice of Underwriting Capital Issues, Together with a Critical Analysis of All the Main Underwriting and Subunderwriting Agreements.* London: Pitman, 1934.

Fischer, Stanley. "Dynamic Inconsistency, Cooperation and Benevolent Dissembling Government." *Journal of Economic Dynamics and Control* 2 (1980): 93–107.

Fishlow, Albert. "Origins and Consequences of Import Substitution in Brazil." In *International Economics and Development,* edited by L. E. DiMarco, 311–65. New York: Academic Press, 1972.

Flandreau, Marc, and Juan Flores. "Bonds and Brands: Foundations of Sovereign Debt Markets, 1820–1830." *Journal of Economic History* 69, no. 3 (2009): 646–84.

Flandreau, Mark, and Nathan Sussman. "Old Sins." In *Other People's Money: Debt Denomination and Financial Instability in Emerging Market Economies,* edited by Barry Eichengreen and Ricardo Hausmann, 154–89. Chicago: University of Chicago Press, 2005.

Florentino, Manolo. *Em Costas Negras: Uma História do Tráfico de Escravos entre a África e o Rio de Janeiro.* São Paulo: Arquivo Nacional, 1997.

Fogel, Robert William. *The Union Pacific Railroad: A Case in Premature Enterprise.* Baltimore: Johns Hopkins University Press, 1960.

Fortune, [E. F.] T[homas]. *Fortune's Epitome of the Stocks and Public Funds.* London: Sherwood, Gilbert, and Piper, 1833.

Fragoso, João, and Ana Rios. "Um Empresário Brasileiro no Oitocentos." In *Resgate: Uma Janela para o Oitocentos*, edited by Hebe Maria Mattos de Castro and Eduardo Schnoor, 197–214. Rio de Janeiro: Topbooks, 1995.

Fragoso, João Luis Ribeiro. *Homens de Grossa Aventura: Acumulação e Hierarquia na Praça Mercantil do Rio de Janeiro, 1790–1830.* Rio de Janeiro: Arquivo Nacional, 1992.

Franco, Afonso Arinos de Melo. *História do Banco do Brasil (Primeira Fase— 1808–1835).* São Paulo: Instituto de Economia da Associação Comercial, 1947.

Franco, Bernardo de Souza. *Os Bancos do Brasil.* 2d ed. Brasília: Editora da Universidade de Brasília, 1984 [reprint].

Franco, Gustavo Henrique Barroso. *Reforma Monetária e Instabilidade Durante a Transição Republicana.* Rio de Janeiro: Banco Nacional de Desenvolvimento Econômico e Social, 1983.

———. *A Década Republicana: O Brasil e a Economia Internacional, 1888–1900.* Rio de Janeiro: IPEA, 1991.

Fratianni, Michele, and Franco Spinelli. "Italian City-States and Financial Evolution." *European Review of Economic History* 10 (2006): 257–78.

Freedeman, Charles Eldon. *Joint-Stock Enterprise in France, 1807–1867: From Privileged Company to Modern Corporation.* Chapel Hill: University of North Carolina Press, 1979.

Furtado, Celso. *A Formação Econômica do Brasil.* Brasília: Universidade de Brasília, 1963.

Gama, Bráz Carneiro Nogueira da Costa. *Regimento Interno do Senado: Acompanhado do Regimento Commum; dos Quadros Demonstrativos da Abertura e Encerramento da Assembléa Geral Legislativa, e das Prorogações, Convocações Extraordinárias, Adiamentos da Assembléa Geral; Bem Como da Dissolução da Câmara dos Deputados; e do Quadro dos Senadores do Império do Brazil, Desde o Anno de 1826 Até 1883.* Rio de Janeiro: Typographia Nacional, 1883.

Garner, Lydia Magalhães. "In Pursuit of Order: A Study in Brazilian Centralization, the Section of Empire of the Council of State, 1842–1889." Ph.D. diss., Johns Hopkins University, 1988.

George, Alexander L., and Andrew Bennett. *Case Studies and Theory Development in the Social Sciences.* Cambridge: MIT Press, 2005.

Gerschenkron, Alexander. *Economic Backwardness in Historical Perspective.* Cambridge: Harvard University Press, 1962.

Giroletti, Domingos. *Industrialização de Juiz de Fora.* 1st ed. Juiz de Fora: Editora da Universidade Federal de Juiz de Fora-MG, 1988.

Gootenberg, Paul. *Between Silver and Guano: Commercial Policy and the State in Postindependence Peru.* Princeton: Princeton University Press, 1989.

Graham, Richard. "A Questão Christie." *Revista de História* 24, no. 49–50 (1962): 117–38, 379–402.

———. *Patronage and Politics in Nineteenth-Century Brazil.* Stanford: Stanford University Press, 1990.

Greif, Avner. *Institutions and the Path to the Modern Economy: Lessons from Medieval Trade.* Cambridge: Cambridge University Press, 2006.

Greif, Avner, Paul Milgrom, and Barry R. Weingast. "Coordination, Commitment, and Enforcement: The Case of the Merchant Guild." *Journal of Political Economy* 102, no. 4 (1994): 745–76.

Grossman, Herschel, and John Van Huyck. "Sovereign Debt as a Contingent Claim." *American Economic Review* 78 (1988): 1088–97.

Guimarães, Carlos Gabriel. "Bancos, Economia e Poder no Segundo Reinado: O Caso da Sociedade Bancária Mauá, Macgregor & Companhia (1854–1866)." Ph.D. diss., Universidade de São Paulo, 1997.

Guinnane, Timothy W. "Delegated Monitors, Large and Small: Germany's Banking System, 1800–1914." *Journal of Economic Literature* 40, no. 1 (2002): 73–124.

Haber, Stephen H. "The Efficiency Consequences of Institutional Change: Financial Market Regulation and Industrial Productivity Growth in Brazil, 1866–1934." In *Latin America and the World Economy Since 1800,* edited by John H. Coatsworth and Alan M. Taylor, 275–322. Cambridge: Harvard University Press, 1998.

Hanley, Anne G. *Native Capital: Financial Institutions and Economic Development in São Paulo, Brazil, 1850–1920.* Stanford: Stanford University Press, 2005.

Harris, Mark. *Rebellion on the Amazon: The Cabanagem, Race, and Popular Culture in the North of Brazil, 1798–1840.* Cambridge: Cambridge University Press, 2010.

Harris, Ron. *Industrializing English Law: Entrepreneurship and Business Organization, 1720–1844.* Cambridge: Cambridge University Press, 2000.

Hellwig, Martin F. "A Model of Borrowing and Lending with Bankruptcy." *Econometrica* 45, no. 8 (1977): 1879–1906.

Hilscher, Jens, and Yves Nosbusch. "Determinants of Sovereign Risk: Macroeconomic Fundamentals and the Pricing of Sovereign Debt." *Review of Finance* 14 (2010): 235–62.

Hoffman, Philip T., and Kathryn Norberg. *Fiscal Crises, Liberty, and Representative Government, 1450–1789.* Stanford: Stanford University Press, 1994.

Jancsó, István, ed. *Brasil: Formação do Estado e da Nação.* São Paulo: Editora Hucitec, 2003.

Jenks, Leland H. *The Migration of British Capital to 1875.* London: Nelson, 1963.

Jequitinhonha, Visconde de. *Reflexões Sobre as Finanças do Brasil, Operações de Crédito do Thesouro e o Empréstimo Contrahido em Londres de Cinco Milhões de Libras Esterlinas no Corrente Ano.* Rio de Janeiro: Typographia Universal de Laemmert, 1865.

Johnson, Noel D. "Banking on the King: The Evolution of Royal Revenue Farms in Old-Regime France." *Journal of Economic History* 66, no. 4 (2006): 963–91.

King, Robert G., and Ross Levine. "Finance and Growth: Schumpeter Might Be Right." *Quarterly Journal of Economics* 108, no. 3 (1993): 717–37.

Klovland, Jan Tore. "Pitfalls in the Estimation of the Yield on British Consols, 1850–1914." *Journal of Economic History* 54, no. 1 (1994): 164–87.

Kohlscheen, Emanuel. "Sovereign Risk: Constitutions Rule." *Oxford Economic Papers* 62 (2009): 62–85.

Kraay, Hendrik. "'As Terrifying as Unexpected': The Bahian Sabinada, 1837–1838." *Hispanic American Historical Review* 72, no. 4 (1992): 501–27.

Kydland, Finn E., and Edward C. Prescott. "Rules Rather Than Discretion: On the Inconsistency of Optimal Plans." *Journal of Political Economy* 85 (1977): 473–91.

La Porta, Rafael, Florencio Lopez-de-Silanes, Andrei Shleifer, and Robert W. Vishny. "Legal Determinants of External Finance." *Journal of Finance* 52, no. 3 (1997): 1131–50.

———. "Law and Finance." *Journal of Political Economy* 106, no. 6 (1998): 1113–55.

Lago, Luiz Aranha Correa do. "Balança Comercial, Balanço de Pagamentos e Meio Circulante no Brazil no Segundo Império: Uma Nota para Revisão." *Revista Brasileira de Economia* 36, no. 4 (1982): 489–508.

Lamoreaux, Naomi R. *Insider Lending: Banks, Personal Connections, and Economic Development in Industrial New England.* Cambridge: Cambridge University Press, 1994.

Lamoreaux, Naomi R., and Jean-Laurent Rosenthal. "Legal Regime and Business' Organizational Choice: A Comparison of France and the United States During the Mid-Nineteenth Century." In *NBER Working Paper,* 2005.

Leff, Nathaniel H. *Underdevelopment and Development in Brazil.* 2 vols. London: Allen and Unwin, 1982.

Levine, Ross. "Financial Development and Economic Growth: Views and Agenda." *Journal of Economic Literature* 35, no. 2 (1997): 688–726.

Levine, Ross, and Sara Zervos. "Stock Markets, Banks, and Economic Growth." *American Economic Review* 88, no. 3 (1998): 537–58.

Levy, Maria Bárbara. "História dos Bancos Commerciais no Brasil." Rio de Janeiro: IBMEC, 1972.

———. *História da Bolsa de Valores do Rio de Janeiro.* Rio de Janeiro: IBMEC, 1977.

———. "O Encilhamento." In *Economia Brasileira: uma Visão Histórica,* edited by Paulo Neuhaus, 191–255. Rio de Janeiro: Campus, 1980.

———. *A Indústria do Rio de Janeiro através de suas Sociedades Anônimas.* Rio de Janeiro: UFRJ, 1994.

———. "The Brazilian Public Debt: Domestic and Foreign, 1824–1913." In *La Deuda Pública en América Latina en Perspectiva Histórica,* edited by Reinhard Liehr, 209–56. Madrid: Iberoamericana, 1995.

Liehr, Reinhard. *La Deuda Pública en América Latina en Perspectiva Histórica.* Madrid: Iberoamericana, 1995.

Lima, Oliveira. *História Diplomática do Brazil.* Rio de Janeiro: H. Garnier, 1901.

Lindert, Peter H., and Peter J. Morton. "How Sovereign Debt Has Worked." In *Developing Country Debt and Economic Performance,* edited by Jeffrey Sachs, 39–106. Chicago: University of Chicago Press, 1989.

Lucas, Robert, Jr., and Nancy L. Stokey. "Optimal Fiscal and Monetary Policy in an Economy without Capital." *Journal of Monetary Economics* 12, no. 1 (1983): 55–93.

Macaulay, Neill. *Dom Pedro: The Struggle for Liberty in Brazil and Portugal, 1798–1834.* Durham: Duke University Press, 1986.

Marichal, Carlos. *A Century of Debt Crises in Latin America: From Independence to the Great Depression, 1820–1930.* Princeton: Princeton University Press, 1989.

———. "Liberalism and Fiscal Policy: The Argentine Paradox, 1820–1862." In *Liberals, Politics, and Power: State Formation in Nineteenth-Century Latin America,* edited by Vincent C. Peloso and Barbara A. Tenenbaum, 90–110. Athens: University of Georgia Press, 1996.

———. "Una Difícil Transición Fiscal: Del Régimen Colonial al México Independiente, 1750–1850." In *De Colonia a Nación: Impuestos y Política en México, 1750–1860,* edited by Carlos Marichal and Daniela Marino, 19–58. Mexico City: El Colegio de México, 2001.

———. "The Construction of Credibility: Financial Market Reform and the Renegotiation of Mexico's External Debt in the 1880s." In *The Mexican Economy, 1870–1930,* edited by Stephen H. Haber and Jeffrey L. Bortz, 93–119. Stanford: Stanford University Press, 2002.

Mathias, Herculano Gomes. *Comércio, 173 Anos de Desenvolvimento: História da Associação Comercial do Rio de Janeiro (1820–1993).* Rio de Janeiro: Expressão e Cultura, 1993.

Mathias, Peter, and Patrick K. O'Brien. "Taxation in England and France, 1715–1810." *Journal of European Economic History* 5 (1978): 601–50.

Mattos, Ilmar Rohloff de. *O Tempo Saquarema.* São Paulo: Editora Hucitec, 1987.

Mattoso, Kátia M. de Queirós. *Bahia, Século XIX: Uma Província no Império.* Rio de Janeiro: Editora Nova Fronteira, 1992.

Mauá, Irineô Evangelista de Souza Visconde de. *Autobiografia ("Exposição aos Credores e ao Público") Seguida de "O Meio Circulante do Brasil."* 3d ed. Rio de Janeiro: Topbooks, 1998.

Maurer, Noel, and Andrei Gomberg. "When the State Is Untrustworthy: Public Finance and Private Banking in Porfirian Mexico." *Journal of Economic History* 64 (2004): 1087–1107.

Mauro, Paolo, Nathan Sussman, and Yishay Yafeh. *Emerging Markets and Financial Globalization: Sovereign Bond Spreads in 1870–1913 and Today.* Oxford: Oxford University Press, 2006.

Mauro, Paulo, and Yishay Yafeh. "The Corporation of Foreign Bondholders." International Monetary Fund Working Paper 03/107, 2003.

Mello, Zélia Maria Cardoso de. *Metamórfoses da Riqueza, São Paulo, 1845–1895: Contribuição ao Estudo da Passagem da Economia Mercantil-Escravista á Economia Exportadora Capitalista.* São Paulo: Hucitec, 1985.

Melo, Hildete Pereira de, and M. B. K. Falci. "Eufrásia Teixeira Leite: O Destino de uma Herança." Paper presented at the 6a Conferência Internacional de

História de Empresas e V Congresso Brasileiro de História Econômica, Caxambu, Minas Gerais, Brazil, 2003.

Michie, Ranald. *The London Stock Exchange: A History*. Oxford: Oxford University Press, 1999.

Milet, Henrique Augusto. *O Meio Circulante e a Questão Bancária*. Recife: Typographia Jornal do Recife, 1875.

Mitchell, B. R. *British Historical Statistics*. Cambridge: Cambridge University Press, 1988.

Mitchener, Kris James, and Marc Weidenmier. "The Baring Crisis and the Great Latin American Meltdown of the 1890s." *Journal of Economic History* 68, no. 2 (2008): 462–500.

Montero Bustamante, Raúl. *Estampas del Montevideo Romántico*. Montevideo: Ediciones de la Banda Oriental, 1968.

Moreira [Barão de Penedo], J. M. Carvalho. *O Empréstimo Brasileiro Contraido em Londres em 1863*. Paris, 1864.

Morgan, E. Victor, and William Arthur Thomas. *The Stock Exchange: Its History and Functions*. 2d ed. London: Elek Books, 1969.

Mosher, Jeffrey C. "Political Mobilization, Party Ideology, and Lusophobia in Nineteenth-Century Brazil: Pernambuco, 1822–1850." *Hispanic American Historical Review* 80, no. 4 (2000): 881–912.

———. "The Struggle for the State: Partisan Conflict and the Origins of the Praieira Revolt in Imperial Brazil." *Luso-Brazilian Review* 42, no. 2 (2005): 40–65.

Musacchio, Aldo. *Experiments in Financial Democracy: Corporate Governance and Financial Development in Brazil, 1882–1950*. New York: Cambridge University Press, 2009.

Naro, Nancy. "Safeguarding Portugal's Colonial Legacies: Pernambuco's 1848." *Portuguese Studies* 17 (2001): 184–99.

Neal, Larry. "The Financial Crisis of 1825 and the Restructuring of the British Financial System." *Federal Reserve Bank of St. Louis Review*, May/June (1998): 53–76.

Needell, Jeffrey D. "Party Formation and State-Making: The Conservative Party and the Reconstruction of the Brazilian State, 1831–1840." *Hispanic American Historical Review* 81, no. 2 (2001): 259–308.

———. "Provincial Origins of the Brazilian State: Rio de Janeiro, the Monarchy, and National Political Organization, 1808–1853." *Latin American Research Review* 36, no. 3 (2001): 132–53.

———. *The Party of Order: The Conservatives, the State, and Slavery in the Brazilian Monarchy, 1831–1871*. Stanford: Stanford University Press, 2006.

Neves, Lúcia Maria Bastos Pereira das. *Corcundas e Constitucionais: A Cultura Política da Independência, 1820–1822*. Rio de Janeiro: FAPERJ: Revan, 2003.

Newton, Lucy, and P. L. Cottrell. "Banking Liberalisation in England and Wales, 1826–1857." In *The State, Financial Systems and Economic Modernisation*, edited by Richard Tilly and Richard Sylla, 75–117. Cambridge: Cambridge University Press, 1999.

Nogueira, Octaciano, and João Sereno Firmo. *Parlamentares do Império*. Brasília: Centro Gráfico do Senado Federal, 1973.

North, Douglass C. *Structure and Change in Economic History*. New York: W. W. Norton, 1981.

———. "Institutions and Economic Growth: An Historical Introduction." *World Development* 17, no. 9 (1989): 1319–32.

North, Douglass C., and Robert Paul Thomas. *The Rise of the Western World: A New Economic History*. Cambridge: Cambridge University Press, 1973.

North, Douglass C., and Barry R. Weingast. "Constitutions and Commitment: The Evolution of Institutions Governing Public Choice in Seventeenth-Century England." *Journal of Economic History* 49, no. 4 (1989): 803–32.

O'Brien, Patrick K. "The Political Economy of British Taxation, 1660–1815." *Economic History Review* 41, no. 1 (1988): 1–32.

———. "Fiscal Exceptionalism: Great Britain and Its European Rivals from Civil War to Triumph at Trafalgar and Waterloo." In *The Political Economy of British Historical Experience, 1688–1914*, edited by Donald Winch and Patrick K. O'Brien, 245–66. Oxford: Oxford University Press, 2002.

Officer, Lawrence H. "Dollar-Sterling Mint Parity and Exchange Rates, 1791–1834." *Journal of Economic History* 43, no. 3 (1983): 579–616.

Oliveira, Cândido Baptista. *Systema Financial do Brazil*. S. Petersburgo: Typographia Privilegiada de Fischer, 1842.

Pang, Eul-Soo. *In Pursuit of Honor and Power: Noblemen of the Southern Cross in Nineteenth-Century Brazil*. Tuscaloosa: University of Alabama Press, 1988.

Paye, Bradley, and Allan Timmermann. "Instability of Return Prediction Models." *Journal of Empirical Finance* 13, no. 3 (2006): 274–315.

Peláez, Carlos Manuel. "The Establishment of Banking Institutions in a Backward Economy: Brazil, 1800–1851." *Business History Review* 49, no. 4 (1975): 446–72.

Peláez, Carlos Manuel, and Wilson Suzigan. *História Monetária do Brasil: Análise da Política, Comportamento e Instituições Monetárias*. Rio de Janeiro: IPEA/INPES, 1976.

Perotti, Enrico, and Paolo Volpin. "Lobbying on Entry." Typescript, 2004.

Pincus, Steven C. A. *1688: The First Modern Revolution*. New Haven: Yale University Press, 2009.

Piñeiro, Théo Lobarinhas. "Negociantes, Independência e o Primeiro Banco do Brasil." *Tempo* 8, no. 15 (2003): 71–91.

Plancher-Seignot, Pedro. *Almanak Imperial do Commércio e da Corporações Civis e Militares do Império do Brasil*. Rio de Janeiro: Casa de P. Plancher-Seignot, 1829.

Portella, Joaquim Pires Machado. *Constituição Política do Império do Brazil*. Rio de Janeiro: Typographia Nacional, 1876.

Potter, Mark, and Jean-Laurent Rosenthal. "Politics and Public Finance in France: The Estates of Burgundy, 1660–1790." *Journal of Interdisciplinary History* 27, no. 4 (1997): 577–612.

Prado Junior, Caio. *História Econômica do Brasil*. São Paulo: Editora Brasiliense, 1967.

Quinn, Stephen. "The Glorious Revolution's Effect on British Private Finance: A Microhistory, 1680–1705." *Journal of Economic History* 61, no. 3 (2001): 593–615.

Rajan, Raghuram G., and Luigi Zingales. "Financial Dependence and Growth." *American Economic Review* 88, no. 3 (1998): 559–86.

Razaghian, Rose. "Establishing Financial Credibility in the United States, 1789–1860: The Impact of Institutions." Typescript, 2001.

Reinhart, Carmen M., Vincent R. Reinhart, and Kenneth S. Rogoff. "Public Debt Overhangs: Advanced Economy Episodes Since 1800." *Journal of Economic Perspectives* 26, no. 3 (2012): 69–86.

Reinhart, Carmen M., and Kenneth S. Rogoff. "The Forgotten History of Domestic Debt." 1–62: NBER Working Paper, 2008.

———. *This Time Is Different: Eight Centuries of Financial Folly*. Princeton: Princeton University Press, 2009.

Reinhart, Carmen M., Kenneth S. Rogoff, and Miguel A. Savastano. "Debt Intolerance." *Brookings Papers on Economic Activity*, no. 1 (2003): 1–62.

Reis, Eustáquio. "A Renda por Capita dos Municípios Brasileiros Circa 1872." Working Paper. Rio de Janeiro: IPEA, 2008.

Reis, Francisco Tito de Souza. *Dívida do Brasil, Estudo Retrospectivo*. São Paulo: O. Ribeiro, 1917.

Reis, João José. "Slave Resistance in Brazil: Bahia, 1807–1835." *Luso-Brazilian Review* 25, no. 1 (1988): 111–44.

Ridings, Eugene. *Business Interest Groups in Nineteenth-Century Brazil*. Cambridge: Cambridge University Press, 1994.

Robinson, James A. "Debt Repudiation and Risk Premia: The North-Weingast Thesis Revisited." Paper presented at the conference "States and Capital Markets in Comparative Historical Perspective," UCLA Center for Economic History, 2006.

Rodrigues, José Carlos. *Constituição Política do Império do Brasil Seguida do Acto Addicional, da Lei da sua Interpretação e de Outras*. Rio de Janeiro: Laemmert, 1863.

Rodrigues, José Honório, ed. *Atas do Conselho do Estado*. Brasília: Senado Federal, 1973.

Roure, Agenor de. "Formação do Direito Orçamentário Brasileiro." *Revista do Instituto Histórico e Geográfico Brasileiro*, Tomo Especial, no. Parte IV (1916): 551–611.

Rousseau, Peter L., and Richard Sylla. "Financial Systems, Economic Growth, and Globalization." In *Globalization in Historical Perspective*, edited by Michael D. Bordo, Alan M. Taylor, and Jeffrey G. Williamson, 373–413. Chicago: University of Chicago Press, 2003.

Rousseau, Peter L., and Paul Wachtel. "Financial Intermediation and Economic Performance: Historical Evidence from Five Industrialized Countries." *Journal of Money, Credit and Banking* 30, no. 4 (1998): 657–78.

Ryan, Joseph. "Credit Where Credit Is Due: The Evolution of the Rio de Janeiro Credit Market, 1820–1900." Ph.D. diss., University of California, Los Angeles, 2007.

Sachs, Jeffrey, and Daniel Cohen. "LDC Borrowing with Default Risk." NBER Working Paper. Cambridge, Mass., 1982.

Salles, Ricardo. *Nostálgia Imperial: A Formação da Identidade Nacional no Brasil do Segundo Reinado.* Rio de Janeiro: Topbooks, 1996.

Salvucci, Richard. *Politics, Markets, and Mexico's 'London Debt': 1823–1887.* Cambridge: Cambridge University Press, 2009.

Sargent, Thomas J., and François R. Velde. "Macroeconomic Features of the French Revolution." *Journal of Political Economy* 103, no. 3 (1995): 474–518.

Schultz, Kenneth A., and Barry R. Weingast. "Limited Governments, Powerful States." In *Strategic Politicians, Institutions, and Foreign Policy,* edited by Randolph M. Siverson, 15–49. Ann Arbor: University of Michigan Press, 1998.

———. "The Democratic Advantage: Institutional Foundations of Financial Power in International Competition." *International Organization* 57 (2003): 3–42.

Schulz, John. *O Exército na Política: Origens da Intervenção Militar, 1850–1894.* São Paulo: EDUSP, 1994.

———. *The Financial Crisis of Abolition.* New Haven: Yale University Press, 2008.

Seckinger, Ron. *The Brazilian Monarchy and the South American Republics, 1822–1831: Diplomacy and State Building.* Baton Rouge: Louisiana State University Press, 1984.

Seignot-Plancher, Emilio. *Almanak Nacional do Commércio do Império do Brasil.* Rio de Janeiro: Typographia Imperial, 1832.

Shaw, Caroline. "Rothschilds and Brazil." *Latin American Research Review* 40, no. 1 (2005): 165–85.

Shepsle, Kenneth. "Studying Institutions: Some Lessons from the Rational Choice Approach." *Journal of Theoretical Politics* 1, no. 2 (1989): 131–47.

Silva, João Manuel Pereira da. *História do Brazil de 1831 a 1840.* Rio de Janeiro: Dias da Silva Junior, 1878.

———. *Memórias do Meu Tempo.* Rio de Janeiro: H. Garnier, 1895.

Silva Torres [de Alvim] [visconde de Jerumerin], Francisco Cordeiro da. *Memória Sobre o Crédito em Geral, Operações de Crédito, Caixas de Amortisação, e suas Funcções.* Rio de Janeiro: Typografia Nacional, 1832.

Sousa [visconde do Uruguai], Paulino José Soares de. *Estudos Práticos Sobre a Administração das Províncias do Brasil.* Rio de Janeiro: B. L. Garnier, 1865.

Sousa, Joaquim Rodrigues de. *Analyse e Commentario da Constituição Política do Império do Brazil, ou Theoria e Prática de Governo Constitucional Brazileiro.* São Luiz do Maranhão: B. de Mattos, 1867.

Stasavage, David. "Credible Commitment in Early Modern Europe: North and Weingast Revisited." *Journal of Law, Economics, and Organization* 18, no. 1 (2002): 155–86.

————. "Private Investment and Political Institutions." *Economics and Politics* 14, no. 1 (2002): 41–63.

————. *Public Debt and the Birth of the Democratic State: France and Great Britain, 1688–1789.* Cambridge: Cambridge University Press, 2003.

————. "Cities, Constitutions, and Sovereign Borrowing in Europe, 1274–1785." *International Organization* 61 (2007): 489–525.

————. "Partisan Politics and Public Debt: The Importance of the 'Whig Supremacy' for Britain's Financial Revolution." *European Review of Economic History* 11 (2007): 123–53.

————. *States of Credit: Size, Power, and the Development of European Polities.* Princeton: Princeton University Press, 2011.

Stein, Stanley. *Vassouras: A Brazilian Coffee County.* Princeton: Princeton University Press, 1985.

Stiglitz, Joseph, and Andrew Weiss. "Credit Rationing in Markets with Imperfect Information." *American Economic Review* 71 (1981): 393–410.

Stone, Irving. "The Composition and Distribution of British Investment in Latin America, 1865 to 1913." Ph.D. diss., Columbia University, 1962.

Sturz, J. J. *A Review, Financial, Statistical, and Commercial, of the Empire of Brazil and Its Resources.* London: Effingham Wilson, 1837.

Summerhill, William R. "Market Intervention in a Backward Economy: Railway Subsidy in Brazil, 1854–1913." *Economic History Review* 51, no. 3 (1998): 542–68.

————. "Institutional Determinants of Railway Subsidy and Regulation in Imperial Brazil." In *Political Institutions and Economic Growth in Latin America,* edited by Stephen Haber, 21–68. Stanford: Stanford University Press, 2000.

————. *Order Against Progress: Government, Foreign Investment, and Railroads in Brazil, 1854–1913.* Stanford: Stanford University Press, 2003.

Surigue, Sebastião Fabregas. *Almanak Geral do Império do Brasil.* Rio de Janeiro: Typographia Commercial Fluminense, 1836.

————. *Almanak Geral do Império do Brasil.* Rio de Janeiro: Typographia Commercial Fluminense, 1838.

Sussman, Nathan, and Yishay Yafeh. "Institutional Reforms, Financial Development, and Sovereign Debt: Britain, 1690–1780." *Journal of Economic History* 66, no. 4 (2006): 906–35.

Suzigan, Wilson. *Indústria Brasileira: Origem e Desenvolvimento.* São Paulo: Editora Brasiliense, 1986.

Sweigart, Joseph Earl. "Financing and Marketing Brazilian Export Agriculture: The Coffee Factors of Rio de Janeiro, 1850–1888." Ph.D. diss., University of Texas, 1980.

Sylla, Richard. "U.S. Securities Markets and the Banking System, 1790–1840." In *Lessons from Financial History: Proceedings of the Twenty-Second Annual Economic Policy Conference of the Federal Reserve Bank of St. Louis,* edited by David C. Wheelock, 83–98. St. Louis: Federal Reserve Bank of St. Louis, 1998.

Sylla, Richard, John B. Legler, and John J. Wallis. "Banks and State Public Finance in the New Republic: The United States, 1790–1860." *Journal of Economic History* 47, no. 2 (1987): 391–403.

't Hart, Marjolein C. *The Making of a Bourgeois State: War, Politics and Finance During the Dutch Revolt.* Manchester: Manchester University Press, 1993.

———. "The Emergence and Consolidation of the 'Tax State.' II. The Seventeenth Century." In *Economic Systems and State Finance,* edited by Richard Bonney, 281–94. Oxford: Oxford University Press, 1995.

't Hart, Marjolein C., Joost Jonker, and J. L. van Zanden. *A Financial History of the Netherlands.* New York: Cambridge University Press, 1997.

Tattara, Giuseppe. "Paper Money But a Gold Debt: Italy on the Gold Standard." *Explorations in Economic History* 40, no. 2 (2003): 122–42.

Tenenbaum, Barbara A. *The Politics of Penury: Debts and Taxes in Mexico, 1821–1856.* Albuquerque: University of New Mexico Press, 1986.

Tirole, Jean. "Inefficient Foreign Borrowing: A Dual- and Common-Agency Perspective." *American Economic Review* 93, no. 5 (2003): 1678–1702.

Tomz, Michael. *Reputation and International Cooperation: Sovereign Debt Across Three Centuries.* Princeton: Princeton University Press, 2007.

Tomz, Michael, and Mark L. J. Wright. "Do Countries Default in 'Bad Times?'" *Journal of the European Economic Association* 5, nos. 2–3 (2007): 352–60.

Tracy, James D. *A Financial Revolution in the Habsburg Netherlands: Renten and Renteniers in the County of Holland, 1515–1565.* Berkeley: University of California Press, 1985.

Trehan, Bharat, and Carl E. Walsh. "Testing Intertemporal Budget Constraints: Theory and Application to U.S. Federal Budget and Current Account Deficits." *Journal of Money, Credit, and Banking* 23, no. 2 (1991): 206–23.

Treisman, Daniel. *The Architecture of Government: Rethinking Political Decentralization.* Cambridge: Cambridge University Press, 2007.

Triner, Gail D. *Banking and Economic Development: Brazil, 1889–1930.* New York: Palgrave, 2000.

Triner, Gail D., and Kirsten Wandschneider. "The Baring Crisis and the Brazilian Encilhamento: An Example of Contagion Among Early Emerging Markets." *Financial History Review* 12, no. 2 (2005): 199–225.

Tsebelis, George. "Veto Players and Institutional Analysis." *Governance* 13, no. 4 (2000): 441–74.

———. *Veto Players: How Political Institutions Work.* Princeton: Princeton University Press, 2002.

Vasconcellos, [Rodolfo Smith] Barão de, and [Jaime] Barão Smith de Vasconcellos. *Archivo Nobiliarchico Brasileiro.* Lausanne: Imprimerie La Concord, 1918.

Versiani, Flávio Rabelo. "Industrial Investment in an 'Export' Economy: The Brazilian Experience before 1914." *Journal of Development Economics* 7, no. 3 (1980): 307–29.

Villela, André. "Política Tarifária no II Reinado: Evolução e Impactos, 1850–1889." *Nova Economia* 15, no. 1 (2005): 35–68.

————. "The Political Economy of Money and Banking in Imperial Brazil, 1850–1870." Ph.D. diss., London School of Economics and Political Science, 1999.

Vizcarra, Catalina. "Guano, Credible Commitments, and State Finance in Nineteenth-Century Peru." *Journal of Economic History* 69, no. 2 (2006): 358–87.

Wallis, John Joseph. "Constitutions, Corporations, and Corruption: American States and Constitutional Change, 1842 to 1852." *Journal of Economic History* 65, no. 1 (2005): 211–56.

Wallis, John Joseph, Arthur Grinath, and Richard Sylla. "Sovereign Default and Repudiation: The Emerging Market Debt Crisis in the United States." NBER Working Paper, 2004.

Weingast, Barry R. "The Economic Role of Political Institutions: Market-Preserving Federalism and Economic Development." *Journal of Law, Economics, and Organization* 11, no. 1 (1995): 1–31.

————. "The Political Foundations of Limited Government: Parliament and Sovereign Debt in 17th- and 18th-Century England." In *The Frontiers of the New Institutional Economics,* edited by John N. Drobak and John V. C. Nye, 213–46. New York: Academic Press, 1997.

————. "The Political Foundations of Democracy and the Rule of Law." *American Political Science Review* 91, no. 2 (1997): 245–63.

White, Eugene N. "The French Revolution and the Politics of Government Finance, 1770–1815." *Journal of Economic History* 55, no. 2 (1995): 227–55.

Willard, Kristen L., Timothy W. Guinnane, and Harvey S. Rosen. "Turning Points in the Civil War: Views from the Greenback Market." *American Economic Review* 86, no. 4 (1996): 1001–18.

Wormell, Jeremy, ed. *National Debt in Britain, 1850–1930.* Vol. 1. Oxford: Oxford University Press, 1999.

Wright, J. F. "The Contribution of Overseas Savings to the Funded National Debt of Great Britain, 1750–1815." *Economic History Review* 50, no. 4 (1997): 657–74.

Wright, Mark L. J. "Reputations and Sovereign Debt." Manuscript, Stanford University, 2002.

INDEX

Note: Page numbers followed by "f" or "t" indicate figures and tables, respectively